Asian America.Net
Ethnicity, Nationalism, and Cyberspace

Edited by **Rachel C. Lee** and **Sau-ling Cynthia Wong**

ROUTLEDGE
NEW YORK AND LONDON

Published in 2003 by
Routledge
29 West 35th Street
New York, NY 10001
www.routledge-ny.com

Published in Great Britain by
Routledge
11 New Fetter Lane
London EC4P 4EE
www.routledge.co.uk

Routledge is an imprint of the Taylor & Francis Group.

"Cyber-Race" by Jerry Kang was originally published in *Harvard Law Review* 113, no. 5
(2000), 1130–1208. Copyright © 2000 by the Harvard Law Review Association.

"North American Hindus, the Sense of History, and the Politics of Internet Diasporism" by
Vinay Lal was originally published as "The Politics of History on the Internet:
Cyber-Diasporic Hinduism and the North American Hindu Diaspora" in *Diaspora* 8, no. 2
(1999), 137–72. Reprinted by permission of University of Toronto Press Incorporated.

"Laughter in the Rain: Jokes As Membership and Resistance" by Emily Noelle Ignacio is
adapted from *Building Diaspora: The Formation on the Internet of a Filipino Cultural
Community,* forthcoming from Rutgers University Press. Used by permission.

"The Revenge of the Yellowfaced Cyborg Terminator: The Rape of Digital Geishas and the
Colonization of Cyber-Coolies in 3D Realms' *Shadow Warrior*" by Jeff Ow was originally
published in *Race in Cyberspace,* edited by Beth E. Kolko, Lisa Nakamura, and Gilbert
B. Rodman (Routledge, 2000), 51–68. Reprinted by permission.

Printed in the United States of America on acid-free paper.
10 9 8 7 6 5 4 3 2 1

Library of Congress Cataloging-in-Publication Data

Asian America.Net : ethnicity, nationalism and cyberspace / edited by Rachel C. Lee and
Sau-ling Cynthia Wong.
    p.   cm.
Includes bibliographical references and index.
    ISBN 0-415-96559-4 (hard cover : alk. paper)—ISBN 0-415-96560-8
(soft cover : alk. paper)
    1. Technological innovations—Social aspects—United States.   2. Internet—Social
aspects—United States.   3. Cyberspace—Social aspects—United States.   4. Minorities in
technology—United States.   5. Asian Americans—Communication.   I. Lee, Rachel C.,
1966–   II. Wong, Sau-ling Cynthia.
T173.8 .A815   2003
303.48'3—dc21   2002153218

CONTENTS

Part 3: Gender, Sexuality, and Kinship through the Integrated Circuit

Preface

RACHEL C. LEE

GOLDSEA visitors are forward-looking and see themselves as among the leaders of today's America. They shape the opinions of the 12 million Asians who make up America's fastest-growing, best-educated and most affluent consumer segment, as well as of their increasingly tech-savvy fellow Americans.

* Age range: 13 to 57; Median age: 32
* Median household income: $104,000
* 10% have $200,000+ household incomes
* 9% are CEOs of their own businesses
* 16% occupy upper- and middle-management positions
* 11% own their own professional practices
* Male/female ratio is 48/52

—<www.goldsea.com>

Husband says he's going to Gold Mountain
And doesn't listen to my pleas.
In the still of the night, full of thoughts, I cannot rest my eyes
Standing before the dresser alone, I face a grieving reflection
I wonder....
We may become rich, but wealth is really nothing!
—from *Songs of Gold Mountain,* trans. Marlon Hom

Cybernetics is already a paradox: simultaneously a sublime vision of human power over change and a multinational's mechanical process of expansion.
—Judith Squires, "Fabulous Feminist Futures and the Lure of Cyberculture"

From the Other Shore of the Y2K Gold Rush

Until the closing years of the twentieth century, both Sau-ling Cynthia Wong and I had never considered ourselves experts or even players in the field of Internet technology. Comfortable in our back-row stadium seats, we were, if not completely on the nether side of the digital divide, then teetering precariously at its edge. And yet, our everyday lives apprised us to the unexamined positions we occupied *within* the digital ballpark. Computers were a workday necessity. More important, the social and cultural fields we, as scholars, had taken as our primary areas of investigation were shifting in relation to a "new" influx of Asian engineers to the United States, in response to the growth of information technology.[1] Like the mothers, wives, and daughters of nineteenth-century Chinese sojourners who kinsmen had rushed to pan for gold in America (and whose constructed sentiments are represented in *Songs of Gold Mountain*), we felt both oceans apart from this second, digital Gold Rush and integrally linked to it as scholars and denizens of the new Asian America both on the World Wide Web and in "real life" sites such as Santa Clara County, California, where Sau-ling, resides. The oceans that separated us in this case were not the vast blue sea coupled with immigration restrictions and social constraints on our female mobility,[2] but rather the sense that Asian American "panethnicity" and coalitional politics were not allegiances shared by the new Asian immigrant families riding the tech boom,[3] and that, conversely, the field of Asian American studies had yet to take into account the impact of cybertechnology on its primary object of analysis. That sense of our own Asian American lives, integrated within digital circuits but only in an unreflective (pragmatic) manner, seemed to carry over to our colleagues and friends as well. Though we could easily locate individuals who were the web technicians for specifically Asian American political and progressive newsgroups, these individuals were not necessarily interested in cyber–Asian America as a research topic. Moreover, it seemed to us that the growing attention to race and cyberspace, for instance in articulations that mapped the digital divide as a racial divide, simply did not take into account the Asian American particularity to specific forms of online life, to cybermediated forms of cultural representation, and to the much-touted "new economy" built on micro-chips.

The compiling of this anthology on the topic of cyber–Asian America, thus, represents an effort not only to discover how Asians in diaspora have thus far used the web—for instance, would Asian Americans approach the web as consumers first;[4] as U.S.-based racial subjects looking for cultural resources;[5] as thrill-seekers searching for a space of fantasy to compensate for constraints on their RL identities; or as a medium to solidify an ethnic bloc vote?[6]—but also to think ahead to how Asian American political activists, researchers, and teachers might begin to shape their use of electronic technology to extend principles enshrined in "third world" politically progressive movements.[7] This volume, in other words, makes manifest another kind of Asian American cybercollectivity distinct from the one most familiar to advertisers, for instance, in the market profile quoted in the epigraph and touted on the still operative website, Goldsea.com. There, community members are celebrated for their "model minority" dimensions. Against such Net profiles that solidify a consumerist-based, Asian American subject, this anthology acts as a portal to another type of Asian

American cyberpractitioner—neither tech utopians nor technophobes (or to use Lee Quinby's terminology, "cyberians" and "cyburbanites")[8]—but comprised of Netizens oriented toward examining and theorizing both the limit and potential for political resistance and social struggle on the net.

Practically speaking, we envision this volume to serve as a resource for those who are teaching courses in new media, cyberculture, media studies, ethnic studies, and women's studies, or have research interests regarding immigration and technology. At the same time, we think it important to note that Asian Americans remain somewhat distinct from other "U.S. people of color" in terms of their adoption of information technology, and in terms of the importance of late-twentieth-century U.S. software and hardware-design industries in materializing conditions for the most recent wave of Asian immigration to American shores. This distinction is only obliquely acknowledged by a number of cybercritics. On the whole, scholars in the field of race and cyberspace remain critically hesitant to emphasize Asian Americans' differences from other racial groups in terms of their cyberpractices, in part due to legitimate worries over the way such claims to distinction can play into old divide-and-conquer tactics that set minorities against (model) minorities (a point further discussed in this volume's introduction). Many of our contributors share such a critical hesitation. However, as editors, we feel it necessary to broach directly, rather than bracket, the difficulties, both analytical and political, inherent in recognizing Asian Americans as minority historical subjects, though ones with a variegated relation to cyberspace.

Our editorial policy reflects the contradictions within Asian America, itself, with respect to a diversity of opinions on cyberspace's "progressive" possibilities or its residual militaristic and corporate structures that hardwire the Internet to further current (early-twenty-first century) modes of racism, sexism, militarism, and capitalism.[9] We chose not to restrict the essays herein to a single political orientation or methodological approach. Instead, this volume approaches the subject of cyberspace and Asian America more as a discovery project, first identifying the kinds of scattered research on cyberspace developing in various disciplinary sites of Asian American studies (e.g., in the fields of law, history, anthropology, sociology, literature, education, gender/sexuality studies, and media studies/communications), and second, asking what, if any, implicit unifying questions motivate Asian American scholars, researchers, and theoreticians of the Net, in their collective inquiry. The coherence of the papers in this volume emerges, then, from the set of inducements and questions that our authors both implicitly and explicitly take up. These common motivations have as their inspiration less a single utopian/dystopian perspective on the Net and more the influence of Asian American political and cultural critique, which habitually remains skeptical of the erasure of a category such as race via the technologies and conceptualizations of the virtual. What also unites the authors are their deep engagements with theoretical debates and conceptual paradigms in their respective fields under the pressure of cyberstudies. As an anonymous reader of the volume put it, "the contributors of *Asian America.Net* wrestle as much with their conceptual frameworks as they do their applied sites on the Net." It is this wrestling with several, traditional disciplinary fields, in addition to engaging cyberracial questions, that sets this volume apart from much of the scholarship produced in cyberculture studies.

As with any collaborative project, the completion of this volume would not have been possible without the enormous collective efforts of a number of individuals and institutions, first among them, the contributors to *Asian America.Net*, to whom we extend our heartfelt appreciation. The task of soliciting material, developing essays, selecting final works, and editing the final manuscript was made easier by the support of the Asian American Studies Center, English Department, and dean of humanities at UCLA, and the Asian American Studies Program, Department of Ethnic Studies, and the Committee on Research at UC Berkeley. Thanks also to able research assistance from Gladys Nubla and Lynn Itagaki.

Finally, a word on the choice to compile an academic print volume on such a fast-changing topic as digital technology and Asian Americans. Much of the writing on cybercommunity formations included in this volume are burdened with the expectation of their being outdated by the fast pace of technological change. We have found, however, that the rush to stay current also results in articles that are mostly surface surveys of what's on the Net rather than deeply engaged, reflective analyses of how computer-mediated technology has and will continue to alter identity-based formations such as Asian America. What this volume presents, then, is a historically located window onto cyber–Asian America, always, and like any other topic, an evolving subject. One sense of the historical location of cyber–Asian America is its discursive difference from prior articulations of the same. As we further discuss in the introduction, this volume emerges at a time when a significant shift is occurring in the way in which Asians and Asian Americans are being figured with respect to their integration into the production process of computer hardware and software, with respect to their Internet practices, and with respect to their cyberrepresentation on the Net. It is this shift that this volume both constitutes and reflects upon, as well.

Notes

1. The changing demographic landscape of one Silicon Valley center—Fremont, California—is profiled by Patricia Brown in "With an Asian Influx, a Suburb finds Itself Transformed," *New York Times*, May 26, 2001, A1+.

2. As suggested by my initial conceit regarding being "oceans apart" (i.e., female counterparts to the male Asian cybertechie), gender is not inconsequential to our sense of cybertechnology and Asian immigrant "cybertechies" as intimate strangers to Asian American studies. Jennifer Terry and Melodie Calvert comment on women's phobia toward technology because of the latter's association with "a masculine pathos of

domination, control, and destruction"; see Terry and Calvert, "Introduction: Machines/Lives," in *Processed Lives: Gender and Technology in Everyday Life,* ed. Jennifer Terry and Melodie Calvert (New York: Routledge, 1997), 8–9. Feminist and post-Enlightenment suspicion toward cybereuphoria also derives from the suspicion of technology as enhancing the alienations of worker subjects. As Andrea Slane puts it, "On the one hand, computers [are] seen to be an extension of the triumph of instrumental reason characterized by the efficiency narratives of Ford and Taylorism. But along with the threat of nuclear annihilation [comes] the concern that rationality [is] not all it [is] cracked up to be, and that instead of representing the height of human accomplishment, the computer [illustrates] the limits of rational thought"; see Slane, "Romancing the System: Women, Narrative Film, and the Sexuality of Computers," in Terry and Calvert, eds., *Processed Lives,* 73. In the end, our decision to act as helmswomen on this project expresses agreement with the feminist pragmatic view voiced by Terry and Calvert regarding the "importance of women's engagement with technology especially as it permeates everyday life. There is no simple way to say no to technology and be a citizen these days"; Terry and Calvert, "Introduction," 9.

3. On panethnicity, see Yen Le Espiritu, *Asian American Panethnicity: Bridging Institutions and Identities* (Philadelphia: Temple University Press, 1992); on coalitional politics, see Lisa Lowe, "Heterogeneity, Hybridity, Multiplicity: Marking Asian American Differences." *Diaspora* 1, no. 1 (1991): 24–44.

4. See <http://www.asianmall.com>.

5. See <http://goldsea.com>.

6. See <http://www.80-20initiative.net>.

7. See Glenn Omatsu, "The 'Four Prisons' and the Movements of Liberation: Asian American Activism from the 1960s to the 1990s," in *The State of Asian America: Activism and Resistance in the 1990s,* ed. Karin Aguilar–San Juan (Boston: South End Press, 1994), 19–70; and William Wei, *The Asian American Movement* (Philadelphia: Temple University Press, 1993).

8. Lee Quinby, "Virile-Reality: From Armageddon to Viagra," *Signs* 24, no. 4 (1999): 1079–87. Lee Quinby's two camps of cyberians (tech utopians) and cyburbanites (technophobes) flattens out a much more ambivalent and multiple/variegated approach to information technology—its aspects not only as a commercial site to "free" the consumer and endanger the innocent surfer; but also its aspects as communicational enhancement for grassroots politics; and, furthermore, its aspect as a materially produced tool, whose availability to more people (by way of lower cost of purchase) is tied to the exploitative practices directed against female workers of color across the globe. The question isn't just how we use the technology, but how the very fact of our using and owning home computers has been enabled by flexible modes of production and accumulation. The engineering design centers in Silicon Valley have enabled a migration and circulation of an Asian-born workforce to American shores, at the same time that tactics to quell and contain dissent of agricultural workers in Malaysia has dovetailed with plans by the state to make their young, "nimble-fingered," obedient women the lure for technology companies to open chip assembly factories.

9. Terry and Calvert, in their "Introduction," remark on cybertechnology's origins in "Cold War strategic military purposes ... created in the interests of military and corporate profit, seldom with the intention of enhancing community participation or individual autonomy" (4). Moreover, Arturo Escobar goes further, grimly asserting that "despite their much touted potential for liberatory and humanizing purposes, the military and profit-oriented applications will undoubtedly remain dominant"; see Escobar, "Welcome to Cyberia: Notes on the Anthropology of Cyberculture" in *Cyberfutures: Culture and Politics on the Information Superhighway,* ed. Ziauddin Sardar and Jerome R. Ravetz (New York: New York University Press, 1996), 118. Taking less of a technologically determinist as much as historical material approach, Irina Aristahrkova,

Maria Fernandez, Coco Fusco, and Faith Wilding stress that while "the digital revolution has engendered more possibilities of disembodiment...[it relies] on a global economic order that impoverishes, uproots and commodifies human beings, most of whom are not white....Celebrating disembodiment need not desensitize us to its physical counterpart"; see Aristahrkova, Fernandez, Fusco, and Wilding, "What is Undercurrents,"<Undercurrents Posting (2/12/2002)>.

Introduction

RACHEL C. LEE
SAU-LING CYNTHIA WONG

The topic of Asian Americans and cyberspace is evolving shaped by the circuits of popular and scholarly discourse that frame Asians' relation to Internet technology and cyberspace. For instance, in the late 1980s and early 1990s, the more common ways that Asians and Asian Americans were construed in relation to computer technologies were as part of the production process—as nimble-fingered workers on the chip assembly lines of Santa Clara County, California, and the Telok Free Trade Zone in Malaysia.[1] The final five years of the last millennium, however, saw more of an ambivalent acknowledgment of Asians and Asian American elites as on the forefront of the tech revolution. As Amitava Kumar points out, Senator Phil Gramm's support for expanding the limit on the number of H-1B visas spurs the imaginative overlay of Asian immigrants and the "cybertechie"—those "rare people whose skills are critical to America's success."[2] Along similar lines, Annalee Saxenian documents the impact of Asian immigrants on the semiconductor revolution, noting that in 1990 one-third of all engineers and scientists in California were foreign born, and of these two-thirds were Asian, predominantly of Indian and Chinese descent.[3] According to Saxenian, this group of engineering "ICs" (a pun on both the "integrated circuits" that they build and the ethnic identities of these "Indians" and "Chinese") constitutes less a new wave of immigrant settlers to the United States and more a transnational, entrepreneurial network that circulates capital through corporate-research nodules situated in cities and institutes across the Pacific Rim.

As these scenes of production and labor make clear, Internet technologies are not mere free-standing tools either for enhancing sociality or reducing human life to a monitored existence, but historically specific inventions dependent upon uneven political relations between the "first" and "third" worlds, and between Northern and Southern Hemispheres. Tech euphoria or tech anxiety might bespeak, not so much politically neutral investments in the patterning of the human psyche and corporeality after a machine-modeled system of flows and stresses, but desires for or disinclinations toward the rather persistent geopolitical borders upon which a borderless world of cyberspatial crossing depends. Asians and Asian Americans, it seems, have become crucial means through which such unacknowledged investments are articulated.

As documented by historians of nineteenth- and twentieth-century immigration to the United States, Asians have been contradictorily imagined as, on the one hand, machine-like workers, accomplishing "inhuman" feats of "coolie" manual labor, and on the other, as brainiac competitors whose technological adeptness ranges from inventing gunpowder to being good with engineering and math.[4] As suggested by Wendy Chun (in this volume), the "Orient"—that oppositional construct of the West—and "oriental women" become hallucinatory figures to manage as well as articulate the perils and pleasures of a "new" generative condition, that of the human-electronic interface. The transnational Asian American border crosser and gender-bending cyborg emerges as a convenient figure to project twenty-first-century anxieties regarding the porosity of national boundaries, the spread of global capital, and the transformation of a large domain of social relations into commodified exchanges. Asian Americans have a complex relation to interrogating, reimagining, and, perhaps, reinhabiting this figure of the Asian (American) cyborg[5]—the yellow body variously jacked into silicon chips and E-bay, to cybersociety and on-line forms of subjectivity.

As proclamations at the website Goldsea.com suggests, the Asian (American) cyborg is not solely the construct of the West, but also a self-invention that can take on model minority dimensions. Asian Americans online, according to this media-marketing outlet, conform to consumerist cyberelites who generously usher their "increasingly tech-savvy fellow Americans" (read: non-Asians who are slightly behind the curve) into twenty-first-century virtual realms.[6] This rhetorical ploy heralds Asian Americans as "leaders of today's America" precisely because of their material and technological wealth.[7] It should be noted that the strategy undertaken by Goldsea.com only partakes of modernity's fetishization of scientific and technical prowess as gauge of civilizational ranking.[8] Although Asians, in this website's estimation, are identified not so much by externally imposed criteria (such as somatic features), they are nonetheless constructed as a (master) race or class apart, distinguished by their technical and economic capital.

The contributors to this volume take a different view: they provide counternarratives to the Asian (American) cyborg invented by the West as they also engage in a struggle *within* Asian America over how "yellows" will be figured on-line. While variously interrogating the ends to which Asian (American) cyborgs and their online communities are made visible, the contributors to this volume all implicitly recognize the specific obligations of Asians and Asian Americans to theorize cyberspatial social questions. This is especially true in light of recent data indicating Asian Americans' quantitatively greater adoption of information technology (IT) compared to other minority racial groups. According to a 2002 report issued jointly by the National Telecommunications and Information Administration and the Economics and Statistics Administration, in September 2001, the computer use rates were highest for Asian American and Pacific Islanders (71.2 percent) and Whites (70.0 percent). Among Blacks, 55.7 percent were computer users. Almost half of Hispanics (48.8 percent) were computer users. During the same year, Internet use among Whites and Asian American and Pacific Islanders hovered around 60 percent, while Internet use rates for Blacks (39.8 percent) and Hispanics (31.6 percent) trailed behind.... From December 1998 to September 2001, Internet use among Blacks grew at an annual rate of 31 percent. Internet use among Hispanics grew at an annual rate of 26 percent. Internet use continued to grow among Asian American and Pacific Islanders (21 percent), and Whites (19 percent), although not so rapidly as for Blacks and Hispanics.[9]

Such research confirming Asian Americans as a majority group in terms of Net access and online presence remains a discomforting subject—a much-avoided detail—in what might be called the burgeoning field of postcolonial cyberracial studies. Typically, acknowledgment of the Asiatic online majority makes an apparitional appearance, first emerging in parentheses, only to be fully disappeared.

Symptomatic of that avoidance is Ziauddin Sardar's otherwise masterful delineation of the links between late-twentieth-century cyberpromotion and earlier conjurings of the "frontier" in the service of Euro-American imperialist expansion.[10] Sardar draws a line of continuity between Western, white colonizers who trammeled native populations and reified their cultures—"wiping out numerous indigenous cultures from the face of the earth"—and the current round of Internet swashbucklers who, in similar fashion, store "primitive" arcana in digital form and imagine cyberspace as a "free" space, a virgin land.[11] Countering the notion of the Internet as "free," Sardar grimly states that "in the U.S... households with incomes above $75,000 are three times more likely to own a computer than households with incomes between $25,000 and $30,000. That leaves most of the household of minorities in the cold: (*But Asian and Pacific Islanders are more likely than whites to own a home computer and therefore have access to the Internet*)" (italics added).[12] Later, claiming that "most of the people on the Internet are white upper and middle-class Americans and Europeans," Sardar finishes effacing the detail which only paragraphs before he places in parentheses.[13]

The eliding of information regarding Asian American "e-proficiency"—and the critical hesitation it bespeaks—might be the current, dominant discursive mode of articulating Asian Americans' vexed relation to cybertechnology. Asians and Asian Americans are imagined as, one the one hand, part of a racial grouping marked as "inferior" to whites—and subject to a long history of disenfranchisement, military destruction of homelands, the sex trade of women and children, and the exploitation of their labor and resources—and, on the other hand, "the heirs apparent to the technological revolution."[14] More to the point is the question of whether there are other ways, besides the parenthetical, through which scholars can acknowledge Asian Americans as minority subjects, though ones with a complex and contradictory relation to cyberspace. Suggesting that there *are* such alternative ways, the essays in this volume both reflect and materialize a significant shift in the way researchers can mine the significance of Asian American Internet practices. This transformation has crucial implications for both Asian American studies' theorization of its own project and for the fields of science and technology studies, race studies, and multicultural studies.

Two groundbreaking anthologies, *Race in Cyberspace* and *Technicolor*,[15] address both the paucity of and hostility toward discussions of race in cyberspace studies and technocultural scholarship. Both volumes employ "race" to designate a particular historically sedimented marking of African American, Latino, Asian American, and Native American bodies as nonnormative. Though such nonnormative "racial" designations are decidedly constructed, they have nonetheless been used to exploit and dominate each of these U.S.-based populations in distinct ways. The materiality of that exploitation has made palpable a "color line" (to recall W. E. B. Du Bois's famous evocation of the same), a paradoxically imaginary and real boundary distinguishing privileged American subjects—white, adult male citizens—from "people of color," in terms of their political orientation, their epistemological perspective, and their access to and disposition toward technology. The absence of race in prior discussions of (Internet) technology serves as the platform to pronounce the importance of the first volume's intervention; whereas the latter anthology takes issue not so much with the absence of race but the narrow figuration of racial subjects as left behind by technology—merely the victims of the much-touted digital divide.[16] However, when thinking about the Asian and the Asian American in relation to technology, Internet or otherwise, not so much absence but overrepresentation, not so much unknowing victimhood but dangerous expertise become the more popular tropes to conjure the relation of *the* racial subject (here, the Asian American) and technology. Asian Americans—though a racial minority group in the United States targeted for historical discrimination, subject to exclusion from the political process and land ownership, subject to group-specific taxes, imprisonment, restrictions on marriage, and unequal protection under the law—also appear askew from other minority groups in America in terms of the popular perception of their tech savvy and "portal-ability" to web entrepreneurial designs.

The possible (real or imagined) technophilic relation of Asian Americans to cyberspace has implications for how we think about the variegated intersection of race and technology, and how we think about the heterogeneity of racial tactics that encompasses such widely differing practices as envisioning Latinos and blacks as technically naive at the same time figuring Asian video junkies through what David Morley and Kevin Robins call "Techno-Orientalism."[17] High-tech orientalism comprises a distinctive type of anxious racializing practice not reducible to the general effacement of race in on-line discussions. Moreover, high-tech orientalism may have oblique articulations alongside low-tech, residual forms of racism. For instance, fears of being taken over by Asiatic geek guys (anxiety over high-tech dominance) may have a relation to the preponderance of Asian female flesh for sale in the formerly low-tech industry of pornography in its recombinant high-tech form: cyberporn. Because Sony is taking over the world, buy American online; better yet, buy Asian women online.

Inquiring into Asian American cultural practices (an endeavor exemplified by the essays in this collection) requires a careful negotiation between, on the one hand, an ideological commitment to U.S. coalitional politics based on the entity "people of color" and, on the other, a post-1965 immigration bias that may be transforming Asian America's population to one that is more technologically "jacked in" and that might conceive of itself more diasporically (as more attached to separate ethnonational groupings) than "panethnically" (allied with other "orientals" in the U.S. and at the same time, other minority groups of color). Thus, while the phenomenological changes exacted by electronic technology and the precise political economy of the web serve as two tech-related, generative axes of this project,[18] it is the notion of the web's deformations or enhancements of identity-based collectives that has been the more significant factor in affirming our convictions with regard to the importance of developing an Asian American cyberanalytics.

This volume also serves as a continuation and extension of scholarship on community formation and collective identity under (post)modern forms of mediation. Some critics of on-line life draw a firm boundary between the identity one enacts by belonging to an electronic newsgroup (or by playing a role in a chat room) and the communal identity that sticks to one in "real life." Ziauddin Sardar, for instance, argues that "communities are shaped by a sense of belonging to a place, a geographical location, by shared values, by common struggles, by tradition and history of a location—not by joining a group of people with common interests."[19] Yet "off line" critics such as Lisa Lowe have argued that the heterogeneous entity known as Asian America might be better conceived as a coalition—very much a collective identity of people with "common interests"—rather than a singular, homogeneous community.[20] If we take Sardar's description of community at its word, it would seem that Asian America is not a local neighborhood or village linked by "history of a location" but more of a virtual fiction. To draw this in another fashion, the rather traditional definition of community and human relations prescribed above would make untenable "Asian American" community, or at least reveal its proleptic virtuality—one prior to the late-twentieth-century explosion of Internet discourse.

Among Asian Americanists, it is a truism that prior to the ethnic consciousness movement of the 1960s there were no Asian Americans; that is, the people we now refer to as Asian Americans used to be known only by their individual ethnic labels: Filipino Americans, Chinese Americans, and so on. Indeed, the *American* term was often absent, suggesting that Asian Americans were to dominant society more notable for their foreign origins than for their national membership in the United States. The notion of a panethnic entity encompassing U.S. resident Asians from vastly different backgrounds is, therefore, an invention, one performed into being and maintained by continued acts of political and cultural intervention, yet under constant challenge from internal heterogeneity and pressures to assimilate. The arrival of Internet technology only intensifies the contestations about the concept of an "Asian American community"—contestations that have, from time to time, erupted into cultural controversies and institutional battles.

As another kind of "consensual hallucination," then, the "Asian American community" exhibits some interesting affinities with the Internet. Both are geographically uncentered, encompassing but also unmoored from, and transcendent of, the physical sites from which their energies emanate. Both have nebulous boundaries and are continually in flux. And both are held together by networks of communication. In the early days of cultural nationalism, Asian American activists valorized geographically specific enclaves (the Little Tokyos, Chinatowns, Manilatowns in various American cities, typically working-class in character and often heavily immigrant) as emblematic of "community"—cohesive, organic, authentic, certain of their identity, easily distinguishable from mainstream America. But even then, at a time of relative homogeneity in the Asian American population, no one would claim a single material location as *the* designated representative territory of the panethnic Asian American community.

With the increasing geographic dispersion of the Asian American population in the 1980s and '90s, and with the massive immigration of new Asian American ethnic subgroups (e.g., Southeast Asians after 1975) and the new prominence of existing subgroups (e.g., Filipino Americans and South Asian Americans), it has become even clearer that the panethnic Asian American community is inherently heterogeneous if not contentious, informally constituted, unterritorialized, centerless, and elastic. Though perhaps not as mercurial as Internet newsgroups or chat rooms, the panethnic Asian American community implies, like them, shared interests, the promotion of which is enabled by communication technology across geographical distances.

Furthermore, because Internet technology crosses national borders easily, the distinction between Asian Americans and "Asian Asians," once jealously defended during the cultural nationalist period, is fast becoming blurry. Because of the need to combat orientalism and secure political clout in the United States, many early theorists of Asian American identity carefully distanced themselves from things and persons Asian. America and no place else was to be home, premised on American nativity, or, in the absence of that for the foreign-born, on a commitment to struggle for full membership in the American nation-state. Nevertheless, the Asian "homeland" cannot be erased from view: the less than enthusiastic treatment received by Asian Americans in the United States, awareness of how such treatment is intimately related to politics in Asia, voluntary desires to maintain cultural ties, and numerous continued interactions with family and friends in Asia combine with recent changes in transportation and communications to keep one's (or one's forebears') land of origin a significant presence in her life, especially for first-generation immigrants and their families. The spread of border-crossing Internet technology highlights the vexed positioning of Asian Americans vis-à-vis the U.S. nation-state and their uncertain relationship to the notion of diaspora.

Asian Americans, in negotiating their heterogeneity (and, more significantly, the histories of enmity between the Asian national groupings that comprise its membership—e.g., Japanese and Koreans, Chinese and Indonesians), have to place an extraordinary amount of faith in the power of Asian America's own "virtualness."[21] To some observers, then, Asian Americans might appear an exemplary group to take advantage of virtual reality's community-building potential given the very "virtualness" built into the group's founding concept. Along similar lines, Mark Poster notes how people of certain ethnic and racial identity—for instance, Jews—incorporate a stage of spatial scattering or "diaspora" into their communal narratives.[22] If *diasporic community* is not an oxymoron, then we must consider how virtual media might be more seamlessly adopted by ethnically or racially defined communities whose geographic proximity has not been (as) crucial to their sense of cohesion. While there is still much debate on the status of Asian America as either a panethnic political coalition forged by Asians in the United States or as an amalgamated cultural entity comprised of many Asian diasporas now settled on American shores, in both cases Asian Americans—like Jews—have a similar deterritorialized communal articulation that may lend itself to virtual mediations.

Important published material on the intersection of Asian America and the Internet already exists,[23] and some of these "early" essays, are reprinted in this volume. The now canonical article that was one of the first to delve into the particular interpolation of Asians in cyberspace, Lisa Nakamura's 1995 "Race in/for Cyberspace," examines the hostility toward racial self-identification in the "cybernetic textual interaction" of MUDs (multiuser domains), particularly the most famous social MUD, LambdaMOO, created by Pavel Curtis in 1990. In an oft-quoted passage from this essay, Nakamura describes how "race in cyberspace is conceptualized as a bug, something which an efficient computer user would eradicate since it contaminates their work/play," noting that "players who elect to describe themselves in racial terms, as Asian, African American, Latino, or other members of oppressed and marginalized minorities, are often seen as engaging in a form of hostile performance, since they introduce what many consider a real life 'divisive issue' into the phantasmatic world of cybernetic textual interaction."[24]

Nakamura's observation on the barrier to exploring race on the Net—except as something to be vanquished—has become a first premise for those insisting on the productive intersection of cyberstudies (or more generally, science and technology studies) and studies of race.[25] While we certainly agree that this site of intellectual exchange is terribly important, we find Nakamura's other observations on how race has been engaged in LambdaMOO as significant as her observation on the implicit banning of "colored" identifications in virtual reality as impolite, unneighborly noise. Asian personae, she tells us, emerge as the most popular nonwhite handles chosen by players in the MUD. Thus, at the same time that racelessness becomes the normative Netiquette on LambdaMOO, cyber-Asian minstrelsy thrives online.[26] Why should the stereotypical Asian be a source of either racial representation or racial impersonation on the Internet?[27] And what is it about "yellowface" that makes this form of minstrelsy a seemingly inoffensive practice to VR participants in ways that putting on burnt cork in "real life," by contrast, would not? How has Asian embodiment and the sociopolitical network of "Asian America" been particularly affected by cybertechnology and this electronic domain of orientalist "play"? And how have Asian American cultural workers addressed the commodification of both the Asian handle and the Asian body in both experimental social domains such as MUDs and the all-too-real (and well-trafficked) commercial pornography websites featuring the sale of Asian flesh?

The essays in this volume variously attempt to answer these questions, even as they differ in their perspectives on the "progressive" possibilities of cyberspace. All share a broad concern with narrative and spatiality, or, more specifically, the way in which narratives of racial difference, orientalism, global power, and Asian nationality enter into that "consensual hallucination" known as cyberspace. They explore the materiality of race and national identity as it is subtly extended—rather than vanquished—in cyberspace (see the chapters by Wendy Chun, Jeff Ow, Aeju Kim, Vernadette V. Gonzalez and Robyn Magalit Rodriguez, John Cheng, Karen Har-Yen Chow, and Pamela Thoma). Across this volume's three parts race emerges not as a mere set of somatic features easily bypassed by the virtual masquerade that the Net affords but rather as (1) a material and gendered relation in the flexible, offshore, capitalist production processes of this wired world (see the chapters by Mimi Nguyen and Thuy Linh Nguyen Tu) and (2) an ethnocommunal kinship category mediated by electronic and other networks of communication (see the chapters by Kim-An Lieberman, Vinay Lal, Yuan Shu, Emily Noelle Ignacio, and Linta Varghese).

Wendy Hui Kyong Chun and Jerry Kang, the two contributors featured in part 1, "Cyberraces, Cyberplaces," share a concern with the way in which spatial tropes (the border, the village, the frontier, the highway, the free or regulated zone) help map and therefore manage the contest over power relations both underwriting and made possible by digital "reality." These articles respond to a question felicitously posed by Rajani Sudan: "In what ways does the endless capacity for representation [on the net] invoke the need for older cartographies of territorialization that crucially depend on histories of marking to make visible an invisible expanse?"[28] In "Orienting Orientalism, or How to Map Cyberspace," Chun reminds her readers that "cyberspace" is a literary invention, making its fictional appearance in William Gibson's *Neuromancer* six years before the creation of the World Wide Web. Mining cyberspace's relation to various articulations of place and space (by Yi-Fu Tuan, Michel de Certeau, and Michel Foucault), Chun finds in the alterity of cyberspace (i.e., the idea that is it not like "real" places and locations) a critical endowment. Cyberspace becomes the figure for a founding alienation in spaces—the alterity that haunts the "real" material locations we inhabit, and at the same time, a compensatory space of projected dreams of perfection, order, and limitless opportunity. Similarly, seeing the Orient as a founding alterity for the West, Chun illuminates the way in which mechanisms of identity, desire, and alienation through which the West engages the Orient, become replicated in cyberspatial representations that negotiate the relation of the nonvirtual to the virtual.

Through a specific reading of the Western cyberpunk novel *Neuromancer* and the Asian anime film *Ghost in the Shell,* Chun examines how feelings of alienation and disembodiment instigated by technology are managed through the "orienting"—that is, the directional *and erotic* touchstone of orientalism. To this end she explores the "entry into cyberspace as entry into world of oriental sexuality" by noting the popularity of oriental pornography sites, some of which include Russian women or mutilated white women in their rosters. The inclusion of Russian women, she astutely points out, "reveals the flexibility of the category 'oriental' to include all economically disadvantaged women." Fiber optics thus disperse orientalism to nonoriental bodies, even as the fleshy meat of the oriental body is necessary as foil for the disembodied possibilities seemingly afforded by cyberspace. It is this circularity and interdependence of the virtual and nonvirtual and the orienting of those categories that Chun deftly dissects.

Sharing Chun's estimation of the primacy of racial discourse to the scaling of cyberspace, Kang's "Cyber-Race" also interrogates the "color line" as spatial and psychological border that motivates both fierce desires for and alienations from cyberspace. Acting as a clarion call to "zone" cyberspace so as to make racial equality a priority, Kang's essay provides legislators, regulatory boards, and other representatives of the state, in conjunction with designers of technology, a heuristic device to grapple with race as a complex phenomenon requiring multiple and sometimes conflicting methods of abolition, integration, and transmutation. In his pragmatic advocacy of a multitiered or variably "zoned" approach to promoting racial equality on the Net, Kang recognizes the often contradictory operations through which race becomes a juridical assignment, a social stigma, and a type of property. Unlike those who sing only one tune—that race is killed on the Net, and that minorities are once again disabled by the cybercall to inhabit the "raceless" body of an abstract Netizen—Kang proposes that the assessment of whether a prescribed racial visibility on the Net goes toward the ultimate goal of unsettling racial stereotypes and racial inequality is highly contingent on the sphere of interaction. No simple formula can be adjudged politically progressive or regressive in an absolute fashion.

The essays in part 2, "The Pixelated Asia/Pacific," have a dual emphasis on web communities formed along the lines of specific ethnonational groupings and on Internet and electronic technologies as media to manage the crises of identification brought on by the migration of people, ideas, and capital across borders. Conflict, dialogue, and debate are key themes in this section, which focuses on both the performative formation of heterogeneous, spatially diffuse "virtual" kinship networks and the management of the psychic and identificatory uncertainties seemingly exacerbated by cyberspace. Kim-An Lieberman's "Virtually Vietnamese: Nationalism on the Internet" provides a theoretical consideration of the Internet's effects on diasporic communities and their "long-distance nationalism," through an intimately knowledgeable account of anticommunist Vietnamese websites all over the world, especially those based in the United States. Taking as her point of departure a relatively idealistic view of the Internet's border-crossing ability, Lieberman begins with an affirmation of its empowering political potential: since the fall of Saigon in 1975, many anticommunist websites have been created by overseas Vietnamese for the purpose of denouncing dictatorship, bearing witness to historical trauma, establishing "protean" self-defined identities, and sustaining an "imagined community" of global reach in the absence of territorial holdings and military might. In Lieberman's view, the very virtuality of the mythic online Vietnam signals not weakness but strength, for this "parallel universe" at once everywhere and nowhere—complete with waving flag and national anthem (of the former Republic of Vietnam), maps, clocks showing local Vietnamese times, and a gallery of national heroes through the centuries—keeps democratic activism alive. Although the author expresses faith in the websites' performative potency, she is acutely aware that unity is not easily achieved. Thus, Lieberman ends her essay with interrogation rather than uncritical celebration.

Offering more of a cautionary perspective on the countering nationalisms that flower on the Net, Vinay Lal's "North American Hindus, the Sense of History, and the Politics of Internet Diasporism" critiques the cyberassisted dissemination of an aggressive Hindu ultranationalism. Lal examines Hindu professionals in the United States who have played "a critical role in shaping a post-scarcity, postindustrial, information civilization." In Lal's portrayal, these United States–based diasporans tend to adhere to an ossified, hypermasculinized version of Hinduism, which is thus turned into "Hindutva," a Hinduism "stripped to its imagined essences." Collapsing the distinction between "Hindu" and "Indian," they reject the notion of a multiethnic, multicultural India where minorities such as Muslims enjoy political rights; they seek to make Hinduism into a world religion; and, within their land of residence, the United States, they remove themselves from the cultural lives and political aspirations of fellow ethnic minorities. In cyberspace—which, Lal argues, is comparable to Hinduism in its "rhizomatic," decentered nature—these typically male, middle-class Hindus, who often work in the high-tech sector, weave together a profusion of websites that present militantly religious claims about the nature of Hindu civilization and history made in the language of modernity, the nation-state, and scientific objectivity. In the postscript to his 1999 essay, written in 2002 specifically for this volume, Lal links his original observations on the cyberassisted transformation of Hinduism into Hinduvatva to the recent anti-Muslim violence in Gujurat.

Pursuing a related critique of the online Chinese transnational community, Yuan Shu's "Reimagining the Community: Information Technology and Web-based Chinese Language Networks in North America" raises explicit questions about Asian American community formation and the growing multilingual, multipolar nature of the Internet. Shu focuses on two North America–based Chinese-language Websites—Chinese News Digest (CND) and Chinese Media Net (CMN); both are heavily patronized by highly educated, technologically savvy professionals who have settled in the United States but travel frequently to East Asia on business. Such transnational professionals, Shu argues, may be seen as part of a loosely defined, supranational Chinese community linked electronically on the basis of a common language, a perception of shared history and culture, and shared stakes in transnational capital flow. Nevertheless, this community's post-Tiananmen depoliticization vis-à-vis "homeland politics" and apparently successful assimilation into the United States are not accompanied by a concomitant growth in activist engagement with the "traditional" Asian American community, as sixties-style Asian American cultural nationalism would predict. Instead, the transnational professionals are quite indifferent to the idea of a panethnic Asian coalition in America, being preoccupied with practical survival and sinocentric cultural transmission. Ironically, the sinocentrism of these transnational professionals is both enabled and made financially lucrative by way of combined offline residence in the United States and online nostalgia. Shu remains acutely aware that the Chinese Americans creators and users of CND and CMN are typically recipients of an elite higher education in the United States. Thanks to protective legislation that the online expatriate Chinese played a role in lobbying for, these professionals have been able to stay in the United States after the 1989 Tiananmen Square Massacre and profit from exercising their expertise and entrepreneurship. Thus, Shu's Chinese American transnational professionals have a physical base in a land of relative political security and material abundance when compared to that of their counterparts elsewhere in the Chinese diaspora.

While Shu figures the sinicization of the Web as a part-economic, part-cultural attempt to intervene in the Web's English dominance, Emily Noelle Ignacio analyzes the Filipino language(s) displayed on another Asian diasporic newsgroup for their humorous tenor. The "laughter" in Ignacio's "Laughter in the Rain: Jokes As Membership and Resistance" emerges precisely because of the crossing of the two or more tongues (Tagalog, English, Spanish, Ilocano) and cultural/geographic positions occupied by the newsgroup's members. As part of her two-year "Nethnographic" study of the Internet-based newsgroup soc.culture.filipino, Ignacio, as participant-observer, finds that jokes can function to close heated debates, especially painful ones, such as those following the execution of Filipina domestic worker Flor Contemplacion in Singapore, a topic generating anger and frustration throughout the Filipino diaspora. In other cases, jokes assuming knowledge of Filipino customs, historical events, foods, and so on can be used to establish membership in a Filipino collectivity and to unify temporarily otherwise disparate individuals. Closely related to these are jokes that demonstrate what Mikhail Bakhtin calls intentional hybridity and what Homi K. Bhabha calls mimicry—ironic appropriations of the colonizer's culture. Such instances of "almost the same, but not quite" (for example, the use of "Taglish") resist assimilation through mockery and assert a common cultural legacy. In Ignacio's view, the anonymous nature of Internet posts, free from face-to-face interactions, allows participants to express their views, even to "flame," with comfort. But interpretation of the posts is always context sensitive: a joke that passes without response or is received enthusiastically in one context may elicit "flames" in another if it is perceived as coming from an "outsider" or is read in conjunction with certain sensitive topics. Ignacio's study gives a ground-level view of how a diasporic community may be formed or challenged in cyberspace.

Shedding light, in related fashion, on how professional communities can be formed or challenged in cyberspace, Aeju Kim's "The Geography of Cyberliterature in Korea" provides a glimpse into the defenses launched by inner circles of professional Korean writers when faced with the perceived erosion of their territory by cyberamateurs. As Kim points out, the growing corpus of Korean cyberliterary texts has proven a boon to marginalized groups such as housewives, who find an easy way to disseminate their works. Leaping over institutionally controlled filters of publication, cyberliterature has much in common with popular literary forms that have been historically denigrated as aesthetically inferior. However, the debate over such literature in Korea is not merely one of offline literary doyens protecting themselves from the onslaughts of damned mobs of scribbling cyberauthors; cyberliterature becomes the occasion for renewed cultural gatekeeping, where Korean national culture is envisioned as under attack by "electronic Americanism." In the debate over Korean cyberliterature, the potential cross-class connectivity of Korean authors publishing online and those publishing through traditional venues is rhetorically constructed as a penetrating, imperialist threat. Rather than seeing cyberliterature as a source of Western invasion, Kim finds in this media another opportunity for Korean literature to join the ranks of global cultural production. Kim's essay reveals how the electronic alteration of traditional formats for writing and reading (and for determinations of literary legitimacy) can become platforms for border wars—for rhetorical defenses of geographic and cultural integrity serving ill-disguised professional interests.

Also addressing cyberspace's mediation of professional networks, "Intercollegiate Web Pedagogy: Possibilities and Limitations of Virtual Asian American Studies," by John Cheng, Karen Har-Yen Chow, and Pamela Thoma, with Rachel C. Lee provides a close-up account of a multicampus pedagogical experiment in which both Asian American and non-Asian American college faculty and students read several common texts, conducted the usual classroom discussions and assignments, then went online to the group's website to compare notes and engage in further conversation. The intention was to use Internet technology to network Asian American teachers and students who work and study on campuses in the northeast, south, and middle United States where Asian American studies, for the most part, has only been recently established. These instructors "East of California" hoped to use the Internet to combat their own relative isolation (and facilitate the sharing of teaching resources) and to introduce their students to an array of peers studying Asian American materials throughout the country (excluding California). Faculty participants were also interested in using Internet technology to foster more demographically diverse virtual classes. What began as a pedagogical initiative, however, became a convenient way to test the so-called disembodying power of the Internet. The study's findings on this point are complex and often surprising. For instance, the chat-room format did not at all eliminate markers of race/ethnicity, gender, or class, as some utopian theorists might predict. Besides detailing technological glitches and pedagogical moves, the authors speculate that the project might have had a legitimizing effect on Asian American curricula by "demonstrating mass"—exposing students in isolated areas to Asian Americans and Asian Americanists elsewhere. Although the electronic pedagogy experiment was small, self-contained, and goal-oriented, its highly concrete and specific findings provoke broader theoretical questions on the nature and dynamics of Asian American "virtual communities." The online pedagogic "community" of teaching professionals and students also represents a coalition forged not through recourse to a territorial homeland but through allegiance to a scholarly multidiscipline—an Asian American book club, if you will. It seems rather set apart from the more predominant ways in which online ethnic communities extend pre-Internet, diasporic modes of policing group boundaries. As feminist critics have pointed out, one of the oldest forms by which a community's border wars are fought is through the regulation of sexuality, particularly women's sexuality. The essays in part 3 of this volume "Gender, Sexuality, and Kinship through the Integrated Circuit," variously weigh in on the cyberspatial representation of the Asian American sexed body and the management of online anxieties through various gendered modes of virtual inhabitation.

If, as we have asserted, Asian Americans suffer more from overrepresentation than exclusion in the digital domain, then this is never more true than when the Asian American is a woman. According to Thuy Linh Nguyen Tu, "in a strange reversal of fortunes, Asian women's invisibility in most cultural arenas has been amply replaced by their hypervisibility in this new virtual arena." Or, as Wendy Chun more starkly puts it, "in this supposedly identity-free public sphere [of the digital landscape] . . . *Asian* has itself effectively become a pornographic category." The authors in this section adopt a range of views regarding the emergence of Asian female flesh for sale on the Net and the Asian (American) hacktivists (Net activists) who intervene into this same terrain. Motivating all of the authors of this section is the implicit question: If the Net were, as claimed, a realm of identity play that enlarges human creativity and consciousness, how is it that the Asian female and/or queer/transgendered body in cyberspace comes to represent a category of ultracommodification and dehumanization—the yellow woman (or transvestite) as reification writ large?

On the pessimistic side of the spectrum, Vernadette V. Gonzalez and Robyn Magalit Rodriguez's "Filipina.com: Wives, Workers, and Whores on the Cyber-frontier" investigates the ways in which typing the word *Filipina* on a variety of search engines transports the e-traveler to several sites for the auction of "maids" and "prostitutes." As the authors point out, the classificatory search engines on the Web, rather than being neutral, reflect a combination of computer-generated algorithms and human indexers, themselves imbricated in global capital flows: "the linking of Filipina to 'sex,' 'mail-order bride,' or 'domestic'. . . is shaped by those who have the capital to hire or buy them as key words. . . ." This informatics of domination also remains deeply gendered. As the authors point out, typing *Filipino* rather than *Filipina* "yields links on culture, the Philippines as a nation, food, and entertainment of the more innocuous type. Filipino men are not a hypervisible commodity to be traded on the Internet." The channeling of Internet flows through such sexualized and colonial signposts that reemphasize the Filipina as so much native plunder shatters overly optimistic renderings of the Internet as a liberatory space for new "androgynous" Asians. The Internet, these authors argue, "eases the processing of Filipina bodies into the circuits of capital." Skeptical of virtual space extending its much-hyped promise of democratic meritocracy to Filipina bodies, Rodriguez and Gonzalez conclude that "the performativity of identities [by which some Asian American cyber-activists and artists parodically "hack away" at the net] is unavailable to most Filipinas who are being reified as 'visual treats.'"

The conflation of Filipinas and Asian with the sex trade and domestic service provides one context for understanding the primary role Asian women are made to play in online discussions of communal boundaries. Cynthia Enloe recounts the ways in which nationalist discourse constructs women as the guardians of communal boundaries. Because women are thought to be the preservers of cultural traditions as well as the physical bearers of the nation's future generations, an entire discourse and apparatus for the hyperregulation of women's behavior and bodies arises as a particularly insidious form of masculinist patriotism.[29] Figures whose sexuality threatens the "pure" reproduction of the nation—e.g., lesbians, feminists, nonmaternal women, mannish women, surgically constructed women, in short, any figure whose desire and/or ontological status as woman could be construed as threatening to the "natural" reproduction of the race/nation—become figures of perversion, subject to forms of punishment and normalization. Linta Varghese's "Will the Real Indian Woman Log On? Diaspora, Gender and Comportment" examines one such effort to police the behavior of an on-line (assumed to be female) signatory "Meera" who posts a "pickup" story—about an Indian American woman called "Heera" and a white man—to the newsgroup alt.culture.us.asia-indian. Varghese traces the way in which discussants in the newsgroup reaffirm a cyberspatial Indian community, scattered across various physical sites yet united in their shared disapproval of Meera's (crucially, *not* Heera's) waywardness, her straying beyond community boundaries and, more generally, flouting the sexual behavior thought necessary to preserve Indianness even outside of India. The cyborg woman "Meera/Heera"—a literal conflation of the offline signatory and online invention—does not emerge a celebrated figure of border-crossing indeterminacy enabled by virtual technology, but instead becomes the occasion for the online community to reassert the priority of offline, historical communal claims and male authority.

The male Western authorities behind the creation of the IBM-PC game *Shadow Warrior* are the objects of Jeff Ow's critique in "The Revenge of the Yellowfaced Cyborg Terminator: The Rape of Digital Geishas and the Colonization of Cyber-Coolies in 3D Realms' *Shadow Warrior.*" Ow suggests that the militarized subject interpellated by this computer application (i.e., PC console game) is not only a gendered subject (expressly male) but a Western one—this despite the fact that the avatar the player inhabits while in the world of the game is an Asian martial artist named Lo Wang. Unlike traditional texts, with their emphasis on psychological depth, computer games retool the player into a mobile subject whose imperial, conquering, and violating movement through space conjures up genocidal fantasies "played" out on real bodies in the age of empire. In *Shadow Warrior's* graphically rich environment, Ow finds only the crassest invocation of Oriental stereotypes that are used to gratify the *gaijin* (Western) player's guiltless pleasure by endowing him with feelings of supremacy and victory in destroying Oriental bodies and landmarks. Ow stylishly renders his essay as part outraged exasperation at the absurd and patently offensive elements of the game and part ironic deflation of 3D Realms' transparent effort to use the game to enact a revenge fantasy upon Asians who comprise not only 3D Realms' primary competitors but also a large portion of their consumer audience. Turning the tables back upon 3D Realms, Ow figures as self-induced the falling profit (hence economic death) of *Shadow Warrior.* In this staging of the academic critic's battle with the racist PC-game producer, Ow also delves into the more troubling aspects of cyberspatial representation, where racial bodies are not visible but only represented in signs of urban uprisings; or where race is elided in the techno-elites' planning of the information superhighway; or where the point seems merely to addict players to the thrill of conquest and exploration—what Donna Haraway has framed as the toxicity of male cyborgs. In a 2002 postscript to his 2000 essay that Ow has written especially for this volume, he updates his handicapping of the battle between corporate high-tech industry (with its large capital investments) and academic critics who are financially limited and dispositionally disinclined to take advantage of post-Fordist decentralization techniques of commodity or intellectual production.

One response to the toxicity of male cyborgs, to the online traffic in pornography, to the speeding of sex-trade circuits enabled by cyberspace, and to the crass orientalism coupled with the online avoidance of substantive engagements with race is to condemn the technology itself.[30] Yet, cyberqueer and cyberfeminist writers warn against any retrenchment into or idealization of a mythic, pretechnological past. They refuse to align the feminine with Mother Earth or with organic community; and they contest the imaginary conflation of the feminine as a space radically cut off from that of industrialized work, postindustrial forms of capital circulation, and technological penetration.[31] Rather than advocate a return to an "organic" past, what kinds of practices of resistance are possible for cyborgian (technologically mediated) women and queers? Moreover, for Asian (American) cyborgettes whose technological enhancements come with reminders of a debilitating commodification of their fleshliness online, what are the psychic ambiguities of embracing cyberspace, even in a resistant fashion? Thuy Linh Nguyen Tu and Mimi Nguyen each mine the possibilities of Asian American artist-activists and theorists negotiating this risky terrain.

If *Asian* has effectively become a pornographic category on the Net, then what's an Asian American girl to do? In "Good Politics, Great Porn: Untangling Race, Sex, and Technology in Asian American Cultural Productions," Tu surveys Web artist Prema Murthy's *Bindigirl* digital art installation, Kristina Wong's deliberately low-tech burlesque of an Asian porn site, *bigbadchinesemama.com,* and Greg Pak's digital short, *Asian Pride Porn!* to provide a provisional answer to that question. Murthy's technologically sophisticated and interactive software is designed to force participants to become part of the exhibit, hence disrupting the "producer-to-consumer relationship made profitable by online pornography." Tu also delves into Wong's and Pak's strategic use of humor to engage an audience "that surely would not suffer through fist-raising lectures on the politics of representation." For both these artists, Asian American political critique must leave the insulated enclaves of like-minded activists, and, interestingly, porn becomes a mediating vehicle to reach a wider audience. Rather than concluding, as Rodriguez and Gonzalez do, that cyberspace is predominately foreclosed to Asian women as a site for enacting their agency, Tu broaches "a productive way to intertwine reality and fiction" by emphasizing not merely how the virtual realm extends the circulation of female flesh for sale but also how Asian American artists themselves employ ironic registers to disrupt the flow of information, metaphorically hacking away at the circuits of consumption upon which online porn sites rely.

One of the Asian American female artists Tu mentions is Mimi Nguyen, whose site <www.worsethanqueer.com> has long enjoyed a following among those interested in cyberAsian American culture. In a previous essay, "Tales of an Asiatic Geek Girl," Nguyen provides an account of her seduction by machines, her hacktivism, and the hate mail that attests to the vulnerability of Asian women constructing themselves in cyberspace.[32] In the article included in this volume, "Queer Cyborgs and New Mutants: Race, Sexuality, and Prosthetic Sociality in Digital Space," she critiques the way in which cybertheorists posit drag (or virtually enabled cross-dressing) as an identity practice that allows the cybertransvestite to resist gendered determinations. Nguyen's article examines the convergence of theories of drag and cyberpassing in their shared focus on "the nonmimetic mapping of bodies." She finds these theories wanting on political grounds, faulting their twin tendencies to define subversion in "gendered and sexual [but not racial] terms" and to celebrate the inhabiting of multiple identities "as insurrection enough." Beginning with her own desire for and identification with the Vietnamese "New Age Mutant" Karma (of the X-Men comic book series), Nguyen suggests that emancipatory politics do not inhere simply in performance and play (these disruptive nonmimetic practices can, themselves, become a fetish), but in the recognition of the density of social history and material relations—the conditions of production—that make possible technologies of such virtual transcendence. Nguyen therefore turns from scrutinizing transgender theorists, scholars of performitivity, and historians of minstrelsy to an account of a friend's buying her first harness at the local sex shop. While recognizing sexuality as mode of transgressive performance (the wearing of the harness a sly commentary on and literalization of the more invisible and pervasive ways sexuality is harnessed or disciplined in codes of heteronormativity, reproduction, and so forth), Nguyen wonders where and by whom such harnesses are manufactured—what are their conditions of production? For Nguyen, the axiom of gender transvestitism as the default setting in cyberspace itself becomes a reified essence, one that obscures the rise of race as a new kind of gendered marking. In this respect, Nguyen extends but also importantly revises insights made by Daniel C. Tsang in his 1996 essay, "Notes on Queer 'N' Asian Virtual Sex" that remarks on virtual reality as a means for "reinvent[ing] sexualities."[33] Nguyen's essay, in combination with Chun's observation of the term *Asian* as a synecdoche for pornography on the Net, indicates that while the default gender and sexual practices in cyberspace are indeterminate, *Asian* has itself become its own kind of sex-gender category, essentially the marked difference that matters and that represents the deprivileged side of a reconstituted binary opposition: genderless versus Asian (the latter synonymous with the sexually determinate category of exploitable sexuality).

The articles in this last section of the anthology might all be construed as responses to Donna Haraway's specifying the "cyborgs" of her famous "Manifesto for Cyborgs" as Asian women, specifically Southeast Asian village women working "in Japanese and U.S. electronics firms...rewriting the texts of their bodies and societies."[34] Haraway's "Manifesto," arguably the founding text of cyberfeminism, advocates taking social responsibility for those bodies unmade and remade by technology, and it is in the spirit of such social engagement that each of the essays—those in part 3 certainly, but also in parts 1 and 2 of this volume—are crafted.

Whether engaged in a dialogue with other cybertheorists or responding to the specifics of an Asian American community online, the essays in *Asian America.Net* demonstrate how Asian Americans have helped define—and are defined by—electronic technology. Taking these essays as a representative example, one can rest assured that Asian American cyberanalytics do not simply "refuse to contemplate that in which we are grounded."[35] They do not, in a sense, seek cyberspace as a way to obviate social process and political critique. Instead, the scholarship compiled in this anthology offers empirical evidence of cyberspace as a zone of power relations. *Asian America.Net* thus emerges from that fluctuating space between the cybersurf and the political shores of Asian America, an effort to reconstitute Asian (American) cyborgs in all their virtual and real dimensions.

Notes

1. Annette Fuentes and Barbara Enrenreich's *Women in the Global Factory* (1983) publicized the Malaysian government's characterization of the "Oriental female" as ideally suited to the intricate assembly-line work of semiconductor manufacture: "The manual dexterity of the Oriental female is famous the world over. Her hands are small, and she works fast with extreme care.... Who, therefore, could be better qualified by nature and inheritance, to contribute to the efficiency of a bench-assembly production line than the Oriental girl?" See Fuentes and Ehrenreich, *Women in the Global Factory* (Boston: Institute for New Communications/South End Press, 1983), 16. They also note that such racial targeting of Asian immigrant women, along with Latina female workers, occurs within U.S. national borders, in the high-tech center of Santa Clara County, California: "On the west coast, Filipinas, Thais, Samoans, Mexicans and Vietnamese have made the electronics assembly line a microcosm of the global production process. Management exploits their lack of familiarity with English and U.S. labor law. Often, companies divide the assembly line according to race and nationality...to encourage competition and discourage cross-nationality alliances" (54). See also Donna Haraway, "A Manifesto for Cyborgs: Science, Technology, and Socialist Feminism in the Last Quarter," *Socialist Review* 80 (1985): 65–107; Rachael Grossman, "Women's Place in the Integrated Circuit," *Southeast Asia Chronicle* 66–*Pacific Research* 9.5 (1979): 2–17;

Karen Hossfield, "'Their Logic Against Them': Contradictions in Sex, Race, and Class in Silicon Valley," in *Workers and Global Restructuring,* ed. Kathryn Ward (Ithaca, NY: Cornell University Press, 1990), 149–78; and Aihwa Ong, *Spirits of Resistance and Capitalist Discipline: Factory Women in Malaysia* (Albany, NY: State University of New York Press, 1987). For a more recent articulation of the geopolitical borders upon which microelectronics firm rely, see Thuy Linh Tu, Debra Wexler Rush, Alicia Headlam Hines, and Alondra Nelson, "Communities on the Verge: Intersections and Disjunctures in the New Information Order," *Computers and Composition* 14 (1997): 289–300.

2. Amitava Kumar, "Temporary Access: The Indian H-1B Worker in the United States," in *Technicolor: Race, Technology, and Everyday Life,* ed. Alondra Nelson and Thuy Linh N. Tu with Alicia Headlam Hines (New York: New York University Press, 2001), 76, 79. Kumar elaborates, "Much of the vaunted success of the Indian cybertechie was spurred in the early 1990s, when U.S. companies hired Indian programmers and consultants in droves. India is overwhelmingly the largest supplier of information technology (IT) professionals to the United States. When the annual cap of H-1B visas was raised from 65,000 to 115,000 in 1998, Indian cybertechies filled 46 percent of that new total. China filled 10 percent of that number; other countries with significant rates of labor immigration to the United States include Canada with 4 percent, the Philippines with 3 percent, the United Kingdom, Taiwan, Pakistan, Korea, Russian and Japan with 2 percent each" (79). Kumar also implicitly notes that these Asian cybertechies are overwhelmingly male: "What is the experience of women who are not engineers, but whose destinies, as a result of marriage, are nevertheless tied to the debates on high-tech immigration?... H-1B visas are granted only to the workers themselves; spouses and children who accompany them are given H-4 visas, which allow them to stay but not to work" (80–81).

3. Annalee Saxenian, *Silicon Valley's New Immigrant Entrepreneurs* (San Francisco: Public Policy Institute of California, 1999), 10–11.

4. According to Michael Adas, Western assessments of technological progress—or the ability to manipulate the material world—preceded race as a mode for the ranking of civilizations. Adas traces the changing attitudes of Westerners to the scientific and technological marvels of Africa, China, and India, before and after the Industrial Revolution. Beginning in the eighteenth century, Westerners started to acknowledge their own technological superiority to Asians, often by conceding a superiority held by these other nations in the past and *only* in the past: "China had been responsible for the three inventions—the compass, printing, and gunpowder—which had been the 'principal material agents of the progress of the modern world... [yet the Chinese had failed] to develop the full potential of these important inventions"; (see Adas, *Machines As the Measure of Man: Science, Technology, and Ideas of Western Dominance* (Ithaca, NY: Cornell University Press, 1989), 188–89). Adas surveys the varying array of attitudes toward China and India's "scientific backwardness," highlighting overstatements such as Robert Knox's that China had "neither 'invented nor discovered' anything" as an effort "to denigrate the one civilization that had clearly rivaled and, in many categories of material achievement, surpassed Europe in the preindustrial era" (192–93). The residue of such ambivalent acknowledgments of Asian scientific advancement and stagnation can be seen in the simultaneous figuring of Asians as technological drones (evoking smug superiority on the part of Westerners) and as technological inventors (whose past technological accomplishments are subject to contemporary denigration).

5. Asian American studies was, at one time, very invested in the distinction between Asians in Asia and Asians in North America (the latter dubbed Asian Americans). As discussed at greater length in the body of this introduction, the addition of "American" to create the compound noun *Asian American* began as a rhetorical ploy to contest a popular association of American citizens of Asian extraction with an eternally foreign presence—always the alien and never the national member. Increasingly, Asian

American studies has questioned both whether the distinction between Asians and Asian Americans is still politically expedient and whether political expediency is reason enough to ignore the increasing blurriness between the two categories. The debate, in short, has not been settled. In relation to Internet technology and cyborgian bodies, this unsettled debate only becomes more vexing. Cyborgs, themselves the metaphors for a hybrid (miscegenated) embodiment at the interface of organic life and technology, are often construed as wholly alien figures—a race apart. When Asian Americans are imagined as cyborgs, it is their Asianness—or foreign metaphoricity—that helps create the association within the Western imaginary of cyborgs as a race apart. In other words, Asian Americans as cyborgs are often registered as Asian cyborgs; the Americanness of these Asian American cyborgs becomes inconsequential to the "alien"(ating) work to which they are enlisted. To acknowledge this complex imaginary formation, we use the term *Asian (American) cyborg*.

6. To quote the online company's self-description, "GOLDSEA is far and away the World Wide Web's biggest and most popular Asian American site. Since opening as the first Asian American media website in April 1995, it has established itself as the preferred site for those affluent Asian Americans for whom their Asian heritage is a source of pride. GOLDSEA's importance reflects the fact that Asians are 12% of the U.S. internet community." See "Goldsea Asian American Supersite, Banner Advertising Information"; online at <http://goldsea.com/Banners/>. No sources are given for their 12 percent estimation of the Asian percentage of the U.S. Internet community.

7. Ibid.

8. See M. Adas, *Machines As the Measure of Man*.

9. National Telecommunications and Information Administration, and Economics and Statistics Administration, "*A Nation Online: How Americans Are Expanding Their Use of the Internet*" (Washington, D.C., February 2002), online at <http://www.ntia.doc.gov/ntiahome/dn/index.html>.

10. Ziauddin Sardar, "alt.civilizaions.faq: Cyberspace As the Darker Side of the West," in *Cyberfutures: Culture and Politics on the Information Superhighway,* ed. Ziauddin Sardar and Jerome R. Ravetz (New York: New York University Press, 1996), 14–41.

11. Ibid., 18.

12. Ibid., 23–24; emphasis added.

13. Ibid., 24.

14. Alicia Headlam Hines, Alondra Nelson, and Thuy Linh N. Tu, "Introduction: Hidden Circuits," in Nelson and Tu with Hines, eds., *Technicolor*, 5–6.

15. See Beth E. Kolko, Lisa Nakamura, and Gilbert B. Rodman, *Race in Cyberspace* (New York: Routledge, 2000); and Nelson and Tu with Hines, *Technicolor*.

16. Nelson, Tu and Hines's volume contests the notion of people of color as primarily victims of technology: "Most often when attention is turned to the implications of race for theorizing technology, people of color are cast as victims. We witness this most commonly in discussions about the digital divide, which characterize people of color—predominantly blacks and Latinos—as victims of either economic and educational constraints, cultural priorities, or their own fiscal irresponsibility.... Unfortunately these accounts sometimes become rationalizations for why people of color fail to have 'productive' relationships with technology, and justifications for the still uneven distribution of technological resources and knowledge." The editors conclude, "Not content to wring our hands about the digital divide, we sought out the many interfaces where technology and race intersect." Ibid., 3, 2.

17. David Morley and Kevin Robins, "Techno-Orientalism: Futures, Foreigners and Phobias," *New Formations,* Spring 1992, 136–56. Drawing out the contradictory elements of high-tech orientalism, Morley and Robins point to its origins in Western fears that "the loss of its technological hegemony may be associated with its cultural 'emasculation'.... If the future is technological, and if technology has become 'Japanified,' then

the syllogism would suggest that the future is now Japanese too. The postmodern era will be the Pacific era" (152–53). These Western anxieties lead to the resuscitation and retooling of older methods of managing the Orient, for instance viewing "*pachinko* and computer games simply as the postmodern equivalents of zen and kabuki." The authors also point to "a more resentful and more aggressively racist side to this Techno-Orientalism. The association of technology and Japaneseness now serves to reinforce the image of a culture that is cold, impersonal and machine-like, an authoritarian culture lacking emotional connection to the rest of the world." The image of "a new breed of 'radically bored' teen information junkies, *otaku*, who shun body contact and spend all their waking hours gathering data on the most trivial bit of media . . . [this image] recreates in a new dimension the image of the Japanese as inhuman" (154).

18. See Vivian Sobchack, "Democratic Franchise and the Electronic Frontier," in Sardar and Ravetz, eds., *Cyberfutures,* 77–89.

19. Sardar, "alt.civilizaions.faq," 29.

20. Lisa Lowe, "Heterogeneity, Hybridity, Multiplicity: Marking Asian American Differences," *Diaspora* 1, no. 1 (1991): 24–44.

21. Other American ethnic "minority" communities exhibit this virtual element, too; but if such things can be compared, a case can be made that "virtuality" is most characteristic of the Asian American. As has often been noted, whereas Native Americans are bound together by the history of conquest, African-Americans by past slavery, and Latinos by a common language, Asian Americans are an uneasy assemblage of members for whom the Asian American identification is never natural—indeed, obviously and recently manufactured—and not always welcome. Such a case could be overstated, of course, as the other groups have their own internal faultlines of difference. On this point, see Stuart Hall, "New Ethnicities," in *Black Film, British Cinema,* ed. Kobena Mercer (London: Institute of Contemporary Arts, 1988), 27–31; and Angie Chabram Dernersesian, "Chicana! Rican? No, Chicana-Riqueña! Refashioning the Transnational Connection," in *Multiculturalism: A Critical Reader,* ed. David Goldberg (New York: Blackwell, 1994), 269–295. But as a gross comparison, it brings out the reason why Internet technology generates as much or even more anxiety as excitement among Asian Americans concerned with panethnic coalition.

22. Mark Poster, "Virtual Ethnicity: Tribal Identity in an Age of Global Communications," in *Cybersociety 2.0: Revisiting Computer-Mediated Communication and Community,* ed. Steven G. Jones (Thousand Oaks, CA: Sage, 1998), 205.

23. Lisa Nakamura, "Race in/for Cyberspace: Identity Tourism and Racial Passing on the Internet," *Works and Days 25/26,* vol. 13, nos. 1–2 (1995): 181–93; Amit S. Rai, "India On-line: Electronic Bulletin Boards and the Construction of a Diasporic Hindu Identity," *Diaspora* 4, no. 1 (1995): 31–57; Daniel C. Tsang, "Notes on Queer 'n' Asian Virtual Sex," in *Asian American Sexualities: Dimensions of the Gay and Lesbian Experience,* ed. Russell Leong (New York: Routledge, 1996), 153–62; Ravi Sundaram, "Electronic Marginality: Or, Alternative Cyberfutures in the Third World," *ZKP4> Beauty and the East> A Nettime Publication;* newspaper "text filter" online at <http://www.ljudmila.org/nettime/zkp4>, 14–15; Ananda Mitra, "Virtual Commonality: Looking for India on the Internet" in *Virtual Culture: Identity and Communication in Cybersociety,* ed. Steven G. Jones (London: Sage, 1997), reprinted in *The Cybercultures Reader,* ed. David Bell and Barbara Kennedy (New York: Routledge, 2000), 676–94; Yuan Shu, "Information Technologies, the U.S. Nation-State, and Asian American Subjectivities," *Cultural Critique* 40 (1998): 145–66; Vinay Lal, "The Politics of History on the Internet: Cyber-Diasporic Hinduism and the North American Hindu Diaspora," *Diaspora* 8, no. 2 (1999):137–72; David Palumbo-Liu, "Asia Pacific: A Transnational Imaginary," in *Asian/American: Historical Crossings of a Racial Frontier* (Stanford, CA: Stanford University Press, 1999), 337–82; Jeff Ow, "The Revenge of the Yellowfaced Cyborg Terminator: The Rape of Digital Geishas and the Colonization of Cyber-Coolies in 3D Realms' *Shadow Warrior,*" in Kolko, Nakamura, and Rodman, eds., *Race in*

Cyberspace, 51–68; Jerry Kang, "Cyber-Race," *Harvard Law Review* 113, no. 5 (2000): 1130–1208; Mark Warschauer, "Language, Identity, and the Internet," in Kolko, Nakamura, and Rodman, eds., *Race in Cyberspace*, 151–70; and Wendy Hui Kyong Chun, "Scenes of Empowerment: Virtual Racial Diversity and Digital Divides," *New Formations* 45 (2001): 169–88. By no means exhaustive, this list represent some of the better-known already published works on this topic. See also the list of works in note 1 as a supplement to these essays cataloged here.

24.   Nakamura, "Race in/for Cyberspace," 190, 183.

25.   Christina Elizabeth Sharpe, "Racialized Fantasies on the Internet," *Signs* 24, no. 41 (1999): 1089–96; and Kolko, Nakamura, and Rodman, eds., *Race in Cyberspace*.

26.   Nakamura places this latter phenomenon in the context of "identity tourism," where adopting the stereotypical oriental identity of a Mr. Sulu or Chun Li does not signal admiration for "real life" Asians as much as a "fantasy of social control" in which the desire to "fix the boundaries of cultural identity and exploit them for recreational purposes" becomes realized; see Nakamura, "Race in/for Cyberspace," 186.

27.   A different kind of disappearing of the Asian majority online also occurs in Nakamura's essay. In her examination of "identity tourism" Nakamura makes a questionable assumption, that "players who choose to perform this type of racial play [picking an Asian stereotypical avatar] are almost always white, and their appropriation of stereotyped male Asiatic samurai figures allows them to indulge in a dream of crossing over racial boundaries temporarily and recreationally. Choosing these [Asian] stereotypes tips their interlocutors off to the fact that they are not 'really' Asian; they are instead 'playing' in already familiar types of performance"; Nakamura, "Race In/For Cyberspace," 185. But how does one ascertain that these players "are almost always white"? Nakamura doesn't entertain the possibility of Asian self-minstrelsy, in which yellows may "play" the Oriental stereotype precisely to distance themselves from the stereotype. Here, the mask is less important than the process of masking itself, the display of ironic distance and depth as a function of knowing and manipulating the stereotype.

28.   Rajani Sudan, "Sexy SIMS, Racy SIMMS," in Kolko, Nakamura, and Rodman, eds., *Race in Cyberspace*, 71.

29.   Cynthia Enloe, *Bananas, Beaches and Bases: Making Feminist Sense of International Politics* (Berkeley and Los Angeles: University of California Press, 1990), 54.

30.   By substantive engagements with race online we do not mean a narrow notion of closing the digital divide by merely facilitating minority and "third world" access to the Net, but instead a deeper engagement with the materialist presumptions and effects underwriting cyberspatial constructions of the online racial subject—all too often reduced to a demographic consumer segment. In her trenchant analysis of websites designed to attract middle-income people of color, Chun remarks, "These tactics cause race as a consumer category to proliferate, not to disappear on the Internet. This category proliferation encourages a kind of consumer racial passing. . . . Jennifer Gonzalez contends that this form of consumption, in which one takes on a marked body rather than an unmarked one . . . merges together the postmodern subject with the transcendent subject of old through the creation of a new cosmopolitanism. Through this one avoids the complex subjectivity of the other [and enacts a racial engagement only in terms of] consuming what the other consumes"; Chun, "Scenes of Empowerment," 180. Against such liberal-consumerist modes of crafting racial (or geopolitical) equality on the Internet in terms of the equal power to buy, Chun claims that "to understand how global telecommunications networks could facilitate social and economic justice . . . we must think about developing nations as producers, rather than as potential consumers or as disposable workers. This would entail the realization that ICT [Information and Communication Technology] does not automatically mean more freedom or democracy" (178–79). See also Tamblyn's elaboration of cyberspace as "strategy of this phase of capitalism" (Christine Tamblyn, "Remote Control: the Electronic Transference," in

Processed Lives: Gender and Technology in Everyday Life, ed. Jennifer Terry and Melodie Calvert (New York: Routledge, 1997), 42; and Palumbo-Liu's critique of cyberspace's mystified promise of (and occlusion of) political democracy by way of touting the Net's facilitation of consumer choices open to all: "we can all shop at our own levels of disposable income and computer access time"; Palumbo-Liu, "Asia Pacific," 369.

31.   Donna Haraway, "A Manifesto for Cyborgs: Science, Technology, and Socialist Feminism in the 1980s" *Socialist Review* 80 (1985): 65–108; Cathy Griggers, "Lesbian Bodies in the Age of (Post)Mechanical Reproduction," in *The Lesbian Postmodern,* ed. Laura Doan (New York: Columbia University Press, 1994), 118–33; and Jennifer Terry and Melodie Calvert, "Introduction: Machines/Lives," in Terry and Calvert, eds., *Processed Lives,* 1–19. As Griggers claims, in the age of (post)mechanical reproduction, "the point is that the bodies that are supposed ground of identity in essentialist arguments— arguments that assert we are who we are because of our bodies—are both internally fragmented in response to the intrusions of biotechnologies and advanced surgical techniques, including transsexual procedures, and externally plied by a variety of technologically determined semiotic registers ranging from the sex toy industry to broadcast [and I would add, computer mediated] representation" (123). See also Anne Balsamo, *Technologies of the Gendered Body: Reading Cyborg Women* (Durham, NC: Duke University Press, 1996); and *Wired_Women: Gender and New Realities in Cyberspace,* ed. Lynn Cherny and Elizabeth Reba Weise (Seattle: Seal Press, 1996).

32.   Mimi Nguyen, "Tales of an Asiatic Geek Girl: *Slant* from Paper to Pixels," in Nelson Tu with Headlam, eds., *Technicolor,* 177–90.

33.   Tsang, "Notes," 155. In Tsang's analysis of a gay Asian bulletin board system, virtual technology appears a facilitator of Asian American sexualities that are "in constant flux." He also argues that "by signing up for the board, one is, in fact, taking the first step toward 'coming out'" (156, 157).

34.   Haraway, "Manifesto," 96.

35.   Judith Squires, "Fabulous Feminist Futures and the Lure of Cyberculture," in *Fractal Dreams: New Media in Social Context* (London: Lawrence and Wishart, 1996), reprinted in David Bell and Kennedy, eds., *The Cybercultures Reader,* 363.

1
Cyberraces, Cyberplaces

1

Orienting Orientalism, or How to Map Cyberspace

WENDY HUI KYONG CHUN

Why cyberspace?

Cyberspace seems an odd name for a communications medium. Unlike *news-paper* (*news* + *paper*) or *film*, cyberspace does not refer to its content or to the physical materials that constitute it. Unlike *cinema*, derived from *cinematograph*, it does not refer to the apparatus that projects it.[1] Further, unlike *television* (*tele* + *vision*; vision from afar), cyberspace does not refer to the type of vision it sup-posedly enables and, unlike *radio*, derived from radiotelegraphy, it not does refer to the physical phenomenon (radiation) that enables transmission. Although all these terms—*newspaper, film, television,* and *radio*—erase sites of produc-tion, *cyberspace* erases all reference to its content, apparatus, process or form, offering instead a metaphorical mirage, for cyberspace is not spatial. Contrary to common parlance, you do not meet someone in cyberspace. Electronic in-terchanges, like telephone conversations but unlike face-to-face ones, do not take place within a confined space. Not only are there at least two "originary" places (the sender's and receiver's computers), data travels as independent pack-ets between locations and can originate from a local cache rather than the "real" location. At most, one could trace the various packet routes and produce a map of the interchange after the fact.

Part of the peculiarity of cyberspace stems from its science-fiction origins. William Gibson coined the term *cyberspace* in 1982, eleven years before Mosaic, the first graphics-based web browser, became available.[2] Although other media forms such as photography and television had literary precursors—or, at least texts that were labeled precursors after the fact—no other form takes its name from a fictional text. Inspired by the early 1980s arcade scene in Vancouver, Gibson sat at his typewriter and outlined a 3-D chessboard/consensual visual hallucination called the Matrix or cyberspace, in which corporations existed as bright neon shapes, and console cowboys stole and manipulated data. In *Neuromancer*, cyberspace is navigable and conceptualizable in a way the Internet, or "real" cyberspace, is not since cyberspace is a "graphic representation of data abstracted from the banks of every computer in the human system."[3] Other than a common fan base driven by a burning desire to see Gibson's vision as the end and origin of the Internet, Gibson's cyberspace has little in common with the Net.[4]

Cyberspace moved most definitively from a science fiction neologism to a legitimate name for communications technology with the U.S. Judiciary's Communications Decency Act decisions' "Findings of Facts" section. In it, the district judges delineated the differences between the various "areas" within cyberspace (cyberspace was chosen over the Internet presumably because it can include configurations, such as local area networks and bulletin boards, not linked to the Net). Even so, cyberspace still remains part science fiction, not only because the high-tech visions of Gibson's Matrix, and later Neal Stephenson's metaverse, have not yet been realized (and they never will), but also because cyberspace mixes science and fiction. Cyberspace is a hallucinatory space that is always in the process of becoming, but "where the future is destined to dwell."[5] Condemning cyberspace for misrepresenting "reality" or "space" thus misses the point—namely, that cyberspace as fact or fiction alters space, cybernetics, and "reality." Most often, cyberspace's alterity has been imagined and examined in terms of disembodiment, with critics and enthusiasts arguing over the fallacies and possibilities of cyberspace as a frontier of the mind. This debate, however, obfuscates the ways that narratives of cyberspace, since their literary inception, have depended on Orientalism for their own disorienting orientation.

Through the orientalizing—the exoticizing and eroticizing—of others, those imagining, creating, and describing cyberspace have made electronic spaces comprehensible, visualizable and pleasurable. In this essay, I expose the ways that cyberspace as mind-to-mind communication relies on another disembodiment—namely, the other as disembodied representation through readings of Gibson's *Neuromancer* and Mamoru Oshii's *Ghost in the Shell*. Conceived before the popularization of the web, these literary and animated texts underscore the rhetorical importance of cyberspace: it is not simply that, until the 1990s, cyberspace's existence has been mainly rhetorical, but also that cyberspace functioned rhetorically—without cyberspace, the Internet would never have become as sexy, utopian and dystopian as it was once represented as being. It also would never have been viewed as so empowering: if online communications threaten to submerge users in representation—if they threaten to turn users into media spectacles—the mind as disembodied construct allows people to turn a blind eye to their own vulnerability, and high-tech orientalism allows them to enjoy themselves while doing so. Significantly, both *Neuromancer* and *Ghost in the Shell* also offer subtle critiques of disembodiment precisely through their portrayal of cyberspace as exotic, erotic, and reductive, critiques that were obfuscated routinely in Internet propaganda.

What is important is to realize that the importance of orientalism to cyberspace is not to dismiss cyberspace and electronic communications as inherently oriental, but rather to understand how narratives of cyberspace seek to manage and engage interactivity, how these narratives fail to protect the self from the public. Not only are oriental myths not always comforting (there is always the danger of "going native"), electronic communications open the self to others. At times, others' representations invade us, and at other times our representations are circulated without our consent or knowledge. Reducing interactivity to "conscious" acts of information exchange elides the ways that our computers operate nonvolitionally and invisibly. Thus, in order to displace orientalist dreams of cyberspace, we must not simply argue that others are selves too, or that everyone should have the right to be a cowboy. Rather, we must displace this disembodying binary by highlighting the ways that the self is always compromised, even within itself. And we must highlight the disconnect between extramedial representations of electronic networks and the networks themselves, between our interfaces and our networks.

Spacing Out

Fundamentally unlocatable, cyberspace functions as a space in which to space out about the difference between space and place.[6] Based on symbolic addresses that are already translations of hexadecimal numbers that also must be translated into binary ones, electronic locations simultaneously impose, obfuscate and displace location, address, area and coordination. Cyberspace disengages name from location while offering the virtue of location. For instance, connecting to arizona.princeton.edu accesses Princeton University's UNIX servers and each specific machine in this system has a name that designates a city within Arizona, such as Flagstaff, Yuma, and Phoenix. Princeton's system does not follow geography: Princeton is not located in Arizona, and yet this state-based naming system makes coherent Princeton's UNIX system (i.e., there is no machine called *arizona*, but one connects to arizona and then is placed in a specific "city" within this state). Further, it is not clear that the original UNIX machine, Phoenix, referred to the city rather than to the mythic bird that consistently died and then rose again (every systems operator would immediately see the connection between this bird and the average server). Once Princeton moved to more than one UNIX machine, however, the state-based system was applied. This naming system reveals the fundamental arbitrariness of geographical names (there is no inherent reason why Arizona should be called Arizona—only historical ones) and calls into question notions of place and space. It is not simply, then, that cyberspace is not spatial, but also that cyberspace, deriving from an attempt to map telecommunications, translates space in such a manner that complicates the map it was once supposed to emulate.

Although space and place are often used interchangeably (one definition for place, according to the *Oxford English Dictionary,* is "a two- or three-dimensional space"), place designates a finite location, whereas space marks a gap. Place derives from the Latin *platea* (broad way), space derives from the *spatium* (interval or period). Place has been tied to notions of civilization and of connected locations, while space has been untied and evokes emptiness. Dave Healy, quoting from Yi-Fu Tuan's analysis of the New World, argues that "place is security, space is freedom: we are attached to one and long for the other."[7] In contrast, Michel De Certeau, while agreeing that place designates stability or proper relations whereas space has "none of the univocity or stability of a 'proper,' argues that space is a practiced place. Place is on the level of *langue;* space is on the level of *parole.* We see places on maps; we articulate space through our everyday lives. Space destabilizes place by catching it "in the ambiguity of an actualization, transformed into a term dependent upon many different conventions, situated as the act of a present."[8] According to Certeau, space is not what one longs for while one is encumbered in place. Rather, it is how we negotiate place—it is how we *do* or *practice* place.

Cyberspace, however, practices space: it rehearses space, it rehearses an actualization. Consider, for instance, the ways in which one "surfs," or "browses" the web. Both popular browsers, Netscape Navigator and Microsoft's Internet Explorer, rely on navigational icons. In 1999, Netscape featured a lighthouse and a nautical steering wheel, while Explorer featured a spinning globe (in recent years, an *e* has replaced the globe). When browsing the web through Netscape, you are at the helm of the ship, with Netscape providing your guiding light. Browsing through Internet Explorer, you are spanning the globe from space, with Microsoft serving as your global positioning system. In either case, by typing in an address, or by clicking from location to location, one teleports rather than travels from one virtual location to another, and one gets lost through typos rather than wrong turns. Traveling through cyberspace takes out the scenery between fixed locations, or, to be more precise, cyberspace reminds us of the temporal aspect of space by converting the "spatial" interval into an often-unbearable space of time in which one anticipates the next page and tries to decipher the page that emerges bit by bit on one's screen.[9] This teleporting does not mean that we no longer catch place "in the ambiguity of an actualization, transformed into a term dependent upon many different conventions, situated as the act of a present."[10] Indeed, through our surfing, through our never-ending caching of webpages, we catch and transform virtual spaces.

If our computer interfaces tend to highlight spatial relations and navigational control, however, it is probably because users usually have little to no navigational control over their data. Even if they know of and use source routing, users cannot always assign their packets' data path successfully: many hosts will refuse to accept their source routed packets, since they are considered to be a security risk. Constantly opened and reopened so that routers may know where to send them next, packets follow paths that are far from efficient and by no means certain. The network operates on the assumption that it is always failing, that packets collide, that packets must be resent. TCP (transmission control protocol) works to ensure the safe delivery of packets by setting up a "virtual circuit" between two machines through features such as the "three-way handshake," in which our machines communicate with each other before any user-initiated data is sent. As well, in order for the system to work, network inter-face cards constantly "listen" to each other and listen for system-wide broadcasts (broadcasts, such as a gateway announcing that it is "up," that have little to do with user messages). There is a real danger that the network will be swamped and rendered inoperable by packets that have nothing to do with the supposed "payload," nothing to do with user interventions.

Critics and pundits usually gloss over cyberspace's rehearsal of space and the noisy network that underlies it in order to reduce it to a terrestrial version of outer space. When understood as an electronic frontier, cyberspace manages global fiber-optic networks by transforming nodes, wires, cables and comput-ers into an infinite enterprise/discovery zone. Like all explorations, charting cyberspace entails uncovering what was always already there and declaring it "new." It obscures already existing geographies and structures so that space is vacuous yet chartable, unknown yet populated and populatable. Like the New World and the frontier, settlers claim this "new" space and declare themselves its citizens (this frontier is relatively guilt free, since there are no natives—or so it seems).[11] Advocacy groups such as the Electronic Frontier Foundation exploited the metaphor of the frontier in the early 1990s in order to argue that cyberspace was both outside and inside the United States, since the frontier effectively lies outside government regulation yet within American cultural and historical nar-ratives. Those interested in "wiring the world" reproduce narratives of "darkest Africa" and of civilizing missions. These benevolent missions, aimed at allevi-ating the disparity between connected and unconnected areas, covertly—if not overtly—conflated spreading the light with making a profit.[12] Cyberspace both remaps the world and makes it ripe for exploration once more. According to David Brande, cyberspace, through its proffering of limitless opportunity and open spaces, reinvigorates capitalism.[13] Cyberspace ends the narratives of the end, ends narratives of postmodern/postindustrial society's ennui and exhaus-tion. Cyberspace proffers direction and orientation in a world disoriented by technological and political change, disoriented by increasing surveillance and mediation, through high-tech orientalism.

Cyberspace's single-minded deflection relies on and perpetuates high tech orientalism. As a frontier of the mind, it seeks to reorient—to steer the self—by making it unrepresentable and by reducing everything else to images. It seeks to reorient the self by turning sexual threat into sexual opportunity. Cyberspace rehearses orientalism in all the meanings of the word *orient*. More precisely, authors refer to the Orient in order to establish cyberspace as an "other space," a compensatory heterotopia.[14]

Edward Said, in *Orientalism*, argues that the Orient—as defined by and for the West—is "the place of Europe's greatest and richest and oldest colonies, the source of its civilizations and languages, its cultural contestant, and one of its deepest and most recurring images of the Other."[15] In *Critical Terrains*, Lisa Lowe, who argues that the "uses" and constructions of the Orient are more multiple than Said allows, agrees that the Orient others space. Pluralizing and merging Michel Foucault's notion of a heterotopia and Said's analysis of the oriental as a "surrogate and even underground self,"[16] Lowe defines oriental spaces as heterotropical, where heterotropical spaces are multiple and interpenetrable rather than singularly defined against normal or utopian spaces.[17] According to Foucault, in "Of Other Spaces," heterotopias are "like counter-sites, a kind of effectively enacted utopia in which the real sites, all the other real sites that can be found within the culture, are simultaneously represented, contested, and inverted. Places of this kind are outside of all places, even though it may be possible to indicate their location in reality."[18] Foucault categorizes heterotopias into crisis heterotopias (the boarding school and honeymoon), heterotopias of deviance (rest homes and prisons), heterotopias of illusion (nineteenth-century brothels) and, most important for our purposes, heterotopias of compensation (colonies).

Heterotopias of compensation are "absolutely perfect other spaces": drawing on Puritan societies in New England and on Jesuits in Paraguay, Foucault describes them as "marvelous, absolutely regulated colonies in which human perfection was effectively achieved . . . in which existence was regulated at every turn." They are "as perfect, as meticulous, as well arranged as ours is messy, ill constructed, and jumbled."[19] In order to set up this compensatory space, Foucault must gloss over the fact that this placing of pure order simultaneously obfuscates, if not annihilates, other spaces/places already in existence—namely, Native America. And these other spaces do not completely dissolve, but rather continually threaten "pure order." Puritan societies had to defend themselves against indigenous populations that threatened their colony, preventing the effective realization of their utopia. Regardless, and perhaps because of the difficulty of maintaining heterotopias, Foucault settles on the figure of the boat as "the heterotopia *par excellence.*" The boat is exemplary because it is "a floating piece of space, a place without a place, that exists by itself, that is closed in on itself and at the same time is given over the infinity of the sea and, from port to port, from tack to tack, from brothel to brothel, it goes as far as the colonies in search of the most precious treasures they conceal in their gardens." Most important for Foucault, "in civilizations without boats, dreams dry up, espionage takes the place of adventure, and the police take the place of pirates."[20]

This displacement of the limitations and promises of occidental societies onto heterogeneous oriental spaces comes with no guarantees, since orientalist narratives cannot entirely displace the actual territories and ships are routinely wrecked. As well, since the Orient serves as one of Europe's first points of identification, it destabilizes the notion of Europe it also grounds. Thus, it is not simply that the Europe stands as subject and the Orient as object, but also that the Orient *haunts* Europe and fissures European identity.[21] This relationship of identification, desire, and alienation serves as a model for the relationship between virtual and nonvirtual spaces—and, just as the multiplicity of "Oriental spaces" works against totalizing myths, so too does the multiplicity of electronic spaces threaten to disorient the user they seek to orient.

Literary Inceptions

Cyberspace, like the Orient, is a literary invention.

Said, arguing for the textual construction of the Orient, writes that "even the rapport between an Orientalist and the Orient was textual, so much so that it is reported of some of the early-nineteenth-century German Orientalists that their first view of an eight-armed Indian statue cured them completely of their Orientalist taste."[22] According to Said, this textual delusion stemmed from the Orientalists' preference for "the schematic authority of a text to the disorientations of direct encounters with the human." In so doing, they assumed "that people, places and experiences can always be described by a book, so much so that the book (or text) acquires a greater authority, and use, even than the actuality it describes."[23] Although Said's assumption that face-to-face encounters are less prone to orientalizing interactions is dubious given the history of face-to-face colonialism, orientalist texts do authorize a simulacrum that they call the Orient. Rather than simply describing the Orient, orientalists have *projected* an Orient that does not easily map onto geographies and cultures deemed oriental. The status of the Orient as fictional yet indexical to an "other" space parallels the status of cyberspace as science fiction made digital, as well as the status of science fiction-based cyberspace.

As noted earlier, William Gibson coined the term *cyberspace* in 1982, but he offered the most compelling description of it in *Neuromancer,* a cyberpunk novel published in 1984. In *Neuromancer,* Case—the console cowboy protagonist— "live[s] for the bodiless exultation of cyberspace," and his "elite stance involve[s] a certain relaxed contempt for the flesh. The body was meat."[24] Case's stance has been mimicked by cyberpunk fiction writers and by the so-called cyberelite who published in and were publicized by magazines such as *Wired* and *Mondo2000* in the 1990s. Like the early-nineteenth-century German orientalists who were disappointed if not repulsed by their first encounter with the "physical" text, most cyberpunk enthusiasts were disappointed by the Internet. Regardless, science-fiction descriptions of cyberspace have been so compelling that people willingly have ignored the differences between electronic networks and science fiction in order to call our networks cyberspace.

The basic plot line of *Neuromancer* is this: As punishment for stealing from one of his employers, Case is injected by the Yakuza (the mythic Japanese Mafia) with a myotoxin that makes it impossible for him to jack into cyberspace. He then travels to Night City (a subsidiary of Chiba City, Japan) in order to find a cure in their infamous nerve shops. Unable to repair the damage and out of money, Case becomes "just another hustler" on a suicidal arc. Before he manages to get himself killed, he's picked up by Molly (a female "street samurai" razorgirl/cyborg) who collects him for a mission directed by Armitage, Gibson's version of a masked man (his standard, handsome, plastic features serve as his mask). Armitage fixes Case's nerve damage in exchange for his cooperation, and, to ensure his loyalty, he lines Case's main arteries with toxin sacs. In order to prevent his nerve damage from returning, Case must be injected with an enzyme possessed by Armitage. The team first breaks into Sense/Net to steal a ROM (read-only-memory) construct (a program that mimics the mind) of Dixie (Case's now dead mentor), who will help Case break into a T-A (Tessier-Ashpool) AI (Artificial Intelligence) called Rio (but whose "real" name is Neuromancer). Molly physically steals the construct while Case, jacked into her sense sensorium via simstim, mans the virtual operation and keeps time. The real boss turns out to be Wintermute, another T-A AI who wishes to merge with Neuromancer in order to form a sentient being: Wintermute is improvisation; Neuromancer is personality. To merge, Molly must enter Villa Straylight—T-A mansion in Freeside (outer space)—and extract the "word" from 3Jane (Tessier's and Ashpool's daughter), while Case hacks into Neuromancer in cyberspace with the help of a Chinese virus program. Things get complicated, but the ending is somewhat happy: Wintermute and Neuromancer merge to become the Matrix; Case gets his blood changed; Molly leaves him to pursue further adventures. Throughout, Case flips between "reality," "cyberspace," and "simstim."

Orientation and disorientation mark cyberpunk worlds. As opposed to science fiction and fantasy novels set in other worlds or universes, cyberpunk plays with the world as we know it, offering different contexts for recognizable places (Boston in Gibson's fiction becomes the endpoint of BAMA—the Boston Atlanta Metropolitan Axis). As Pam Rosenthal notes, "the future in the cyberpunk world, no matter how astonishing its technological detailing, is always shockingly recognizable—it is our world, gotten worse, gotten more uncomfortable, inhospitable, dangerous, and thrilling."[25] Gibson writes that cyberpunk is "all about the present. It's not really about an imagined future. It's a way of trying to come to terms with the awe and terror inspired in me by the world in which we live."[26] As with BAMA, Gibson effects this shocking recognizability through seemingly gratuitous descriptions, and descriptions embedded in specialty language (as Gibson explains in an interview: "it was the *gratuitous* moves, the odd, quirky, irrelevant details, that provided a sense of strangeness"[27]). Consider the opening to *Neuromancer:*

> The sky above the port was the color of television, tuned to a dead channel.
>
> "It's not like I'm using," Case heard someone say, as he shouldered his way through the crowd around the door of the Chat. "It's like my body's developed this massive drug deficiency." It was a Sprawl voice and a Sprawl joke. The Chatsubo was a bar for professional expatriates; you could drink there for a week and never hear two words in Japanese.

Ratz was tending bar, his prosthetic arm jerking monotonously as he filled a tray of glasses with draft Kirin. He saw Case and smiled, his teeth a webwork of East European steel and brown decay. Case found a place at the bar, between the unlikely tan of one of Lonny Zone's whores and the crisp naval uniform of a tall African whose cheekbones were ridged with precise rows of tribal scars. "Wage was in here early, with two joeboys," Ratz said, shoving a draft across the bar with his good hand. "Maybe some business with you, Case?"[28]

As these three opening paragraphs reveal, the "gratuitous" details Gibson uses usually entail the surprising juxtaposition of the natural and technological, the "primitive" and the high tech, written matter-of-factly. He also uses foreign (mainly Japanese) brand names (such as Kirin) in the place of more familiar American ones (such as Budweiser), or some very odd mix (such as the Mitsubishi Bank of America, Hosaka, Ono-Sendai, Tessier-Ashpool, Maas-Neotek). Corporate names as modifiers have become essential: it is never simply a coffee maker, but a "Braun coffeemaker" and later a "Braun robot device." He also insists on unfamiliar proper names, such as Lonny Zone and the Sprawl. Gibson's "explanations" or descriptions are perhaps appropriate in a series all about "information": they are noninformative, but written in such a way that one would think they would be informative. The peppering of description with specialty jargon such as "joeboy" furthers this informatic effect since presumably to those "in the know" such language would make sense. This combination of jargon with foreign and made-up trademarks gives the impression that this world should be knowable, or that some subject (or reader) who knows should exist or emerge.

Significantly, the most important markers are racial and ethnic ones, that both refer to and complicate notions of nationality and race. Although Gibson argues that nation-states in his new world have mainly disappeared or become reconfigured, nationality or continentality (when it comes to non-American white characters) has become all that stronger: Ratz's teeth are a webwork of East European steel and brown decay, and Case's fellow bar inhabitant is a tall African whose cheekbones were ridged with precise rows of tribal scars. In general, racial otherness is confined to stereotypes that serve as local details (which thus proves the "global scope" of this future) and that offer no movement, a limitation that Gibson works hard to improve upon in *Count Zero*. Although Case eventually moves outside his profile (and thus becomes more than a "case"), the Zionites are constantly high, always touching and completely romanticized by and incomprehensible to our cowboy, Case. Maelcum, Case's soon to be sidekick serves as an erotic object of sorts, with Case constantly staring at Maelcum's muscular back and describing him in the same manner that he describes Molly. And these "dark" others in *Neuromancer* are marked as technologically outside, as somehow involved in an alternative past of tribal scars, and the shock value of the prose lies in this juxtaposition of their past with our future. Istanbul—the classically "oriental" space—is described as a sluggish city that "never changes," seeped in history and sexism.[29] Certain things that never change anchor the reader and serve as her orienting points.

The future world, "gotten worse, gotten more uncomfortable, inhospitable, dangerous, and thrilling," however, invariably translates into the world gotten more Japanese.[30] Gibson magnifies the 1980s burgeoning economic power of Japan so that, as Yoshimoto Mitsuhiro notes, "the future world does not seem to be able to function without things Japanese."[31] Whereas golden-age science fiction incorporated Greek togas into their sunny futures, *Neuromancer* incorporates parts of the Japanese past, such as ninjas, in their dystopian ones. As Lisa Nakamura argues, "anachronistic signs of Japaneseness are made, in the conventions of cyberpunk, to signify the future rather than the past."[32] These anachronistic signs of Japaneseness are not chosen randomly. Rather, samurais, ninjas, and shonen are drawn from Japan's Edo period and they confine the Japanese past to the period of first contact between the West and Japan. Cyberpunk thus mixes images of the mysterious yet-to-be-opened Japan (which eventually did submit to the West) with the conquering corporate Japan of the future. In addition, the "near" Japanese past (i.e., the present) is represented by technological badlands produced through contact with the West. Describing Night City, Case says, "the Yakuza might be preserving the place as a kind of historical park, a reminder of humble origins."[33] But Night City, as the opening page of *Neuromancer* makes clear, is filled with gaijin paradises, places where "you could drink . . . for a week and never hear two words in Japanese."[34] Night City, the "deliberately unsupervised playground for technology itself," is not entirely Japanese.[35] Rather, the past that Night City marks is the moment of fusion between East and West, the moment of the Japanese adopting and surpassing Western technology.

This denial of the coeval, as Johannes Fabian has noted, is how anthropology constitutes its object—the native other, who is consistently treated as though his existence does not take place in the same time. This "time machine" effect of anthropology is magnified within cyberpunk in its literal construction of a time machine, in which the reader is supposedly transported into the "near" future— a future whose recognition and misrecognition is created by juxtaposing archaic (non-Western) pasts with present (Western) pasts. Thus, the much-lauded ability of cyberpunk to enable us to finally "experience" our present depends on the construction of those others as past and future (which is just as much a "failure" as—Fredric Jameson argues—their inability to imagine the future).[36]

Within the grim Japanified landscape of *Neuromancer*, the software industry marks the last vestige of American superiority. In cyberspace, American ingenuity wins over Japanese corporate assimilation. In "reality," those who succeed efface their own individuality and become part of the corporate machinery.

Power means incorporation into a larger organism: "The zaibatsus, the multi-nationals that shaped the course of human history, had transcended old barriers. Viewed as organisms, they had attained a kind of immortality. You couldn't kill a zaibatsu by assassinating a dozen key executives; there were others waiting to step up the ladder, assume the vacated position, access the vast banks of corporate memory."[37] Corporate power—power somehow tied to real bodies rather than virtual ones—seems immortal because power is depersonified. Instead of relying on individual talent or rewarding the individual, power breeds endless replacement parts, forcing people to accommodate to its machine-like rhythm. We read that "Case had always taken it for granted that the real bosses, the king-pins in a given industry, would be both more and less than *people*. He'd seen it in the men who'd crippled him in Memphis, he'd seen Wage affect the semblance of it in Night City, and it had allowed him to accept Armitage's flatness and lack of feeling. He'd always imagined it as a gradual and willing accommodation of the machine, the system, the parent organism. It was the root of street cool, too, the knowing posture that implied connection, invisible lines up to the hidden levels of influence."[38] More or less than people, the real bosses are cyborgs who meld together to form a superorganism not unlike *Star Trek*'s master enemy, the Borg. Gibson relies on the 1980s mythology of Japan as "the greatest 'machine-loving nation of the world,' a culture in which 'machines are priceless friends,'"[39] by portraying the zaibatsus as master cyborgs. Because of their unnatural love of machines, the Japanese have fused into a mass organization dominated by machine rhythm and this mass organism happily assimilates all. Importantly, Gibson uses the term *zaibatsu* rather than multinational corporation. This use of the Japanese for what seems to be a particularly American phenomenon does not simply imply that only Japanese corporations assimilate their workers. Rather, Gibson projects this process onto the Japanese partly in order to de-familiarize his readers, to dislodge their assumption that multinationals mean American superiority.

Cyberspace seems to stand as a Western frontier against this world of ac-commodation and assimilation. The meatless console cowboy is an individual talent: he paradoxically escapes this machine-organism fusion by escaping his body—by becoming a disembodied mind—when he merges with technology. Navigating the digital world and manipulating its code take bravado and skill, and cowboys steal data for their employers by manipulating ICEbreakers (ICE = intrusion countermeasures electronics). Cyberspace, as a consensual hallucination, as "a graphic representation of data abstracted from the banks of every computer in the human system," allows for freelancing.[40] As a space in which the body disappears, it rewards anonymity rather than assimilation. As Pam Rosenthal argues, "The hacker mystique posits power through anonymity. One does not log on to the system through authorized paths of entry; one sneaks in, dropping through trap doors in the security program, hiding one's tracks, immune to the audit trails that were put there to make the perceiver part of the data perceived. It is a dream of recovering power and wholeness by seeing wonders by not being seen."[41]

In effect, cyberspace allows the hacker to assume the privilege of the imperial subject—"to see without being seen."[42] This recovery of wholeness and power also recovers American ideals. As Frederick Buell argues, through the console cowboy, "a cowboy on the new frontier of cyberspace, he [Gibson] brings a pre–Frederick Jackson Turner excitement into a postmodern, hyperdeveloped world; if the old frontier has been built out thoroughly and its excitements become guilty ones in the wake of contemporary multi-cultural/postcolonial rewritings of western history, try, then, cyberspace in an apparently polycultural, globalized era."[43] More succinctly, Buell argues, "cyberspace becomes the new U.S. Frontier, accessible to the privileged insider who happens to be a reconfigured version of the American pulp hero."

Perhaps, but not because cyberspace is outside the Japanified world; cyberspace in *Neuromancer* is not a U.S. frontier and good old American cowboys cannot survive without things Japanese. First, cowboys cannot access cyberspace without Japanese equipment (Case needs his Ono-Sendai in order to jack in). Second, cyberspace is still marked by Asian trademarks and corporations. However, cyberspace—unlike the physical landscape—can be conquered and made to submit: entering cyberspace is analogous to opening up the Orient. *Neuromancer* counters American anxieties about "exposure to, and penetration by, Japanese culture" with a medium that enables American penetration.[44] Cyberspace as disembodied representation rehearses themes of oriental exoticism and Western penetration. Consider, for instance, the moment that Case is reunited with cyberspace:

A gray disk, the color of Chiba sky.
Now—
Disk beginning to rotate, faster, becoming a sphere of paler gray. Expanding—And it flowed, flowered for him, fluid neon origami trick, the unfolding of his distanceless home, his country, transparent 3D chessboard extending to infinity. Inner eye opening to the stepped scarlet pyramid of the Eastern Seaboard Fission Authority burning beyond the green cubes of the Mitsubishi Bank of America, and high and very far away he saw the spiral arms of military systems, forever beyond his reach.
And somewhere he was laughing, in a white-painted loft, distant fingers caressing the deck, tears of release streaking his face.[45]

Cyberspace opens up for him, flowers for him—a fluid neon origami trick. Reuniting with cyberspace is a sexual experience: he has tears of release as he enters once more his distanceless home. As Molly (the all black-clad "street samurai" razorgirl who collects Case for his mission) notes, "I saw you stroking that Sendai; man, it was pornographic."[46] This flowering cyberspace draws on and disseminates pornographic Orientalist fantasies of opening Asian beauties.

As one pornographic website put it, "You are welcome to our dojo! Look no further, traveler. You have found the Clan of Asian Nudes, filled with gorgeous Asian women in complete submission. Take them by becoming a samurai. Our dojo houses the most incredible supermodels from Japan, Vietnam, China, Laos, and San Francisco's Chinatown! Their authentic, divine beauty will have you entranced nightly. New girls are added almost every day, their gifts blossoming before you on the screen."[47] Not only cyberspace blossoms for the console cowboy, so do Oriental ICEbreakers. When Case breaks into the T-A AI, he uses a Chinese Kuang Grade Eleven ICEbreaker and this "big mother" unfolds around them. "Polychrome shadow, countless translucent layers shifting and recombining. Protean, enormous, it tower[s] above them, blotting out the void."[48] The *translucent* shifting layers surround them and evoke images of oriental mystery and penetrability.[49] This oriental "big mother" blots out the void, filling it with its shadow and revealing its secret to the occidental male who maneuvers it to perform his will. If the Yakuza—the "sons of the neon chrysanthemum"—have altered his system so that Case could no longer jack in to cyberspace, by reentering it he takes over their territory; he unites with their flowering mother.[50] This link between cyberspace and blossoming oriental female positions the viewer as samurai and contains the "modern" threat of Japan by remapping it as feudal and premodern. If, as David Morley and Kevin Robins argue, Japan "has destabilized the neat correlation between West/East and modern/pre-modern," this feudal portrayal reorients the cowboy by reorientalizing Japan;[51] hence the allusions to the Edo and Meiji periods, which undermine the future global power of Japan.

Entering cyberspace thus allows one to conquer a vaguely threatening oriental landscape. As Stephen Beard in his reading of Ridley Scott's *Blade Runner* argues, "through the projection of exotic (and erotic) fantasies onto this high-tech delirium, anxieties about the 'impotence' of western culture can be, momentarily, screened out. High-tech Orientalism makes possible 'cultural amnesia, ecstatic alienation, serial self-erasure.'"[52] In *Neuromancer,* high-tech orientalism allows Case to erase his body in orgasmic ecstasy. Or, to be more precise, high-tech orientalism allows one to *enjoy* anxieties about Western impotence. It allows one, as Gibson puts it, "to try to *come* to terms with the awe and terror inspired in me by the world in which we live."[53] That is, ecstasy does not obliterate impotence, but rather allows one to make do with it. This portrayal may also highlight the limitations of such sexual fantasies and conquest, for this orgasmic ecstasy constructs cyberspace—the supposed consensual hallucination—as a solipsistic space.

In cyberspace, Case runs into no other people—or perhaps more precisely no other disembodied minds: Case's mind is the only human one out there. On the Matrix, Case communicates with artificial intelligences, computer viruses, and computer constructs. This American superiority depends on American disembodied brains combating representations, virtual shapes and programs rather than people. In order to preserve the cowboy, cyberspace is "a drastic simplification" that not only limits sensual bandwidth; it also reduces others to code.[54] In effect, these others—these codes—that Case encounters are mimics. The Chinese ICEbreaker does the methodical hacking work, going "siamese" on the computer defense systems. Glowing and colorful cubes in cyberspace represent Japanese corporations such as the Mitsubishi Bank of America. The closest things to sentient beings Case encounters online are Dixie (the ROM construct of his deceased hacker mentor), Linda Lee (whose ROM construct he encounters when Neuromancer attempts to trap him), and the T-A AIs Wintermute and Neuromancer.

This empty high-tech orientalist space parallels the textual construction of the Orient in early scholarly studies that focused on ancient civilizations. These studies, as Said has argued, treated the Orient as empty; the "real" Egyptians orientalist scholars encountered—if these scholars traveled to Egypt at all—were treated as background, as relics or as proof of the degeneration of the Oriental race.[55] In cyberspace, then, as in all orientalist spaces, there are disembodied minds on the one hand and disembodied representations on the other. There are those who can reason online and those who are reduced to information. *In cyberspace, there is disembodiment, and then there is disembodiment.* Via high-tech orientalism, the window of cyberspace becomes a mirror that reflects Case's mind and reduces others to background, or reflects his mind via the others it constructs as mimics. High-tech orientalism, like its nontech version, "defines the Orient as that which can never be a subject," since nonsubjecthood is the condition of possibility of the Occidental subject.[56] In order to preserve the American cowboy, it reinforces stereotypes of the Japanese as mechanical mimics (imitators of technology). This is not to say that in order to portray a more "fair" version of cyberspace, Gibson should have included Japanese cowboys within *Neuromancer* (or even more Japanese characters); nor is it to say that Gibson celebrates cyberspace as orientalist. It *is* to say that this influential version of cyberspace mixes together frontier dreams with sexual conquest: it reveals the objectification of others to be key to the construction of any "cowboy" and any James A. Michener–esque American samurai. This is, perhaps, a brilliant critique of Orientalism in general. Perhaps.

Significantly, Case navigates both cyberspace and Night City through a relentless paranoia- and drug-induced datafication. When he and Molly play a cat-and-mouse game through Night City, he describes his adventure in terms of his previous virtual experiences. We read, "In some weird and very approximate way, it was like a run in the matrix. Get just wasted enough, find yourself in some desperate but strangely arbitrary kind of trouble, and it was possible to see Ninsei as a field of data, the way the matrix had once reminded him of proteins linking to distinguish cell specialties. Then you could throw yourself into a highspeed drift and skid, totally engaged but set apart from it all, and all around you the dance of biz, information interacting, data made flesh, in the mazes of the black market."[57] When one finds oneself in some desperate but strangely arbitrary trouble—when the world no longer makes sense—the virtual and physical landscapes converge. More specifically, Ninsei becomes the Matrix, a world in which others are reduced to information or data. As in cyberspace, these reductions to code enable a certain self-direction; they enable one to throw oneself into a high-speed drift and skid. Parallels between cyberspace and Ninsei are sprinkled throughout *Neuromancer*. The gray disk that marks Case's entry into cyberspace is the color of the Chiba sky (the color of television tuned to a dead channel). When Case remembers Ninsei, he remembers "faces and Ninsei neon," a neon that is replicated in the bright red and green online representations of corporations. Ninsei people are similarly reduced to light and code. Case always remembers his former lover Linda Lee as "bathed in restless laser light, features reduced to a code."[58] The easy codification of things and people breaks down when Case confronts his other "home," BAMA; hence, when he is thrown into the metropolis again, when everything no longer mimics him, Case notes that "Ninsei had been a lot simpler."[59] Ninsei had been a lot simpler because this space had always been data, been Oriental for Case. To Case, the Orient had always been "a library or archive of information."[60]

Importantly, Gibson portrays Case as a *bad* navigator in order to show the inadequacies of Ninsei as information. In the high-speed chase I cited earlier, Case correctly assesses that Molly is following him, but incorrectly assumes that she is out to kill him on Wage's behalf (a misconception based on faulty information given to him by Linda Lee). Linda Lee also moves from being an easily codified character, to a woman who embodies the complex patterns of the human body. As well, although Case eventually wins in cyberspace, he "flatlines" several times and is almost seduced by Neuromancer into dying there. Finally, the neat separation between cyberspace and the physical world collapse at the end, when Wintermute's plans go astray and Case must enter the T-A villa to help Molly. In other words, the cowboy and the datafication of others do not always work; Case's rehearsing of orientalism as a means of navigation and understanding does not always work. If anything, this rehearsal is—to repeat once more—an attempt to *come* to terms with awe and terror, not necessarily to eradicate awe and terror (if such a thing were possible). This rehearsal is intimately linked to the desire to contain the foreign, to render comprehensible a "new space" if only through desire. As Said argues, "In essence such a category is not so much a way of receiving new information as it is a method of controlling what seems to be a threat to some established view of things. If the mind must suddenly deal with what it takes to be a radically new form of life—as Islam appeared to Europe in the early Middle Ages—the response on the whole is conservative and defensive. Islam is judged to be a fraudulent new version of some previous experience, in this case Christianity. The threat is muted, familiar values impose themselves, and in the end the mind reduces the pressure upon it by accommodating things to itself as either 'original' or 'repetitious.' "[61] Orientalism, like cyberspace, emerges from contact with something new and reduces the new to previous experiences. In terms of the genesis of cyberspace, the *newness* of cyberspace has been rendered old through orientalism. This conservative response constructs what it seeks to explain and control. As a defensive response, orientalism offers critics of cyberspace a means by which to attempt to contain a cyberspace that does not yet exist. Thus, given that *Neuromancer* precedes the web, the "new" has been produced as a way to create nostalgia for the old, for the good old American present.

Thus, cyberpunk's twin obsessions with cyberspace and the Orient stem from the ways that the Orient serves as a privileged example of the virtual. The Orient serves to orient the reader/viewer, enabling her to envision the world as data. This twinning sustains—barely—the dream of self-erasure and pure subjectivity. The reduction of the Japanese to mimic sustains the image of the Imperial subject. Most simply, others must be reduced to information in order for the console cowboy to emerge and penetrate. The dream of bodiless subjectivity must be accompanied by bodiless representivity. Since its very inception, then, cyberspace—as orientalist heterotopia—has perpetuated and relied on differences that it claims to erase.[62]

Looking Back

Despite its focus on American underdogs-come-heroes, cyberpunk has global appeal. Most significantly, cyberpunk has influenced an already existing genre of anime, or Japanese animation, by the name of *mecha* (a Japanese transliteration and transformation of the word mechanical); through mecha, anime has gained cult status in nations such as the United States and France.[63] In Japanese cyberpunk, however, the American cowboy disappears and "bad" technology stems from American, rather than Japanese, companies. The future, though, is still Japan's, and in this section I turn to Mamoru Oshii's animated rendering of Masamune Shirow's *Ghost in the Shell* in order to see what happens to cyberpunk when it travels *home,* so to speak.

Arguably the most "westernized" anime, *Ghost in the Shell* was released simultaneously in Europe, America and Japan and marks anime's American debut in major movie theaters. It reached No. 1 on *Billboard* magazine's video sales chart and earned the rather limited title of New York's highest-grossing film shown exclusively on a single screen in one theater.[64] *Ghost in the Shell* was a hallmark in anime production for both aesthetic and corporate reasons: it was "the most expensive and technically advanced Japanese animated feature yet made," although it still only cost $10 million—a tenth of that for "*The Hunchback of Notre Dame.*"[65] It was also cofinanced and produced by Japan's Bandai and Kodansha and Chicago-based Manga Entertainment.

The net is vast and limitless.

Figure 1.1   The "new Major" leaving Batou's safehouse.

The plot of *Ghost in the Shell* parallels *Neuromancer*—except that, rather than an artificial intelligence seeking to be free by merging with its better half, an artificial life form (the Puppet Master) seeks to free itself by merging with the cyborg Major Motoko Kusanagi. Set in Hong Kong in 2029, *Ghost in the Shell* follows the adventures of the Major, who leads Section 9—a secret intelligence agency filled with cyborgs of "a strange corporate conglomeration called Japan"—as she pursues the Puppet Master. A titanium "Megatech Body" has replaced the Major's entire body, or "shell." The human essence is encapsulated in one's "ghost," which holds one's memories. The "Puppet Master" is so dangerous a criminal because he ghost-hacks people, inserting false memories, controlling their actions, and reducing them to puppets. After various plot turns and chase scenes, they merge: the Puppet Master dies, and the Major receives his powers. The anime ends with her studying the expanse of the Net before her. Although she asks herself, "where shall I go now? The net is vast and limitless," the "camera" pans through the landscape of Hong Kong (see figs. 1.1, 1.2, 1.3).

Like *Neuromancer, Ghost in the Shell* is set in a foreign locale—this time Hong Kong instead of Japan. As well, both films were produced at a time of economic anxiety and impotence. Toshiya Ueno argues that "the choice of Hong Kong represents an unconscious criticism of Japan's role as sub-empire: by choosing Hong Kong as the setting of this film, and trying to visualize the information net and capitalism, the director of this film, Oshii Mamoru, unconsciously tried to

Figure 1.2 The Major overlooking the city.

criticize the sub-imperialism of Japan (and other Asian nations)."[66] Perhaps, but the choice of Hong Kong also orientalizes. Faced with the task of representing basically invisible networks of information, director Mamoru Oshii chose a location that could easily be conflated with information. He chose Hong Kong because, he explains, In "Ghost in the Shell," I wanted to create a present flooded with information, and it [Japan's multilayered world] wouldn't have lent itself to that. For this reason, I thought of using exoticism as an approach to a city

Figure 1.3 The last frame; Hong Kong as vast net.

of the future. In other words, I believe that a basic feeling people get perhaps when imagining a city of the near future is that while there is an element of the unknown, standing there they'll get used to this feeling of being an alien. Therefore, when I went to look for locations in Hong Kong, I felt that this was it. A city without past or future. Just a flood of information."[67] But, as the film's last sequence shows, rather than inherently having no past or no future, Hong Kong's landscape is *made* into a flood of information in order to represent the vast expanse of the Net. In order to "explain" cyberspace, the threatening city/region (Hong Kong, and by extension China) becomes data.

To function as data, the city must also be readable. The "basic feeling" portrayed by Hong Kong, then, must be an oriented disorientation. The basic feeling that Oshii strives for is that of a *tourist* rather than a resident: tourists, not residents, *stand* in a public space, in order to get used to the feeling of being alien. In other words, it is not simply that Tokyo is more multilayered than Hong Kong, but rather that Oshii's audience is too familiar with Tokyo to be adequately disoriented.[68] After all, what city—to the tourist—is not a flood of information? By this, I do not mean to imply that all cities are alike; indeed, some are more disorienting than others. However, an unknown city confronts one with the task of navigation, and one is confronted with the necessity and inadequacy of maps. The city both inundates and leaves one looking for more information, for a way to decipher the landscape in front of oneself.

In order to effect this paradox of familiar alienation, Oshii relies on street signs: "I thought that I could express networks which are invisible to all through drawing not electronic images but a most primitive low-tech group of signboards piled like a mountain, that this would work well in drawing a world being

Figure 1.4   Street scene in the first chase scene.

Figure 1.5 Hong Kong signs in the extended musical interlude.

submerged under information, in which people live like insects."[69] *Ghost in the Shell* thus relentlessly focuses on street signs that function as literal signposts for the foreign audience (see figs. 1.4, 1.5, and 1.6). Oshii glosses over the fact that the street signs' ability to invoke information networks depends on literacy: a Japanese audience can read these signs, which are written in Chinese characters and in English. Just as "getting used to the feeling of being alien" in American cyberpunk depends on Japanese trademarks—words that have

Figure 1.6 Signs in English as well as Chinese characters.

Figure 1.7 Overhead view of the market.

become recognizable and readable in other languages—unalienating alienation in *Ghost in the Shell* depends on literacy enabled by historic connections between East Asian countries via Confucian study and modernization.[70]

Oshii also juxtaposes past and primitive artifacts with modern architecture in order to make Hong Kong legible. In order to construct Hong Kong as a city without history, without the complexity associated with one's home environment, he deploys historical images. As in *Blade Runner,* scenes of Oriental "teeming markets" punctuate *Ghost in the Shell.* Just as American cyberpunk's vision of Japan mixes together Edo images and ideas with high-tech equipment, Japanese cyberpunk visions of Hong Kong mix together traditional Chinese hats and teeming markets with high-tech office towers (see figs. 1.7 and 1.8).[71] The Chinese "present" marks a low-tech future that enables the viewer to make sense of this high-tech future.

This exoticism of the city of the near future enables the reader to navigate cyberspace and to view it as a guiding, yet visually poor, map. Cyberspace makes unfamiliar space mappable and understandable. If at first the viewer is confused by the views of cyberspace that begin the anime, the viewer soon relies on them to understand the action; it helps the viewer orient herself. The frequent segues between cyberspace and real space emphasize the ways that jacking-in serves as a means for navigation, and the ways in which cyberspace erases local particularities by translating locations into a universal video player screen (see fig. 1.9). Featured prominently and, in fact, solely—in chase scenes, cyberspace reduces the pursuit to game and hunter, and the game into a green arrow. For instance, when tracking down a garbage truck driven by one of the Puppet Master's puppets, the anime morphs from street view to cyberspace view, in

Figure 1.8 Hong Kong market, replete with stereotypical Chinese figures and technology.

which the foreign street appears as a benign green line. In cyberspace, one moves from being inundated with information to being presented with the bare necessities of direction. Thus, cyberspace and the city of the near future combine differing versions of orientalism: they play with both exotic dislocation and navigational desire (the desire to reduce other locations to navigable maps). At the same time, Oshii's version of cyberspace points to the limited means of

Figure 1.9 Cyberspace view of a car chase.

Figure 1.10   Image from movie poster for *Ghost in the Shell.*

orienting oneself: the visual simplicity of the cyberspace scenes alerts the viewer to the fact that manageable information is often poor information.

Oshii also uses the Major and the city to represent cyberspace. As he notes, "networks are things that can't be seen with the eyes, and using computers, showing a gigantic computer, would definitely not do the trick. Showing something like a humongous mother computer would be scary."[72] In order to represent the network in a less "scary" way, he uses instead a humongous mother figure (see fig. 1.10). In this image (taken from the *Ghost in the Shell* movie poster), the Major's enormous mutilated form blots out the void in the same manner the "big mother" virus program does in *Neuromancer.* The wires attached to her body highlight her network connections and her broken form reveals her as a cyborg. Her form represents power: she dominates the scene, holding her phallus, and the cityscape shrinks in light of her connected body. Her jacked-in bare body makes cyberspace sexy rather than completely scary and impersonal. Thus, Oshii's rendering of cyberspace is both erotic and simplistic, or perhaps erotic in its simplicity.

Like *Neuromancer,* then, *Ghost in the Shell* represents cyberspace by relying on maps and by reducing others and other locations to information. Both American and Japanese versions of cyberpunk, that is, rely on *other* locations that are fictional yet recognizable in order to render comprehensible their vision of cyberspace. At the same time, both Oshii and Gibson point out the limitations of such an orientation by also presenting the ways in which foreign, exotic—oriental—locations exceed such a reduction. Whereas cyberspace, to use Certeau's definitions, reduces these locales to places (ordered), the disorienting yet orienting near city invokes ambiguity. These "oriental sites," importantly, are sources of economic anxiety and fears of economic emasculation. As Japan's economy soured in the 1990s, Hong Kong—and as a result, China—loomed as the next big economic power, and China should be the country with the largest gross domestic product sometime soon in this century. Thus, this insistence of the "soulless" informatics or mechanization of the seeming burgeoning other, combined with dreams of conquering, serve as a way to cope with, to fantasize about, to relieve perhaps barely concealed anxieties over economic impotence.

Who's Zooming Who?

Given the merging of the Puppet Master and the Major at the end of *Ghost in the Shell*, it would be easy to read this anime as celebrating the emergence of Japan as a technological powerhouse. Just as the Major receives technological advances from the Puppet Master, Japan takes technology from a dying West— and there is no American cowboy with which Americans can identify. If this is so, why would anime be so popular within the United States, and especially among "minority" Americans, such as Korean-Americans, who have no special fondness for Japan? Annalee Newitz argues that American boys are feminized by watching anime and placed in a capitulatory position to Japanese culture. Newitz, however, also suggests that translating and viewing anime may be a means by which viewers "convert a Japanese product into a uniquely American one. What might be satisfying for Americans about this is that it essentially allows them to 'steal' Japanese culture away from Japan."[73] This conversion supports the notion of anime producing a "Peeping Tom" or spying effect. Indeed, Antonia Levi, who argues that anime enables a great cultural exchange,[74] also portrays it as enabling a penetrating view into Japanese society. Anime, she posits, "can show you a side of Japan few outsiders ever even know exists. Unlike much of Japanese literature and movies, *anime* is assumed to be for local consumption only. That's important, because most Japanese are highly sensitive to outside pressure.... They write for and about Japanese. As a result, their work offers a unique perspective, a peeping Tom glimpse into the Japanese psyche.... But be warned. What you learn about Japan through *anime* can be deceptive. This is not the way Japanese really live. This is the way they fantasize about living. These are their modern folk tales, their myths, their fables. This is not a peep into the conscious Japanese mind, but into the unconscious."[75]

The viewer, looking over the Major's shoulder, peeps into the Japanese un-conscious, penetrating down to the very ghost in the shell. Similarly, Frederik Schodt, who argues for anime as a rosetta stone for mutual understanding,[76] also argues that the form allows one to see beyond "the surface or *tatemae* level of Japanese culture."[77] The great mirror, or illusion, of anime gives the impression of looking beyond surfaces, to what *really is*—which is, appropriately enough, fantasy.

More concretely, the American subject gets inserted into *Ghost in the Shell* through the gaze and through fantasy. In this film the "camera" often highlights the viewers' presence. When asked why he uses the fisheye effects, Oshii replied, "If you pressed me, you could say that these are the 'eyes' that look at the world of the film from the outside—that these are the eyes, in fact, of the audience."[78] The eyes of the audience often coincide with the view of the Major—enabling the viewer to see through her eyes—but, even more often, this coincidence enables the viewer to see over her shoulder. This effectively puts the gaze on the screen, so that the viewers identify with the camera's gaze rather than with specific characters. As Kaja Silverman argues, "fantasy is less about the visualization and imaginary appropriation of the other than about the articulation of a subjective locus—that is 'not an *object* that the subject imagines and aims at but rather a *sequence* in which the subject has his own part to play."[79] The viewer's role is made explicit in the last scene, when the camera comes online again after fading out with the Major going "offline." When it does come online, instead of offering us a view through the Major's eyes, we come online as an audience with an entirely new line of vision that does not coincide with anyone else's. In the over-the-shoulder shots, the gaze sometimes skips over the Major to rest on the viewer.

The viewer's role as voyeur has a precedent within cyberpunk fiction itself, namely in Case's relationship with Molly in *Neuromancer*. Case literally jacks into Molly, seeing what she sees and feeling what she feels. Similarly, the viewer jacks into the Major and the portrayal of the Major's connections to cyberspace makes this explicit: in *Ghost in the Shell*, jacking into cyberspace is not portrayed as ejaculating into the system or penetrating the Net. Rather, the trodes emerge from the other and penetrate the Major (see fig. 1.11). Unlike Gibson's version of merging with the Net, *Ghost in the Shell* portrays a feminine connection where the cyborg is the female connector and the computer is the male connector. And the camera becomes the network connection—when we look over the Major's shoulder we are literally in the position of the Net/console cowboy logging into her and seeing what she sees. This jacking in functionally parallels "passing" on the Internet. Rather than offering people an opportunity for others to lose their body or to understand others to be whoever or whatever they want to be, cyberspace offers simstim—the illusion of jacking into another being, seeing what they see and pretending to be who they are, and being invisible while doing so. There is always an option of jacking out, of leaving whenever things get too uncomfortable or difficult, yet also the illusion of being the person you take on. Again, as in *Neuromancer*, there is the ability to see what they see, to be treated as they are treated, but not access their minds and their emotions.

Thus, anime allows viewers to employ cyberpunk fantasies about the Orient already in place in order to insert themselves into narratives that do not seem

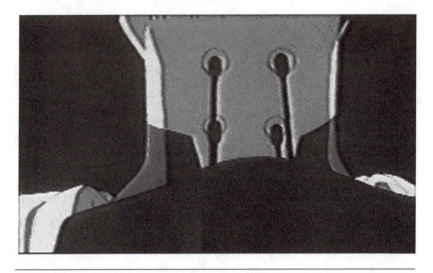

Figure 1.11 Cyberspace "jacked into" the Major.

to offer them a character with which to identify. If, "through fantasy, 'we learn how to desire'" through works like *Neuromancer* and *Blade Runner,* we learn to jack into anime; we learn to enjoy exotic orienting disorientation and to identify with the gaze. The viewer identifies with protagonists such as Case and Deckard (the protogonist of *Blade Runner*), who are faced by a world dominated by technology and all things Asian. The uncompromising nature of anime, the sense of being thrown into another culture and not being able to completely understand the situation, again reiterates Case's position in *Neuromancer.* The arbitrariness of the trouble one finds oneself in, combined with the green cyberspace view that makes things comprehensible in terms of a cat-and-mouse chase (again an American theme), is exactly what anime offers its American viewers. The inability to comprehend Japanese and to read all the signs afforded him, rather than alienating the viewer, places him a position structurally mimicking cyberpunk heroes. The viewer in *anime* puts into place lessons learned from Western cyberpunk. Moreover, the position of the viewer—who sees without being seen—strengthens this parallel.

Thus, cyberspace—or more properly, *narratives* of cyberspace—rely on the incomprehensibility of the Orient for their comprehensibility. Faced with making computer networks readable to others, influential writers such as Gibson draw on Asia (mistakenly collapsed into Japan, even though in Japan, Asia does not equal Japan) as a land easily reduced to information, yet also exotic enough to overload the viewer with information. To be clear, I am not arguing that cyberspace is limited to Gibson's, Oshii's, or Shirow's conception of it; nor am I arguing that orientalism is the only "other space" relied on to make cyberspace comprehensible. I *am* arguing that the conjunction of narratives about cyberspace and orientalism domesticates fiber-optics narratives. Narratives of cyberspace that make reference to orientalism seek to contain what they also create, even if they show cyberspace as exceeding information. That is, these narratives view the Orient as challenging one's navigational assumptions, but still rely on the logic of the navigable, of the symbolic as readable. The confusion the viewers feel stems from their position as tourists viewing the exotic. The unreadability of these locations serves to enhance their exoticism rather than challenge the viewers' assumptions about the symbolic and about orientation and orientalism. The point, then, is to see the ways in which this challenge of disorientation in the face of the foreign can disrupt everyday locations and understandings rather than being reserved for those *other.* spaces. The point is to see the ways in which heterotopias disrupt "normal" spaces, rather than lie neatly outside them.

Going Native

This orientalizing of the digital landscape, this entry into cyberspace as entry into world of oriental sexuality, is not limited to literary and animated conceptions of the Internet. Marty Rimm, whose senior thesis became the notorious Carnegie Mellon report on the consumption of pornography on the information superhighway, argues that cyberspace introduces nine new categories of pornography, two of which are "Asian" and "interracial." What is interesting in this supposedly identity-free public sphere is not simply that Asian pornography has emerged as a popular genre, but rather that *Asian* has itself effectively become a pornographic category.[80]

The Internet also revises our understandings of orientalism, disengaging it from the Orient. Through high technology, orientalism is made to travel: it is cited and disseminated in ways that untether the relationship between orientalism and the Orient. Oriental mail-order-bride sites such as *Asian Rose Tours* offer women from the former Soviet Union as well as the Philippines. Some oriental pornography sites offer pictures of white women, albeit women who are either bound or mutilated. The conceit behind these oriental pornography sites is that oriental women are submissive and in some way lacking the independence and status of their female contemporaries (notably, the visitors to these sites are predominantly American and Japanese men). The inclusion of Russian women exposes the economic base behind this assumption, but also reveals the flexibility of the category *oriental* to include all economically disadvantaged women. It relies on Michener's Oriental dreams: fantasies of white men and Asian women brought together by World War II. The inclusion of mutilated and economically disadvantaged white women disturbingly highlights the image of Oriental women as submissive and lacking. Those who produce Oriental websites that include these "other" white women on their sites assume that the desire for submission, rather than a certain aesthetic preference, drives desire for Asian women. High-tech orientalism, then, disperses orientalism, in all the meanings of the word *disperse*. High-tech orientalism seems to be all about dispersal—specifically, the dispersal of global capitalism.

These attempts to contain the Internet, to restrict it via techno-orientalism, do not guarantee safety either fictionally or factually. Orientalist narratives are not always comforting: they do not always orient. Rather, they carry with them fear of the yellow peril or uncontrollable and contagious intercourse; they carry fears of overwhelming contact, of being taken over by the very thing they seek to control. They carry with them the fear of "going native". According to U.S. Senator Jim Exon, among others arguing for Internet regulation, cyberspace has spread obscene pornography, pornography that goes beyond naked women. Exon, when arguing on the Senate floor for Internet regulation, admitted he had never surfed the web. Rather, he had an intern or friend collect the vilest online pornography and then print it out. He carefully compiled these printouts into a little blue binder and brought then to the Senate chamber. Before the vote on the Communications Decency Act, his peers came over to his desk, peered at the pictures, and then overwhelmingly supported the CDA. His notebook, in many ways, served as a perverse version of "look at my pictures from my friend's last vacation." Exon's horror at "hard-core" pornography and his desire to censor such materials is analogous to European reactions to "excessive" oriental intercourse. As Said argues, "Every European traveler or resident in the Orient has had to protect himself from its unsettling influences . . . In most cases, the Orient seemed to have offended sexual propriety; everything about the Orient— or at least Lane's Orient-in-Egypt—exuded dangerous sex, threatened hygiene and domestic seemliness with an excessive 'freedom of intercourse,' as Lane put it more irrepressibly than usual."[81] What ruffles legislators' feathers about the Internet is freedom of intercourse—in all senses of the word *intercourse*. Faced with the information superhighway and the massive deregulation of the telecommunications industry in 1996, the reason seized upon for government regulation was pornography—"excessive" sexuality.

So, what happens when we take freedom of intercourse seriously, even if it is within the rubric of high-tech orientalism? Take, for instance, the case of virtual sex; in many ways it epitomizes the orientalist dreams of the Internet. As Cleo Odzer argues in *Virtual Spaces: Sex and the Virtual Citizen*, "western men play with Thai prostitutes with the same nonchalance we play with our cyber-lovers."[82] The guiding metaphor of the web—namely, virtual travel—feeds into the notion of the Internet as a vacation space, a space in which responsibility is temporarily suspended in favor of self-indulgence; a space in which our formal identities are left behind in favor of our secret ones. Virtual sex seems always to verge on the risqué: bondage, domination, sadism and masochism dominate it, thus furthering the theme of submissive and deviant oriental sexuality.

Virtual sex and all so-called real-time communications cannot be safely cordoned off, because they are not limited to the self and because cyberspace cannot be limited to narratives of it perpetuated by works in other media that try to tell the truth about cyberspace. Instead, these real-time communications enable a form of contact that disables the notion of disembodied communication. By now, we've all heard stories of people addicted to chat rooms and virtual sex— people whose lives and marriages have been destroyed by virtual infidelities or obsessions, or people whose definition of community has been redefined by their online participation. Further, rather than marking a disembodied space, MOOS (multiuser object oriented environment) and MUDS (multiuser domains) create spaces in which people pass rather than imagine themselves as everywhere yet nowhere. Although I elaborate on this in my larger project, *Sexuality in the Age of Fiber Optics,* I would like to flag real time as a place where dreams of exploration and domination are put to the test—as a space that is fundamentally public in the sense that it belongs to no one but is also constantly contested. The fact that real-time communications are never *really* real time, that there is a considerable time lag between question and response, also serves to make this space disorienting, and it is this disorientation, I argue, that enables the Internet to verge on the disruptive, on the truly public—although this potential is always mediated by software. Indeed, software online works as cyberpunk fiction does offline—both provide a means for comprehension; they offer images and words that must surround the "real bytes" and hardware before they can be accessed and experienced.

To conclude, the Internet is not *inherently* oriental, but has been made oriental. The narrative of the Internet as orientalist space accompanies narratives of the Internet as disembodied space. In other words, the Internet can only be portrayed as a space of the mind if there is an accompanying orientalizing of difference, if there is an accompanying display of orientalized bodies. However, this binary of disembodied mind on the one hand, and embodied and orientalized other on the other is not sustainable. This binary breaks down not because the orientalized other is suddenly afforded the status as subject, but rather because the boundary between self and other, self and self, breaks down whenever one jacks in. Or, to be more precise, this division between self and other is itself a response to connectivity, which means that connectivity precedes the "user"—which means that this boundary is a screen rather than a shield.

Notes

1. *Cinematograph,* a neologism introduced in the late nineteenth-century, itself refers to the process by which "films" are experienced. Coined by Auguste and Louis Lumière and originally spelled *kinematograph,* it is comprised by two Greek words: *kinhma, kinhmato* [motion] + *graph* [written].
2. Gibson first coined the term in his short story "Burning Chrome," which was published in the July 1982 edition of *Omni.* He developed the concept of cyberspace more fully in his 1984 novel *Neuromancer* (New York: Ace Books, 1984).

3. Gibson, *Neuromancer*, 51.
4. The term *burning desire* refers to Geoffrey Batchen's analysis of the conception of photography, *Burning with Desire: The Conception of Photography* (Cambridge, MA: MIT Press, 1997).
5. John Perry Barlow, "Across the Electronic Frontier," (7/10/1990), online at <http://www.eff.org/Publications/John Perry Barlow/HTML/eff.html>. This earnest conflation of the future and cyberspace would become key to the selling of the Internet as an endless space of opportunity for individualism and/or capitalism.
6. Dave Healy argues in "Cyberspace and Place: The Internet As Middle Landscape on the Electronic Frontier," in *Internet Culture*, ed. David Porter (New York: Routledge, 1997), 66, that cyberspace is "'middle landscape' between space (empty frontier) and place (civilization) that allows individuals to exercise their impulses for both separation and connectedness." He sees us as "heirs not only of the primitivist philosopher Daniel Boone, who 'fled into the wilderness before the advance of settlement,' but also the empire-building Boone, the 'standard bearer of civilization'" (66). However, placing cyberspace as a middle landscape assumes that the Internet is a landscape to begin with, and this overlooks the work needed to construct the Internet as such. Rather than mediating between space and place, the Internet allows us to space out about the difference between space and place. For more on the space and cyberspace, see Kathy Rae Huffman, "Video, Networks, and Architecture," in *Electronic Culture: Technology and Visual Representation*, ed. Timothy Druckrey (New York: Aperture, 1996), 200–207; Chris Chesher, "The Ontology of Digital Domains," in *Virtual Politics: Identity and Community in Cyberspace*, ed. David Holmes (London: Sage, 1997), 79–93; and Mark Nunes, "What Space is Cyberspace? The Internet and Virtuality," in Holmes, ed., *Virtual Politics: Identity and Community in Cyberspace*, 163–78.
7. Healy, "Cyberspace and Place," 57.
8. Michel de Certeau, *The Practice of Everyday Life*, trans. Steven Rendall (Berkeley and Los Angeles: University of California Press, 1984), 117.
9. Thinking of electronic spaces in terms of "time" rather than "space" nuances our understandings of Internet space and brings out the repressed similarities and differences between the Internet and television. This is elaborated in more detail in my *Sexuality in the Age of Fiber Optics* (forthcoming).
10. Certeau, *The Practice of Every day Life*, 117.
11. For settlers' claims, see John Perry Barlow, "A Declaration of the Independence of Cyberspace" (February 8, 1996), online at <http://www.salon1999.com/08/features/declaration.html>; Cleo Odzer, *Virtual Spaces* (New York: Berkley Books, 1997); and Howard Rheingold, *The Virtual Community: Homesteading on the Electronic Frontier* (Reading, MA: Addison-Wesley, 1993).
12. For *Wired*'s version of the civilizing mission, see Jeff Greenwald, "Wiring Africa," *Wired* 2.06 (1994), online at <http://www.wired.com/wired/archive/2.06/africa.html>; and John Perry Barlow, "Africa Rising," *Wired* 6.01 (1998), online at <http://www.wired.com/wired/archive/6.01/barlow.html>; Nicolas Negroponte, "The Third Shall be First."*Wired* 6.01(1998), online at <http://www.wired.com/ wired/archive/6.01/negroponte.html>; and Neal Stephenson, "Mother Earth Mother Board," *Wired* 4.12 (1996), online at <http://www.wired.com/wired/ archive/4.12/ffglass.html>.
13. David Brande, "The Business of Cyberpunk: Symbolic Economy and Ideology in William Gibson," in *Virtual Realities and Their Discontents*, ed. Robert Markley, (Baltimore: Johns Hopkins University Press, 1996), 100–102.
14. In defining cyberspace as a heterotopia instead of an utopia, I am responding to critics who insist that the Internet is not utopia, and that the mythology of the Internet must be debunked/demystified. Whereas they seek to put "sociology before mythology" and

look at the Net's relation to the "real world," I argue that its mythology is precisely what links it to the real world, not as a regression or fantasy, but rather as a public space. This is not to say that sociology is unimportant, but that cyberspace must not be either sociology or mythology, but both at once.

15. Edward Said, *Orientalism* (New York: Vintage Books, 1978), 1.

16. Ibid., 3.

17. Lisa Lowe, *Critical Terrains: British and French Orientalisms* (Ithaca, NY: Cornell University Press, 1991), 15.

18. Michel Foucault, "Of Other Spaces," trans. A. M. Sheridan Smith, *diacritics* 16, no. 1 (1986), 24.

19. Ibid., 27.

20. Ibid. Boats, of course, also have an alternate history that place them as dystopian heterotopias. The Middle Passage and the Vietnamese boat people also show the dreams enabled by boats as nightmares. Neal Stephenson plays on both images of boats in *Snow Crash* (New York: Bantam, 1992).

21. For more on disruptive identifications, see Diana Fuss, *Identification Papers* (New York: Routledge, 1995).

22. Said, *Orientalism*, 52.

23. Ibid., 93.

24. Gibson, *Neuromancer*, 6.

25. Pam Rosenthal, "Jacked-in: Fordism, Cyberspace, and Cyberpunk," *Socialist Review* 21, no. 1 (1991): 85.

26. Gibson, quoted in Rosenthal, "Jacked-in," 85.

27. Larry McCaffery, ed., *Across the Wounded Galaxies: Interviews with Contemporary American Science Fiction Writers* (Urbana: University of Illinois Press, 1990), 141.

28. Gibson, *Neuromancer*, 3.

29. This juxtaposition of Turkey's open sexism with the bad-ass coolness of Molly allows *Neuromancer* to project the (false) image of a world without sexism, since some women can opt to augment their bodies so they can be as physically tough as many men, again naturalizing technology and portraying it as empowering by pinpointing it onto a body of a woman: What difference would it make if Molly were a man?

30. For other "Japanified" futures, see Ridley Scott's 1982 film *Blade Runner;* William Gibson, *Count Zero* (New York: Ace, 1986); William Gibson, *Mona Lisa Overdrive* (New York: Bantam, 1988); William Gibson, *Idoru* (New York: G. P. Putnam's Sons, 1996); and Stephenson, *Snow Crash.*

31. Yoshimoto Mitsuhiro, "The Postmodern and Mass Images of Japan," *Public Culture* 1, no. 2 (1989): 18.

32. Lisa Nakamura, "Techno-Orientalism and Cyberpunk: The 'Consensual Hallucination' of Multiculturalism in the Fiction of Cyberspace," paper delivered at the 1999 Association of Asian American Studies conference, Philadelphia, n.p.

33. Gibson, *Neuromancer*, 11.

34. Ibid., 3.

35. Ibid., 11.

36. See Fredric Jameson, "Progress versus Utopia; or, Can We Imagine the Future?" *Science-Fiction Studies* 9, no. 2 (1982): 147–58.

37. Gibson, *Neuromancer*, 203.

38. Ibid.

39. David Morley and Kevin Robins, "Techno-Orientalism: Futures, Foreigners and Phobias," *New Formations* 16 (1992): 153.

40. Gibson, *Neuromancer*, 51

41. Rosenthal, "Jacked-in," 99.

42. Fuss, *Identification Papers*, 149.

43. Frederick Buell, "Nationalist Postnationalism: Globalist Discourse in Contemporary American Culture," *American Quarterly* 50, no. 3 (1998): 503, 566.

44. Morley and Robins , "Techno-Orientalism," 139.

45. Gibson, *Neuromancer,* 52.

46. Ibid., 47.

47. Asian Nudes website, <http://www.asiannudes.com/tour1.html>. In these "Asian" pornography sites, the spectator is usually hailed as a "papasan" or "samurai," so that everyone must act as a mythic Asian patriarch (even Asians or Asian Americans—a demographic at which many of these pornography sites are directed). For more on this, see Wendy Hui Kyong Chun, "Scenes of Empowerment: Virtual Racial Diversity and Digital Divides," *New Formations* 45 (2001): 169–88.

48. Gibson, *Neuromancer,* 168.

49. For more on orientalism and translucent layers see David Henry Hwang's *M. Butterfly* (New York: Dramatists Play Service, 1988).

50. Gibson, *Neuromancer,* 35.

51. Morley and Robins , "Techno-Orientalism," 146.

52. Beard, quoted in Morley and Robins, "Techno-Orientalism," 154.

53. Gibson, quoted in Rosenthal, "Jacked-in," 85; emphasis added.

54. Gibson, *Neuromancer,* 55.

55. Said, *Orientalism,* 52

56. Naoki Sakai, quoted in Morley and Robins, "Techno-Orientalism," 146.

57. Gibson, *Neuromancer,* 16.

58. Gibson, *Neuromancer,* 8. In his 1996 novel *Idoru,* Gibson takes this datafication of Asians to the extreme: Rei Teio is a virtual construct. She "grows"—i.e., becomes more complicated—by absorbing information and mimicking others. People "see" her as a hologram.

59. Gibson, *Neuromancer,* 69.

60. Said, *Orientalism,* 41.

61. Ibid., 59.

62. Although Gibson consistently uses Japanese as mimics, other cyberpunk authors such as Neal Stephenson do not, even as they employ Japanese and East Asian geographies. Stephenson's *Snow Crash* is especially interesting since his cyberspace is not empty and characters become avatars online. In effect, his characters pass as others rather than as disembodied minds. In *Snow Crash,* racial stereotypes serve as prototypes for such online avatars as Brandy.

63. Although popular Japanese mecha series such as *Robotech* and *Astroboy* predate cyberpunk, mecha is now most often translated as cyberpunk, with posters for such popular series as *The Bubblegum Crisis* prominently featuring the English word "cyberpunk." For the "global" popularity of *mecha,* see Anime Web Turnpike, online at <http://www.anipike.com>; and Laurence Lerman, "Anime vids get Euro-friendly," *Variety,* June 24, 1996, 103.

64. Elizabeth Lazarowitz, "COLUMN ONE: Beyond 'Speed Racer,'" *Los Angeles Times,* December 3, 1996, 1.

65. Ibid.

66. Toshiyo Ueno, "Japanimation and Techno-Orientalism," online at <http://www.t0.or.at/ueno/japan.htm>.

67. "Interview with Mamoru Oshii," *ALLES* (n.d.), online at <http://www.express.co.jp/ALLES/6/oshii1.html> (5/1/99). The portrayal of Hong Kong as a city with no past or future is problematic. First, it denies the colonial history of Hong Kong; second, it perpetuates an image of a timeless Hong Kong at a time when Hong Kong's identity is at stake. As Ackbar Abbaz argues in *Hong Kong: Culture and Politics of Disappearance* (Minneapolis: University of Minnesota Press, 1997), in the period

before the 1997 handover there was a fast and furious attempt to delineate a Hong Kong culture—a problematic attempt that focused on such culture as disappearing.

68. Abbaz divides Hong Kong's architecture into three forms: merely local, anonymous, and placeless; Abbaz, *Hong Kong*, 79–90.

69. "Interview with Mamoru Oshii." Ridley Scott previously used this technique in *Blade Runner*. Although Oshii does not comment directly on his citations of *Blade Runner*, they are numerous and mostly relate to questions of representing technology. For instance, the long musical scene in which the Major tours Hong Kong ends with mannequins similar to those that appear in *Blade Runner* when Deckard tracks down the snake-stripping replicant Zhora.

70. Abbaz argues that signs have the opposite effect on Hong Kong city dwellers. If tourists gaze at these signs and in some way try to read them, "Bilingual, neon-lit advertisement signs are not only almost everywhere; their often ingenious construction for maximum visibility deserves an architectural monograph in itself. The result of all this insistence is a turning off of the visual. As people in metropolitan centers tend to avoid eye contact with one another, so they now tend also to avoid eye contact with the city." (Abbaz, *Hong Kong*, 76).

71. Further, to link this to the mixing of high- and low-tech in cyberpunk, Japanese anime often features a trip into "Chinatown" or Chinese tea rooms that are marked as inferior or perpetrating bad employment practices. In the popular *Bubble Gum Crisis* series, for example, the two women bond over a trip to Chinatown. In the "prequel" to the *Bubble Gum Crisis*, the *AD Police Files*, bad labor practices at a Chinese tea room marks the onset of a crisis with boomers. In *Ranma 1/2*, Ranma turns into a girl when splashed with cold water—female Ranma has red hair, and the male Ranma has black hair. As Annalee Newitz argues in "Magical Girls and Atomic Bomb Sperm: Japanese Animation in America," *Film Quarterly* 49, no. 1 (1995): 11, "Ranma is not only feminized, but also associated with China, a country invaded and occupied by Japanese imperialist forces several times during the 20th century. Ranma's 'curse' is in fact a Chinese curse, which he got during martial arts training with Genma in China. Moreover, Ranma wears his hair in a queue and his clothing is Chinese: at school, the students often refer to him as 'the one in Chinese clothing.'" As well, Chinese and Korean characters are visually marked as different from Japanese characters through eye size. Only the Japanese characters are given the enormous eyes that many critics mistake for a "racially ambiguous" look.

72. "Interview with Mamoru Oshii."

73. Newitz, "Magical Girls and Atomic Bomb Sperm," 2.

74. According to Antonia Levi, "The new generations of both Japan and America are sharing their youth, and in the long run, their future. However much their governments may argue about trade and security in the Pacific, American's Generation X and Japan's *shin jinurui* will never again be complete strangers to one another. The connection is not only with Japan. *Anime* has already spread across most of Asia. Future social historians may well conclude that the creation of the American *otaku* was the most significant event of the post-Cold War period." See Levi, *Samurai from Outer Space: Understanding Japanese Animation* (Chicago: Open Court, 1996), 1–2.

75. Ibid., 16.

76. Frederik Schodt argues, "Ultimately, the popularity of both anime and manga [Japanese comic books] outside of Japan is emblematic of something much larger—perhaps a postwar "mind-meld" among the peoples of industrialized nations, who all inhabit a similar (but steadily shrinking) physical world of cars, computers, buildings, and other manmade objects and systems. Patterns of thinking are still different among cultures, and different enough for people to be fascinated by each other, but the areas of commonality have increased to the point where it is easier than ever before to reach out

and understand each other on the deepest levels of human experience and emotion." (See Schodt, *Dreamland Japan: Writings on Modern Manga* (Berkeley: Stone Bridge Press, 1996), 339.

77. Ibid., 31.
78. Carl Gustav Horn, "Interview with Mamoru Oshii," in *Anime Interviews: The First Five Years of Animerica, Anime and Manga Monthly (1992–97)*, ed. Trish Ledoux (San Francisco: Cadence Books, 1997), 139.
79. Kaja Silverman, *Male Subjectivity at the Margins* (New York: Routledge, 1992), 6.
80. As of 2002, an Internet search on Google for "Asian + woman" produced porn sites, whereas a search for "pornography" failed to produce pornography in the first ten answers. For more on this, see Chun, "Scenes of Empowerment."
81. Said, *Orientalism*, 166–67.
82. Odzer, *Virtual Spaces*, 239.

2
Cyber-Race

JERRY KANG

Introduction

When we built the interstate highway system, we celebrated the possibilities. This national transportation network would facilitate commerce, promote defense, and better the welfare of all Americans. But in the planning, we did not seriously explore what the concrete network would do to community life.[1] When television rolled out in the 1940s and 50s, we again celebrated the possibilities. And again, we failed to see how television would become a "vast wasteland,"[2] serving up stock images folded into agreeable entertainment and sensational news.

Both highway and television have had unforeseen impacts on human relations generally and race relations specifically. We should remember these lessons as we build-out cyberspace. Part (information super-) highway,[3] part (web-) TV, cyberspace has already had enormous political, economic, and social impact. It may eventually dwarf the significance of both highway and television. What unintended consequences will it have on American race, racism, and race relations? Put another way, can cyberspace change the very way that race structures our daily lives? To see why this might be possible, consider the following:

Car purchase: I have bought my last two cars through a buying agent, who charges me a flat fee of three hundred dollars over dealer's invoice. I use this service mostly because I am too busy to negotiate with car dealers. But there is another reason: I worry that I may receive worse offers than a similarly situated white male.[4] By using the buying agent, I skirt the aggravation of wondering, "Am I being discriminated against?"

Tennessee roommate: One college summer, I was hired at Oak Ridge National Laboratories. Unfamiliar with Tennessee, I found housing over the telephone. I arranged to live with a graduate student, who was kind enough to pick me up at the airport. I told him my height, what kind of jacket I had, and that I wore glasses. He told me that he had red hair, which would make him easy to spot. I later learned that neither he nor my immediate supervisor knew that I was Asian American until we met face to face. My phone voice, grammar, and accent did not prompt them to flip out of the default assumption: white. As for my name, they somehow heard "Jerry *King.*"

Fighting words: In researching this paper, I began participating in graphical virtual communities. In these communities, one picks an avatar (a graphical representation of the self), navigates visually depicted environments, and chats with other individuals. In one world, I play a black man who looks young, muscular, bald. My virtual skin tone, which can be altered, is very dark. One afternoon, a character who appeared as a white woman asked me whether I was an "African American" in real space. When I said "yes," I was sprayed with racist bile. Here is a partial log:

PERPETRATOR: hey nigger
PERPETRATOR: betta watch out we got an eye on you and others do to your reported to the aryan nation KKK mutherfucker!!
PERPETRATOR: eine mine mo catch a nigger by his toe and if he hollers let him go! HEHEHE
PERPETRATOR: KKK
ME: Why don't you come out to play? [The perpetrator had been sending me these messages privately, after disappearing from the room that I was in. I was trying to get her to reappear.]
PERPETRATOR: run nigger run <grin> [This was in response to my leaving the room in which I was originally attacked.]
ME: Are you afraid to show yourself even in the virtual world?
PERPETRATOR: were are you at>??
ME: I'm at the teleporter, near Temple St.
PERPETRATOR: answer monkey boy
ME: So why are you so filled with hate?
PERPETRATOR: Im not just dont like niggers thats all
PERPETRATOR: white power!!
ME: Is it all of us or just some?
ME: Why did you leave? [The perpetrator had reappeared, but then disappeared.]
ME: Have you ever met one of us in the real world?
ME: Do you care whether I'm an American Black or a Carribean [sic] or Nigerian immigrant?

These three anecdotes illustrate how race still functions in American society—what I call "racial mechanics." Each anecdote also demonstrates how the architecture that mediates an interaction can alter racial mechanics in different ways. For example, in the *car purchase* anecdote, I used an economic architecture that removed racialized negotiations from the car buying ritual. In the *Tennessee roommate* anecdote, the telephone's architecture inadvertently cloaked my race until I met my roommate face-to-face. Finally, in the *fighting words* anecdote, cyberspace enabled me to present myself as a black man, something I could not do face-to-face.

Cyberspace enables new forms of social interaction. How might these new communicative forms affect racial mechanics? To answer this question, I begin in part 1 by examining how race continues to have a significant impact in American life and society. Exploring a central theme of critical race theory—that race is a social construction—I offer a social cognitive account of American racial mechanics. Next, in part 2, I explore how cyberspace can alter racial mechanics. Social interaction mediated through cyberspace differs significantly from social interaction in real space. These architectural differences make possible interesting disruptions of racial schemas.

The next three parts investigate specific strategies of schema disruption. In part 3 I discuss how cyberspace-enabled racial anonymity might prevent us from applying the rules of racial mapping. It is a strategy of racial *abolition*. In part 4, I discuss how cyberspace-enabled social interactivity can reform the troublesome racial meanings associated with each racial category. This is a strategy of racial *integration*. In part 5, I discuss how cyberspace-enabled racial pseudonymity, or "cyberpassing," can disrupt the very concept of racial categories. I call this strategy racial *transmutation*.

In part 6, I explore in more practical terms what we might do. Interestingly, in cyberspace, we do not have to choose a uniform design strategy. Instead, we can adopt a policy of diversification that racially zones different cyber spaces differently, as the circumstances warrant.

1. Race

Race continues to be a fundamental axis of social, economic, cultural, and political organization. Race affects both the symbolic and material realms of our lives, shaping our self-conceptions and altering our life chances.[5] How does race structure our lives so powerfully? To answer this question, we need a theory of race, especially one that can parse the specific nexus of race and cyberspace. In particular, such a theory must be able to explore the significance of whether we transmit racial signals at all, how we transmit those racial signals that we do convey, and the impact of racially integrated environments on race and racism.

A promising theoretical approach is social cognitive, which is empirically well grounded and has impressive explanatory and critical power.[6] Applying this method, I offer the following descriptive model of racial mechanics: In any social interaction, we *map* each other into racial *categories* that trigger associated racial *meanings*. As shorthand, I use the term *racial schema* to refer to the interaction of all three elements: (1) *racial categories,* through which the basic concept of race is understood; (2) rules of *racial mapping,* which are used to classify individuals into categories; and (3) *racial meanings,* which are cognitive beliefs about and affective reactions to the categories.

Race is a familiar concept within our culture. Most people understand race as a biological characteristic, inherited from our parents and manifested in physical appearance. Integral to the concept of race is the typology of *racial categories*. In fact, the way that many people define race is simply to list categories. Consider, for example, the category "Asian" or "oriental."

Upon encountering an individual, we collect data through our senses to map the individual to a racial category. *Racial mapping* can be based on physical appearance, such as hair color or shape of eyes, but it can also take place discursively, such as disclosing a surname. Racial mapping then triggers *racial meanings*—cognitive beliefs about and affective reactions to—people in these racial categories. They may include, for instanced, assumptions about foreignness ("Where are you from? No, really?"), intelligence, and physical attractiveness. Often, these meanings are triggered automatically, without self-awareness, and once triggered, they alter our behavior. In these ways, racial mechanics alter interpersonal interactions. These microlevel changes then accumulate over time and people to produce enduring macrolevel effects on our culture, economics, and politics.

These brief comments do not provide a complete account of racial mechanics, especially regarding how the microalterations aggregate into the macrostructural and -institutional imbalances in wealth and power among racial categories. Nonetheless, the description of racial mechanics I offer—because of its simplicity—gives us practical tools with which to solve problems. This social cognitive model also particularizes a fundamental theme of critical race theory that "race is a social construction." "Race," in the sense of its racial *categories,* is a social construction that lacks meaningful biological bases; the same is true for the rules of racial *mapping,*[7] and the social *meanings* we infuse into racial categories.

2. Cyberspace

For those who see cyberspace as the digital union of Federal Express and the Home Shopping Network, any claim about cyberspace affecting race must sound ludicrous. How can a computer connected to a telephone line change something as monumental as race and race relations? *It can do so by disrupting racial schemas.* Before exploring how, I provide a primer on the communicative forms of cyberspace.

Cyberspace enables multiple forms of computer-mediated interactions.[8] A taxonomy can be generated along the following axes:

1. *Temporal Engagement—Asynchronous versus Synchronous:* Asynchronous communications, such as e-mail, do not require simultaneous participation of sender and receiver. By contrast, a standard voice telephone call (without voicemail) is synchronous. The phone call is useless unless the other person picks up.

2. *Communication Initiation—Push versus Pull:* "Push" communications arrive at the receiver without any special effort on the part of the

receiver to obtain that particular communication item. E-mail is a good example. Once one has established an account and publicized the address, e-mails will arrive without any special effort by the receiver. By contrast, "pull" communications require more focused effort by the receiver to retrieve particular information. Surfing the World Wide Web is a common example of pull technology.

3. *Audience Scope—One versus Many:* One may send or make a communication available to just one person, to a few, or to millions. Importantly, on the Internet, transmitting information to multiple receivers often costs no more than sending it to a single person. A familiar "push"-like example is an e-mail distribution list; a familiar "pull"-like example is a personal home page on the web.

4. *Media Richness—Text-only versus Multimedia:* Communications differ in media richness, ranging across plain text, formatted text, pictures, audio, and video. A single piece of communication may mix multiple forms and thus be "multimedia."

In this taxonomy, the familiar e-mail would be categorized as asynchronous, push, one-to-one, and text-only. A message sent to a group of people, such as all subscribers to an academic list, would make audience scope one-to-many. E-mails that include graphics, audio, or movie clips would change media richness to multimedia. Browsing a webpage would be asynchronous, pull, one-to-many, and typically multimedia (because webpages generally include graphics as well as text).

Less familiar than e-mail and standard webpages are threaded discussion fora (asynchronous, pull, one-to-many, and generally text-only), which are available on the Usenet or on the web.[9] On these fora, people post messages and replies on matters of mutual interest, such as computer operating systems, daytime soap operas, or affirmative action. These posts generate a threaded discussion through which participants share thoughts, experiences, and expertise with each other. Although many participants simply search these fora for specific information on a need-only basis, others participate far more regularly, not only taking but also giving information.

Even less familiar than these forms of cyberspace communication are real-time chat, instant messaging, and MUDs (multiuser domains or multiuser dungeons). Most chat is synchronous, push/pull, one-to-many, and text-only. An individual runs a software program called a chat client, connects to a chat room delivered by a chat server, then sees a screen of scrolling text typed by the room's inhabitants. While chat is like a large, often unruly, common room for discussion, instant messaging is more like a real-time textual pager (synchronous, push/pull, one-to-few, and principally text, although increasingly voice). Finally, MUDs are spatially elaborated chat rooms. In addition to enabling instantaneous communicative exchange, MUDs have a geographical structure in which individual participants can move from room to room, finding new persons to meet and new areas to explore. Most MUDs are text based, but some are graphically mediated through the use of avatars.

Through these various computing-communication technologies, cyberspace helps people maintain social relationships originally constructed in real space. Used in this way, cyberspace is a speedy postal service that supplements the handwritten letter and telephone. Cyberspace also facilitates relationships that originally form in cyberspace. Typically, these relationships form in virtual communities of common interests, experiences, and fates. Such communities can be large, and often their members have not met face-to-face. Examples include academic e-mail distribution lists, Usenet newsgroups, chat rooms, and instant messaging. In these examples, cyberspace functions less like Federal Express and more like sidewalk cafés with different themes or milieus. People already participate extensively in virtual communities of one sort or another. Those drawn to the Internet are often drawn to its sociality, not its data. The "killer application" of the Internet turns out to be other human beings.[10]

The way that cyberspace facilitates social relationships will change as computing-communications technologies develop. As we move from communications that are text-only to text-plus, avatars will become more popular.[11] Think how a single, simple creation in the early 1990s—the World Wide Web—made the Internet a household term. Consider how much our lives have changed in just a decade. In two more decades, future innovations of greater significance await us. By 2020, cyberspace will allow us to navigate graphically mediated environments of stunning complexity, detail, and realism.[12] These advances have the potential to change everything. Our racial schemas may not be exceptions.

In the following three parts I outline three different strategies of disrupting racial schemas. Specifically, we can adopt a strategy of abolition, which disrupts racial mapping by promoting racial anonymity; integration, which reforms racial meanings by promoting social interaction; or transmutation, which disrupts racial categories by promoting racial pseudonymity. I present the merits of each design strategy as forcefully as I can; however, each path suffers from severe limitations. We should not presume that by logging into cyberspace, we enter some digital promised land that deletes centuries of racial conflict or downloads into our brains an antiracist patch that encodes us all to "get along."

3. Abolition

In my *car purchase* anecdote, I took a self-help measure to disrupt racial schemas by preventing racial *mapping*. In this way, I sought to avoid even subconscious triggering of racial meanings—a phenomenon the social cognitive literature has well-documented. Can cyberspace generalize this solution by abolishing race in most cyber-interactions?[13]

Cyberspace makes visual appearance and verbal self-identification harder to access. First, because of bandwidth limitations, most cyberinteractions take place through typed text. In contrast to a face-to-face encounter, text need not disclose morphology. Second, the conversation norms in most Internet chat rooms and MUDs generally discourage racial identification.[14] By making it easier for us to wear a racial veil, cyberspace promotes *racial anonymity*. This prompts fantasies about realizing Martin Luther King, Jr.'s dream in cyberspace.[15] In the digital remix version, people are judged by the content of their text characters, not the color of their skin.

I find such claims naive. For instance, just because race is not signaled in cyberspace does not mean that race ceases to matter in cyberspace or, certainly, in real space. Race will continue to influence the "content" of one's communications even if the audience is not aware of the nature of that influence. Moreover, technological and demographic changes make blanket abolition infeasible.

To begin with, even text permits racial mapping. One's language, grammar, and diction may also suggest race.[16] In addition, a text-only stance has little future. The most engaging chat rooms and MUDs have graphical interfaces that use avatars, which are typically racialized. Audio, growing more and more popular in chat rooms and MUDs, also reveals accent, which in turn may signal national origin, geography, or race.[17] When video exchange goes mainstream, a cyber-interaction will be no more racially anonymous than a face-to-face encounter. I am not claiming that text will disappear. Often, plain old text is best—for example, for lengthy or complex expositions as well as group communications. Still, I believe that preserving text-only communication throughout cyberspace, in the hopes of preserving racial anonymity, is a losing proposition.

One could imagine society mounting an aggressive campaign to abolish race in cyberspace, even prohibiting racial self-identification. But doing so across the board, through official legal action, would amount to an unconstitutional restraint on speech. Instead of clumsy law, we could imagine more subtle social norm and technological interventions. For instance, when we transmit voice, we could create an architecture that applies speech-to-text; translation and/or grammar checking; and then text-to-speech algorithms to generate a computer-synthesized voice that strips away racialized voice cues. Similarly, avatar interfaces could have default characters that are nonhuman—for example, animals, cartoon characters, or robots.[18] Even with videophones, one could imagine an architecture that allowed morphing of the transmitted image into a nonracialized human face.

Yet such interventions seem implausible. What market forces would lead to widespread adoption of such deracing technologies, such as the voice-to-text-to-voice filter, when they introduce additional costs and inefficiencies? And especially with increasing numbers of racial minorities entering cyberspace, not to mention the globalization of the Net, why would a social norm of abolition grow in acceptance?

Moreover, any heavy-handed attempt to pressure people into an abolition environment would inflict disparate burdens on people of color. For many racial minorities, their racial identity is an integral facet of their self-conception. To strong-arm them into repressing that self-conception, even if only in cyberspace, is to ask some Americans to silence a part of themselves. Even worse, when "colorblind" strangers interact in cyberspace, racial minorities will understand that the default assumption is not that each is raceless: The assumption instead is that each is white. This is what happened in my *Tennessee roommate* anecdote. But this means that not only would racial minorities be gagged in their self-representation, they would also be mistaken for white. Finally, in addition to individual psychic harms, there may be collective political harms. Often, racial minorities need to engage in collective politics based on race to resist injustice heaped upon them based on race. Heavy-handed abolition would undermine such politics just as cyberspace is maturing into a serious political medium.

One might respond that whites would also be prevented from representing their race. But for most whites, racial identity is less significant. As recent work in critical white studies has emphasized, whiteness is unapparent, inconspicuous, and invisible.[19] Further, although abolition identically silences whites from presenting their racial identity, the default assumption is descriptively accurate as applied to them.[20] In sum, designing cyberspace to abolish race rigidly and completely would be both impossible and unwise.

4. Integration

So if race cannot and should not be quarantined from cyberspace, can we adopt an integration design strategy instead? Instead of trying to disrupt racial mapping, can cyberspace help reform racial meanings by promoting social interactions? This approach teleports the social cognitive strand of *Brown v. Board of Education* into the twenty-first century.[21] At the core of the integration approach is faith in the contact hypothesis, which claims that increased social contact between the races, under the right conditions, dissolves racial prejudice.[22]

A. Quantity

As a threshold matter, will cyberspace increase social contact between the races? Cyberspace makes geographical proximity less relevant.[23] This partially lifts residential segregation's choke-hold on interracial social contact.[24] In addition, cyberspace also makes talking with strangers easier because individuals are less fearful in cyberspace.[25] One's physical body is never at risk. One's mental welfare is also less at risk given the option of easy exit. Further, one often enjoys reputational safety. This may be because one is interacting anonymously or pseudonymously.[26]

All this, of course, assumes that racial minorities have access to cyberspace. If they do not, then we have simply replaced geographical segregation with electronic segregation. The National Telecommunications and Information Administration (NTIA) provides recent comprehensive data on this point.[27] As of September 2001, 50.5 percent of all U.S. households had access to the Internet.[28]

The NTIA's study did, however, find racial differences in using the Internet (from any location): Asian/Pacific Islanders (60.4 percent); whites (59.9 percent); blacks (39.8 percent); and Hispanics (31.6 percent).[29] In previous studies, the NTIA found racial differences in household subscription to Internet services even adjusting for household income.[30] For some skeptics, this divide is a fatal objection.

This is an overreaction. First, in absolute numbers, there is substantial minority presence in cyberspace, and that presence is increasing every year. New business models and decreasing costs may increase these numbers substantially. Second, for the problem I address, relative numbers are not as important as absolute ones. Altering racial schemas is not the same political project as promoting high-tech distributive justice. The existence of a large gap between whites and nonwhites (relevant to the latter project) does not necessarily say much about the opportunities for social interaction enabled by cyberspace (relevant to the former project). It is myopic to renounce cyberspace because of current disparities in technological and cultural access.[31] That is akin to renouncing universities, and their redesign, because of disturbing racial disparities in admissions.

One final objection to my quantity claim could be that even if racial minorities are in cyberspace and even if residential segregation matters less in guiding social encounters, members of each racial group will associate only with other members of that group. It is true that virtual communities specifically designed for racial and ethnic groups are popular. But we should not exaggerate the problem of self-segregation. Virtual communities are centered around common interests, experiences, and fates. There is, however, no perfect identity between one's race and one's interests, experiences, and fates: Think hip-hop,[32] Nintendo,[33] partner dancing, or golf. Consider instead how powerfully these matters are shaped, for instance, by socioeconomic class, gender, or generation. People who are drawn together by such commonalities will hardly be all of the same race.[34]

As well, cyberspace, with its fundamental metaphor of a hyperlink, invites exploration. Even if people start in isolated race-specific communities, which may be comfortable ports of entry for racial minorities, they will undoubtedly explore other cyberrealms. That is cyberspace's seduction. As folks navigate cyberspace, going from hyperlink to link, they will likely encounter a diversity of ideas and peoples.

B. Quality

Increased social contact is necessary but not sufficient to reform racial meanings. That contact must also have certain qualities that lessen our self-interest in maintaining negative racial meanings of others. Such meanings serve deep-seated needs of belonging, superiority,[35] and self-esteem.[36] Taking account of these factors, a broad consensus in the social psychological literature has developed on the environmental characteristics crucial to decreasing negative racial meanings: (1) exposure to disconfirming data, (2) interaction among people of equal status, (3) cooperation, (4) nonsuperficial contact, and (5) equality norms.[37]

Disconfirming Data   First, during the social contact, "[t]he attributes of the disliked group members with whom the contact occurs must disconfirm the prevailing stereotyped beliefs about them."[38] Why might cyberspace deliver more disconfirming data than real space? In real space, we navigate racially segregated communities; therefore, our cache of racial meanings is informed mostly by vicarious experiences with other races—imagined experiences, provided by mass media.[39]

Vicarious experiences are, however, often stereotypical. Take television broadcasting, for example, which sells consumer attention to advertisers. To capture the greatest number of eyes and ears, commercial broadcasters peddle products that will attract the largest number of viewers. This means pitching to the mainstream.[40] In telling a story in thirty minutes or thirty seconds, simpler characters that tap into preexisting assumptions work best because exaggerated generalizations of racial "others" are more easily processed than complicated images.[41] Even in nonfictional news, we see similar biases. For example, photo editors disproportionately use photographs of African Americans to illustrate stories about poverty because the racial category *black* is already connected to poverty, thus making the story and images easier to consume.[42]

By contrast, in cyberspace, we navigate less segregated communities, which means that we will potentially engage in more direct experiences with other races—experiences with actual people, not mediated by third parties. And direct experiences are less stereotypical than vicarious ones since there is less economic pressure for raical minorities to perform stereotypically for any audience. In this way, cyberspace will expose us to relatively more disconfirming data.

Cyberspace will not magically reform vicarious experiences. This is evident from the huge zones of cyberspace that look no different from more traditional mass media such as newspapers, magazines, and television. However, cyberspace will increase the proportion of direct experiences we consume, and individuals will thereby be exposed, on balance, to more disconfirming data.[43]

Equal Status   The social psychological consensus also points out that increased contact will do little good if it is configured by drastic hierarchies. Consider, for example, the intimate socioeconomic and personal contact between African Americans and whites throughout slavery and the Jim Crow era. Some commentators contend that cyberspace naturally generates ideal, antihierarchical environments. I am more skeptical. For instance, if cyberspace is used simply as a communications device, akin to a fancy telephone, then cyberspace will still reflect the preexisting hierarchy between sender and receiver. In other words, if an employer sends an instruction to a temporary worker through e-mail, the hierarchy between employer and temp is not erased simply because the communication traversed a computer network.

Fortunately, a substantial amount of cybersocial contact takes place in contexts not configured by any master-servant relationship. On bulletin boards, chat rooms, and MUDs, the vast majority of participants relate on equal terms, as if they were all patrons of a virtual café. Each participant generally has no special power over the others, no special capacity to communicate in ways that others cannot. If participants are treated differently, it is usually on the basis of their reputations within that virtual community.

One might complain that differences in socioeconomic status present in real space will surely manifest themselves in cyberspace. No doubt they will. However, this may actually be a blessing in disguise. In real space, because residential segregation cuts across income levels, rich white folks do not generally live next to rich black folks.[44] In cyberspace, however, both groups will congregate in virtual communities centered around fancy wines, stock tips, vacation spots, and the like. Regardless of the classist aspect of this interaction, it is an example of cyberspace promoting direct interracial experiences among people of similar socioeconomic status.

Cooperation   Third, there must be cooperation toward a joint goal. Participation in cooperative projects is important because it defuses competition and highlights group membership defined by common project, not common race. Is there reason to think that cyberspace might promote cooperative relationships?

Perhaps the commonalities underlying cybercommunities could act as a foundation for cooperation. Plenty of anecdotal evidence speaks to impressive acts of cooperation based on common interests, experiences, and fates: pregnant women share experiences; the elderly console each other after losing loved ones;[45] patients fighting cancer provide information and support; disabled children find friends who do not judge them immediately on their disability; users share stories about drug addiction;[46] and gay and lesbian people on the brink of coming out give each other emotional shelter.[47]

An entirely separate mechanism with which we can encourage cooperation is to design short-term delays in racial disclosure. Recall my *Tennessee roommate* anecdote. The telephone delayed the triggering of racial meanings associated with the category *Asian American*. Assume that, contrary to fact, my roommate would have resisted rooming with an "oriental": imagine a gallon jar of *kimchi* stinking up your refrigerator, or better yet, consider rooming with another Wen Ho Lee. The telephone's architecture would have prevented those racial meanings from affecting his housing decision. Over that summer, by cooperating with me as a colleague and roommate, his views of "orientals" would likely have grown more complex, less exaggerated.

Thus, even if cyberspace cannot (and should not) be kept colorblind, a short-term delay might make sense. By embedding some such delay into the architecture, we could prevent racial meanings, which are often biased, exaggerated, and unduly negative, from setting (often subconsciously) the initial terms of the social interaction. After race is disclosed—and this must eventually occur for integration to succeed—one or both parties may be surprised, as my Tennessee roommate was surprised at the airport. However, the relationship will have already been framed by the interaction that took place before disclosure.

But what about my *fighting words* experience? The same technology that enables us to talk to strangers without fear also enables us to type slurs without the threat of physical retribution. The same technology that enables us to join together based on commonalities also enables us to avoid and abuse those marked as different. Racism is the common interest for neo-Nazis who feed each other's paranoia on the Internet.

Cyberspace is no panacea. Environmental spaces need to be specifically designed to promote accountability, sometimes through authentication of identity. I should, however, highlight a few silver linings in these dark clouds. First, witnessing racist "flames" may be educational for the rest of us. Second, the same factors that make extremists comfortable launching hate speech will also embolden the more moderate to talk frankly about race.

Clearly, both "silver linings" are speculative and hard to measure. Balkanization should concern us in cyberspace, as in real space; on balance, however, cyberspace does not pose any greater threat. If we want environments of cooperation in cyberspace, then we must intentionally design and build them—as in real space. Cyberspace does not intrinsically encourage cooperation. That would be an error of technological determinism. However, the fact that cyberspace enables people to join together based on common interests, experiences, and fates provides a substantial foundation upon which we can build environments of cooperation.

Social Depth   Even if racial minorities are online, one might be sharply skeptical about the true value of virtual "communities." Can they generate the sorts of sustained, emotionally powerful relationships that are necessary to change racial meanings? Worse, what are their opportunity costs? Do they take us away from more valuable projects and relationships in real space?

Some studies suggest a correlation between increased use of the Internet and small declines in social environment, as well as increases in loneliness and depression.[48] However, other studies and myriad anecdotes point in the other direction—toward the positive power of social relationships mediated through cyberspace.[49] Clearly more research is needed. In the interim, we can avoid in confusion. For instance, the question of whether cyberspace impairs psychological health is largely irrelevant to the wisdom of adopting an integration environmental design. Even if cyberspace increases depression across the board, racial meanings may nevertheless be reformed. There is nothing logically or psychologically inconsistent with becoming both less racist and more depressed.

Equality Norms   Finally, "[t]he social norms of the contact situation must favor group equality and egalitarian intergroup association."[50] On this last factor, cyberspace has no necessary advantage over real space. That said, in certain cyberspace realms, social norms can be more clearly delineated and more efficiently enforced than in real space. For instance, the registration process could require acceptance of "social contracts" that prohibit foul language and racial slurs.

Moreover, in virtual communities that require some form of registration, enforcement of such social norms may prove easier than in real space. First, the fact that all cyberspace interactions are computer mediated makes resolving factual disputes easier. Second, virtual community hosts can empower system operators, guides, or wizards to boot offline those who egregiously violate social norms of equality. If technically feasible, behavior akin to the *fighting words* incident should lead to permanent exile. Third, the very software supporting the virtual community can be designed to promote these social norms. For instance, if particular epithets violate the community's equality norms, then the underlying software can prevent transmission of these epithets to a single individual. This code can be fine-tuned such that epithets could still be spoken in some public realm, or even to a specific individual, as long as that individual chose to decline the "racist filtering" option.

Some readers will be concerned about the power of private censorship and how it might be used to promote only "politically correct" speech. In the abstract, one cannot decide which is the greater threat: the private power of individuals making racist comments that flaunt social norms of equality or the private power of virtual community hosts trying to enforce such norms. However, these concerns should be assuaged by the amazing diversity of the Internet, which guarantees that those kicked out of one community will land in another where it is politically correct to be politically incorrect, or where hosts exercise no editorial control.

At bottom, my claims amount to a cybersocial contact hypothesis, which requires empirical testing. Although cyberspace does not naturally or inherently encourage integration spaces, they can be consciously designed. And when well built, there is good reason to believe that these spaces will help reform unwarranted racial meanings.

5. Transmutation

Recall my *fighting words* anecdote. There, I was broadcasting a different racial signal in cyberspace than in real space—what I call "cyberpassing."[51] In real space, this sort of passing is restricted to those persons whose physical appearances straddle racial categories. By contrast, in cyberspace, passing is potentially available to all: it is far easier to wear racial masks. The transmutation approach argues that we should take advantage of this opportunity and all engage in cyberpassing as a transgressive challenge to American racial mechanics. This approach draws from the real-space passing literature. As Elaine Ginsberg explains, "In its interrogation of the essentialism that is the foundation of identity politics, passing has the potential to create a space for creative self-determination and agency: the opportunity to construct new identities, to experiment with multiple subject positions, and to cross social and economic boundaries that exclude or oppress."[52]

Although Ginsberg is discussing real-space passing, her comments apply at least as well to cyberpassing. To evaluate the transmutationist claim, we need to examine more carefully what lessons cyberpassing teaches.

Suppose that I decide to cyberpass as an African American out of honest curiosity. Imagine that I develop this African American character seriously, as if I were engaged in method acting. The threshold act of choosing race may itself have some pedagogical value. In real space, the racial *category* I have been assigned seems to be a natural, biological characteristic, based on immutable morphology and ancestry. I cannot cease to appear Asian to my audience. But in cyberspace, the racial signal I broadcast becomes the product of voluntary choice and intentional experimentation. This might prompt me to look at race differently, as less fixed.

Over many months, this African American character could develop a reputation by becoming active on a software application bulletin board and regularly posting helpful advice. He could chat "as a regular" in a graphically mediated MUD. He could even exchange e-mails and instant messages with a small circle of "friends." Through these experiences, I might learn a great deal about myself.[53] More important, assuming that the audience accepts my cyber passing I might learn something about being a black man in American society.[54] This is what I felt I learned through my *fighting words* encounter.[55]

Such experiences might help corrode the presumed connection between identity and biology. In particular, I might no longer see the ancestry and morphology of my single physical body as constricting my identity. I may eventually come to internalize the idea that multiple identities can map to a single physical body.

This upbeat story about transmutation relies on numerous controversial assumptions. For instance, one might question how many people will engage in serious transmutation. Worse, transmutation has significant downsides, which can be seen most clearly from the audience's perspective. On the one hand, suppose that the audience never discovers the cyberpassing. Then, racial meanings may be reworked in dangerous ways. Above, I posited that my purpose for cyberpassing was to satisfy honest curiosity. But, what if it were to perpetuate a racist caricature? Then, in Amos and Andy–like blackface, I could have broadcast a black racial signal in cyberspace and acted as an ignorant buffoon speaking "jive."

Reinscription of stereotypical racial meanings may occur even without intentional parody. How do I know what it means to "act black"? Given residential and social segregation, my knowledge will be predominantly based on the messages and themes promulgated in the mass media. Because the mass media resonates with stereotypes, my understanding and presentation of blackness risks stereotype. So how does the audience react to this unintentionally stereotypical performance? It will experience my performance as authentic because it will hold the same stereotypes that I hold. Moreover, the audience's credulous reception will reinforce my own stereotypes about what blackness means. Because of cyberpassing, we may unwittingly consume black/red/yellowface, while believing it to be an "authentic" direct experience.

On the other hand, consider what happens if the audience discovers the cyberpassing. Once the audience discovers that cyber-passing is common, it will start questioning the value of the racial signal transmitted in cyberspace. Perhaps individuals will expend greater effort to identify cases of cyberpassing. Or they may simply stop crediting all racial signals in cyberspace. Racial *mapping* based on such signals would be deemed useless.

Perhaps this is a good thing. People would no longer be judged by the color of their (virtual) skin. But we have seen this argument before. Transmutation has collapsed into a form of abolition: the racial mask now functions as a racial veil. In this environment of transmutation collapsed into abolition, I will learn no lesson in empathy. Even the racists will not trust the racial signal. This environment will also negate any benefits of integration by introducing uncertainty about one's real-space racial signal.

In sum, the transmutation approach hopes that cyberpassing will, among other things, disrupt the very notion of racial categories and decouple biology from identity. Unfortunately, transmutation poses the substantial risk of reinscribing stereotypical racial meanings into our racial schemas.

6. Diversification

I have outlined three design strategies for cyberrace: abolition, integration, and transmutation. These strategies are in tension with each other. As just explained, transmutation conflicts with integration. Integration also conflicts with abolition: The entire point of abolition is to be blind to race, whereas integration requires people to see each other's race and to interact with members of different races.[56] Finally, abolition conflicts with transmutation. Abolition permits individuals to express every facet of their identity save one: race. Thus, the space of identity experimentation is significantly restricted. The transmutation approach finds this counterproductive because it flattens the number of dimensions of identity to explore generally, and it removes the one specific dimension—race—that needs to be experimented with the most.

Given such conflicts, which design philosophy shall we adopt for cyberspace? Luckily, we do not have to choose a *single* architecture for all of cyberspace. Instead, we can "racially zone" cyberspace by adopting different racial environments for different cyberspaces.

A. *Racial Zoning*

Zoning cyberspace—a space without physical geography—might seem odd. However, recent cybersocial theory has argued that the concepts of location, borders, and distance translate into a cybergeography.[57] Location in cyberspace can map to a unique Internet protocol (IP) address and any associated domain names, which exist for each computer on the Internet. A more specific location for any object stored on such a computer can be referenced by a universal resource locator (URL). This location information can be represented visually or aurally through the user interface, thereby providing "notice" of one's cyberlocation. A cyberspace can also have clear borders that explicitly notify visitors about the nature of the place they are about to enter. Borders can also be secured, not by installing barbed wire, but by requiring registration and passwords to gain entry.[58] Instead of physical fences, we have password screens and system firewalls. Finally, even distance translates to cyberspace, though it must be understood in transaction cost—not physical—terms. The distance between any two cyberlocales is measured by the ease with which one can navigate from source to destination. Thus, a location that is bookmarked within a web browser is closer than another location whose URL has to be looked up or typed manually. A location that has a prominent hyperlink is closer than another location not linked at all or linked deeper within the website. Accordingly, cyberspatial distance is subjective. For the individual with good searching skills, all locations are closer than for the neophyte. With these translations, the possibility of zoning different cyberspaces begins to make sense.

Although the state plays the central role in real-space zoning, in cyberspace zoning, a wider range of public and private actors jointly wield the zoning power. They include legislatures, standard-setting bodies, Internet service providers (ISPs), virtual-community hosts, technology companies (both hardware and software), and individual users. Depending on the context, different actors can use different techniques to achieve specific zoning objectives.

Having explained how racial zoning *can* be done, let me now address why it *should* be done. In cyberspace, a pragmatic, case-by-case racial zoning approach will be superior to a one-size-fits-all strategy. The racial zoning approach gives us the flexibility to tailor specific cyber environments to specific racial environments. We may thus be able to capture important synergies by combining all three strategies. Moreover, a "racial zoning" approach provides policy portfolio diversification, which is wise whenever we design cyberspace. Cyberspace is too novel and dynamic a medium for anyone to be confident that she has gotten policy just right. We must therefore be careful to avoid irrevocable decisions.

B. Marketplaces

Recall again my *car purchase* anecdote. Even if abolition is not appropriate generally for cyberspaces, it makes plenty of sense for those realms that are marketplaces.[59] For most discreet marketplace transactions, society has rightly decided that being race-conscious produces no net positive benefit. For example, when buying a car, no one argues for race-based affirmative action. Consider then the impact of abolition on large economic transactions, such as automobile purchases, insurance, personal loans, and mortgages. These transactions are today negotiated face-to-face, thereby triggering racial schemas. If they were instead executed through communication systems that filtered out race and its proxies, then racial discrimination (of the disparate treatment variety, conscious or unconscious, statistically or animus-based) would decrease. Ending today's disparate treatment would do nothing to rectify the material legacy of a racist past. Still, this would not be a trivial contribution to racial equality. But what of the criticisms I had made of the abolition approach?

First, I suggested that abolition was untenable because of rapidly changing technologies and demographics. Although this would be true if the goal were to make *all* of cyberspace colorblind, it is less true if we are talking about zoning the narrow subspace of market transactions.

Second, I suggested that any heavy-handed attempt to abolish race would inflict disparate costs on racial minorities by gagging their expression of identity. That is not the case here. Racial identity, although sometimes relevant to deciding whether to engage in a particular market transaction, is irrelevant to the transaction mechanics once the decision has been made. In other words, although my racial self-conception may be implicated when deciding whether to buy a Ninja or a Harley, once I have made the decision, nothing much turns on my buying the motorcycle in a colorblind way. Also, the default assumption that each transactor is white presents little insult to nonwhites in economic space. For racial minorities concerned about economic discrimination, it actually serves our interest for others to assume that we are white. This assumption grants "most favored race" status, in which minorities are treated as well as members of the most favored racial group, whites.[60] By avoiding racial discrimination, racial minorities will incur real economic payoffs, redeemed in real space.

Thus, our challenge is to generate a technolegal infrastructure that encourages racially anonymous e-commerce transactions. In designing such systems, it is useful to divide the transaction into three phases: preliminary research, risk assessment, and final execution. To illustrate each phase, I use a home-purchase example.

Real estate information is now easily accessible on the Internet.[61] Therefore, I can engage in the *preliminary research* of available housing inventory without being steered by any third party. Fortunately, web browsing does not generally disclose information about identity that can be mapped back to race. This ability to research anonymously, however, faces threats from two corners. First, improved surveillance technologies make it easier to collect and link the personal data generated in the course of navigating cyberspace. Second, the rise of database marketing has created strong economic incentives to collect such information. In light of these two converging forces, cyberspace privacy is increasingly at risk.[62] As I have argued elsewhere, the U.S. Congress should enact cyberspace-specific privacy legislation.[63]

Large, complicated economic transactions often involve a second phase, in which some party must make a *risk assessment* of the buyer, for example, regarding creditworthiness. Unfortunately, in the course of my providing that data, the institution also receives irrelevant information, such as race. Can the relevant data be provided without lifting the racial veil?

Digital credentials, supported by public key cryptography, provide a potential solution.[64] If there were some agency that could be trusted to make fair creditworthiness judgments and not to discriminate on the basis of race, then I could go to that agency, provide all relevant financial data, and then receive a digital credential of creditworthiness up to some dollar amount, with specified interest rates and a given term of years. This credential would automatically expire after some time. With my credential in hand, I could approach lending institutions in cyberspace, identify the house I would like to purchase,[65] and request mortgage offers—with all responses to be sent to a pseudonymous e-mail account.

Such digital credentialing systems will be adopted, if at all, at the behest of private sector actors. However, the state could encourage their widespread implementation. First, the state could decrease business uncertainty surrounding the legal significance of digital credentials. For instance, statutes could clarify the legal significance and acceptability of digital signatures.[66] Second, the state could subsidize investment in this e-commerce infrastructure not only through applied research grants, but also indirectly through statutory safe harbors that immunize credentialing agencies and other trusted third parties.[67] Third, if for some reason the market does not generate enough enthusiasm, the state could create an agency that itself issues creditworthiness credentials. In addition, the state could require lending institutions to accept these government-issued credentials if they are in the business of making comparable loans or benefit from federal insurance programs.[68]

In the last phase, the *final execution,* I must ensure that race, which has been filtered out of the first two phases, does not sneak back in. Therefore, I cannot meet the seller face-to-face; otherwise, racial schemas will again be triggered.[69] How can I make an offer on the house without disclosing my race? I could employ a human agent, like the human agent in my *car purchase* anecdote. Two decades from now, our society may use electronic agents, which are software programs with limited artificial intelligence, capable of negotiating transactions on our behalf. In the short term, we could adopt an "auction" system that would accept anonymous bids on homes backed by some earnest money and a digitally signed mortgage certification.

But a skeptic may argue that the racial signal will still get through. The buyers who take advantage of the race-blind option, the argument goes, will mostly be racial minorities because only they have anything to gain from such a system. By contrast, whites will buy homes the old-fashioned way.

The actual story is more complicated. In the short term, those who try to buy a home through cyberspace will be the self-selecting few who are early adopters of technology. There is little reason to think that racial minorities will be disproportionately represented in this group. Moreover, it is possible that the racially anonymous system will provide such substantial efficiency advantages that no one, including whites, will buy homes the old-fashioned way.

Still, the racial signal may somehow bleed through, for example, via a requested face-to-face meeting between the buyer and the seller of the property. If this becomes a large problem, the law could intervene. Sellers could be required not to discriminate against anonymous offers. The state might also create positive incentives, such as tax benefits, that would encourage sellers to opt for the race-blind transaction system.

Total abolition of the buyer's race and all its proxies will not eliminate residential segregation.[70] Moreover, these reforms will not help those racial minorities who are worst off—those who lack the money to buy cars or homes and lack the technological access, intellectual wherewithal, and emotional desire to log on to cyberspace. Nonetheless, we have before us an opportunity to abolish race in significant economic transactions that affect the lives of racial minorities. To the extent that disparate treatment still prevents minorities from enjoying equal economic opportunities, abolition delivers a concrete payoff we should pursue.

C. Social Spaces

In more social spaces, abolition would be not only difficult but also inappropriate. Two design options remain: integration and transmutation. Integration requires authentication—confidence that the racial signal broadcast in cyberspace is the same racial signal broadcast in real space. By contrast, transmutation shuns authentication.

As between the two strategies, I am more sanguine about integration. My concerns about transmutation should become obvious upon reading the description of a cyberspace persona called "Geisha_Guest," controlled by a white American male living in Japan, that describes her as "a petite Japanese girl in her twenties. She has devoted her entire life to the perfecting the tea ceremony [*sic*] and mastering the art of lovemaking. She is multi-orgasmic. She's wearing a pastel kimono, 3 under-kimonos in pink and white. She is not wearing panties, and that would not be appropriate for a geisha. She has spent her entire life in the pursuit of erotic experiences."[71]

This is not to say that I would try to forbid transmutation environments, which would be impossible even if we tried. I would, however, encourage general education of cyberspace users to alert them to the possibility of cyberpassing. Similarly, I would not forbid abolition environments. Such tolerance arises from my digital diversification model of racial zoning. That said, I see the greatest potential in generating integration spaces.

Authentication   As a threshold matter, any integration environment requires some degree of racial authentication. In other words, people must feel relatively secure that the racial signal broadcast in cyberspace is the same signal broadcast in real space. Such authentication could be effected through designing architecture and social norms. First, any virtual community could make clear that its ground rules preclude cyberpassing. In other words, every member of the community is expected to present his real-space name and identity within the cyberspace community: This Is a "No (Cyber)Passing Zone." Reputational sanctions attach to violations of this norm. Second, this clear ground rule could be enforced by members of the community through various verification strategies that can take place through some regime of registration and peer interrogation.[72]

Within any virtual community, authentication generates accountability. Even if authentication is far from perfect, as long as there is sufficient accountability, the relationships that form within that virtual community will tend not to be fictional. Accordingly, individuals will generally decline to cyberpass. Moreover, a small amount of passing will not destroy an integration environment.

Smart Design   As explained in part 4, smart design of integration spaces requires attention to both quantity and quality of interracial social contact.

QUANTITY   An obvious smart design practice includes promoting racial minority access to cyberspace. As a society, we should carefully consider subsidization, education, and anti-redlining (in the build-out of high-speed data networks) strategies to facilitate access. Another reason to fight the digital divide, then, is to increase the number of viable integration spaces.

In addition, ISPs, virtual community operators, and technology companies (both software and hardware) should develop user interfaces that promote chance encounters with other people. Consider the following two possible interfaces for a graphical world: In World 1, one can move instantly between locations by clicking on a menu of available rooms; by contrast, in World 2, the only way to move from room to room is by walking your avatar (even if quickly) through intervening hallways and public spaces. World 2 is a superior integration space because walking increases the number of common spaces regularly traversed. Along the way, we might encounter interesting people and unexpected places to explore—something less likely to happen if we simply "teleport" from location to location. For similar reasons, many people in real space prefer walkable cities to those that require driving.

QUALITY   Recall that the five environmental factors that help decrease racial prejudice are (1) exposure to disconfirming data, (2) interaction on terms of equal status, (3) cooperation, (4) social depth, and (5) equality norms. I have already argued that cyberspace will likely expose us to more disconfirming data because it will increase the ratio of direct-to-vicarious interracial experiences. In addition, I have explained how the self-selecting and social (as opposed to master-servant) nature of these interactions may generate interracial contact on terms of equal status. What about the other factors? Are there ways to implement "smart design" principles to promote them?

Cooperation One source of entertainment in these social spaces could be team games, in which teams are selected randomly and groups compete against each other for prizes, virtual or real. These games could range from the intellectual (akin to *Trivial Pursuit* and *Scrabble*) to the visceral (e.g., team *Doom*). What is essential here is that the virtual community forms teams somewhat randomly, so that individuals do not stick only to those players they already know. The hope is that by repeatedly playing these games in teams, with individuals of other races, we might alter—even if only slightly—racial meanings for the better.

Also, virtual community hosts and users should experiment with strategically delaying racial disclosure. To repeat, there is troubling evidence that, notwithstanding good intentions, stereotypes are triggered simply by exposure to the object of the stereotype.[73] So even though integration requires that participants eventually reveal their race, race need not be the first thing that people see. Consider, for example, how a text-based troubleshooting bulletin board might be designed. Next to each posting can be the following: (1) screen name, (2) first name, (3) first and last name, or (4) first and last name with photograph. My recommendation is to display authorship information in just this order. This delay strategy may have limited usefulness. Still, it seems worthwhile to experiment with this technique while we can. To be clear, I am not arguing in favor of abolition, which would run counter to an integration space. However, especially in spaces where race seems marginally relevant to the conversation, I would consider inserting a pause in the racial mapping process.

Social Depth In addition, we should foster the social interactions in virtual communities that have depth and meaning. This is basic to good community design, regardless of integration concerns.[74] At the very least, the virtual community host should encourage individuals to return often and to become "regulars." This makes it more likely that multiple interactions among individuals over time will generate deeper social bonds. Economic incentives could promote such behavior. For example, for every minute that you are in the virtual community, you might be credited with a monetary token to use within that virtual community. Or, just as we accrue frequent-flier points with airlines, we could have frequent "presence" points in a virtual community, redeemable for tangible goods and services in real space.

Another technique is to export cyberspace social interaction to real space. In other words, the individual members of the cybercommunity could arrange real-space gatherings, such as picnics or annual reunions. We could make real-space contact more probable by creating cybercommunities based on real-space geography. We could encourage users to provide geographical information within their profiles, which could be easily indexed and searched. As always, all such personal information exchanges must be consistent with good information privacy practices. Obviously, by making real-space geography relevant, we risk importing the significance of residential segregation into cyberspace. Accordingly, we must balance the ways in which real-space meetings can enrich the social depth of cyberspace interactions without replicating real-space residential segregation.

Equality Norms   Finally, the virtual community should espouse basic norms of equal dignity and respect for all members. I have already discussed how virtual community hosts have the power to promulgate such equality norms clearly and with some bite, for instance, by writing the behavioral norms into the underlying software. Here, private firms such as America Online will have to take the lead since they, not the state, create and administer the various social spaces that might be designed with integration in mind. Still the state can actually make it easier for virtual community hosts to promulgate and enforce equality norms. An excellent example is Section 230 of the Telecommunications Act of 1996,[75] part of the original Communications Decency Act that was not declared unconstitutional. This section establishes that "interactive computer service" providers are not to be considered the publisher or speaker of comments made by "another information content provider," which includes members of the virtual community.[76] Moreover, these providers are not civilly liable for good faith attempts to restrict access to objectionable material. This statutory immunity gives virtual community hosts great flexibility in punishing members who flaunt the community's equality norms, without subjecting themselves to civil liability.

Conclusion

America's racial problems, centuries old, persist into the present. At a microlevel, the racial schemas in our heads—racial categories, racial mappings, and racial meanings—continue to alter the path of social interactions, often in troublesome ways. These alterations, when aggregated, produce large, societal effects at the macrolevel. If we add these macrolevel effects to the sediments of America's racist past, we have good reason to think that America's racial problems will persist for centuries more.

Yet here and now we are afforded an intriguing opportunity, made possible by the coming of the "information society," brought by the convergence of computing and communication technologies. Cyberspace creates novel communication platforms that open up new possibilities in both individual identity and social interaction. By designing cyberspace appropriately, we may be able to alter American racial mechanics.

We can choose among three design strategies. Abolition seeks to keep race out of cyberspace. It invokes *racial anonymity* in cyberspace to prevent racial *mapping*. Depending on the context, this approach makes sense to those who believe that (white) racism is incorrigible, as well as to those who insist that the best way to get beyond race is to blind ourselves to it.

By contrast, integration seeks to increase interracial *social interaction* through cyberspace, thereby altering the cache of racial *meanings* in our heads.

Integration sees in cyberspace the possibility that all Americans might be exposed to a lower ratio of stereotypical data. It also sees how cyberspace could promote social interactions based on cooperative projects among people of equal status. Integration envisions cyberspace communities as antiracist pedagogical tools similar to our idealized integrated neighborhood or university.

The last path, *transmutation*, is the most fantastic. It *seeks racial pseudonymity*, or cyberpassing, in order to disrupt the very notion of racial *categories*. By adopting multiple racialized identities in cyberspace, individuals may slowly dissolve the one-to-one relationship between identity and the physical body. Traditional social categories, such as race (as well as gender), may begin to lose their oppressive rigidity.

We need not choose a single path for all of cyberspace. Instead, we can racially zone cyberspaces more selectively, at a space-by-space level. For many marketplaces, abolition is most appropriate. For many social spaces, integration is most appropriate. The terms *marketplace* and *social space* are mere labels: For each there must be a contextual analysis about the merits of representing race; the labels do not short-circuit that analysis.

By adopting all three paths in cyberspace, we adopt a policy of digital diversification. We cannot know which path will have which consequence. By implementing all three design strategies, in different zones and in different proportions, we make certain that the legal/social/architectural combination necessary to support any one of these paths remains a policy option.[77]

In this essay I have presented my vision of what cyberrace may come to be. Many readers will write this vision off as science fiction. If this dismissiveness prevails, in fifty years we will look back upon cyberspace in the same way that we look back upon the interstate highway system and television—with regret, as opportunities not seized and therefore lost. There are novel opportunities here, configured not only by new technologies but also by new politics. For example, consider how Americans along a broad political spectrum could agree on zoning most marketplaces as abolitionist. In addition, consider how cyberspace offers a way to increase direct interracial social interaction without the actual and perceived zero-sum conflicts inherent to busing or race-conscious admissions.

The thoughts I present here are not science fiction, but they are tentative. I share them in the hope of provoking users, software engineers, hardware designers, virtual community hosts, ISP providers, policy analysts, regulators, and lawmakers to think through cyberrace.[78] I do so with urgency because decisions made—or not made—now, with little thought of racial consequences, may haunt us later. If we view cyberspace as a mere tool, like a glorified fax machine, we underestimate its transformative potential.

We should see cyberspace instead as a new universe, which we build potentially without the constraints that bind real space. Even if that potential is lost to us, it may not be lost to the next generation. Some readers will complain that I have been too optimistic about cyberrace. Let me be clear: I genuinely fear that cyberspace will reinscribe a repressive racial mechanics even deeper into our nation. This essay is a plea to build toward redemption instead.

Notes

This is a substantially redacted and slightly revised version of *Cyber-Race, Harvard Law Review* 113(2000): 1130–1208. The original article struggles with various complexities that have been edited out of this chapter.

1. *See* Kenneth T. Jackson, *Crabgrass Frontier: The Suburbanization of the United States* (New York: Oxford University Press, 1985), 249.
2. Newton Minow, "Address to the National Association of Broadcasters" (May 9, 1961), in *Abandoned in the Wasteland: Children, Television, and the First Amendment*, ed. Newton N. Minow and Craig L. LaMay (New York: Hill and Wang, 1995), 185, 188.
3. For another comparison between the interstate highway system and cyberspace, see Steven G. Jones, "Understanding Community in the Information Age," in *CyberSociety: Computer-Mediated Communication and Community*, ed. Steven G. Jones (Thousand Oaks, CA: Sage, 1995), 10–11. For a related discussion of the automobile, see Douglas Schuler, *New Community Networks: Wired for Change* (Reading, MA: Addison-Wesley, 1996), 178.
4. Ian Ayres has demonstrated statistically significant differences in the average offers received by car purchasers as a function of gender and race (white versus black). See Ayres, "Fair Driving: Gender and Race Discrimination in Retail Car Negotiations," *Harvard Law Review* 104 (1991): 817–19; and Ian Ayres, "Further Evidence of Discrimination in New Car Negotiations and Estimates of Its Cause," *Michigan Law Review* 94 (1995): 109–10.
5. See Ralf Dahrendorf, *Life Chances: Approaches to Social and Political Theory* (Chicago: University of Chicago Press, 1979), 28, 31, 34 (discussing the concept of life chances); Andrew Hacker, *Two Nations: Black And White, Separate, Hostile, Unequal* (New York: Ballantine Books, 2d ed. 1995), 99–111 (comparing the earnings of black Americans to white Americans); Paul Ong and Suzanne J. Hee, "Economic Diversity," in *The State of Asian Pacific America: Economic Diversity, Issues, and Policies*, ed. Paul Ong (Los Angeles: LEAP Asian Pacific American Public Policy Institute and UCLA Asian American Studies Center, 1994), 31–56 (comparing the earnings of Asian Americans to whites).
6. See generally Ziva Kunda, *Social Cognition: Making Sense of People* (Cambridge, MA: MIT Press, 1999) (surveying the social cognition field). Readers new to race literature should not assume that critical race theory generally adopts social psychological explanations of race. Two prominent pieces that do use social psychological research, however, are Linda Hamilton Krieger, "The Content of Our Categories: A Cognitive Bias Approach to Discrimination and Equal Employment Opportunity," *Stanford Law Review* 47 (1995): 1161; and Charles R. Lawrence III, "The Id, the Ego, and Equal Protection: Reckoning with Unconscious Racism," *Stanford Law Review* 39 (1987): 317, 336–39.
7. The rules of racial mapping are configured by politics, social conventions, and law. Not surprisingly, there has been great fluidity in racial mapping rules applied by the federal government. See generally Ian F. Haney López, *White by Law: The Legal Construction of Race* (New York: New York University Press, 1996), 118–19 (cataloging the history of legal racial definitions). These rules have been challenged in court; see López, *White by Law*, 42–46 (discussing cases prompted by the federal laws that, until 1952, maintained racial bars on naturalization); and Ariela J. Gross, "Litigating Whiteness: Trials of Racial Determination in the Nineteenth-Century South," *Yale Law Journal* 108 (1998): 109, 111–23 (discussing the law's role in defining the cultural meaning of racial identities.

These challenges have continued to the present, see *Jane Doe v. Department of Health and Human Resources, Office of Vital Statistics*, 479 So. 2d 369, 372 (La. Ct. App. 1985) (deciding that Suzy Guillory Phipps is not white).

8.   At its broadest, the term *cyberspace* encompasses the entire web of computing-communication technologies that enmesh the globe. It includes every computing processing unit connected through every type of telecommunications, both wired and wireless. It includes every telecommunications and mass media industry, such as land line and wireless telephony, broadcast radio and television, satellite, and cable. In this paper, however, I use the term more narrowly to apply to all computer networks that interoperate with the Internet. See Peter Kollock and Marc A. Smith, "Communities in Cyberspace," in *Communities in Cyberspace* eds. Marc A. Smith and Peter Kollock (New York: Routledge, 1999), 3, 4–8 (describing the cyberspace landscape).

9.   For good descriptions of the Usenet, see Marc A. Smith, "Invisible Crowds in Cyberspace: Mapping the Social Structure of the Usenet," in Smith and Kollock, eds., *Communities in Cyberspace*, 195; and Paul K. Ohm, "Comment: On Regulating the Internet: Usenet, A Case Study," *UCLA Law Review* 46 (1999): 1941. According to Smith, as of 1999, there were 14,347 newsgroups, on which an average of 20,000 people post 300,000 messages daily, generating six gigabytes of messages (197).

10. See, e.g., Susan C. Herring, "Two Variants of an Electronic Message Schema," in *Computer-Mediated Communication: Linguistic, Social and Cross-Cultural Perspectives*, ed. Susan C. Herring (Philadelphia: J. Benjamins, 1996), 81, 103–5 (finding that both men and women used two Internet mailing lists more for social interaction than for information exchange); Kollock and Smith, "Communities in cyberspace," 6 (describing the popularity of chat rooms on America Online); Robert Kraut, Vicki Landmark, Sara Kiesler, Tridas Mukopadhyay, and William Scherlis, "Internet Paradox: A Social Technology That Reduces Social Involvement and Psychological Well-Being?" *American Psychologist* 53 (1998): 1017, 1029 (reporting that a major reason people use the Internet is "to keep up with family and friends through electronic mail and on-line chats and to make new acquaintances through MUDs, chats, Usenet newsgroups, and listservs"); Barry Wellman, Janet Salaff, Dimitrina Dimitrova, Laura Garton, Milena Gulia, and Caroline Haythornthwaite, "Computer Networks As Social Networks: Collaborative Work, Telework, and Virtual Community," *Annual Review of Sociology* 22 (1996): 213, 220 ("[W]hile most of the elderly users of the 'SeniorNet' virtual community joined to gain access to information, their most popular on-line activity has been companionable chatting.").

11. Such interfaces are often more compelling and functional. For example, the standard interface for chat rooms includes a window of rapidly scrolling text—the chatter of room inhabitants. But this text is hard to follow because multiple conversations are taking place among multiple people, and all comments are interlineated into one streaming transcript. By contrast, in a graphical chat room, characters having a conversation can simply move their avatars to a different corner of the room. Comments made by each character appear in a "balloon" above the avatar's head. Through visual mediation, multiple conversations in a single room can be spatially separated. See, e.g., "Avaterra.com, Inc. Backgrounder," (describing the graphical MUD Dreamscape), online at <http://www.worldsaway.com/aboutus/backgrounder.html> and on file with the Harvard Law School Library.

12. For futuristic visions of virtual reality, see Howard Rheingold, *Virtual Reality* (New York: Summit Books, 1991), 345–76.

13. I do not align abolition thinking with either the political Left or Right. On the one hand, opponents of affirmative action contend that race is no longer a salient factor in society, with the exception of affirmative action programs. On the other hand, cultural critics such as Anthony Appiah argue that the continuing use of race, even acknowledging it as a social construct, is a dangerous reliance upon an illusion; see Appiah, "The

Uncompleted Argument: Du Bois and the Illusion of Race," in *"Race," Writing, and Difference* ed. Henry Louis Gates Jr. (Chicago: University of Chicago Press, 1986), 21, 35–36. In addition, my discussion of abolition should not be confused with the new abolitionism movement represented, for example, by Noel Ignatiev and John Garvey's magazine, *Race Traitor*. The goal of this movement is to abolish the *white* race and its related privilege, not the notion of *all* races. See, e.g., "Abolish the White Race—By Any Means Necessary (editorial), reprinted, " in *Race Traitor*, ed. John Garvey and Noel Ignatiev (New York: Routledge, 1993), 1.

14. See Lori Kendall, "Meaning and Identity in 'Cyberspace': The Performance of Gender, Class, and Race Online," *Symbolic Interaction* 21 (1998): 129, 142, 145–47 (describing MUD norms of not presenting or discussing race); compare Lisa Nakamura, "Race in/for Cyberspace: Identity Tourism and Racial Passing on the Internet," *Works and Days 25/26*, vol. 13, nos. 1–2 (1995): 181, 183 (stating that in LambdaMOO, a multiuser domain, "[r]ace is not only not a required choice, it is not even on the menu").

15. See Earl Babbie, "We Am a Virtual Community," *American Sociologist* (1996): 65, 66.

16. See, e.g., Byron Burkhalter, "Reading Race Online: Discovering Racial Identity in Usenet Discussions," in Smith and Kollock, eds., *Communities in Cyberspace*, 60, 65 (discussing how the subject line "Sisters please explain" may suggest that the author is black).

17. In one experiment, individuals—some with identifiably black voices—called a wrong number, tried to explain that their car had broken down, then asked for assistance in contacting a garage. The study organized its subjects by political affiliation, and both conservatives and liberals were less likely to help blacks than they were to help whites. See Samuel L. Gaertner and John F. Dovidio, "The Aversive Form of Racism," in *Prejudice, Discrimination, and Racism*, ed. John F. Dovidio and Samuel L. Gaertner (Orlando: Academic Press, 1986), 61, 68–69.

18. See, e.g., Elizabeth M. Reid, "Text-Based Virtual Realities: Identity and the Cyborg Body," in *High Noon on the Electronic Frontier: Conceptual Issues in Cyberspace*, ed. Peter Ludlow (Cambridge, MA: MIT Press, 1996), 317, 339 (describing FurryMUCK, a highly popular MUD in which all characters are nonhuman, and most are furry animals).

19. See generally Richard Delgado and Jean Stefancic, eds., *Critical White Studies: Looking behind the Mirror* (Philadelphia: Temple University Press, 1997).

20. See, e.g., Ruth Frankenberg, *White Women, Race Matters: The Social Construction of Whiteness* (Minneapolis: University of Minnesota Press, 1993), 6 (discussing whiteness); Barbara J. Flagg, "Was Blind, but Now I See": White Race Consciousness and the Requirement of Discriminatory Intent," *Michigan Law Review* 91 (1993): 953, 971 (noting that whites' social dominance allows them to "relegate [their] own racist specificity to the realm of the subconscious"); see also Devon W. Carbado, "Epilogue: Straight Out of the Closet: Men, Feminism, and Male Heterosexual Privileges," in *Black Men on Race, Gender and Sexuality: A Critical Reader*, ed. Devon W. Carbado (New York: New York University Press, 1999), 420, 426 (noting how men do not think about gender and heterosexuals do not think about sexual orientation).

21. *Brown v. Board of Education*, 347 U.S. 483 (1954). *Brown* had an equally if not more important material strand, which I do not emphasize here. "Separate but equal" was a sham not only symbolically but also in terms of the material resources made available to black institutions.

22. See, e.g., Norman Miller and Marilynn B. Brewer, "The Social Psychology of Desegregation: An Introduction," in *Groups in Contact: The Psychology of Desegregation*, ed. Norman Miller and Marilynn B. Brewer (Orlando: Academic Press, 1984) 1, 2. For a summary of studies lending support to the social contact hypothesis, see Gordon Allport, *The Nature of Prejudice* (Garden City, NY: Doubleday, 1958), 252–60; Thomas F. Pettigrew, *Racially Separate or Together?* (New York: McGraw-Hill

1971), 274–78; and Thomas F. Pettigrew, "Prejudice," in *The Harvard Encyclopedia of American Ethnic Groups*, ed. Stephan Thernstrom (Cambridge, MA: Balknap Press of Harvard University, 1980), 820–29.

23. See, e.g., David R. Johnson and David Post, "Law and Borders—The Rise of Law in Cyberspace," *Stanford Law Review* 48 (1996): 1367, 1370–76 (explaining how cyberspace undermines the relationship between physical location and legal governance).

24. See, generally, Douglas S. Massey and Nancy A. Denton, *American Apartheid: Segregation and the Making of the Underclass* (Cambridge, MA: Harvard University Press, 1993), 81, 109–14; see also Richard H. Sander, "Housing Segregation and Housing Integration: The Diverging Paths of Urban America," *University of Miami Law Review* 52 (1998): 977–79 (describing the persistence of black segregation).

25. See Pavel Curtis, "MUDding: Social Phenomena in Text-based Virtual Realities," in Ludlow, ed., *High Noon on the Electronic Frontier*, 347, 357–58.

26. For an explanation of the differences between cyberspace anonymity and pseudonymity, see A. Michael Froomkin, "Flood Control on the Information Ocean: Living with Anonymity, Digital Cash, and Distributed Databases," *University of Pittsburgh Journal of Law and Commerce* 15 (1996): 395, 417–24.

27. See National Telecommunications and Information Administration (NTIA), "A Nation Online: How Americans Are Expanding Their Use of the Internet" (Washington, DC: U.S. Department of Commerce, NTIA, Economics and Statistics Administration, 2002).

28. Ibid., 3.

29. Ibid., 21.

30. See National Telecommunications and Information Administration (NTIA), "Falling through the Net: Defining the Digital Divide: A Report on the Telecommunications and Information Technology Gap in America" (Washington, DC: U.S. Department of Commerce, NTIA, Economics and Statistics Administration 1999), xv–xvi.

31. See Anthony G. Wilhelm, "A Resource Model of Computer-Mediated Political Life," *Policy Studies Journal* 25 (1997): 519, 531 nn. 2, 4 (emphasizing the importance of human capital and other antecedent resources necessary to engage in computer-mediated political life).

32. Hip-hop is wildly popular among Asian youths, both in America and in Asia. See Kimberly Chun, "Asian Artists Put New Spin on Hip-Hop; Filipino Rappers Rewrite Ghetto Music to Own Experience," *San Francisco Chronicle*, May 21, 1999, 5 (describing Asian American hip-hop).

33. See Arturo Escobar, "Welcome to Cyberia: Notes on the Anthropology of Cyberculture," *Current Anthropology* 35 (1994): 211, 218 (noting the globalization of Nintendo in youth culture).

34. See Oscar H. Gandy Jr., *Communication and Race: A Structural Perspective* (London: Oxford University Press, 1998), 241 (citing statistics demonstrating that in 1996, 60 percent of the audience for Black Entertainment Television was not black).

35. See Kunda, *Social Cognition*, 314.

36. Substantial experimental evidence supports this view. Studies reveal, for example, that people who have recently received negative feedback are more likely to activate negative racial stereotypes, in order to promote their own self-esteem. Ibid., 362–64 (summarizing studies by Steven Fein and Steven Spencer).

37. See Miller and Brewer, "Social Psychology," 2.

38. Ibid.

39. See Adeno Addis, "'Hell Man, They Did Invent Us': The Mass Media, Law, and African Americans," *Buffalo Law Review* 41 (1993): 523, 530 (explaining that whites and blacks know about each other largely through the media, not through direct individual contact); Robert M. Entman, "Representation and Reality in the Portrayal of Blacks on Network Television News," *Journalism Quarterly* 71 (1994): 509, 517 (suggesting that

whites with limited personal contact with blacks assume that TV news portrayals of blacks are representative).

40. See, generally, C. Edwin Baker, "Giving the Audience What It Wants," *Ohio State Law Journal* 58 (1997): 311, 320 (describing the distortions caused by the advertiser-driven model of broadcasting).

41. Racial caricatures are common in advertisements; see Gandy, *Communication and Race*, 100, and also 186 (discussing the Frito Bandito). Films also contribute to racial stereotyping; Gandy, 178–79 (explaining how stereotypes are easy to capture on film and are also easily processed by the audience). See also Jesse Algeron Rhines, *Black Film/White Money* (New Brunswick, NJ: Rutgers University Press, 1996), 70 (arguing that black films must include stereotypes in order to generate enough crossover appeal to garner funding). See, generally, Kathy Russell, Midge Wilson, and Ronald Hall, *The Color Complex: The Politics of Skin Color among African Americans* (New York: Harcourt Brace Jovanovich, 1992), 244 (describing the "dominant gaze" as "the tendency of mainstream culture to replicate, through narrative and imagery, racial inequalities and biases which exist throughout society").

42. See Gandy, *Communication and Race*, 114–15; see also Howard Kurtz, "Time's 'Sinister' Simpson: Cover Photo Was Computer-Enhanced," *Washington Post*, June 22, 1994, D1 (describing *Time Magazine's* decision to darken O. J. Simpson's skin color in a photograph).

43. Ringo Ma, "Computer-Mediated Conversations as a New Dimension of Intercultural Communication between East Asian and North American College Students," in Herring, ed., *Computer-Mediated Communication,* 173, 177 (concluding that computer-mediated communication between students in Asia and America "tends to demystify some distorted mass media reports"—for example, regarding the U.S. educational system).

44. See Sander, "Housing Segregation," 984 ("[T]he most affluent blacks experience roughly the same degree of segregation as the least affluent blacks.").

45. See Mary S. Furlong, "An Electronic Community for Older Adults: The SeniorNet Network," *Journal of Communication* 39 (1989): 145, 149 (describing "SeniorNet's online grief counselor, [who] provides support for persons who have lost a spouse or loved one").

46. See Barry Wellman and Milena Gulia, "Virtual Communities As Communities: Net Surfers Don't Ride Alone," in Smith and Kollock, eds., *Communities in Cyberspace,* 167, 172.

47. See Bruce Bower, "Marginal Groups Thrive on the Internet," *Science News* 154 (1998): 245.

48. See, e.g., Kraut, et al., "Internet Paradox," 1017.

49. For example, a survey by James Katz and Philip Aspden found that "[f]ar from creating a nation of strangers, the Internet is creating a nation richer in friendships and social relationships"; see Katz and Aspden, "A Nation of Strangers?" *Communication of the ACM,* December 1997, 81, 85. Interestingly, of the 601 Internet users interviewed, fourteen percent had met at least one person through the Internet whom they considered a "friend"; moreover, 60 percent of these people reported meeting at least one Internet friend in real space (85, 86).

   See also Elizabeth Reid, "Virtual Worlds: Culture and Imagination," in Jones, ed., *CyberSociety,* 164, 175 (quoting a posting from someone who wrote, "I don't care how much people say they are, muds are not just games, they are *real*!!! My mud friends are my best friends, they are the people who like me most in the entire world. Maybe the only people who do. . . . They are my family, they are not just some dumb game.").

   There are numerous supporting testimonials. For example, Sherry Turkle describes "Peter," who in real life had few friends. The MUD he participated in became a part of his everyday life. In that virtual world, he successfully courted a female player, something he could not readily do in real space. See Sherry Turkle, "Constructions and Reconstructions of Self in Virtual Reality: Playing in the Moods," *Mind, Culture, and Activity* 1 (1994): 158, 161–62.

Another MUD enthusiast, who is a man (in real space) playing a woman who is pretending to be a man (in cyberspace), proclaimed that "this [online life] is more real than my real life." See Sherry Turkle, "Multiple Subjectivity and Virtual Community at the End of the Freudian Century," *Sociological Inquiry* 67 (1997): 72, 73.

50. Miller and Brewer, "Social Psychology," 2; see also Yehuda Amir, "Contact Hypothesis in Ethnic Relations," *Psychological Bulletin* 71 no.5 (1969): 319, 334 ("The effectiveness of interracial contact is greatly increased if the contact is sanctioned by institutional support. The support may come from the law, a custom, a spokesman for the community or any authority which is accepted by the interacting group. In many cases, institutional support comes simply from a social atmosphere or a general public agreement").

51. See Elaine K. Ginsberg, "Introduction: The Politics of Passing," in *Passing and the Fictions of Identity*, ed. Elaine K. Ginsberg (Durham, NC: Duke University Press, 1996), 1 (introducing literature on passing). By this I mean *only* that in cyberspace (1) graphically, I used an avatar that most Americans would map into the category black, and (2) textually, I self-identified as black. By contrast, in real space (1) visually, my appearance leads most Americans to map me into the category Asian American, and (2) verbally, I self-identify as Asian American. I exclude from my definition of "racial signal" any judgment about whether I was "acting black" in my linguistic patterns, mannerisms, aesthetic sensibilities, consumer preferences, and political commitments.

52. Ginsberg, "Politics of Passing," 16.

53. See Elizabeth M. Reid, "Communication and Community on Internet Relay Chat: Constructing Communities," in Ludlow, ed., *High Noon on the Electronic Frontier*, 336 (describing how a man, by playing a woman, felt liberated from having to act macho); Turkle, *Multiple Subjectivity*, 79–80 (describing how a timid man learned to become more assertive in real life by playing an aggressive female in cyberspace).

54. Many commentators have claimed that cyberspace teaches empathy across genders. For example, men who cyberpass as women realize that women in cyberspace are presented with unwanted sexual attention and unsolicited assistance. See, e.g., Curtis, MUDding, 355; compare Sherry Turkle, *Life on the Screen: Identity in the Age of the Internet* (New York: Simon and Schuster, 1995), 211 (reporting that when she played a male character in a MUD: "I finally experienced that permission to move freely I had always imagined to be the birthright of men. Not only was I approached less frequently, but I found it easier to respond to an unwanted overture with aplomb. . . .").

55. Here is another mechanism for learning interesting lessons. Imagine that I cyberpass as a white person. In so doing, I may become privy to comments, jokes, and conversations that would not normally take place in front of me. This too would have pedagogical value. See, e.g., Adrian Piper, "Passing for White, Passing for Black, in Ginsberg, ed., *Passing and the Fictions of Identity*, 234, 264 (describing insulting descriptions of blacks made in front of the author, a woman who self-identifies as black but who is generally mapped—by whites and blacks—as white).

56. For a concrete example of this conflict, consider that abolition would discourage the inclusion of photographs on personal home pages, but integration might approve of such a practice.

57. See, e.g., Lawrence Lessig, "The Zones of Cyberspace," *Stanford Law Review* 48 (1996): 1403, 1409 (describing the Communications Decency Act of 1996 and the National Information Infrastructure (NII) White Paper as attempts to "induc[e] a technology for zoning").

58. See Johnson and Post, "Law and Borders," 1379 (describing how cyberspace boundaries may be defined by reference to screens and passwords).

59. Readers will rightly ask how I define marketplaces. For example, is an investment club a marketplace or something else? I use this term only as shorthand, not as an analytic concept that helps us zone. *Marketplaces* is a conclusory label I attach to those cyberspaces that involve an exchange of property, goods, or services that society has decided should be colorblind. This term, in and of itself, does not help us make that decision.

60. See 42 U.S.C. § 1981(a) (1994): "All persons within the jurisdiction of the United States shall have the same right in every State and Territory to make and enforce contracts . . . and to the full and equal benefit of all laws and proceedings for the security of persons and property as is *enjoyed by white citizens* . . ." (emphasis added).

61. See, e.g., Realtor.com, online at <http://www.realtor.com>.

62. Excellent introductions to the legal landscape of information privacy can be found in Marc Rotenberg, *The Privacy Law Sourcebook 1999: United States Law, International Law, and Recent Developments* (Washington, DC: Electronic Privacy Information Center 1999); Paul M. Schwartz and Joel R. Reidenberg, *Data Privacy Law: A Study of United States Data Protection* (Charlottesville, VA: Michie, 1996); and Peter P. Swire and Robert E. Litan, *None of Your Business: World Data Flows, Electronic Commerce, and the European Privacy Directive* (Washington, DC: Brookings Institution Press, 1998).

63. See Jerry Kang, "Information Privacy in Cyberspace Transactions," *Stanford Law Review* 50 (1998): 1193, 1246–94.

64. A readable introduction to cryptography in general and public key cryptography in particular can be found in Simson Garfinkel, *PGP: Pretty Good Privacy* (Sebastopol, CA: O'Reilly, 1995), 33–58. The definitive source on the subject is Bruce Schneier, *Applied Cryptography: Protocols, Algorithms, and Source Code in C* (New York: Wiley, 2d ed. 1996). For an introduction to these concepts as applied to electronic commerce, see Froomkin, "Flood Control," 449–79.

65. If the lending institution knows the address of the home, then it can practice geographical redlining without knowing the race of the home buyer. We could try to engineer economic systems that take even this bit of information away from lending institutions. However, lenders would actively resist losing so much of their financial discretion, which typically depends on information about the home buyer (removed by the third party credentialing system), the property to be purchased, and the property's neighborhood.

66. See, e.g., The Electronic Signatures in Global and National Commerce Act, 15 U.S.C. § 7001 *et. seq.* (2002).

67. Trusted third parties are necessary to any e-commerce system established on public key cryptography. An excellent overview of trusted third parties is A. Michael Froomkin, "The Essential Role of Trusted Third Parties in Electronic Commerce," *Oregon Law Review* 75 (1996): 49. A practical overview appears in Thomas J. Smedinghoff, "Electronic Contracts and Digital Signatures: An Overview of Law and Legislation," *Third Annual Internet Law Institute* (New York: Practicing Law Institute, 1999), 125.

68. This proposal would go beyond the Community Reinvestment Act of 1977, which uses federal financial regulatory institutions to monitor lending practices, such as the geographical distribution of loans. Supervisory government agencies are required to consider this information, which is available to the public, in approving any application for a bank charter, deposit insurance, merger or acquisition, or office relocation. See Deanna Caldwell, "An Overview of Fair Lending Legislation," *John Marshall Law Review* 28 (1995): 333, 340–42.

69. The seller may not be as comfortable selling her home to an Asian American man. Faced with multiple offers at the same price, the seller may prefer to sell her home to a "nice" couple, who happen to be white. Maybe she will think, "That Chinese fellow might paint his house pink. I know those Chinese like pink. I couldn't do that to my neighbors."

70. For example, even if sellers and lenders do not know the buyer's race, buyers will know the racial makeup of the neighborhood. If whites prefer to live in a mostly white neighborhood—as opposed to an all-white neighborhood or a predominately black neighborhood—then white buyers will pay a premium for such neighborhoods. This premium might indirectly price blacks, who simply do not place as much value on a predominately white neighborhood, out of such communities. See David M. Cutler, Edward L. Glaser, and Jacob L. Vigdor, "The Rise and Decline of the American Ghetto," *Journal of Political Economy* 107 (1999): 455, 495–96 ("[W]hites still prefer to live with other whites more than blacks prefer to live in white areas"); Sander, "Housing Segregation," 986–88. Moreover, after moving in, the neighbors will obviously discover the race of the new residents. A family may fear harassment, hostility, and even violence and thus may decline to move into a neighborhood that is predominately of another race (985; see also 1009–10, citing additional reasons why reducing discrimination in housing sales may not significantly affect residential segregation.

71. Nakamura, "Race in/for Cyberspace," 187.

72. *See, e.g.*, Kira Hall, "Cyberfeminism," in Herring, ed., *Computer-Mediated Communication,* 147, 161–62 (describing a women's community whose members occasionally undertook real-space verification of a new member's gender). Some system operators will make unannounced telephone calls to registrants to listen to their voices to determine whether they are male or female; see, e.g., Jodi O'Brien, "Writing in the Body: Gender (Re)production in Online Interaction," in Smith and Kollock, eds., *Communities in Cyberspace* 86.

73. See John A. Bargh, Mark Chen, and Lara Burrows, "Automaticity of Social Behavior: Direct Effects of Trait Construct and Stereotype Activation on Action," *Journal of Personality and Social Psychology* 71 (n.d.): 230 ("Stereotypes become active automatically on the mere presence of physical features associated with the stereotyped group, and categorizing behavior in terms of personality traits and then making dispositional attributions about the actor's personality have both been shown to occur automatically to some extent"); (citations omitted).

74. See, e.g., Peter Kollock, *Design Principles for Online Communities,* online at <http://www.sscnet.ucla.edu/soc/faculty/kollock/papers/design.htm> (identifying general design principles for successful online communities, which include internal economy, a coherent sense of place, rituals, history of community, identity persistence, moderate risk, and likelihood of unplanned interaction).

75. 47 U.S.C. § 230(c)(1) (Supp. III 1998).

76. Ibid.; *Blumenthal v. Drudge,* 992 F. Supp. 44, 50–53 (D.D.C. 1998); *Zeran v. America Online, Inc.,* 958 F. Supp. 1124, 1132–33 (E.D. Va. 1997).

77. Perhaps this pragmatic approach toward racial zoning can be imported back into real space. For example, many opponents of race-based affirmative action in higher education argue that the state sends mixed messages when it tells employers, on the one hand, to ignore race, but admissions officers, on the other hand, to consider race. This contradiction can be seen as an example of real-space racial zoning. Certain employment spaces can be zoned "abolition," at the same time that certain education spaces are zoned "integration."

78. This attempt is an exploration of what I call *critical race technologies,* rooted in what Eric Yamamoto calls "critical pragmatism." Eric K. Yamamoto, *Interracial Justice: Conflict and Reconciliation in Post–Civil Rights America* (New York: New York University Press, 1999), 133. A critical race technology takes into account the power of architecture, digital as well as spatial, in the construction of racial mechanics. For examples of the latter, see Keith Aoki, "Race, Space, and Place: The Relation between Architectural Modernism, Post-Modernism, Urban Planning, and Gentrification," *Fordham Urban Law Journal* 20 (1993): 699; and Richard

Thompson Ford, "Geography and Sovereignty: Jurisdictional Formation and Racial Segregation," *Stanford Law Review* 49 (1997): 1365.

Critical Race Theorists should also recall C. P. Snow, who warned, "It is dangerous to have two cultures which can't or don't communicate. In a time when science is determining much of our destiny, that is, whether we live or die, it is dangerous in the most practical terms. Scientists can give bad advice and decisionmakers can't know whether it is good or bad. On the other hand, scientists in a divided culture provide a knowledge of some potentialities which is theirs alone." See Snow, *The Two Cultures: and a Second Look: An Expanded Version of the Two Cultures and the Scientific Revolution* (Cambridge: Cambridge University Press, 1964), 98; internal citation omitted.

2
The Pixelated Asia/Pacific

3
Virtually Vietnamese: Nationalism on the Internet

KIM-AN LIEBERMAN

We are in the epoch of simultaneity: we are in the epoch of
juxtaposition, the epoch of the near and far, of the side-by-
side, of the dispersed.
—Michel Foucault, "Of Other Spaces"

Beyond the impossible, we are the possible.
—Hoang Viet Cuong, Coalition of Vietnamese
National Parties Homepage

The Republic of Vietnam: "Everywhere and Nowhere"

The fall of Saigon to Hồ Chí Minh's communist army in 1975 triggered an exodus of over two million Vietnamese who disagreed with or feared for their lives under the new regime. They scattered across the globe, resettling in Australia, France, the United States, and many other countries. Support for a Vietnamese democracy, however, remained strong. With the 1989 unification of Germany and the subsequent dissolution of communism in Eastern Europe, political change in Vietnam seemed increasingly tenable. Vietnamese nationalists, although dispersed, began forming several democracy movements. Their common goal: a free Vietnam. Among the most efficient and effective tools in their cause has been, and continues to be, the Internet.

As David Lamb points out, "anyone with a computer and $20 for subscription fees to a service provider can become a dissident activist these days."[1] Dorothy Dunning echoes, "The Internet is clearly changing the landscape of political discourse and advocacy."[2] Unlike older forms of public discourse, the large majority of Internet space still lacks an overt power structure. There are no editors, critics, sponsors or other authority figures mediating access. Not only do authors get unlimited air time, but they have a ready-made audience of millions. Publication is immediate, worldwide, and (beyond access to a computer) independent of material or social status; the transfer of information is instantaneous and simultaneous. With a vastly wider and faster range of transmission than photocopied manifestos, short-wave radio, or public access television, the Internet has become a essential grassroots medium for expressing dissent, even altering the very nature of civil war. Peter Eng notes, "In fighting Burma's brutal military government Lwin Moe used to wear combat fatigues, wield an AK-47 rifle and roam the jungles with Regiment 201 of the All Burma Students Democratic Front. Today, in business jackets and from an office in neighboring Thailand, he still fights the same enemy but a very different type of war. His weapons now are two 233 MHz desktop computers. His battle ground is Cyberspace."[3] Moe much prefers the computer because "We can fight without bloodshed. We can send statements to the entire world and we can send a virus to the [government] machine."[4] Another Burmese opposition group, with only "a single computer powered by a 286 chip," applied for a grant to buy additional computers "and now has become a potent anti-government force. At times it has crippled the government's e-mail system with a flood of junk messages."[5] China's communist government is contending with its own self-proclaimed "hacktivists."[6] In Indonesia, protesters used "literally hundreds of e-mail lists" to rally support for an underground movement that successfully ended President Kemusu Suharto's thirty-two-year rule.[7] Other world regions with volatile political climates, such as east central Europe and northern Africa, have found themselves battling conflict on land as well as in cyberspace.[8]

Overseas Vietnamese have also harnessed online free speech for political ends. The Internet has become a springboard for their dissent from Vietnam's current government. "Accurate information," asserts one organization, "must be one of the most effective and peaceful weapons to conduct the struggle for democracy and freedom against that worst tyranny in the history of Vietnam."[9] Claims another, "by utilizing the Internet for information and suggestions from people around the world, [we] may also have invented a new way of fighting for Human Rights, Freedom and Democracy for Vietnam."[10] Self-directed, uncensored, and globally broadcast, online media such as webpages and e-mail are the perfect complements to Vietnamese political activism—especially since the activists cannot easily gather together on physical ground. Journalist David Case explains that "for years, [overseas Vietnamese] have been separated from Vietnam and one another by the vast geography of the globe. The Internet has changed that, bringing them as close as the nearest modem." He concludes that "Next century, Vietnam's battles will be fought in cyberspace."[11]

There are over two dozen websites devoted entirely to Vietnamese anticommunist activism. Among them: homepages for the fifty-year-old Việt Nam Quốc Dân Đảng (Vietnamese Nationalist Party, known as "Việt Quốc" for short);[12] the southern California–based Đoàn Thanh Niên Phan Bội Châu (Youth For Democracy Group);[13] and the Đại Việt Cách Mạng Đảng (Vietnam Revolution Party) with its battle cry of "humanism, democracy, prosperity."[14] The outspoken Phong Tráo Thống Nhất Dân Tộc và Xây Dựng Dân Chủ (Movement to United the People and Build Democracy) uses its Internet space to announce that "*blind* adherence to Marxist doctrine led to an totalitarian state at the expense of the health and welfare of the [Vietnamese] people. Communism has now proven to be [a] miserable failure."[15] Other online declarations detail specific steps toward the reestablishment of a Vietnamese Democratic Republic, ranging from the self-titled Government of Free Vietnam's "A Program to Save the Nation and Build the Nation"—a series of "whereas" and "because" statements that reads strikingly like Abraham Lincoln's Emancipation Proclamation[16]—to the Free Vietnam Alliance's step-by-step outline for "the Democratization Process," with different directives for the leadership of the Vietnamese Communist Party and its "progressive" members, Vietnamese in Vietnam and overseas, and "all democratic forces."[17] A handful of websites even propose restoration of the Nguyen Dynasty's monarchical descendents (within a democratic structure, of course) as remedy to communism.[18]

The Internet has become the central switchboard for Vietnamese activists exchanging and disseminating information. Many organizations, including the Vietnam Human Rights Network (Mạng Lưới Nhân Quyền) and the International Committee for Freedom (Cao Trào Nhân Bản), use the Internet to monitor political violence and persecution in Vietnam.[19] Others—like the recently retired Vietnam Insight, maintained throughout the 1990s by an activist who worked from her home in suburban San Jose[20]—function as a general clearinghouse of news articles "carrying the voice of opposition against the oppressive regime in Vietnam to the outside world."[21] All are accessible from any country that is linked to the Internet; their authors might come from the United States or Germany; their host computers might be located in New Zealand or Taiwan. "The Internet and e-mail are fantastic for crossing borders," says Doan Viet Hoat, a prominent Vietnamese dissident, because "no dictator could stop it."[22] As webpage author Lý Thanh Bình proclaims, "This new political party will be everywhere and nowhere."[23]

Even if not political in purpose, the webpages for many Vietnamese communities and associations include their own anticommunist mission statements or reference other sites with corresponding agendas. A recent posting on the general-interest Vietnamese American web portal Kicon Vietspace provides a direct link to the Committee For Religious Freedom in Vietnam, along with information about the organization's upcoming protest against the new China-Vietnam border agreement.[24] The international Vietnamese Professionals Society—a forum hoping "to facilitate the exchange of professional information, the interaction between Vietnamese and non-Vietnamese professionals, and between groups of Vietnamese of different professions"—lists among its primary goals "to contribute to . . . the formation of a democratic Vietnam" and avers that "its members oppose all activities that benefit the dictatorial regime."[25] Vietnamese university student groups often use the Internet to vocalize political opinions: in October 1997, UCLA's Vietnamese Student Union homepage highlighted its protest of an on-campus performance by Hanoi's Thăng Long

Water Puppet Troupe, a movement spread by e-mail to Vietnamese student associations at Berkeley and elsewhere.[26] Likewise, the soc.culture.vietnamese Usenet newsgroup, easily accessible through web-based services like DejaNews, has become an active arena for anticommunist debate and information exchange. One posting lists the "top websites" of "free Vietnamese people all over the world," informing interested readers about their online options for activism and information.[27]

Taking advantage of the web as multimedia, Vietnamese online express their political opinions visually as well as textually. Anticommunist icons, sounds, and speech abound in Vietnamese Internet space. The Việt Quốc webpage, for instance, depicts the "Mourning Soldier" statue that stood in South Vietnam's National Military Cemetery until dismantled at the end of the war by Communist forces.[28] Online maps of Vietnam often have "Saigon" prominently labeled where "Hồ Chí Minh City" should be.[29] Real-time audio technology enables politically minded broadcasts like Radio Free Vietnam and Vietnamese Public Radio to reach a global audience.[30] Perhaps most boldly, the yellow and red striped flag of the Việt Nam Cộng Hoà (Republic of Vietnam), displaced in 1975 by the Communists' five-point star, still waves—literally, through the use of animated graphics—on a website proudly claiming to represent the late South Vietnamese armed forces.[31] Adorning the large majority of political and even nonpartisan Vietnamese webpages, the decommissioned Republican flag has become a commonplace motif online.[32] The education reference page for the ABC Interactive World Factbook includes former South Vietnam in its "Flags of all Countries" section, "By Popular Demand."[33] There is even a website whose sole purpose is "Protection of the Flag of the Republic," waving its own flag graphic to a rousing MIDI-synthesizer rendition of the South Vietnamese national anthem.[34] As this last site explains, its fanfare of sight and sound is deliberately meant to capture attention: "We do know our flag does not exist on the international map, that is why we have to protect and keep [it] alive...."[35] Technically, the Republic of Vietnam fell with Saigon, but in many senses it has been resurrected on the Internet.

This essay is an exploration of how the Internet both enables as well as shapes Vietnamese democratic activism. I am especially interested in the Internet as a site of imagination and empowerment, of possibility for change—and how that environment can affect the formation of individual identity. With cyberspace standing as proxy for the unobtainable space of Vietnam, how do those of the Vietnamese diaspora define themselves and their nationality? How does Vietnam itself respond? I look closely at the online manifestations of common national markers: language, history, and homeland. This is all uncharted territory; my hope is that future researchers will further explore these issues. We all know that the Internet is changing the way that we shop, work, communicate. How is it changing the way that we envision ourselves in political and geographic space?

Imagining Things

It may be dictator-proof, but an idealized online manifestation of Vietnam still has its complications. After all, the efficacy of a political movement without central leaders or tangible presence is questionable. Especially when its opponents are an all-too-real and powerful communist government firmly ensconced in the homeland, online activists are vulnerable to the accusation that their democratic alternative is (and has always been) a fantasy. How do you prove the validity of social structure, of actual and significant achievement, in a physical unreality located "everywhere and nowhere"? For Vietnamese activists on the Internet, the answer has been to take conscious control of the imagined ideal. This alone is a source of empowerment: the ability to determine the way that the Vietnamese democratic community conceives itself. As Guobin Yang writes of a parallel online movement among overseas Chinese, "Their success story is a story of connection: they provide points of entry and connection for a dispersed population."[36]

The process of imagining community, to borrow Benedict Anderson's term, is a pivotal hinge for "entry and connection." Vietnamese activists build national and political allegiance by remaining cognizant of the larger context in which they operate—using the literal network of the Internet to reach their symbolic network of compatriots. Like Anderson's newspaper reader, who is "well aware that the ceremony he performs is being replicated simultaneously by thousands (or millions) of others of whose existence he is confident, yet of whose identity he has not the slightest notion,"[37] the Việt Quốc party explicitly recognizes its widespread but anonymous audience: "The primary objective of this homepage is to provide those who read English with profound insights into the true situation in Vietnam and the conflict between the communists and non-communists.... With such better knowledge, we hope the readers would lend their strong support to the right causes of our Vietnamese non-communist bloc."[38] Similarly, the Government of Free Vietnam invokes "the Holy Spirit of the Fatherland, our glorious Ancestors ... our heroes ... seventy million compatriots, inside the country and abroad."[39] If we start with Anderson's definition of the newspaper as "an 'extreme form' of the book, a book sold on a colossal scale, but of ephemeral popularity,"[40] then the Internet takes it one step further, an "extreme form" of the newspaper which achieves an even greater scale, and is not even ephemeral but instantaneous.

As "extreme" newspapers, webpages and e-mail help project national identity. The subjects of Anderson's study, however, arrive at their nationalism through a relatively passive and ambient awareness of neighbors. The Vietnamese online community, as a product of diasporic experience, must actively manufacture its sense of interconnection. As John Rex explains, "A diaspora is said to exist when an *ethnie* or nation suffers some kind of traumatic event which leads to the dispersal of its members, who nonetheless, continue to aspire to return to the homeland."[41] Just like Anderson's newspaper nation, the dispersed nation is a concept fabricated by self-identifying members. The role of imagination in diasporic nationalism, however, is differently inflected. Anderson places the crux of imagination in community formation: "It is *imagined* because the members of even the smallest nation will never know most of their fellow-members, meet them, or even hear of them, yet in the minds of each lives the image of their communion."[42] The diaspora, by contrast, are a globally disbanded network of former neighbors, a collective that has ostensibly fallen apart: "two million Vietnamese had to escape by any means possible, scattering all over the world."[43] It is a patchwork of cross-continental span that embraces but cannot effectively unite its members. What they have in common, I suggest, is the image of their *separation.*

In place of communion, the diaspora construct what James Clifford calls "a history of dispersal, myths/memories of the homeland, alienation in the host (bad host?) country, desire for eventual return, ongoing support of the homeland, and a collective identity importantly defined by this relationship."[44] The diasporic framework shifts emphasis from imagined community to imagined origin, from notions of fellow newspaper-readers to "myths/memories of the homeland."[45] Online, Vietnamese activists take control of this act of imagining. The homeland is made mythic and memorable on the Internet through the active and collaborative presentation of personal anecdotes, photo montages, nostalgic or epic histories. On the Vietnamese Boatpeople Connection webpage, former refugee Binh D. Dao collects "Untold Stories" of "perilous escapes to freedom that no one could have imagined," valorizing the anecdotes as a vital act of remembering: "I decided to set up this website, hoping that many fortunate survivors would be willing to share their stories. I know many stories are just too painful to recall. I just hope that you would somehow find the courage to share. Now that it is a thing of the past, only its legacy remains..."[46] Tuan Nguyen's effusive webpage, "Vietnam: The Land of Hope and Prosperity," also solicits collective participation in the act of construction: "Welcome all. Together we are going to discover the beauty of our homeland." Nguyen then goes on to figure Vietnam in mythic proportions, "a precious stone which can never be shattered. Each struggle of this lovely land is like a polishing, and after each polishing it becomes clearer and brighter.... When the wave of democracy washes over Vietnam, it will polish down all the flaws and the Vietnam Jade will become ten times brighter and more refined."[47]

Awareness of imagining is key to the Vietnamese activists' agenda. Even if they no longer reside in the Vietnamese nation, they can still claim national allegiance to a Vietnam that has been deliberately idealized through memories of the past or hopes for the future. Edward Said posits that "there is no doubt that imaginative geography and history help the mind to intensify its own sense of itself"; it is precisely recognition of this "imaginative geography and history" upon which Said's argument about orientalism as the crystallization of occidental identity hinges.[48] For the diaspora, who remain by definition politically and geographically marginalized, imagination has everything to do with identity—and the Internet helps them to extend their imaginative grasp. Ananda Mitra notes that "the determinate moment in the process of voicing on the Internet is the moment of creating the utterance and not so much the moment at which the utterance is heard. This perspective is particularly important for marginal groups who might not have had the opportunity to express themselves in their own authentic voice until the Internet was available. In making that possibility available, the Internet empowers the marginal in ways that no other media technology has been able to do before.... [and] makes that empowerment particularly significant since many such traditionally powerless voices can now connect with each other to empower each other."[49] If not immediately effecting the desired political change, Vietnamese online expression does something equally important: it enables Vietnamese expatriates as authors of their own collectively imagined identity.

Monique T. D. Trương, in one of the only existing studies of Vietnamese American identity by a Vietnamese American, writes that "For the majority of Americans, Vietnam as a self-defined country never existed."[50] Instead, Vietnam signifies a war, an era, a landmark in American (but not Vietnamese American) historical and social consciousness. "Vietnamese Americans" are consequently stereotyped as boat people, ambiguous enemy-victims, martyrs from the "other side"—marked by war, not cultural heritage. The general conception of Vietnamese American life and identity remains one wholly divested of individual choice: "Immigrants *choose to come* to a new life, whereas refugees *are forced to flee*—often for their lives. Vietnamese refugees left their old life, not freely, but because they were persecuted or feared being persecuted on account of their ethnic, religious, or political affiliations; had they not felt threatened, they would not have left."[51] Paul James Rutledge echoes that "a significant factor in the Vietnamese flight from their homeland is the fact that they left as refugees and not as immigrants."[52] The distinction, of course, is shaky. Historically, the experiences of "immigrant" and "refugee" overlap; each decision to leave the homeland (Vietnam or otherwise) is almost always part choice, part crisis. There is no room in this model of emigration for those who *choose* to flee. As one disgruntled reader penciled into the margin of my library copy of Rutledge's *The Vietnamese Experience in America,* "even refugees have time to prepare."

A glance at the scholarship on Vietnamese diasporic identity in general indicates a significant lag between public perceptions and actual demographics. Thomas A. DuBois acknowledges the need for a new model, something that moves past the problematic litany of "refugees, migrants, immigrants, ethnics, and ... racial minorities."[53] The refugee rubric, in particular, encourages "the tendency to view Southeast Asians as passive, immobilized, and pathetic."[54] While DuBois does not provide any immediate answers for the problems that arise from such categorization and stereotyping, he does point out the need for refocusing academic attention on "discursive models of the Southeast Asian as invented and reinvented by scholars, the general American populace, and Southeast Asians themselves."[55] DuBois's request simply underscores the extent to which individual choice has been defused. Including "Southeast Asians themselves" in a discourse about Southeast Asian identity should be axiomatic.

Not only has the ability of Southeast Asians to participate in scholarly discourse about themselves been underestimated, but the refugee model, flawed in the first place, is quickly becoming irrelevant. A second, post-1975 generation of overseas Vietnamese, predominantly born and raised in their "host" countries, is emerging as a separate voice. The term *refugee* simply does not apply to them, literally or figuratively. But the persisting problem in the creation of Vietnamese diasporic identity is not just inaccurate terminology: it is a lack of Vietnamese agency in shaping the entire discourse. In this light, I believe that online political activism becomes an important statement of self-determined Vietnamese American (and other overseas Vietnamese) identity. Mitra suggests that "diasporic communities are increasingly embracing the Internet system to produce a new sense of community where they can textually create images of their own national and tribal communities."[56] The Internet has become a crucial forum for the expression of ideas that before were suppressed either actively, in the case of communist censorship of Vietnamese democracy, or passively, in the case of Western stereotypes of Vietnamese identity.

Establishing a Cartography

Because all of this active imagining and self-determination ultimately passes through the filter of online communication, I would like to return to a more detailed consideration of the Internet itself. Both Anderson's imagined community and the Vietnamese diasporic nation still maintain specific physical and political ties to the tangible world, whether through daily actions (of reading a newspaper) or assertions (of feeling patriotic toward one's homeland). The Internet, by contrast, transcends bodily and geographic boundaries. It is imagination unharnessed; it is a public sphere where public authority does not intrude. People can do, say, and be whatever they want. Like the economically booming "Pacific Rim," the Internet is a fabricated space of promise, of opportunity, of modernity and change.[57] For the idealized democracy of Vietnamese diasporic activism, which exists in direct opposition to the spatial realities of a fragmented population and a communist-governed Vietnam, cyberspace seems a perfect fit.

Karim H. Karim notes that "the phenomenon of inter-continental diasporic communication has existed for centuries," exploiting almost every possible medium: mail, telegraph, telephone, fax, audio- and videotape, film, television, satellite. The Internet, however, "is particularly suited to the needs of diasporas" because of its unprecedented accessibility and global reach.[58] All webpages are created equal: the online world has unlimited room for divergent voices, and assigns everyone the same status. It is the global village, the information superhighway, "the new middle landscape, the garden in the machine, where democratic values can thrive in a sort of cyber-Jeffersonian renaissance."[59] Sherry Turkle suggests that cyberspace presents an escape from static and hierarchical paradigms of identity: "When people adopt an online persona, they cross a boundary into highly charged territory. Some feel an uncomfortable sense of fragmentation, some a sense of relief. Some sense the possibilities for self-discovery, even self-transformation."[60] Similarly, Shawn P. Wilbur sees "virtual community" as a revolutionary act of imagination: "With their eyes wide open and using the tools we have inherited . . . researchers may be able to carry forward the study of community in directions which we had not previously ever imagined."[61] The online explorer must be prepared not only to imagine self and community in a number of new ways, but also to uncover conclusions that fall outside that initial imagining. In a specifically ethnic context, this slippage even allows for release from racial markers: "If being Vietnamese today is not what you want to be, you could pick some other category."[62]

The boundless extremity of this freedom, however, can also give way to instability. In the absence of physical markers—when it is quite possible to misrepresent age, gender, ethnicity, or any other traditional touchstone of identity—how do you form genuine communities based on common experience? How do you keep disguised intruders out of spaces reserved for a specific group such as Asian Americans or women? Even if you suspect that someone is lying, by what authority can you demand the truth? These fears of misrepresentation expose the shaky underpinnings of online representation. The Internet is, at a basic level, a world of imagined interpersonal connections. This complicates a project like the Web-based spread of Vietnamese democratic activism, which depends so much on real individual identity in relation to an urgent collective cause. It presents a situation where foreknowledge of the mechanisms of imagination do not empower but paralyze: the same freedom that makes room for the authentic voice also allows for its possible impersonation and usurpation.[63]

Anxiety about multiplicity and duplicity is not unique to the Vietnamese online community, but is a symptom of the broader, technology-infused narrative of postmodernity: urban disarray, global diversity, media blitz, millennial anarchy. Robert Jay Lifton, in *The Protean Self: Human Resilience in an Age of Fragmentation*, writes, "We are becoming fluid and many-sided. Without quite realizing it, we have been evolving a sense of self appropriate to the restlessness and flux of our time. This mode of being differs radically from that of the past, and enables us to engage in continuous exploration and personal experiment. . . . The protean self emerges from confusion, from the widespread feeling that we are losing our psychological moorings. We feel ourselves buffeted about by unmanageable historical forces and social uncertainties."[64] A similar sentiment, attributed more pointedly to technology, is echoed by Kenneth Gergen, who writes, "As a result of advances in radio, telephone, transportation, television, satellite transmission, computers, and more, we are exposed to an enormous barrage of social stimulation. Small and enduring communities . . . are being replaced by a vast and ever-expanding array of relationships . . . this massive increment in social stimulation—moving toward a state of saturation—sets the stage both for radical changes in our daily experiences of self and others. . . ."[65] Gergen writes about a "saturated" self, not able to support much more change, while Lifton envisions a "protean" self, adapting to new situations. In either case, there is a sense of fragmentation within the self and of distance from history, a breaking off from one's roots. The self is being reinvented, and perhaps overloaded, by "restlessness and flux," a "vast and ever-expanding array of relationships."

Internet culture, as ultimate pastiche, is a prime example of "restlessness and flux." It is certainly "vast and ever-expanding," and infamous for its unreliability: in any given day, hundreds of webpages undergo makeovers, relocate to new servers, or disappear completely. The web also makes a strong case for rootlessness; it is "outside of the human experiences of space and time."[66] It is geographically unbounded, a virtual space not subject to landlocked necessities. It is inherently ahistoric, because everything exists on the Internet simultaneously in an identical state of newness. In the face of so much disorder, writes critic Scott Bukathman, "There is an ongoing attempt to explore and cognitively map the new terminal spaces, to establish a cartography."[67] Even the jargon of the Internet suggests a desire for spatial orientation: people "navigate" the web, "visit" a webpage, use "links" and "frames" to organize information. The personal webpage, the starting point, is comfortably called "home." Physical terminology helps to anchor the shifting modalities of online existence in recognizable, familiar concepts. As Ananda Mitra and Rae Lynn Schwartz propose, "It is no longer possible to live within the metaphors of maps, movements, and nations, but it is important to move away from these signifiers to ones that address the more authentic lived experience of web-maps, hyperlinked-spaces, and cyber-communities. . . ."[68] Traditional notions of location and place, in other words, have been dramatically altered by the development of Internet culture; but basic human concerns with self-location and self-placement remain highly relevant nevertheless.

For Vietnamese online activists, the desire to "establish a cartography" has materialized in their webpages, which often connect political efforts to undeniably "real" phenomena. The Free Vietnam Alliance's homepage, for example, includes links to "Vietnam Time," which displays the current local time in "Hanoi-Saigon, Vietnam" in relation to current Greenwich Mean Time;[69] and to "Vietnam Weather," which brings up the current and extended forecast for multiple Vietnamese cities, complete with windspeed, visibility, and a satellite overview.[70] A more literally cartographic approach can be found on websites like the Vietnam Picture Gallery and Lien Hoa's Vietnam My Country. Both sites invite users to click anywhere on a map of Vietnam in order to produce a page of full-color photographs depicting the individual city of interest.[71] Through associating the map's representative outlines with vivid real-life images, these websites assert the tangibility and visibility of an online Vietnam. Similarly, Cuong Nguyen's Maps of Vietnam page exhibits an array of twenty-eight "various maps of Vietnam that I have collected," with no further explanation. Each mini-map in the grid can be clicked for "an enlarged fullscale image." Gathered together, Nguyen's twenty-eight maps insist that Vietnam is not simply an imagined place, dreamed up in the nebulous realm of cyberspace, but a land with physical shape and charted coordinates.

Many other websites conjure Vietnam through illustration. Vietnam's Knowledge Base offers sixteen postcard-quality "Images of Vietnam,"[72] while both Chi D. Nguyen's elegant viettouch.com and Dang Anh Tuân's French-and-English Pays D'Eau (Land of Water) make extensive use of graphics to help outline Vietnamese culture and history.[73] Taking things one step further, the VietScape homepage is designed not only to display temporary pictures online, but to let the user actually affix a "Vietnam landscape" on the desktop of his computer screen: "With mouse over image, click mouse right button and select 'Set As Wallpaper' or 'Set This As Background Image.'" The mobile landscape, with point-and-click rapidity, brings "Vietnam" right into the user's own room. Additionally, Internet images help overseas Vietnamese to visualize one another. Extensive online archives of photographs and videos taken at anticommunist rallies, demonstrations, and speeches around the world allow individual members of the Vietnamese diaspora—no matter how isolated or far-flung—to experience the excitement of united political protest.[74] Like Nguyen's maps, these images help to confirm tangible Vietnamese realities. They refresh memories, revive cultural connections, and strengthen nationalist sentiment. Through online visualization of a commonly remembered homeland and a collectively mobilized cause, Vietnamese democratic activists promote their political survival.

In this capacity, anticommunist icons on the Internet become pivotal stand-ins for physical evidence. The waving Republican flag of South Vietnam, for instance, validates a political regime that today's communists demean as a "puppet government"; the relabeled map asserts the geographical reality of Saigon despite the official name change that effaced that city's existence in modern-day Vietnam. Pointedly defiant, one webpage displays a tattered, fragmentized image of Vietnam's "communist bloody flag"—just under a healthily waving Republican flag—with a list of "the exact location and date of any Vietnam communist flags which were brought down" in the United States. The graphics are strategically arranged on the screen to emphasize the contrast between the proudly hoisted, upright Republican banner and its flattened communist counterpart. Another webpage uses flashing red dots on a map to indicate the locations of recent uprisings against the communist government by Vietnamese citizens in Thái Bình and Xuân Lộc.[75] On its own site, Vietworld publishes a Virtual Memorial Wall of the names, occupations, and locations/circumstances of death for 898 of the political prisoners verified to have perished in Vietnam's "reeducation camps" after the war's end. The sheer length of this document, divided into nine sections "for your viewing convenience," speaks for itself.[76]

As its title indicates, the Vietworld Wall also makes deliberate reference to the Vietnam Veterans Memorial Wall in Washington, D.C. Introducing each section of the Vietworld is a picture of a candle held up to a black granite slab, in which the camp victims' names appear to be engraved—just as veterans' names are carved in the actual black granite of the D.C. monument. The Vietnam Oral History Project has a similar Cyber Wall displaying against a gray marble background the names of several South Vietnamese soldiers killed in battle.[77] Like the flashing maps and waving flags, these simulated monuments function as online forms of visible "proof." They locate Vietnamese diaspora within a physically tangible geographical and historical absolute—and, at the same time, undermine the communist-specific version of that geography and history. They stamp political messages with the iconic solemnity and solidity of names carved in stone.

VNI, VIQR, VISCII

Perhaps the most vivid illustration of the desire for concretized affirmation amid online flux has been the push to reproduce the Vietnamese language—for many overseas Vietnamese, the authentic voice—in a computerized environment. Because it has a Roman alphabet, Vietnamese can be approximated with American standard code for information interchange (ASCII) characters, the international Internet standard that comprises all the letters, numbers, and symbols found on a normal English-language keyboard. The diacritic marks that differentiate tonal variants and thus determine meaning for Vietnamese words cannot, however, be fully represented in ASCII text. Without the proper tonal designations, reading Vietnamese becomes an exercise in guesswork.

As a temporary solution, people posting Vietnamese-language messages in newsgroups and other computerized contexts devised the Vietnamese quoted-readable (VIQR) convention, which uses ASCII marks to connote diacritics.[78] Basically, the diacritics are represented with similar-looking keyboard symbols, typed after (instead of over or under) the letters themselves: *ế* becomes *e^´* and *u* becomes *u+* in VIQR. The process is admittedly awkward, as the official example illustrates:

> *Vietnamese:* Tôi yêu tiếng nước tôi tứ khi mói ra đòi.
> *VIQR:* To^i ye^u tie^^ng nu + o + ´c to^i tu + `khi mo + `i ra ddo + `i.

I should note that the official example is fortified with a heavy dose of nationalism. The opening line of a famous folksong by Vietnamese American composer Phạm Duy, it reads: "I have loved the language of my country since the first moment of my life."[79]

In 1989, the nonprofit Vietnamese-Standard Working Group (Viet-Std) was formed "to promote the standardization of Vietnamese character encoding and to monitor ongoing work of international bodies in this regard."[80] Viet-Std proposed the Vietnamese standard code for information interchange (VISCII), which made possible the keyboard entry of Vietnamese words with properly placed diacritics. Another nonprofit group, TriChlor Software, helped to make special computer programs for the composition and viewing of Vietnamese documents widely available.[81] With appropriate software and fonts installed, anyone could now write and read a webpage in neatly formatted Vietnamese. Viet-Std announced its accomplishments in a 1992 report: "It is our dream one day to be able to read, write, and exchange Vietnamese data of a common format on any machine, any platform, and to take advantage of all the processing tools that have been produced by the computing world. That dream, once a pure exercise in imagination, has today come many steps closer to realization."[82]

Unfortunately, several other people had the same idea. VISCII is perfectly viable, but it contends with a host of other Vietnamese-font options. The main competitors are VPS (from the Vietnamese Professionals Society[83]) and VNI (from a flashy for-profit software company by the same name[84]), but countless others exist: the latest version of VietKey typing software recognizes an astounding forty-four options.[85] As a result, one webpage might use VISCII conventions, while another might use VPS, and still another might offer a choice between VIQR and VNI. To vex matters, most of these fonts are incompatible, requiring additional software simply to convert from one to the next. The problem has become not *how* to put Vietnamese on the Internet, but *which* Vietnamese to use. New developments in typography software such as Unicode (which allows a single standard font, like Times New Roman, to support multiple languages[86]) and web font embedding (which allows the author to control exactly how a webpage will appear on the user's screen[87]) are helping to overcome some of these barriers by replacing ASCII with a new universal standard that happens to support Vietnamese-language type. Still, these improvements remain version-specific. That is, without the right software and fonts installed on both ends—for both author and user—a Vietnamese webpage is rendered unreadable.

The quandary would be easier to dismiss as a technological glitch were it not for the large resonance that Vietnamese nationalism has with the online restoration of the language. As Anderson indicates, the Vietnamese language has long been integral to Vietnamese national identity: "French and American imperialists governed, exploited, and killed Vietnamese over many years. But whatever else they made off with, the Vietnamese language stayed put."[88] Even before Western colonization, a thousand years of Chinese rule managed to influence but not replace the Vietnamese language. The word for written script—*quốc ngữ*—contains the Sino-Vietnamese radical *quốc*, or "nation," and literally means "national language." In this light, VNI language software is hailed by its supporters as "an honor for all Vietnamese people, and a major contribution to the Vietnamese community abroad";[89] its efforts "deserve being recorded on the pages of Vietnamese history,"[90] and it is deemed "something . . . valuable to the Vietnamese at home and abroad, Your good name VNI will be remembered generations after generations."[91] One user "was moved to the point of tears when I first saw Vietnamese writing appear on my monitor and from my printer."[92] Another expressed hope that "come some fine day, perhaps a day in the not-too-distant future, the work of VNI will constitute a truly significant contribution to the restoration of our homeland."[93] Meanwhile, given this context, it is unsurprising that the Vietnamese communist government chose to develop its own national typing system, TCVN (also known, suggestively, as "ABC"). Equally unsurprising is the fact that TCVN, the universal standard within Vietnam, is rarely used outside of the country.[94]

If language is a conduit for national sentiment—literally, in terms of person-to-person communication, and figuratively, as an emblem of commonality—then the electronic labyrinth of Vietnamese-language software frustrates any move toward a unified front for those working online. Instead of "restoration," the proliferation of Vietnamese(s) results in a deeper splintering and separateness. Instead of a single "national language," there are suddenly several dozen incompatible versions. This conscious attempt to pin down a shared reality produces only uncomfortable instability and a breakdown in communication. Vietnamese and all its cultural meanings are crudely reduced to a "standard code for information interchange." At the same time, the myriad versions of computerized Vietnamese also enable a form of democratic choice. Like the separate development of Vietnam's official TCVN system, the decision of members of the Vietnamese diaspora *not* to use that particular make of "language" on their webpages—and to offer, instead, forty-four different options—becomes a fundamental statement of political position and dissent.

Vietnam: "The Great Leap Forward into Cyberspace"

Amid the plans and efforts of Vietnamese overseas activists, the Socialist Republic of Vietnam itself is facing a critical dilemma: what to do about the Internet? Cyberspace, as a fundamentally unmediated forum, presents a direct threat to a one-party regime wishing to keep tabs on the flow of imported media and cultural exposure; the busy "hacktivists" of Burma, China, and Indonesia provide object lessons. At the same time, Internet-based communication is arguably the single most significant part of modern business and industrial growth, and a country already struggling economically cannot afford to get left behind. Vietnam's approach to the Internet, consequently, has been "an acute contradiction. On the one hand, it is eager to facilitate knowledge of business nature.... On the other hand, Vietnam cannot drop its obsession to maintain control over information both within the country and with the outside world."[95] Alternately, as the Hanoi-based *Vietnam Investment Review* phrases it, "The problem is control, or more precisely, how to integrate with the rest of the world without suffering the ills, such as moral ambiguity, alienation, consumerism, and homogenisation of culture."[96] Ironically, many of Vietnam's misgivings about the Internet stem directly from the strong online presence of the Vietnamese diaspora.

Politics aside, globalization (and Westernization) of culture is a concern for many countries, not just Vietnam, and is a process intimately tied to advances in modern technology. As Vu Dinh Cu notes, "Traditional arts are flooded and sometimes swept away by a powerful wave of Western movies, videotapes, CDs. Folklore is seemingly dead or dying, theaters are empty of any audience.... the money cult reigns, extreme individualism and egoism are manifest, serious damages occur to community institutions, the three-generation family (children, parents, grandparents) is breaking down, and the inter-generation gap is widening."[97] International media, mass production, and widespread consumerism—the same postmodern conditions that generate Gergen's "saturated" or Lifton's "protean" self—are major issues confronting any culture that attempts to participate in the modern marketplace. Vietnam's concerns are echoed by other members of the Association of South East Asian Nations (ASEAN), as expressed in a 1996 agreement: "[T]he trans-border nature of the Internet would open individual countries to external influences and [this] affirmed the importance of having safeguards against easy access to sites which ran counter to our cherished values, traditions and culture."[98] ASEAN member Singapore addressed this problem by using firewall software that blocks access to certain politically or culturally objectionable websites.[99] Malaysia, on the other hand, has decided to make the Internet an integral part of its "cherished values": prepaid cards are available to access the Internet from public kiosks,[100] and in the further interest of industry, Prime Minister Dato Mahatir announced a commitment to "developing the necessary [online] infrastructure" and "not censoring the Net."[101] Vietnam is still ironing out its own approach—vacillating all the while between Singapore's caution and Malaysia's enthusiasm.

Even among ASEAN nations, Vietnam has been particularly slow to accept online technology. In 1992, the Viện Công Nghệ Thông Tin, or Institute of Information Technology (IOIT), began tentatively "researching its Internet options."[102] Two years later, the Vietnam Academic Research Educational Network (VAREnet) was established for the exchange of academic and scientific information. Assisted by the Australian National University, VAREnet established a rudimentary e-mail system, using only nine telephone lines; messages were received via Australia in five daily batches and then hand delivered around the city.[103] VAREnet next teamed with a Canadian sponsor to create Netnam, a Hanoi-based computer network providing e-mail, bulletin board, and informational database services to businesses and other government-approved organizations in Vietnam.[104] Until November 1997, Netnam would remain the only point of contact between Vietnam and the Internet. Faster and larger than the original VAREnet, Netnam managed to attract several hundred subscribers. Still, it was a highly unreliable method of communication, approved for use by a very limited audience. To address the government's concerns about their "control over information," Netnam's system administrators routinely censored messages before sending them out.[105]

Moving beyond Netnam was inevitable, however, with the Internet playing an increasingly crucial role in economics, politics, education, and social interaction worldwide. At the end of 1997, Vietnam finally decided "to open up to the Internet and take the great leap forward into Cyberspace."[106] After months of "near-weekly proclamations in the country's official press herald[ing] the imminent arrival of the Internet, amid much ballyhoo about how it will help propel Vietnam into the new millennium,"[107] the Vietnamese government granted licenses to four in-country, state-regulated Internet service providers: Vietnam Data Communication (VDC), Saigon Postel, Finance Promoting and Technology (FPT), and the Institute of Information Technology (IOIT/Netnam).[108] The "great leap forward" was heralded as a new age of Internet freedoms, a virtual perestroika; November 19 was officially declared Vietnam Internet Day.[109] There was even a formal introduction, as Vietnam unveiled its "first public website" to the rest of the world. Written almost exclusively in English, Vietnam Online targeted an audience of non-Vietnamese tourists, workers, and investors as "a comprehensive site covering the ins and outs of life and doing business in Vietnam." Still, Vietnam Online was not all together "public": though free of charge, visitors were asked to sign up for a username and password so that their presence could be monitored.[110] Again, information control remained a priority.

Vietnam Online was the first of many projected advances: instantaneous e-mail, access to the "real Internet," first-rate educational and economic benefits for Vietnamese citizens.[111] These advances, however, have yet to materialize fully. A number of factors continue to hinder development. First, the luxury of Internet access is more than most Vietnamese can afford. A personal computer is beyond the reach of the typical family, and the financial barrier is aggravated by Vietnam's prohibitive telecommunications costs (which remain among the highest in the world).[112] Users also have to contend with an outdated and congested network. The entire country has a bandwidth of sixty megabits per second—a respectable speed for a single desktop computer, but not much when divvied up nationwide—and connections often drop or freeze without warning.[113] Despite regular government-mandated reductions to Internet access charges and the addition of a fifth service provider (Vietel), Vietnam's online population remains extremely low. There are only 200,000 registered users, representing a negligible 0.2 percent of the country's eighty million inhabitants.[114]

For those willing and able to deal with the drawbacks, the government's insistence on "control over information" remains an added obstacle to forward movement. While "certain organisations and corporations" enjoy online privileges, "regular users will have to wait for more cautious trials, and the step-by-step process that comes with access to outside information from Vietnam."[115] Personal or private homepages are not allowed; Vietnamese webpages are all government, corporate, or academic. E-mail accounts are often shared by entire businesses, limiting their use to work-related transactions, while the accounts themselves remain subject to regular search and censorship.[116] Citizens are only allowed to access "culturally acceptable" sites,[117] and are blocked from using e-mail accounts, newsgroups, or networks which originate outside Vietnam.[118] The consequences of not following government restrictions on Internet usage can be harsh: large monetary fines, denial of online service, seizure of computer equipment, and even imprisonment.[119]

The government's hard-line policy is aimed, in large part, at foiling the efforts of the community of democratic Vietnamese activists, which continue to flourish online. Vietnam's reluctance to embrace "outside information" undoubtedly references the Free Vietnam Alliance webpage and the CyberWall of political victims, the tracts calling for democracy in Vietnam and the point-by-point condemnations of the Vietnamese Communist Party. Even the 1997 decision to go online was steeped in explicit distrust of Vietnamese diaspora on the Internet. Concurrent with the "great leap forward" press release,

> The *Nhan Dan* Communist Party daily [newspaper] . . . blasted Voice of America radio, saying it had called on Vietnamese living abroad and opposed to communism to send information on the Internet which could be harmful to the regime.
>
> "It's clear that someone with their black plot is deliberately blocking our peoples' steps towards building and defending the country," it said in a commentary.
>
> It added that the Internet was a double-edged sword for any country, including the United States.[120]

To fight back, *Nhan Dan* launched its own procommunist website in June 1998, aimed specifically at overseas Vietnamese.[121] An April 2002 meeting of the Committee for Overseas Vietnamese in Hanoi had a parallel discussion about "the need to upgrade transmission equipment, improve the quality of T.V. and radio programmes, and diversify the content of electronic publications" in order to reach those Vietnamese living abroad and, presumably, to communicate the government's viewpoints more effectively to them.[122] Asserts one Ministry of Culture and Information official, "The information must not distort the truth"[123]—that is, the Communist Party version of the "truth."

Attacking the problem of unwanted information on an even broader level, Vietnam (like neighbors Singapore and China) has chosen to surround itself with "a restrictive firewall used to block access to select websites deemed or viewed as a 'social evil.'"[124] All Internet transactions pass through the firewall's filtering software, which blocks out "politically, religiously or sexually offensive" material. The government routinely adds to its list of censored web addresses—including, of course, most anticommunist sites by overseas Vietnamese.[125] To see the firewall in action, *Wall Street Journal* reporter Stan Sesser attempted to access freeviet.org directly from a computer in Hồ Chí Minh City: "When I typed in the address, a box came up asking me for an ID and an authorization code."[126] This "Internet Iron Curtain," as it has been called,[127] is not infallible, however—as Sesser discovered when he was able to access FreeViet after all, fooling the firewall by using an indirect link on a third-party website.[128] Pham Ngoc Lan, who runs the webpage for another overseas Vietnamese organization on the government's blacklist, claims that "temporary holes" in the firewall occasionally allow his friends in Vietnam to visit his site.[129] The Libertarian website Revolution, meanwhile, "extends a hearty welcome to any Vietnamese citizens who have thwarted their government in reaching this page."[130]

As one Vietnamese official states, "Control through the firewall is no longer effective. . . . If anyone who has a wish to get over the wall, they will. It is just a technical measure. If we put all our future hopes on the firewall, we will fail."[131] Concrete evidence of firewall breaching appears in the increasing reluctance of Vietnamese youth to accept the status quo: "We want personal freedom, we want to be able to achieve our full potential without the mistakes of incompetent leaders. CNN and the Internet tell us that is possible."[132] Inside the firewall, things are not serene, either. Political dissidents within Vietnam have discovered that the Internet can be a powerful resource and soapbox, and "a disturbing new phenomenon" of renegade websites and online transmissions has been plaguing the country's network.[133] Nor has the Communist Party itself escaped the online-aided spread of internal criticism: "e-mail and Internet [internal dissident] texts fly around the world so that increases the heat. . . . the broad dissemination . . . adds to the amount of angst the party feels, [and] puts them under more pressure so therefore they have to respond."[134]

Within Vietnam, circumventing official constraints on Internet accounts has ironically been facilitated by the government's tight grip on online access fees. The high cost of maintaining a personal computer and e-mail account has led to a boom in Internet cafés, where the Vietnamese public at large can cheaply (and often anonymously) log onto the web.[135] Also, because accounts are usu-ally shared by several people, administrators cannot easily regulate use by an unauthorized outsider or trace the author of an offensive e-mail—generating what Dang Hoang-Giang describes as a "kind of Wild West behavior among the user community."[136] The very act of constructing firewalls is, furthermore, economically counterproductive. By blocking certain kinds of computer com-munications, the firewall frustrates attempts at developing software, running ordinary office applications, and launching cooperative business ventures—hindering Vietnam's bid for the lucrative technology market and scaring off potential partners from overseas.[137] The constant monitoring of Internet trans-actions also slows down the nation's already sluggish network, causing occa-sional system-wide crashes.[138]

The bumpiness of Vietnam's attempts at moderating online access seems to be a consequence of a backfired policing. At the same time, it attests to the inexorable overlap between the Internet and free speech. As it links to the global online network, Vietnam is agreeing to join a discussion that, until now, it has essentially dismissed. There are no sure safeguards to prevent overseas Vietnamese activists—like the Burmese insurrectionists in Thailand—from challenging, attacking, or sabotaging the Socialist Republic of Vietnam's online presence. Furthermore, Vietnam is entering a forum that has significant meaning for the structure of the country in terms of political reality as well as the citizen's imagination; for the role of representation and language in the construction of national consciousness; and for the formation of Vietnamese identity in relation to the rest of the world. The power to negotiate these issues of national and cultural strength, as overseas Vietnamese have demonstrated through their patriotic interconnection online, is no longer restricted by geography.

Meanwhile, the reluctance of Vietnam and other nondemocratic countries to join the online club (or, in China's recent curtailment of Hong Kong Internet activity, to take a member away) remains hotly debated within the Internet community—a group dominated, naturally, by countries with a strong investment in unimpeded information exchange. One Asian journalist declares that Vietnam's Internet policy "could only draw laughter from foreign reporters, who would point to its contradictory nature. For what meaning could a controlled Internet have? After all, it is meant to allow users to freely surf through waves of information."[139] Another paints a mocking analogy: "It is said that there is a big, fat and lazy Dinosaur sitting on Vietnam's Information Highway that will bite everyone daring to pass it. If the Government cannot solve this problem, it will forever be sitting on and trying to hatch what may eventually turn out to be a fossilized egg.[140] For the same reason that political dissidence and individual expression thrive on the web, governments wishing to "hatch" a streamlined cultural approach to the Internet are constantly patching holes in their firewalls. Whether or not they achieve their goals within Vietnam proper, Vietnamese democratic activists are making significant impact with their online presence. They have managed, through the creation of a strong Internet community with its own take on being "Vietnamese," to affect strategically the ways in which Vietnam will conduct and evaluate itself in an international context.

What I am interested to see, and call for future researchers to explore, is the reciprocal effect of Vietnam's online presence on Vietnamese overseas. The country, until recently nonexistent on the Internet, has been the organizing factor and determining memory around which the diasporic Vietnamese online community defines itself. Anderson argues that the imagined community is made possible because "a fundamental change was taking place in modes of apprehending the world, which, more than anything else, made it possible to 'think' the nation."[141] How does this new fundamental change—the addition of Vietnam to the Internet—impact the "thinking" of Vietnamese diasporic nationalism? The successful construction of the Vietnamese activist network has been largely dependent upon Vietnam's absence from the web. What does it mean to have the communist side of the debate fully represented on the web, on equal par with the democratic? Does this shift the focus of dissident webpages, or alter the tenets of the activist cause? How does the nature of authentication and spatiality change as the mythic homeland itself becomes a physical entity on the Internet? Hopefully, these new lines of communication between Vietnam and its former citizens will further a better appreciation, on both sides, of the different ways in which individuals and communities can imagine their national identities.

Notes

Because many Vietnamese names and terms are not published with the proper diacritics, I only provide tonal marks when they are printed in the source. All of the online information was current and accessible as of May 12, 2002, unless otherwise specified; where possible, I also indicate posting dates.

1. David Lamb, "The Right to Surf in Vietnam," *Los Angeles Times,* October 6, 1997, home edition, D3.
2. Dorothy E. Dunning, "Activism, Hacktivism, and Cyberterrorism: The Internet As a Tool for Influencing Foreign Policy," Nautilus Institute, December 10, 1999, online at <http://www.nautilus.org/info-policy/workshop/papers/denning.html>.
3. Peter Eng, "A New Kind of Cyberwar—in Burma, Thailand, Indonesia, Vietnam: Bloodless Conflict," *Columbia Journalism Review* 37 no. 3 (1998): 20.
4. Ibid.
5. Lamb, "The Right to Surf," D3.
6. Maggie Farley, "Dissidents Hack Holes in China's New Wall" *Los Angeles Times,* January 5, 1999, record edition, 1. For a more detailed look at the "hacktivism" phenomenon worldwide, see Julie L. C. Thomas, "Ethics of Hacktivism," SANS Institute, January 12, 2001, online at <http://rr.sans.org/hackers/hacktivism2.php>.
7. Eng, "Cyberwar," 20. See also Bertil Linter and Ashley Craddock, "Indonesia's Net War," *Wired News* (May 29, 1998), online at <http://www.wired.com/news/topstories/0,1287,12609,00.html>.
8. Laura B. Lengel, "New Voices, New Media Technologies: Opportunity and Access to the Internet in East Central Europe," *Convergence* 4, no. 2 (1998): 27–30, online at <http://www.v2.nl/~arns/Projects/Converge/Cleng.html>; and Laura Lengel and Daniel P. Fedak, "The Politicization of Cybernetic Discourse: Discourse Conflict and the Internet in North Africa," (c. 1998), online at <http://www.vptech.demon.co.uk/lengell/research/africa2.htm>. Dunning's work is also helpful here.
9. "Introduction," Việt Quốc Home Page, <http://www.vietquoc.com/INTRODUC.HTM>.
10. Khanh K. Chau, "Austin Texas: VN Refugees Protest—Human Rights for VietNam," April 12, 1999, online at <http://www.ampact.net/vietnetworks/chinhtri/Austinprotest.htm>.
11. David Case, "Big Brother Is Alive and Well in Vietnam—and He Really Hates the Web," *Wired,* (November 1997), online at <http://hotwired.lycos.com/collections/connectivity/5.11_vietnam1.html>.
12. Việt Quốc Home Page, <http://www.vietquoc.com>.
13. DTN Phan Bội Châu, <http://members.aol.com/dtnpbc>.
14. DVCMD Main Page, <http://www.daiviet.org>.
15. Nguyen Viet Thang, "Manifesto," PTTNDT (July 16, 1992), online at <http://www.pttndt.org>.
16. Government of Free Vietnam, "Chương Trình Cứu Nước & Xây Dựng Đất Nước" (A Program to Save the Nation and Build the Nation) (April 30, 1995), online at

<http://www.vntd.org/vietnamese/chuong_trinh_cndn/ctcndn1.htm>. My comments are based upon the English-language translation posted on the Government of Free Vietnam website in November 1999; currently, the document is available only in Vietnamese. A new English-language website, however, is slated for launch in May 2002.

17. Free Vietnam Alliance, "A Proposal to Build a Democratic Society in Vietnam," (November 16, 1991), online at <http://www.fva.org/document/propose.htm> and "Roles of the Vietnamese from Different Strata in the Democratization Process," at <http://www.fva.org/document/prop4.htm>.

18. See the Website of the Vietnamese Constitutional Monarchist League, <http://www.geocities.com/vietmonarchy/home.html> or Imperial Vietnam: A Website for the Restoration of the Nguyen Dynasty, <http://www.geocities.com/imperialvietnam/mainpage.html>.

19. Vietnam Human Rights Network (Mạng Lưới Nhân Quyền), online at <http://www.vnhrnet.org>; International Committee for Freedom (Cao Trào Nhân Bản), online at <http://www.ctnb.org>. Many organizations also track human rights in Vietnam as a function of their global activism. See, for example, the Vietnam sections on the Human Rights Network's United Nations "For the Record" System, online at <http://www.hri.ca/fortherecord2001/vol3/vietnam.htm>, or Amnesty International's website, <http://web.amnesty.org/ ai.nsf/COUNTRIES/VIET%20NAM>.

20. Tim Karr, "Dial-In Diasporas: Firewalls and Filters Fail to Halt Vinsight.org Penetration into Opinion-Sensitive Vietnam," *WorldPaper Online* (April 2000), <http://www.worldpaper.com/ 2000/April00/karr.html>. Vietnam Insight, which was established in 1992 by Chan Tran and remained one of the most important and well-known Vietnamese democratic activist websites throughout the 1990s, was formerly posted at <www.vinsight.org>. As of April 2002, however, it was no longer available.

21. See note 20; this mission statement, quoted from the original Vietnam Insight homepage, still appears on many sites that continue to reference the now-defunct site—including the Yahoo! web directory, <http://dir.yahoo.com/Regional/Countries/Vietnam/News_and_Media>.

22. "'Frustrations Are High': Dissident Doan Viet Hoat Speaks His Mind," *Asia Week* (January 29, 1999) online at <http://www.asiaweek.com/asiaweek/99/0129/nat7.html>.

23. Lý Thanh Bình, "A Declaration of Freedom for Viet-Nam," Viet-Nam Freedom Party website, <http://home.navisoft.com/vfp/statemt.htm>; no longer available as of May 2002.

24. Kicon Vietspace (April 2002), online at <http://vietspace.kicon.com>; Committee For Religious Freedom in Vietnam (Ủy Ban Tự Do Tôn Giáo Cho Vietnam), online at <http://www.crfvn.org>.

25. Vietnamese Professionals Society, "Mission Statement and Goals" (January 1, 2002), online at <http://www.vps.org/article.php3?id_article=191>.

26. The webpages that supported this cause no longer exist. Some coverage of the protest, however, can still be found on the UCLA student newspaper website. See Jonathan Pham, "Controversial Water Puppet Show Spreads Communist Propaganda," *Daily Bruin Online* (October 16, 1997), <http://www.dailybruin.ucla.edu/DB/issues/97/10.16/view.pham.html>; and Tram Linh Ho, "Vietnam Needs A Change," *Daily Bruin Online* (October 16, 1997), <http://www.dailybruin.ucla.edu/DB/issues/97/10.16/view.ho.html>.

27. Lý Thanh Bình, "Top Vietnam's Government: Politics Websites on Yahoo! (none from CSVN)," (October 24, 1997), online at <news: soc.culture.vietnamese>.

28. "The Wandering Statue," Việt Quốc Home Page, <http://www.vietquoc.com/thngtiec.htm>.

29. See, for example, the "Vietnam Clickable Map" in Hoàng Khai Nhan'sVietnam Picture Gallery, online at <http://www.saigonline.com/hkn/queviet/main/index.html>

or Cuong Jake Tran's homepage, <http://www.geocities.com/Athens/Crete/4888>. Tran underlines the point with a message to his readers: "Notice that some provinces' names here are the names were used to be used [*sic*] in Vietnam before 1975. Thank you!"

30. Radio Free Vietnam (Đài Phát Thanh Việt Nam Tự Do) is based in Westminster, California, and is online at <http://www.rfvn.com>; Vietnamese Public Radio (VPR / Đài Tiếng Nói Việt Nam Hải Ngoại) is based in Falls Church, Virginia, and online at <http://www.vietnamradio.com>. For a list of other Vietnamese-language radio broadcasts available on the Web, see *Kicon Vietspace,* online at <http://www.kicon. com>.

31. Army of the Republic of Vietnam (ARVN), or Quân Lực Việt Nam Cộng Hoà (QLVCH), online at <http://www.vnet.org/qlvnch>. The animated gif (graphic image file) is called "cobay," short for "cờ bay" or "flying flag."

32. To give an idea of how widespread and varied the uses of Republican flag graphics have become on the web, I present a small sampling:

    - ARVN Army Ranger, <http://www.bdqvn.org>
    - Federation of Overseas Free Vietnamese Communities (Cộng Đồng Người Việt Quốc Gia Hải Ngoại), <http://kicon.com/freevietnam>
    - *Gọi Dân* (*Call to the People*) radio program, <http://www.goidan.com>
    - Liên Hội Người Việt Quốc Gia Bắc California (Coalition of Nationalist Vietnamese Organizations of Northern California), <http://www.lienhoi.com>
    - Liên Minh Dân Chủ Việt Nam (Alliance For Democracy In Vietnam), <http://www.lmdcvn.org>
    - Tan Le, Vietnam's Knowledge Base, <http://www.geocities.com/Tokyo/5673/index.html
    - Tuan Nguyen, VIETNAM: Land of Hope and Prosperity, <http://www.plumsite.com/vietnam>
    - Vietnamese American Business Association, "*Sống Trên Đất Mỹ* (*Living in America*) radio program, <http://songtrendatmy.net>
    - Vietnamese National Military Academy Alumni, Association, <http://www.vobi-vietnam.org>

33. Information Technology Associates, "Vietnam through Yugoslavia," (May 1, 1996) at the Flags of All Countries website, <http://www.theodora.com/flags_20.html>.

34. Ủy Ban Bảo Vệ Quốc Kỳ Việt Nam Cộng Hoà (Committee for Protection of the Flag of the Republic of Vietnam), online at <http://chaocovnch.8m.com>. To hear the anthem, click on the first link at the bottom of the page ("National Anthem—Digital Sound"), or go directly to <http://chaocovnch.8m.com/chao_Quocky.htm>.

35. Committee for Protection of the Flag of the Republic of Vietnam, "Why Do We Have To Protect Our Flag?" online at <http://chaocovnch.8m.com/dear_young_patriotism.htm>.

36. Guobin Yang, "Information Technology, Virtual Chinese Diaspora, and Transnational Public Sphere," (April 23, 2002) Nautilus Institute, Virtual Diasporas website, <http://www.nautilus.org/virtual-diasporas/paper/Yang.html>.

37. Benedict Anderson, *Imagined Communities: Reflections on the Origin and Spread of Nationalism* (London: Verso, 1991), 35.

38. "Introduction," *Việt Quốc* home page.

39. Government of Free Vietnam, "Chương Trình Cứu Nước."

40. Anderson, *Imagined Communities,* 34.

41. John Rex, "The Nature of Ethnicity in the Project of Migration," in *The Ethnicity Reader: Nationalism, Multiculturalism and Migration,* ed. Montserrat Guibernau and John Rex (Cambridge: Polity Press, 1997), 274.

42. Anderson, *Imagined Communities,* 6.

43. Ngo T. Duc, speech at Stanford University, (April 27, 1995), online at <http://www.fva.org/0595/speech.html>.

44. James Clifford, "Diasporas," in Guibernau and Rex, eds., *The Ethnicity Reader,* 284.

45. Stuart Hall addresses the issue of the "presence/absence" of the original country as "a necessary part of the [national] imaginary"; see Hall, "Cultural Identity and Diaspora," in *Identity: Community, Culture, Difference* (London: Lawrence, 1990), 222–37.

46. "Vietnamese Boatpeople Stories," Vietnamese Boatpeople Connection website, <http://www.boatpeople.com/stories>.

47. Tuan Nguyen, "Vietnam: The Land of Hope and Prosperity," online at <http://www.plumsite.com/vietnam/hope.htm>.

48. Edward Said, *Orientalism* (New York: Vintage, 1978), 55.

49. Ananda Mitra, "Creating Immigrant Identities in Cybernetic Space," paper presented at the Media Performance and Practice across Cultures Conference at University of Wisconsin-Madison, (March 14–17, 2002), online at <http://polyglot.lss.wisc.edu/mpi/conference/mitra.htm>.

50. Monique T. D. Trương, "Vietnamese American Literature," *An Interethnic Companion to Asian American Literature,* ed. King-Kok Cheung (Cambridge: Cambridge University Press, 1997), 220.

51. James M. Freeman, *Hearts of Sorrow: Vietnamese-American Lives* (Stanford: Stanford University Press, 1989), 11.

52. Paul James Rutledge, *The Vietnamese Experience in America* (Bloomington: Indiana University Press, 1992), 9.

53. Thomas A. DuBois, "Constructions Construed: The Representation of Southeast Asian Refugees in Academic, Popular, and Adolescent Discourse," *Amerasia Journal* 19, no. 3 (1993): 1–25. Note, however, that DuBois still favors the term *refugee,* at least insofar as the title indicates.

54. Ibid., 5.

55. Ibid., 21.

56. Ananda Mitra, "Nations and the Internet: The Case of a National Newsgroup, 'soc.cult.indian,'" *Convergence* 2, no. 1 (1996), abstract online at <http://www.luton.ac.uk/convergence/volumetwo/numberone/abstracts.shtml>. Amit S. Rai explores a parallel point in "India On-line: Electronic Bulletin Boards and the Construction of a Diasporic Hindu Identity," *Diaspora* 4, no. 1 (1995): 31–57.

57. For a discussion of the imagined space of the Pacific Rim, see Arik Dirlik, "Introducing the Pacific" and Donald M. Nonini, "On the Outs on the Rim: An Ethnographic Grounding of the 'Asia-Pacific' Imaginary" in *What Is In a Rim? Critical Perspectives on the Pacific Region Idea,* ed. Arik Dirlik (Boulder, CO: Westview, 1993).

58. Karim H. Karim, "Diasporas and Their Communication Networks: Exploring the Broader Context of Transnational Narrowcasting," (April 23, 2002) Nautilus Institute, Virtual Diasporas website, <http://www.nautilus.org/virtual-diasporas/paper/Karim.html>.

59. Shawn P. Wilbur, "An Archaeology of Cyberspaces: Virtuality, Community, Identity," in *Internet Culture,* ed. David Porter (London: Routledge, 1997), 14.

60. Sherry Turkle, "Who Am We?" *Wired,* (January 1996), 198.

61. Wilbur, "Archaeology," 20.

62. Daniel C. Tsang, "Notes on Queer 'N' Asian Virtual Sex," in *Asian American Sexualities: Dimensions of the Gay and Lesbian Experience,* ed. Russell Leong (New York: Routledge, 1996), 156.

63. While somewhat overwrought, many of the essays in *Resisting the Virtual Life: The Culture and Politics of Information,* ed. James Brook and Iain A. Boal (San Francisco: City Lights, 1995), are also concerned with these same issues of the Internet as potentially dangerous or destabilizing to individual identity.

64. Robert Jay Lifton, *The Protean Self: Human Resilience in an Age of Fragmentation* (New York: Basic Books, 1993), 1.

65. Kenneth J. Gergen, *The Saturated Self: Dilemmas of Identity in Contemporary Life* (New York: Basic Books, 1991), xi.

66. Scott Bukathman, *Terminal Identity: The Virtual Subject in Postmodern Science Fiction* (Durham, NC: Duke University Press, 1993), 2.

67. Ibid., 117.

68. Ananda Mitra and Rae Lynn Schwartz, "From Cyber Space to Cybernetic Space: Rethinking the Relationship between Real and Virtual Spaces," *Journal of Computer-Mediated Communication* 7, no. 1 (2001), online at <http://www.ascusc.org/jcmc/vol7/issue1/mitra.html>.

69. "Vietnam Time," Free Vietnam Alliance, online at <http://www.fva.org>; link to "Local Time in Hanoi-Saigon, Vietnam," online at <http://www.hilink.com.au/times/bin/time.sh?offset=0700& loc=Hanoi-Saigon,+Vietnam>.

70. "Vietnam Weather," Free Vietnam Alliance, online at <http://www.fva.org>; link to "Yahoo! Weather by WeatherNews Inc., Weather: Asia: Vietnam," online at <http://weather.yahoo.com/regional/Vietnam.html>. As of May 2002, this link as listed on the Free Vietnam Alliance is actually outdated: the correct URL is <http://weather.yahoo.com/regional/VMXX.html>.

71. "Vietnam Clickable Map"; Lien Hoa, "mapvn.gif," Vietnam My Country website, <http://disc.cba.uh.edu/~lienhoa>.

72. Tan Le, "Images of Vietnam," Vietnam's Knowledge Base website, <http://www.geocities.com/Tokyo/5673/images.htm>.

73. Chi D. Nguyen, VIET NAM (Vietnam) website, <http://www.viettouch.com>; Dang Anh Tuân, Pays D'Eau (Land of Water) website, <http://www.limsi.fr/Recherche/CIG/menu.html>.

74. For example, see the Free Vietnam Alliance website's "Pictures," <http://www.fva.org/imgindex.html> or Kicon Vietscape's "Flag Protest in Little Saigon," <http://kicon.com/flagprotest>.

75. "Lửa Thái Bình & Xuân Lộc" (Thái Bình & Xuân Lộc Uprisings), online at <http://ampact.net/ uybanyemtrodongbaoquocnoi>. The political message is incontrovertible: clicking anywhere on the map automatically launches a RealAudio music file of the South Vietnamese national anthem. For more background, see the news clips on THAIBINH'S Home Page, <http://www.geocities.com/CapitolHill/Lobby/4417>.

76. "Re-education Camps Memorial Wall," *VietWorld* (April 24, 1999), online at <http://www.vietworld.com/Holocaust/index.html>.

77. "The Cyber Wall," Vietnam Oral History Project website, <http://www.viet.org>. Most of the names also act as hyperlinks to information about the individual soldier's rank and date/place of death.

78. See "The VIQR Convention," *Non Sông Magazine* (October 23, 1996) online at <http://www.nonsong.org/viqr.html>; or the Vietnamese-Standard Working Group's official "Viet-Std Bilingual Report," (September 1992), online at <http://www.vietstd.org>. VIQR bears resemblance to the common online methods of using abbreviations or smiley faces to express the cadences of natural conversation. For further discussion of ASCII chat language, see Elizabeth Reid, "Virtual Worlds: Culture and Imagination," in *CyberSociety: Computer-Mediated Communication and Community,* ed. Steven G. Jones (Thousand Oaks, CA: Sage, 1995), 164–83.

79. "The VIQR Convention"; my translation. The song is called "Tình Ca" ("Love Song"); written in 1953, it presents a patriotic and romanticized vision of Vietnam with tacit disapproval of the country's split into Northern and Southern halves.

80. "The Vietnamese Standardization Working Group," (October 23, 1996), Vietnamese-Standard Working Group website, <http://www.vietstd.org/document/vietstd.htm>; no longer available as of April 2002.

81. TriChlor Organization website, <http://www.vnet.org/trichlor>.

82. "Viet-Std Bilingual Report."

83. Vietnamese Professionals Society website, <http://www.vps.org>.

84. VNI Software Company website, <http://www.vnisoft.com>.

85. Đặng Minh Tuấn, *VietKey 2000,* build 10727 (Hanoi: Vietkey Group, 2001).

86. Unicode Home Page, <http://www.unicode.org>. See also *Non Sông* magazine's "Unicode FAQs," online at <http://www.nonsong.org/Unicode>, for a specific discussion of how Unicode enables Vietnamese-language type.

87. Steve Mulder, "Embedding Fonts Tutorial" at the Webmonkey website, <http://hotwired.lycos.com/webmonkey/design/fonts/tutorials/tutorial2.html>, provides a helpful overview and discussion of embedded web fonts.

88. Anderson, *Imagined Communities,* 148.

89. Cao Anh Nguyet, "Comments," VNI Software Company website, <http://www.vnisoft.com/english/comments.htm>.

90. Nguyen Thanh Long, "Comments," VNI Software Company.

91. Le Ai Ly, "Comments," VNI Software Company.

92. Truong Tan Loc, "Comments," VNI Software Company.

93. Brother Nguyen Van An, "Comments," VNI Software Company.

94. TCVN, which stands for "Tiêu Chuẩn Việt Nam" or "Vietnam standard," refers to a series of several thousand benchmark regulations issued by the state's Ministry of Science, Technology and Environment—ranging from industrial safety requirements to the technical specifications for an electric rice cooker (TCVN 5393-91). More information can be found on the official TCVN website, <http://www.tcvn.gov.vn>. Starting in July 2002, however, Vietnam began using Unicode as its official typing system.

95. Dang Hoang-Giang, "Internet in Vietnam: From a Laborious Birth into an Uncertain Future," *Informatik Forum* 1 (1999), online at <http://www.interasia.org/vietnam/dang-hoang-giang.html>. Another helpful overview is John S. Quarterman's anecdotal "Internet in Vietnam," *Matrix News* 8, no. 2 (1998), online at <http://www.mids.org/mn/802/vn.html>.

96. "Surfers Stand By for the First Wave," in "Internet: A Special Vietnam Investment Review Advertising Feature," *Vietnam Investment Review,* June 9–15, 1997, 13.

97. Vu Dinh Cu, "I.T. in Vietnam: Opportunities and Challenges," Interasia Organization, at Le Viet Nam, aujourd'hui website, <http://perso.wanadoo.fr/patrick.guenin/cantho/internet/dinh.htm>. This particular article is not dated, but since it mentions Vietnam's involvement with the Internet, we can safely assume that it was written in the late 1990s.

98. ASEAN Statement, quoted in Joel Deane, "Asia and the Internet: Why Are Vietnam, Singapore and China Practicing Cybercensorship?" (June 30, 1997) ZD-Net Products website, <http://www5.zdnet.com/products/content/articles/199706/np.asia>; no longer available as of May 2002. Dang, "Internet in Vietnam," also discusses the impact of the 1996 ASEAN agreement, which was signed by all member countries except for the Philippines.

99. Deane, "Asia and the Internet." Singapore is using proxy servers, which control what users can access from inside the firewall but not what they receive from external parties (via e-mail, newsgroups, etc.). For more information on the elements and construction of a network firewall, see the Firewalls FAQ website, <http://www.faqs.org/faqs/firewalls-faq>.

100. Lamb, "The Right to Surf," D3.

101. Deane, "Asia and the Internet."

102. Nguyen Tri Man and Sam Korsmoe, "Linking Up to the World," *Vietnam Economic Times Online* (March 13, 1997); the *Vietnam Economic Times* archives for 1996–2000, originally stored at <www.batin.com.vn>, are no longer available. More recent back issues, from September 2001 to the present, can be found on the *Vietnam Economy* website, <http://www.vneconomy.com.vn>.

103. Dang, "Internet in Vietnam."
104. Netnam website, <http://www.netnam.vn>. As the possibilities for Vietnamese Internet access have improved, the service has expanded to support home users as well.
105. In my own experience with Netnam during the summer of 1997, about 50 percent of my incoming and outgoing messages were either "lost" or delayed by several days.
106. "What's Ahead on Vietnam's Web: Vietnam Online—A Sneak Preview," in "Internet: A Special Vietnam Investment Review Advertising Feature," 13.
107. Case, "Big Brother."
108. "Four ISPs Begin Operations in Vietnam," *New York Times* (December 13, 1997), at VietGATE Internet News from Vietnam, online at <http://www.vietgate.net/news>; "Internet Users in Vietnam on the Rise to 15,000," *AsiaBizTech* (December 9, 1998), at Le Viet Nam, aujourd'hui website, <http://perso.wanadoo.fr/patrick.guenin/cantho/internet/itnews.htm>.
109. "Net, Toilets Slow to Reach Vietnam," *Wired News* (November 18, 1997), online at <http://www.wired.com/news/politics/0,1283,8622,00.html>.
110. "Welcome Page," Vietnam Online, <http://www.vietnamonline.net>; no longer available as of May 2002. The site stopped requiring user registration after a few years of operation.
111. "Surfers Stand By."
112. Michelle Castillo, "Telecommunciations Infrastructure," *Information Technology Landscape in Vietnam*, MBA report, American University, c. 2001, online at <http://american.edu/carmel/mc5916a/telecommunications.htm>.
113. "Vietnam Catches Up" (April 2, 2002), Asia.internet.com, <http://asia.internet.com/asia-news/article/0,3916,161_1001841,00.html>. I base this observation on personal experience as well. While traveling throughout Vietnam in April 2002, I rarely managed to find a stable Internet connection.
114. "Software and Internet Promise New Economy: Despite Internet Censorship, IT Imperative Drives Nation," *Washington Times* International Reports: Vietnam 2002, online at <http://www.internationalreports.net/asiapacific/vietnam/2002/software.html>. Compare Vietnam's 0.2 percent to regional averages: 3 percent of Chinese, 7 percent of Thais, 9 percent of Malaysians, and 30 percent of Singaporeans are online. At the other end of the spectrum, 45 percent of Canadians and 53 percent of Americans use the Internet—as does 54 percent of Hong Kong ("Geographics: The World's Online Populations" *CyberAtlas* (March 21, 2002), online at <http://cyberatlas.internet.com/big_picture/geographics/article/0,,5911_151151,00.html>).
115. "Surfers Stand By."
116. Dang, "Internet in Vietnam."
117. "Four ISPs."
118. Dang, "Internet in Vietnam."
119. See Adam Creed, "Vietnam Govt Readies New Internet Rules," *Newsbytes* (August 30, 2001), online at <http://www.newsbytes.com/news/01/169564.html>; Reporters San Frontières, "Two Dissidents Arrested for Publishing Documents on the Internet" (March 15, 2002), online at <http://www.rsf.org/article.php3?id_article=575>.
120. Reuters News Service, "Vietnam Sets Mid-November for Full Internet Access" (October 13, 1997), at University of Saskatchewan Vietnamese Students' Association website, <http://duke.usask.ca/~ss_vsa/news16.html>.
121. Nhân Dân website, <http://www.nhandan.org.vn>.
122. "Society," *Voice of Vietnam News* (April 12, 2002), online at <http://www.vov.org.vn/2002_04?12/english/xahoi.htm>; no longer available as of May 2002.

123. Kristin Huckshorn, "Hanoi, Eager for Links with World, Still Suspicious of Internet," *San Jose Mercury News* (June 1, 1998), at Internet, Vietnam website, <http://www.hf.ntnu.no/anv/HjemmesiderIFAS/Olafstoff/Internet,Vietnam.html>.

124. "Software and Internet Promise New Economy."

125. Mark McDonald, "Vietnam Heavily Filters Content, but Firewalls Are Leaking," *Mercury News* (August 12, 2001), online at <http://www.landfield.com/isn/mail-archive/2001/Aug/0087.html>.

126. Stan Sesser, "Internet Cafes Flourish in Vietnam, Presenting a Puzzle about Policy," *Wall Street Journal Interactive* (January 18, 2000), online at <http://interactive.wsj.com/articles/SB948137265699680614.htm>.

127. "Vietnam: Asian's Next IT Success Story?" (November 2, 2001) Global Sources Computer Products website, <http://www.globalsources.com/MAGAZINE/CP/0112/PVIET.HTM>.

128. Sesser, "Internet Cafes." Increasingly, third-party websites that allow users to duck firewalls (like www.anonymizer.com, which Sesser used in this instance) are themselves being targeted for censorship by the Vietnamese authorities.

129. McDonald, "Vietnam Heavily Filters Content." Pham runs *Thông Luận* <http://www.thongluan.org>, an online newsletter for the international Vietnamese activist group Rally for Democracy and Pluralism.

130. Addendum to "Vietnam Prepares to Join the Internet," *Revolution* (1996), online at <http://www.boogieonline.com/revolution/express/techno/internet/vietnam.html>.

131. Do Quy Doan, qtd. in McDonald, "Vietnam Heavily Filters Content."

132. Huw Watkin, "Restless Youth Yearn for Change" (July 21, 1999) Vietnam Insight website, at <http://www.vinsight.org/1999news/0721.htm>; no longer available as of April 2002. Also helpful is Tim Larimer's article "Disquiet among the Quiet," which discusses the growing discontent among Vietnamese youth as well as the Vietnamese public at large; *Time Asia* (January 18, 1999), online <http://www.time.com/time/asia/asia/magazine/1999/990118/vietnam_dissidents1.html>.

133. McDonald, "Vietnam Heavily Filters Content."

134. Andy Solomon, "ANALYSIS—Mixed Signals From Hanoi General's Ouster," (January 13, 1999); originally at Vietnam Insight, <http://www.vinsight.org/1999news/0113.htm>; no longer available as of April 2002.

135. Sesser, "Internet Cafes." See also Mary Kelly, "Internet News: Getting Wired in Vietnam," (November 2000) Vietnamese-American Chamber of Commerce Hawaii website, <http://www.vacch.org/ecom_112200.htm>.

136. Dang, "Internet in Vietnam."

137. Ibid. See also "What's the Rush? Vietnam Reacts Slowly to Technology Wave," *Far Eastern Economic Review* (July 15, 1999), online at <http://perso.wanadoo.fr/patrick.guenin/cantho/internet/itnews.htm>. For a Vietnamese perspective on the software industry, see the Research Vietnam website, <http://www.researchvietnam.com>.

138. Huckshorn, "Hanoi"; and McDonald, "Vietnam Heavily Filters Content."

139. Yomiuri Shimbun, "Vietnam Tries to Have It Both Ways," *Daily Yomiuri* (December 3, 1997); originally at Vietnam Insight, <http://www.vinsight.org/1997news/1203.htm>; no longer available as of April 2002.

140. Dao Yen, "Can Vietnam Hatch The e-Commerce Golden Egg?" *E-Commerce News* (August 21, 2001) online at <http://www.internetnews.com/ec-news/article/0,,4_869671,00.html>.

141. Anderson, *Imagined Communities,* 22.

4

North American Hindus, the Sense of History, and the Politics of Internet Diasporism

VINAY LAL

Democracy and Authoritarianism in Cyberspace

Nothing has been as much celebrated in our times as the information super-highway. Everyone is agreed that never before has information proliferated so profusely, diminishing as is commonly thought the boundaries and barriers that have held people apart—though many voices have sought to distinguish between "knowledge" and "information," while others have railed at how the overwhelm-ing surfeit of information has made some people incapable of thinking beyond trivia and the "factoid." We speak with unreflective ease of the "information revolution," and in this clichéd expression there is the most unambiguous asser-tion of confidence in the benign telos of history. Some commentators, alluding to more recent developments such as *e-commerce*, speak even of going "beyond the information revolution," but there is something of a consensus that the in-formation revolution has been to our age what the Industrial Revolution was to the eighteenth century.[1]

The advocates of the information superhighway have been prolific in voic-ing the view that cyberspace embodies immense revolutionary possibilities for creating democratic polities and enfranchising those communities that have so far existed only at the margins of the tremendous information explosion of recent years. The Internet, so argue its unabashed votaries, creates a polyphony of voices, allows the hitherto silenced to speak,[2] offers forums for dissenting views, destroys the monopoly of old elites, disperses the sources of informa-tion and knowledge, empowers the dispossessed, and assists in the formation of new identities—constituted not only by such obvious markers as race, gender, and ethnicity, but also by religious freedom and sexual orientation, linguistic affiliation, political ideologies, intellectual interests, customs, shared traditions and histories, and hobbies. The "imagined communities" of which Benedict Anderson spoke flower in unprecedented ways on the Internet; the shackles that chained the working classes 150 years after Karl Marx invoked the cry of revolution and urged them to take destiny into their own hands, now seem broken. In the then hip voice of *Mondo 2000*, to quote from the inaugural issue in 1989, "The cybernet is in place. . . . The old information elites are crumbling. The kids are at the controls. This magazine is about what to do until the *millennium* comes. We're talking about Total Possibilities. Radical assaults on the limits of biology, gravity and time. The end of artificial Scarcity. The dawn of a new humanism. High-jacking technology for personal empowerment, fun and games."[3] Just when boredom appeared to be the most pressing problem for the affluent West, and the usual sources of entertainment seemed to have exhausted their potential to amuse, the Internet arose to offer a jaded people a new source of enchantment. Cyberspace has restored to the West that ludic element that was once so essential an element of its being, to vanish when confronted with the unrelenting demands—whether upon the family, the workplace, or social institutions—of modernity. Meanwhile, boredom, a disease that is inextricably linked to Western notions of time, is now poised to find its newest victims in the developing world.

The enthusiastic advocates of cyberspace have stretched the case for its allegedly democratic properties much further. The futurist Alvin Toffler and his associates speak of the post-scarcity information civilization as a Third Wave of humankind. If in the First Wave civilization was predominantly agricultural, and the Second Wave ushered in the age of industrial production, in the Third Wave "the central resource—a single phrase broadly encompassing data, information, images, symbols, culture, ideology and values—is actionable knowledge."[4] Cyberspace is universal, it is its own ecosystem; it is "inhabited by knowledge, including incorrect ideas, existing in electronic form."[5] As one might expect, that perennial American language of the *frontier* is incurably a part of the language of cyberspace enthusiasts: thus, Toffler and his cohorts speak of the "bioelectronic frontier," which has emerged just as the American dream of the limitless, yet again contracting, frontier seemed doomed to extinction.[6] The bioelectronic frontier points to the death of that fundamental embodiment of centralized values—namely, the bureaucratic organization of which the government is the supreme instantiation; and consequently cyberspace is the space of unregulated freedom, the logical culmination of the human hunger for liberty from constraints and access to limitless markets. "Cyberspace is the land of knowledge," write Toffler and his associates, "and the exploration of that land can be a civilization's truest, highest calling."[7] Here, at the frontier of knowledge, one can create one's own basket of the fruits of wisdom: "Demassification, customization, individuality, freedom—these are the keys to success for Third Wave civilization." In cyberspace is writ large the continuing story of America's espousal of the values of individuality over conformity, achievement over consensus, and the celebration of difference—all typified, if only as an instance of the occasional negative excess of American democracy, in the figure of the hacker, a near impossibility in "the more formalized and regulated democracies of Europe and Japan." If the destiny of the world is to follow the example and leadership of the United States, as Francis Fukuyama and other exponents of the end of history have repeatedly reminded us, then the values of cyberspace, which are none other than expressions of the American ethos, become the values of the world. Cyberspace confers on humankind a "Magna Carta for the Knowledge Age."[8]

If the conquest of the Americas furnished the Spaniards with a charter for conquest and colonization, the enthusiasts of cyberspace point—five hundred years after the conquistadors first began to leave behind a trail of charred ruins, shattered lives, and decapitated Indians—to the Americas as the site for new forms of resistance to global capitalism, as the originary point from where a truly new world order can be envisioned at the cusp of the millennium. The laboratories and universities of the United States may have seeded the script for the cyberspace revolution, but it was enacted in the relatively remoter areas of Mexico, when the Zapatista National Liberation Army led the people of Chiapas in an insurrection on New Year's Day 1994. Occupying San Cristobal de las Casas and five smaller towns, the Zapatistas declared war against the Mexican government, issued a manifesto of demands, invited foreign observers, monitors, and sympathizers to Chiapas, and initiated an international media campaign to gain support for their cause. Vastly outnumbered by the army and security forces that were rushed to Chiapas within a couple of days of the insurrection, the Zapatistas nonetheless not only held out, forcing the government to the negotiation table, but also introduced a new element in revolutionary warfare. Writing in April 1995, the Mexican foreign minister, José Angel Gurria, doubtless bewildered at the developments of the previous year, noted that "Chiapas . . . is a place where there has not been a shot fired in the last fifteen months. . . . The shots lasted ten days, and ever since the war has been a war of ink, of written word, a war on the Internet."[9] Subcommandante Marcos, the energetic and mystery-shrouded leader of the Zapatistas, himself remarked that "one space . . . so new that no one thought a guerilla could turn to it, is the information superhighway, the Internet. It was territory not occupied by anybody . . . the problem that distresses Gurria is that he has to fight against an image that he cannot control from Mexico, because the information is simultaneously on all sides."[10] It is this phenomenon, of a war inspired by the battle tactics of Genghis Khan but made possible by the "information revolution," which RAND researcher David Ronfeldt has variously described as "cyberwar" when the conflict takes on a military aspect, and "netwar" when the conflict is at the "societal" level.[11] Though from his standpoint the advent of netwar is scarcely to be welcomed, as it poses new threats to American national security, "digital Zapatismo" has gained many voluble adherents,[12] who construe the rhizomatic characteristics of the Internet as the most likely font of new forms of insurrectionary activity.[13] The advocates of cyberspace do not, however, have the field to themselves. Their critics have constructed a less elaborate, but by no means insignificant, account of the deleterious consequences of the new computer-based information and communication technologies. They are more inclined to describe the information superhighway as a charter for the disenfranchisement of those who are already underprivileged, authorizing the further polarization of the rich and the poor. The grave inequities between the postindustrial nations and the rest of the world will be further aggravated, and cyberspace, argue its detractors, can only sharpen the boundaries between the haves and the have-nots in the industrializing nations. In even as large a country as India, the largest democracy in the world, only a million people have Internet connections, and they are the ones who already have at their disposal fax, telephone, and other means of communication, just as they are the ones who are privileged to take overseas trips: Net surfers and tourists are two classes of people who largely coincide. It is their views, which are wedded to transforming India in the image of the West and making India into a strong modern nation-state, that predominate among Indian policy makers and are critical in shaping the view of India in the West. It is the agenda of the "Internet elites," if they may be so termed, that dictates the modernization and liberalization of the Indian economy, and it is their interests and ambitions that have led to the emergence of a cellular phone culture, while the greater part of the country remains without reliable ordinary telephone service. The emergence of an internationally renowned software industry even while nearly 50 percent of the Indian population remains mired in poverty is yet another one of the anomalies engendered by the culture of the Internet elites. Their mobility in cyberspace furnishes them with those opportunities that allow them to work within the world of international finance and business; like the elites of the "first world," they are beginning to live in time, and space poses no barriers for them.[14] The time-space compression that cyberspace typifies only works to the advantage of these elites. Cyberspace, then, is yet another mode of self-aggrandizement, and it is calculated, certainly in India and the rest of the "developing" world, to narrow a franchise which was achieved with great struggle.[15]

Questions of political economy aside, it has been argued that cyberspace represents a more ominous phase of Western colonialism, the homogenization of knowledge and, in tandem, the elimination of local knowledge systems. Cyberspace stands for the renewed triumph of all those categories of thought by means of which the West has been able to establish its dominance over other parts of the globe. "Western civilization has always been obsessed with new territories to conquer," writes Ziauddin Sardar on cyberspace, and cyberspace is the newest domain that it seeks to colonize.[16] Where the long arm of the colonial state and fascist organizations could not reach, there cyberspace has made inroads; those remote spots that were inaccessible to missionaries and colonial administrators, where the Coke bottle could not be dropped from the air, now enter the stream of globalization. Where before the notion of "place" was displaced by "space" to render local histories indistinct and so pave the way for colonialism,[17] now "space" is regurgitated back into "place," the place from where the browser is guided into unknown domains. Radical dissent—which is only possible with incommensurability and profits from inassimilation into dominant strands of thought—is brought into the marketplace; and so, dissent itself becomes homogenized, and those very modalities of thought that held out the possibility of 'interrogating' received notions arrive in packaged forms. Cyberspace renders complete that colonization that sheer force and military might could not achieve; indeed, while cyberspace may not entirely obviate the necessity of a military-industrial complex, as the immensely technologically driven NATO assault upon Serbia visibly demonstrated, it enlists more hegemonic and insidious categories to eliminate dissent and create new hierarchies. Some critics of cyberspace, even while agreeing with Carlos Fuentes that the Zapatista insurrection was no "Sandinista-Castroite-Marxist-Leninist" rebellion, but rather the first postcommunist and postmodern insurgency,[18] have profound misgivings that anything postmodern, most eminently cyberspace, can be anything other than a sign of imperialism.[19]

Though the activists who staged a marvelously disruptive demonstration against the World Trade Organization (WTO) on the occasion of its ministerial meetings in late November 1999 were summoned to Seattle by messages widely dispersed on the Internet,[20] it is doubtful that these activists, buoyed by their Internet successes, have reflected sufficiently on the ironic fact that the Internet is avowedly the most expressive realization of that very idea of 'globalization' against which they militate. To make the point more sharply, though scattered intellectuals and activists might, say, militate against development as perhaps the most unfortunate idea to afflict humankind, cyberspace is itself intrinsically disposed toward the idea of development, effortlessly hospitable to the idea of limitless growth. Similarly, though proponents of cyberspace speak of its role in creating communities, particularly in societies where the family is presumed to have broken down and where other traditional institutions have been unable to offer the succor that people require in the course of daily life, critics argue that cyberspace trivializes the notion of "community."

It is the particular feature of real—or, shall we say, grounded—communities that they are born amidst conflict and must thrive amidst conflicting interests: they must perforce accommodate the fat and the slim, the healthy and the diseased, women and men, white and colored, the aged and the young; cybercommunities, contrariwise, are founded on the principle of exclusion, and inclusion in the community is only a mode of signaling someone else's marginalization. Cybercommunitarians, who have no appetite for pluralism, recognize no community that does not exist to do their own bidding, or that would ask of its members the fulfillment of responsibilities. With the click of a mouse, the community can be shut out. As for the notion that cyberspace heralds the arrival of a post-scarcity civilization, the detractors can only mock at the presumptuousness and hubris of the affluent. True, there is no "scarcity" of information, but it is foolish to confuse information with knowledge, and far more depraved to imagine that knowledge can substitute for wisdom. Put rather plainly, the so-called information revolution seems to be little better than what one writer,

David Shenk, has described as "data smog."[21] There is yet the cruel irony that while the advocates of cyberspace work to create the rules governing the post-scarcity information civilization that they inhabit, in many parts of the world a new scarcity has emerged as the grinding reality for the masses. Surprisingly, even when the realization has dawned that starvation, famines, and the short-ages of food are political problems, the supposed surfeit of information has done nothing to diminish the supposed scarcity of food.[22]

One of the iron rules of cyberspace, suggests Shenk, is that it is intrinsically Republican, or inegalitarian; its most keen enthusiasts are white, upper-class males.[23] There is the obvious consideration that if cyberspace can be deployed to enfranchise marginalized people and communities, it also services the ambitions and designs of racist ideologues, misogynists, anti-Semites, and other white male supremacists. As the recent, ominously massive, compilation in a CD-ROM by the Simon Wiesenthal Center in Los Angeles of over five hundred websites devoted to white supremacy indubitably suggests, in this matter as in most others, the supporters of racism, fascism, and Nazism have been more diligent in turning to new technologies than those people committed to more democratic and egalitarian forms of politics. Against this, the proponents of cyberspace can point to the mobilization of tribal peoples throughout the world, and the effectiveness of the Internet in yielding a possibly emancipatory Fourth World politics, a worldwide coalition of aboriginal people. But if cyberspace is what its enthusiasts admit—namely, a deregulated and decentralized zone with minimal rules for engagement—those are the very conditions under which the Republican paradise would flourish. Never did presumptive savagery, or the customs of the heathen, prevent a multinational corporation from conducting business. In this paradise, in the name of freedom, all dissenting histories are absorbed, commemorated only as relics of a previous age. Could these be the conditions under which certain histories will predominate, while other histories are erased? And could these be the conditions under which a cyberdiasporic politics of Hinduism has found comfortable refuge and a refurbished home? To ponder how the politics of Hinduism has played itself out in cyberspace, and Hinduism itself gradually merged into what is very nearly its opposite, namely Hindutva politics, it is well to consider first the Indian diasporic presence in the United States.

The Post-Industrial Vedic Diaspora: Hindus in the United States

More than 1.3 million Indians reside in the United States, and of these the pre-ponderant number are Hindus. Most Indians have done exceedingly well for themselves in, to appropriate the Biblical metaphor of a people who are the very embodiment of a diasporic sensibility, the land 'flowing with milk and honey' (Exodus 3:8); numerous studies have established that their per capita income is among the highest of any racial or ethnic group in the United States, and for some years they were the most affluent community.[24] Almost everywhere in the professions, Indians are well represented, and in some they have created an enviable niche for themselves. Though they make up less than 0.8 percent of the American population, as far back as the early 1990s they comprised 5 percent of the investment bankers and financial consultants on Wall Street. Their contribution to the sciences and engineering is even more formidable, perhaps even overwhelming; and it has become something of a cliché, at least among Indians, to speak of Silicon Valley as though it were a part of an Indian landscape. In middle-class homes in India, particularly where English is routinely spoken, it is not uncommon to find parents anticipating and even planning a future for their children not merely in Silicon Plateau (the new name for the "garden city" of Bangalore, where the software explosion in India took place a few years ago), but in Silicon Valley.[25] It may not even be long before Indians, like a previous generation of first-time visitors from Bombay and Calcutta to London who saw in the metropole a copy of their home town, might start thinking of Silicon Valley as the Bangalore (or Hyderabad, if future trends may be predicted) of the West Coast. In the crucible of this culture of Silicon Valley and Plateau, Indians have even generated their own postmodern and cyberdiasporic jokes: thus, the Hindi film villain Ajit, around whom an entire industry of jokes has developed, commands his henchman Robert to render extinct the life of the hero by placing him in a "microprocessor," so that he can die "byte by byte."[26] From these manifold computer companies a sizable number of Indians have moved into venture capital, in a spirit that is perhaps reminiscent of the entrepreneurship, trading acumen, and financial ambitions of earlier generations of Indian traders and businessmen who once dominated the Indian Ocean trading networks. Finally, in the domain of medicine, where over 4 percent of the doctors are estimated to be of Indian origin, a similar tale of Indian success is easily told, and the strength of an organization such as the American Association of Physicians of Indian Origin can be gauged by the fact that its 1995 annual meeting was addressed by no lesser a luminary—however disgraced—than President Bill Clinton.[27]

Along with some other Asian Americans, Indian Americans are often characterized as a model minority; and yet they construe themselves as "invisible." In the United States, the Sinic element has always predominated over the Indic in the understanding of what was meant by "Asian," and the presence of the Chinese and the Japanese antedates the presence of Indians by one generation. The Asian American, in the imagination of the white American, is an oriental figure of Mongoloid features; and Asian Americans themselves, viewed as a whole, appear to have been largely indifferent, except very recently, to claims that Indian Americans should be accommodated under that rubric. Nor is "Indian" very useful as a marker of identity, since that is liable to render the Indian into a specimen of a Native American tribe. It is only a very slight exaggeration to suggest that from "India" one easily moves on to "Indiana", a rather more familiar terrain to Americans, though no one, if optimism be allowed, ought to think of India as similarly nondescript as its near namesake. Nor, in the matter of color, is the Indian easily positioned. In the early part of the century, Indians (or "Hindoos" as they were then called, regardless of their religious faith) endeavored to be treated as whites;[28] in more recent years, when affirmative action was more warmly received than it is in the present political climate, Indians strove to be considered nonwhite, a minority people. In Britain, they are lumped with 'black' people; in South Africa under apartheid, Indians were distinguished from white, black, and colored people. This apprehension of 'invisibility' is compounded by other psychological and cultural factors, far too numerous for any detailed consideration at present. Suffice to note that since India has for some time been "the largest most unimportant country in the world,"[29] Indians in the United States fear that this stigma is attached to their own persons; and since South Asia has historically been the only home of Hindus, with the exception of Hindu communities that as far back as a millennium ago came to be established in Bali, Java, and some other parts of Southeast Asia, Indians do not doubt that India is condemned to oblivion, unless of course Hinduism can somehow be construed as a threat to the Stars and Stripes. I suspect that at times devout Hindus, whose piety is in no way incompatible with a barely concealed interest in wanting the emergence of a powerful Indian nation-state, have wanted nothing more than that India should turn staunchly communist, or into a hotbed of 'Islamic fundamentalism': their anxieties about invisibility would certainly disappear. India might then even be the beneficiary of the kind of monumental aid that was pumped into Pakistan when neighboring Afghanistan came under Soviet influence. Such is the Hinduism of some Hindus that even communism can be construed as a form of Hinduism: not only are Hindu deities multiarmed, but Hinduism can be fruitfully and ecumenically multipronged.

However acute the problems Indians Americans appear to have in nominating themselves and in allowing themselves to be named, they indubitably belong as well, or so one might think, to a postindustrial civilization. In several respects, the Cold War climate was propitious for Indians desirous of settling in the United States. As the principal political and economic power, the United States was bound to spend increased amounts on research and development to retain its edge in military technology, aerospace engineering, telecommunications, medical research, and "big science." The American military, notwithstanding the conclusion of the Cold War, has continued to display a monstrous and insatiable appetite for new and ever more sophisticated hardware, and with the exponential growth of the computer industry over the last decade, the need for professionals with backgrounds in science, engineering, computers, and medicine has persisted. In Indians, American universities, industries, scientific organizations, and other public and private enterprises found a people who, while proficient in English, also had the requisite skills and professional training. Thus, unlike Indians in many parts of the globe where their presence arose from circumstances of indentured servitude, or the labor shortages in the aftermath of World War II, Indians in the United States are predominantly professionals, playing a critical role in shaping a post-scarcity, postindustrial information civilization. It is only very recently that they have thought their professional services, which have earned them considerable affluence, also entitled them to some measure of political influence and thereby to lessen that invisibility, the fear of which shadows every successful Indian American. Indeed, it endlessly rankled these successful Indian American professionals that Pakistan and Pakistani Americans were, as they perceived, more successful lobbyists on Capitol Hill; and the reverse suffered by Pakistan in 1999, when the United States unequivocally condemned Pakistani adventurism in the Himalayan heights of Kargil, was assessed by professional Indians, who waged a tremendous and ultimately successful campaign to have Congress pass a resolution condemning Pakistan's abrogation of the Line of Control as the first sign of the political influence that they feel they can rightfully exercise among American lawmakers.[30] It is these same professional Indian Hindus who, now mindful of the strength of their numbers, their professional standing in society, and the power of the Internet, orchestrated with success a campaign to have Warner Brothers, producers of Stanley Kubrick's *Eyes Wide Shut,* delete from the film verses from the Hindu scripture *Bhagavad Gita* that had been inserted in the midst of an orgy scene.[31]

The postindustrial civilization of North American Hindus is also, if a paradox may be entertained, a Vedic civilization. Its conception of India, as I argue later, is largely derived from the texts and practices of remote antiquity, which supposedly furnish us with a vision of Hinduism in its pristine state. There are indubitably those Hindus who, without the least trace of humor or irony, fervently argue that there is virtually no scientific advancement that was not already anticipated in the Vedas or other ancient Hindu texts, and that in the visions of Indian seers are to be found the blueprints for rocket science, satellites, and the supersonic jet fighters of our times. The very term *stealth fighters* seems to evoke subliminal memories among the unamused Hindus of awe-inspiring and magical weapons wielded—often treacherously, as if by stealth—by Brahma, Vishnu, or Shiva, usually with incalculable and devastating effect. These Hindus are dedicated to the proposition that the highest truths of Hinduism are easily reconciled with the highest truths of science, and that the ancient seers and nuclear physicists have intuited the same ultimate reality. These Hindus point to Robert Oppenheimer's famous invocation, at the precise moment of the first nuclear test, of a passage from the Bhagavad Gita, or to the interest that the most eminent physicists, such as Albert Einstein and Subrahmanyan Chandrasekhar, have taken in Indian philosophical thought.

However, this is scarcely the most substantive sense in which the Hindu diaspora in the United States is a harbinger of Vedic civilization. Though in Uttar Pradesh a dalit woman,[32] who not long ago would have been resigned to having herself viewed as part of a collective of "untouchables," rose a few years ago to become the chief minister of the state, a position only second to that of the prime minister in any traditional reckoning of Indian political fortunes in the electoral age, in the Vedic Diaspora of Hindus such an outcome is considered to be well beyond the ken of contemplation. It defies their sense of Hindu hierarchies that a lower-caste person, and a woman at that, could be elevated to such eminence. To gain an inkling of what this Vedic civilization of diasporic Hindus looks like, one has only to consider the activities of the Saiva Siddhanta Church in the northern California town of Concord. A few years ago, the *pujari*, or priest, of this temple placed a rope about ten feet away from the deity, and strung a sign on it that loudly proclaimed, "Vegetarians only beyond this point." At a slightly greater distance, another rope was strung across the room, and the sign on this advised the worshippers, "Hindu clothing only beyond this point."[33] Numerous devotees suddenly found themselves out in the cold, denied *darshan* [that is, the gaze, and thus the blessing] of their deity, condemned to be pariahs. While it is true that this particular Hindu institution is headed by an American swami who is based in Hawaii—where a magnificent Hindu temple is being constructed according to the stipulations of the ancient *shilpasastras*, or Hindu temple-architecture manuals—its following consists largely of Indian Hindus.[34] Though Marxist scholarship has, with reasonable certainty, established that the ancient Aryans were beef-eaters,[35] and this continues to be at least a matter of debate in India, among Hindus in the United States it is an article of faith to suppose that vegetarianism has been critical to Vedic civilization from the outset. On "Hindu clothing," the innovation here is a reversion to the practice, common among the most orthodox Hindu temples in South India, whereby men must shed themselves of leather products and stitched clothes before entering the temple and drape a *dhoti* around them. It is well to argue that one must come before God unstitched and untethered, but the Hindus in the United States show every tendency to adopt the literalism that is so characteristically an American trait.

To suggest that the Hindu diaspora in the United States aspires to be Vedic is to point to the manner in which Hindu devotees here have developed an ossified conception of their faith, frozen in time. Though "homeland" Hinduism continues to evolve, and deities are born and die, and the faith acquires new resonances while shedding some of its older emphases, the Hinduism of its Indian American devotees, one can reasonably maintain, displays the most retrograde features. Certainly, as far as I am aware, there is nothing to suggest that Hinduism in the United States has jettisoned some of the rituals that accompany the faith in India; quite to the contrary, as even a cursory examination of *India-West*, a California-based newspaper with a circulation of twenty thousand suggests, the Hindus here have embraced forms of worship pursued by only the most dedicated Hindus in India. The religion pages of the weekly newspaper are full of announcements about various obscure *pujas*, (acts of religious worship) many conducted to celebrate rites or in honor of one or more deity, when these particular *pujas* are scarcely celebrated by any but the most orthodox Hindus in India itself. Whether in the political, cultural, or psychosocial domain, the

Hinduism of North American Hindus can in no manner be viewed as a "lighter" form of the faith.

Indeed, it would be no exaggeration to argue that Hinduism in the United States has been transformed, to a degree that is not merely unhealthy but politically undesirable, into what is known as Hindutva, a Hinduism stripped to its imagined essences, and purportedly reinvigorated by arming it with attributes commonly thought to belong to the more "masculine" faiths of Christianity, Islam, and Judaism. It is no accident, I might note parenthetically, that relations between India and Israel, which is seen by admiring proponents of militant Hinduism as a no-nonsense masculine state that knows how to deal with terrorists, secessionists, and disgruntled rebels, have improved vastly over the last two years that the Bharatiya Janata Party, which openly advocates Hindu rule in India, has been in political power. While the rise of militant Hinduism in India is a phenomenon too well-known and well-documented to require any elaborate discussion, it merits discussion, that the consolidation of identity around the notion of highly differentiated religious communities, a process that was first set in motion by the colonial state in the nineteenth century, began to acquire ominous overtones around the mid-1980s. With the increasing turn to history—among a people typically characterized in colonial discourses as devoid of the historical sensibility—as a mode of living with the present and acquitting oneself for the tasks of citizenship, Hindus began to think of the wrongs, as they thought, committed against them by Muslim invaders. The burden of a cruel past, in which they had been reduced to subjection, and their faith trampled upon by those 'foreigners' who had acquired political power, began to weigh heavily upon them; and the colonial argument—that the Hindus were a supine people incapable of defending their own interests—left its impression upon them.

The sense of grievance among Hindus began to crystallize further when the government was seen as pandering to the economic and cultural demands of minority communities, particularly Muslims, from the grossest political calculations. Militant Hindus speak disparagingly of Indian secularism, and proclaim that the Indian state is wedded to "pseudo-secularism"; the minorities are said to be the beneficiaries of government largesse, and certain Hindus, belonging to a community that accounts for about 78 percent of India's population, complain of how they have been reduced to a minority in their own country. Drawing upon the writings of Veer Savarkar, Madhav Sadashiv Golwalkar, and other Hindu ideologues who defined India as the eternal land of the Hindus and insisted that the "blood of Hindus" streamed through everyone born in the motherland (*janmabhoomi*), the advocates of a renewed Hindu militancy have endeavored to turn India—to deploy Islamic terminology—into the land of the "pure and the faithful." Muslims and exponents of other faiths are asked to understand that they are Hindus, and they are enjoined to return to the bosom; and as for those who unremittingly cling to their faith, they must perforce understand, so argue militant Hindus, that they live in India at the pleasure of the Hindus. While loudly declaring themselves to be tolerant of other faiths, in keeping with the idea that Hinduism has been an intrinsically pluralistic religion, these Hindutvavadis or militant exponents of Hinduism have sought to shape their faith in the image of those very other faiths that they decry. Consequently, both Islam and Christianity are seen as displaying an admirable unity and rationality not stricken by the effeminacy, devotional excess, or the needless multiplicity—whether in the arena of deities, or sources of doctrinal authority—that are construed as having crippled Hinduism. The militant Hindus have no greater desire than to turn Hinduism into a more masculine faith, more vigorous and uncompromising in the defense of its devotees; and the destruction of the Babri Masjid in December, 1992, was the most visible sign of that ferocious intent.[36] Thus has Hinduism, in their hands, become Hindutva ideology.

Among Hindus in the United States, the Hindutvavadis appeared to have gained ascendancy. Though Hindus in the United States are just as fragmented and dispersed as anywhere else, their organizations torn apart by common rifts over ethnic and linguistic affiliations or other anxieties about their "identity," over the last few years they have shown signs of being able to cohere together, carried forth by pride in those features of Indian civilization that are seen as specially emblematic of Hindu tradition and culture. Indeed, they have collapsed the distinction between *Indian* and *Hindu,* and some might also be inclined to altogether jettison the category *Indian.* One of the most prominent of the Hindutva ideologues, Ashok Singhal, the general-secretary of the Vishwa Hindu Parishad (VHP), an organization set up to perform the cultural work of Hinduism and make it into a religion with a worldwide presence, has written that "the Hindu Rashtra can only be a state where there must be Hindu churches and Hindu mosques, for Hinduism is not a religion. It is the collective experience of thousands of individuals[,] unlike Christianity and Islam which are experiences of single individuals. In Hindu India, every one has to call himself a Hindu."[37] The RamJanmabhoomi movement, leading to the destruction of the aforementioned Babri Masjid, received considerable support from Hindus settled overseas, and the funding of Hindu institutions, temples, and other purportedly 'charitable' enterprise by nonresident Indian (NRI) Hindus, particularly those from the United States, can be established beyond doubt.[38] Strikingly, though in the aftermath of the destruction of the mosque nearly two thousand Indians were killed in Hindu-Muslim riots, the Hindus in Southern California, describing themselves as "concerned NRIs," could think of no more reasoned intervention than to take out an advertisement in the *Indian Express,* one of the largest English-language daily newspapers in India, deploring the government's short-lived ban of "nationalistic [Hindutva] organizations" and urging their "brothers and sisters in India" to aim at the "restoration of common sets of values and laws based on the 6,000 year heritage."[39] As if in anticipation of questions about their entitlement to intervene in the politics of the homeland, they argued that "of the one million NRI's living in the United States, over 900,000 call Bharat [India] as [*sic*] their Mother. Hindus have only one place (other than Nepal) to call home. Their roots are in Bharat."[40]

If in India the clarion call of militant Hindus is that "another Pakistan" must at all costs be avoided, in the United States they insist that their children be spared the evils and excesses of American culture (which Indians seldom consider to *be* culture), and be exposed to the incontestable virtues of Hindu civilization. In the United States, where proximity to the Muslim can be avoided, and views about the fanaticism of Islam are seen as receiving the endorsement of the wider culture, Vedic India appears in illumined glory as the opposite of all that is evil. An extraordinary, but by no means atypical, illustration of the besieged Indian-American Hindu mentality at work can be seen in a book published recently by the Federation of Hindu Associations (FHA), a Los Angeles–based organization, of which over ten thousand copies were distributed free at the November 1999 Diwali *mela,* or celebrations in the Indian neighborhoods of Cerritos and Artesia. Entitled *Bhagwan's Call for Dharma Raksha,* or *God's Appeal for the Protection of the [Hindu] Faith,* this book purports to set out the facts about the truly destructive nature of Islam and the unique innocence of Hinduism. Over the course of "The Last (1000) Dreadful Years," the Hindu readers are reminded, "We have lost more than half of our Vedic land"; "Crores [tens of millions] of Hindus were converted to Islam and other religions"; "Thousands of our temples were demolished"; "Temples of Hindus, some of whom [*sic*] like Mathura and Kashi, are half temple–half mosque, indicating destruction by the invaders and establishment of their mosques," stand forth as signs of the humiliation of Hindus; and "The % of non-Hindus in India increased dramatically whereas Hindus continued family planning."[41] Hindus are reminded that merely because their forefathers survived the genocidal onslaught of Muslims and other invaders, they should not be complaisant, thinking that Hinduism "will anyhow survive"; and they are asked to reflect on the ominous fact that, "by all calculations" given the Muslim's alarming propensity to breed hordes of children, "Hindus could become [a] minority in [the] very near future." Consequently, Hindus are enjoined to engage in "Dharma Raksha," the protection of the faith, so that:

- Rigid religions may not harm this flexible way of Hindus.
- Revelations may not harm this philosophical religion of Hindus.
- Fanatics may not destroy the compassionate Hindus.
- Narrow-minded many not spoil the broad-minded Hindus.
- Theocracies may not destroy the secular & democratic Hindus.
- There is at least one Vedic land.
- Cultural experience, known as Hindutva, may not go waste.[42]

The alarming susceptibility of NRI Hindus in the US to resurgent Hinduism is nowhere more clearly exemplified than in their admiration for the most intolerant Hindus to have gained public eminence in India over the last few years. In 1994 the FHA took it upon itself to institute a new award, called the Hindu of the Year Award, which was then promptly conferred upon Bal Thackeray and Sadhvi Rithambara. The citation accompanying the award commended Thackeray (an avid admirer of Hitler who has acquired immense notoriety for his part in instituting pogroms against Muslims in Maharashtra) and Rithambara (whose shrill rantings against the *yavanas* (foreigners) have left many wounded and trembling) for their role in, of all things, "the creation and preservation of Hinduism."[43] The FHA could well have pondered on the longevity of an ancient faith, and wondered how such a faith has fared so well in the absence of such defenders in the past; rather, in the following year, the award was bestowed upon Uma Bharati, who summons Hindu men to arms with the observation that Hindus want no cut-up (partitioned) nation any more than they want cut-up (circumcised) men in their midst.[44] The speeches of Uma Bharati and Sadhavi Rithambara, whom Hindutvavadis doubtless see as modern-day Durgas, wielders of that immense feminine energy that in Hindu theology is seen as generating the universe and undoing the wrongs that even the Hindu male gods are incapable of arresting, are so incendiary that they have been subjected to repeated bans in India.

What, then, is this postindustrial civilization of diasporic Hindus, particularly those settled in the United States and the "advanced" West? Hindu communities in the United States appear to know the contours and meaning of Hinduism better than do Hindus in India, and these diasporic Hindus can routinely invoke Indian civilization with a self-assurance that, in an Indian in India, would at once provoke mockery and consternation. Far removed as these Hindus are from the lived practices of the faith, their Hinduism is ossified; equally distanced in their adopted country from the cultural life and political aspirations of black people, Hispanics, and other racial or ethnic minorities, and often xenophobically proud of the allegedly unique spiritual qualities of their own Hindu traditions, one wonders if their sense of the moral community is not inadequate. Most trenchantly, Indian-American Hindus have taken to cyberspace to press forth their own claims about the nature of Hindu civilization, and they have been unrelenting in their attempt to give shape to a new Hindu history. This history, which aggressively sets itself against the long trajectory of colonial histories, the "pseudo-secular" agenda of the Indian state, the secularism of the Indian left, the nefarious designs of the Pakistani state, the Western contempt for Hindu culture, and the intellectual pusillanimity and moral cowardice of the Indian academy, furnishes a point of entry into debates about the political uses of cyberspace just as it suggests that the battle for contending versions of history, which had appeared to reach its acme in the debate surrounding the Babri Masjid, will surely intensify as it is played upon new turfs in the homeland and the diaspora alike.

Cyberdiasporic Hindu Militancy and Revisionist Indian Histories

It is perhaps apposite that the North American proponents of Hindutva, as well as revisionist Hindu historians, should have found the Internet an agreeable avenue for the propagation of their worldview. More than any other religion, Hinduism is a decentered and deregulated faith, and in this it appears akin to cyberspace. It has no one prophet or savior, nor are Hindus agreed upon the authority of a single text. Only in the older Indian diaspora created by indentured labor, such as in Fiji and Trinidad, did a single text—namely Tulsidas's *Ramacaritmanas*—become supremely authoritative, and here, too, for reasons that had to do with the cultural, political, and economic characteristics of the migration, its point of origin mainly in the Gangetic plains where Tulsidas's devotional book was deeply revered, the illiteracy of the laborers, and so on. Moreover, if Trinidad or Fiji Hindus even for a moment thought they had become the people of the book, their distinctly second-class status in these societies was enough to disabuse them of that far-fetched notion. Hinduism not only has multiple sources of doctrinal authority, it is polycentric. Varanasi (Benares) is not to Hinduism what Mecca and Medina are to Islam, and the pilgrimage sites of Hindus are almost as numerous as their deities. While for Muslims the pilgrimage to Mecca can be nothing other than a literal visit to Mecca, for Hindus the sacred river Ganga can be fully re-created by mixing Ganga *jal* in any body of water.[45] The circumambulation around any number of temples or sacred lakes could, for a Hindu, stand in place of the circumambulation around the Kaaba: even Hinduism's most sacred sites are largely places of myth rather than history.

In the language of the cybernetic postmodernists, one could say that Hinduism is rhizomatic, with multiple points of origin, intersection, and dispersal. If the modular form for Netwar conforms to what one early analyst described as "a segmented, polycentric, ideologically integrated network" (SPIN), where "segmented" means "cellular, composed of many different groups," and "polycentric," "many different leaders or centers of direction,"[46] then Hinduism most certainly inhabits those very properties that characterize cybernetworks. In a manner of speaking, Hinduism even makes the head *spin;* and if "electronic civil disobedience" consists in "swarming" and "flooding" the websites of the foe, popular Hinduism displays a similar tendency to create an immense sensory overload and swarm one's sensibilities. Hinduism and the Internet, one might conclude, were happily made for each other; even the millions of websites evoke the "330 millions gods and goddesses" of Hinduism.[47] The Internet, it could also be argued, is a particularly happy medium for those who construe themselves as members of a diaspora, or who have what might be termed *diasporic sensibilities.* Though the Indian diaspora is much smaller than the Chinese or African diasporas, it has perhaps a greater geographic reach, and is represented in virtually every country of the world: in the clichéd saying, the two things that are found everywhere in the world are "a potato" and "a Sikh." Through cyberspace, Hindus have found a new awareness of themselves as part of what they now imagine is a global religion, and nothing could be more calculated to augment Hindu pride than the perception that Hinduism is on the verge of arriving as a "world religion," to take its place alongside Islam, Christianity, and even Buddhism. Though the adherents of Hinduism are still overwhelmingly confined to the subcontinent, what Arjun Appadurai has called "the globalization of Hinduism" was evidently on witness in 1995 when the news spread that *murtis*, or images of Ganesh, the elephant-headed God, had been seen drinking prodigious amounts of milk in Hindu temples; and so from Delhi and Bombay this news was rapidly flashed to Leeds, London, Leicester, Chicago, New York, Los Angeles, and elsewhere.[48] Reflecting on the "milk miracle" of September 1995, one long-time scholar of the Hindu overseas population observed that a "South Asian religious diaspora was now linked through advanced global telecommunications."[49]

Moving to more mundane considerations, it is an empirical observation that in the United States many professional Indians, and particularly Hindus, earn their living in the computer and software industries, and they take readily to the culture of the Internet. It is not in the least coincidental that a preponderant number of the people associated with what may be termed Hindutva websites owe their livelihood to computer industries or are drawn from the hard sciences, and that their Hinduism is without those soft and porous edges that gave the religion its historically amorphous and ecumenical form. Significantly, very few professional historians, if any, contribute to these websites, which is hardly to say that the expertise of professional historians is reliable. Judging from recent events in India, such as the endeavor to reduce professional historical associations—the Indian Historical Records Commission being a case in point—to mouthpieces of the Vishwa Hindu Parishad (VHP) and the Bharatiya Janata Party (BJP), which correspondingly perform the cultural and political work of the militant Hinduism whose militaristic expression is found in the cadres of the Rashtriya Swayamsevak Sangh (RSS), one might feel relieved that Hindutva websites are largely amateurish undertakings, however much scientific credibility their creators might attach to such enterprises. While no complete sociological profile of the people who labor on such websites—whether in a technical capacity or by way of providing substantive content—is available, typically they are male graduate students from middle-class backgrounds, drawn evidently to revisionist histories of India; they are also the ones who contribute most frequently to various listservs and bulletin boards, such as alt.hindu and soc.culture.indian.

Though the subjects on which the most substantial contributions to the websites are made vary considerably, the webmasters and their associates are united in their resolve to offer radically altered accounts of even the most common verities of Indian history. Thus, while it is generally agreed that the Mughal emperor Akbar (reigned 1556–1605) was, especially for his times, a just ruler, whose policies of tolerance were conducive to the expansion of his empire and the good of his subjects, and who is said to have introduced elements of Hinduism into his own practices of worship and even the culture of the court, in Hindutva websites he appears as a "tyrannical monarch"; not unexpectedly, then, Aurangzeb (reigned 1658–1707), who has always been disliked by Hindu historians as a sworn enemy of the Hindus and breaker of idols, is viewed as entirely beyond the pale. The Taj Mahal, which no serious historian doubts was built at the orders of Shah Jahan (reigned 1628–1658), is transformed into a Hindu monument by the name of Tejomahalay, as though its history as one of the finest examples of Mughal architecture is wholly inconsequential, a malicious invention of Muslim-loving Hindus. Lest these revisionisms be considered merely arbitrary and anomalous, the systematic patterning behind these rewritings is also evidenced by the attempt to argue, for example, that the Aryans, far from having migrated to India, originated there.[50]

Turning to a lengthier consideration of these websites, they weave their own intricate web of links, conspiracies, and nodal points: at one moment one is at one website, and at another moment at another. Even Krishna, who by his *leela* or divine magical play could be among several *gopis* (lovers) simultaneously, might have found his match in the World Wide Web; he might have gazed with awe at rhizomatic Hindutvaness at its propagandistic best. Among the most remarkable and most comprehensive of the sites are those created by the VHP and students who have constituted themselves into the Global Hindu Electronic Network (GHEN). Links take the surfer to such sites as hindunet, the Hindu Vivek Kendra, and the various articles culled from the archives of *Hinduism Today*, a glossy magazine published by the white *sadhu* (mendicant) who, as previously mentioned, is constructing a lavish temple amidst the rich tropical green of Hawaii's Kaui island. There are links to other spiritual matters of interest to nonresident Hindus, such as the teachings of Swami Chinmayananda,[51] whose associations with the VHP have been explored by scholars at some length, and to comparatively more esoteric sites on Indian philosophy, devotional literature, the legends of gods and goddesses, and the like. The importance attached to cyberspace communication and politics and the nonresident Hindu factor is, incidentally, nowhere better illustrated than in the fact that the BJP, which used to shout itself hoarse over *swadeshi* (self-reliance) and is nauseatingly jingoistic, locates its website in the United States, as does the paramilitary RSS.[52]

GHEN is sponsored by the Hindu Students Council, and the astuteness of its creators, no less than their zeal and ardor, can be gauged by the fact that it had developed into the most comprehensive site on Hindutva philosophy and aggressive Hindu nationalism at least six years ago, when such work in cyberspace was in its infancy. GHEN was the recipient in 1996 of an award from *IWAY*, then one of the leading Internet magazines, for the "Best Web Page Award" in the religious category, and one of GHEN's members described himself as pleased that the world was finally "taking cognizance of the most important movement in this century, 'The Hindutva Movement.' "[53] The home page takes one into predictable categories, namely "Introductions," "Scriptures," "Temples," "Organizations," "Latest News," and the bulletin board alt.hindu; another link opens what is called the "Hindu Universe" and is graced by the sign of *aum,* which believing Hindus describe as the primal sound that stands for the Supreme Godhead, and this in turn leads to pages on five categories, enumerated as follows: "Latest News from Bharat (India)," "Kashmir," "Terrorism in Bharat (India)," "Hindutva: Nationalist Ideology," and "Shri Ramjanmabhoomi Movement." Each page, in turn, furnishes links to a dozen or more related articles: the aspiration to be comprehensive, and to leave the surfer with an impression that neutrality is being maintained, is suggested by the characterization of each page as a "reference center."

Though the page on Kashmir offers a Hindu perspective on the rebellion that has been taking place in that valley over the last few years; highlights the suffering of Kashmiri Pandits (Brahmins); and reiterates the role of Pakistan in aiding and abetting the rebellion, it is the manner in which Kashmir is assimilated into the "Hindu universe" that is deserving of comment.[54] The assumption is that one can ignore the largely Muslim population of the state, and presumably the Buddhists of the Ladakh region of Kashmir are construed as belonging to the Hindu fold; and while there is undoubtedly a Saivite (Hindu) substratum as well, the positioning of Kashmir within a "Hindu universe" betrays an acute anxiety about the reality of Kashmir as a composite culture and the eventual disposition of what is generally termed the "Kashmir problem." Moreover, though Kashmir is recognized as a matter of jurisdiction for the Indian nation-state, its transposition into a Hindu universe signifies the ease with which "India" can effortlessly be elided into "Hindu," maneuver that is repeatedly encountered in Hindutva websites.[55] Similar sleights of hand are visible throughout the GHEN site. Thus, in the "Shree Ramjanmabhoomi Reference Center" page, which like much of GHEN offers an array of articles culled from Indian newspapers, in this case about the dispute over the Babri Masjid, it is quite baldly stated that the "Ramjanmabhoomi movement is carried out by hundreds of millions of Hindus in Bharat (India)."[56] Far too many studies have already established that the movement leading to the destruction of the mosque drew its membership from precisely those elements of society from which the BJP, RSS, and VHP draw their support—namely, the trading castes, the petite bourgeoisie, and small-town dwellers.[57] The destruction of the Babri Masjid itself was an affair orchestrated to the extreme, and as with many riots that require careful engineering, volunteers had to be drawn upon from the outside.[58] It is also an indubitable fact that there are millions of Hindus in Bharat, and that Rama is one of the principal deities, particularly in the so-called cow belt in north India; yet this does not inescapably lead to the logic that the preponderant number of Hindus put their weight behind the movement, or that the millions of Rama *bhaktas* (devotees) can be safely described as adherents of the movement.

If GHEN shares something ominous in common with Hindutva websites, it is the deliberate attempt to obfuscate the distinction between Hinduism and Hindutva. Swami Vivekananda, to take one instance, becomes in their histories an exponent of Hindutva ideology, not an advocate of a mere Hinduism; and this, perhaps, receives some credence from the circumstances surrounding the life of Vivekananda, who, as the sole representative of Hinduism at the World Parliament of Religions in Chicago in 1893, can be described as playing a not inconsiderable role in furnishing Hinduism something of a place on the world stage.[59] Though Hindutvavadis do not care much for Gandhi—finding it fit even to dismiss him as something of a *hijra* (eunuch) and father of Pakistan, or even for Vivekananda's own spiritual master Ramakrishna, whose spirituality they admire but whose androgyny poses something of a problem to their own sense of masculinity—they have ferociously struggled to claim Vivekananda as one of their own. For some years now, even within the Ramakrishna Mission, it has been apparent that Vivekananda has been gaining more prominence, and when he began to be championed in Rajiv Gandhi's India as a model for Indian youth, it became imperative for the VHP and its friends to declare themselves as the true inheritors of Vivekananda's legacy. In Hindu communities, from Port of Spain to Chicago, it is the image of Vivekananda that looms large over the landscapes that Hindus inhabit.[60] He is seen, in the first instance, as the prophet who energized the Indian nation, urged his brethren to social action, critiqued the devotional excess of the faith (what he would have made of his master, one cannot say), strove to make Hinduism a more rational and masculine religion, and won Hinduism its first devotees in the West. It is Vivekananda's stridency and proselytizing that, doubtless, make him an attractive feature to Hindutva advocates, who are prone to take the view that Hindus have, for too long of their history, remained a pacific and tolerant people upon whom others trod none too gently. "The message has reached far and wide throughout the world," states Ashok Singhal, the general-secretary of the VHP, "that the Hindu will no more be subdued. Eventually the world at large will come to the conclusion that after all now they have to deal with a Hindu India."[61]

Judging from GHEN's Swami Vivekananda Study Center," which presents the RSS as the fulfillment of Vivekananda's ideas, the Swami was a militant Hindutvavadi who desired "the conquest of the whole world by the Hindu race."[62] If Argentina is nothing other than "Arjuna town," where Arjuna—one of the five Pandava heroes who in the *Mahabharata* are condemned to spend thirteen years in exile—went for the year that he was enjoined to remain incognito; if Denmark, rich in dairy products, is none other than "Dhenu Marg," the cow pathway; if the "Red Indians" are the signposts for the advance of an Indian civilization in remote antiquity; and if Vivekananda's own name, "Vive! Canada," is a ringing testimony to his reach over the world, then surely it is not too far-fetched to imagine that Vivekananda desired the worldwide supremacy of the Hindu race.[63] His militancy is highlighted with his observation that the

Bhagavad Gita, which Gandhi would interpret as a text counseling nonviolent resistance, would be better understood with the "biceps," by "strong men with muscles of steel and nerves of iron inside of which dwells a mind of the same material as that of which the thunderbolt is made."[64] Yet in their haste to turn Vivekananda into the apostle of Hindutva, the defender of the faith, the VHP and its allies appear to have forgotten his admonition to others who would dare to be the guardians of Hinduism. Once, on a visit to Kashmir, Vivekananda felt pained at seeing the ruins of temples and the idols of Hindu deities scattered around the country. Approaching the goddess with anger and trepidation, Vivekananda bowed before her, and asked in an anguished tone, "Mother, why did you permit this desecration?" Vivekananda reports that Kali whispered to him, "What is it to you if the invaders broke my images? Why do you trouble yourself over it? Do you protect me, or do I protect you?"[65]

Evidently, if one is to consider the rather gargantuan website of VHP-America, the Hindutva advocates, quite oblivious to Vivekananda's teachings, dwell on the ruins of temples and the Muslim hatred of idolaters. No one who has looked at the VHP site can fail to be impressed by the fact that its home page, which takes surfers to GHEN's "Hindu Universe," to a list of temples in the United States, and other activities of interest to Hindus, also takes readers to the "History of Hindu Temples," which in turn features a section on "Temple Destruction." Though readers can rejoice in the presence of monumental temple complexes as varied as Angkor Wat and Hampi, the engagement with the history of destroyed temples appears to be more intense; the destruction of Somnath evokes greater passion than the dancing stones of Belur, Halebid, Konarak, and other temples. Here, again, the cue may have come from Vivekananda, who reminded his countrymen and women that their "forefathers underwent everything boldly, even death itself, but preserved their religion. Temple after temple was broken down by foreign conquerors, but no sooner had the wave passed than the spire of the temple rose again."[66] If the valiant Hindu woman, by the very act of choosing self-immolation (*jauhar*) and immortality rather than the ignominy of sexual violation by the Muslim invader, bore in negation the mark of the Muslim upon her body, so the Hindu temple carried the history of regenerative violations: "Mark how the temples bear the marks of a hundred attacks and a hundred regenerations, continually destroyed and continually springing out of the ruins, rejuvenated and as strong as ever! That is the national life current."[67]

Vivekananda had, however, asked the Hindu to look to his own resources, and to consider what weaknesses in Indian society, and in particular in the Hindu social structure, made the country vulnerable to invasion and attack. For the Hindutvavadi in the diaspora, the alterity of the Muslim—the "Indian Muslim" is something of an anomaly from that perspective, because the Muslim in India is never sufficiently Indian, and as a Muslim he is seen as having promised his loyalty to the *qaum,* the worldwide community of Muslims—is paradoxically the sine qua non of Hindu identity and history. Sometimes the expression of Hindu identity is expressed by waging a virulent attack on Islam, as in the website, located in the United States, that takes its name from the Sanskrit phrase "*Satyameva Jayate*" ("The Truth Alone Triumphs"), which is the national motto of sovereign India.[68] Though viewers are invited to send e-mail to a person carrying a Muslim name, Zulfikar, the website is almost certainly operated by a Hindu. The site is linked to the home page of a "Vedic astrologer,"[69] and the remarks about Islam and its prophet are so slanderous that it is nearly inconceivable that any Muslim, howsoever much an unbeliever, would have dared to be so foolishly offensive. Four of the twenty articles, all unsigned, available on this website purport to establish that Muhammad was the "Prophet of Terror," two document Islam's supposed worldwide network of terrorism, and some others venture into descriptions of Islam as a religion of lust, murder, rape, and genocide. Attempting to unmask the "sadistic cruel nature of Prophet Mohammed," the author argues that "Mohammed was in fact a terrorist, criminal and murderer whose entire life was based on victimizing innocents and indulging in mindless violence, carnage and massacre."[70] The author alleges that the Prophet's sexual appetite for young boys and beautiful virgins could never be satiated; he enticed the Arabs with sex slaves and booty, and "to please the homosexuals among his followers he promised them pre-pubescent boys in Paradise."[71]

More often, the Hindutva notion of history comes wrapped around a tale of Hindu innocence, and more precisely the tale of the destruction of Hindu temples. This is quite transparent in the Satyameva Jayate website, where four of the twenty articles are devoted to an enumeration of the "Destruction of Hindu Temples by Muslims." The very sense of history, by no means unique to Hindutvavadis, is marked by violence, wars, and technological achievements: historians have become habituated to speaking of World War I, World War II, the Vietnam War, and the Indo-Pakistan War of 1971 as "watersheds,"[72] and it is this language that is absorbed into Hindutva websites, where the "watersheds" are those periodic invasions of India that led to the destruction of Hindu temples. What remains evokes no sense of history; the present is always transcendental, and is less easily hitched to the anguished sense of a past where one was wronged—and all this is not in keeping with the VHP's ideological interests, which are to transform Hinduism, viewed by Hindutvavadis as having been wrongly condemned as a form of myth-making, into a religion of history. No Hindutvavadi is prepared to countenance the observation that the particular genius of Hinduism may lie in none other than its mythicity, and the ire expressed at the recent website inaugurated by the "Indian Express," www.hindumythology.com, suggests how far militant Hinduism remains captive to the mode of historical thinking.[73]

The historical sensibility has, fortunately, from a civilizational standpoint, never been a marked feature of Indian thinking; indeed, it is a commonplace to argue that the historical sense was severely underdeveloped in ancient India, and the view of Jawaharlal Nehru, not only India's first prime minister but a man with a distinctly historical sensibility whose *Discovery of India* still serves as one of the better introductions to Indian history, may be taken as representative. He writes, "Unlike the Greeks, and unlike the Chinese and the Arabs, Indians in the past were not historians. This was very unfortunate and it has made it difficult for us now to fix dates or make up an accurate chronology. Events run into each other, overlap and produce an enormous confusion. . . . the ignoring of history had evil consequences which we pursue still. It produced a vagueness of outlook, a divorce from life as it is, a credulity, a woolliness of the mind where fact was concerned."[74] A number of scholars have attempted, in an overdetermined reaction to save India from the orientalist structures of thought,[75] to provide a more complex scenario of India's engagement with historical thinking, but they have been less attentive to Nehru's observation that "this lack of historical sense did not affect the masses ... they built up their view of the past from the traditional accounts and myth and story that were handed to them from generation to generation. This imagined history and mixture of fact and legend became widely known and gave to the people a strong and abiding cultural background."[76] But the attack on the Indian Express website, by those who purport to speak for Hindu civilization, displays precisely this profound anxiety that Hinduism should in no manner be construed as a religion of myth, an unscientific and unhistorical enterprise; and even the slight nuances of Nehru's view are lost in the Hindutvavadi's unabashed celebration of the historical mode. Notably, it is only the destruction of temples that, in the VHP's mistaken view, serves to distinguish Hinduism from other faiths: it is what renders the Hindus singularly into victims, and gives them a history they otherwise are said to lack.

GHEN's home page on Hindu temples disavows any interest in "the politicization of temples and the[ir] history" but nonetheless avers that "those who do not learn from history are condemned to relive it."[77] Should there be any doubt as to what history might be in store for those obdurate Hindus who do not comprehend the evil genius and mental psyche of the Muslim, a page reminds readers of "what happened" to Hindu temples. The "Moslem behavior pattern as recorded by Moslem historians of medieval India," we are told, furnishes a decisive account of the murderous activities of "Islamized invaders." Why these "invaders" are represented as "Islamized" rather than "Islamic" is not certain, but it is surely not for the charitable reason that they were not true Muslims, who had merely the veneer of Islam around them. One Islamic chronicle after another, it is maintained, documents the hatred of the invaders for the faith of the infidels, their contempt for idols, and their destruction of the idolater's temples. (This is doubtless the case, though the author of the webpage scarcely understands that these chronicles betray a characteristic tendency of the oppressors to leave behind an archive, even an exaggerated one, of their own ill-doings.) The invading Muslims, in brief, engaged in "mass slaughter of people not only during war" but after they had "emerged victorious"; they captured noncombatants and sold them throughout the Islamic world, thus rendering a free people into slavery and violating the convention whereby civilians are spared the retributions due to soldiers; they engaged in "forcible conversion to Islam of people who were in no position to resist," and stripped those who could not be so converted of their citizenship, turning them into "zimmis," or noncitizens; and on these "zimmis" they imposed "inhuman disabilities," appropriating their wealth and "holding in contempt all their institutions and expressions," cultural, religious, and social.[78] In this narrative, which seeks to etch in bold the "magnitude of Muslim Atrocities," (a webpage derived from yet another site that calls itself the "Library of Hindu History"),[79] it becomes wholly unnecessary to consider the politics of conquest, and a vocabulary inherited from modern institutional practices and political theories is introduced as the benchmark by which the conduct of Muslim invaders is to be judged. What, for instance, was the theory of "citizenship" in pre-Muslim India, and was there any notion of "rights," a term that everywhere is of relatively recent vintage? In that paradise called Aryavarta, the land of the Aryas or Hindus before Islam rudely entered into the scene, who conferred "citizenship" on whom, by what criteria, and with what consequences?

Not unexpectedly, the destruction of Hindu temples by Aurangzeb—who for Hindus has been iconic of Muslim barbarity since the colonial histories of the eighteenth century began enumerating the despotic tendencies of Islam—is enumerated at great length, but far more significant is the clustering together, on this home page, of tales of the destruction or appropriation of Hindu temples throughout the subcontinent and into the far-flung parts of the Indian diaspora. If one were to ask what makes the Indian diaspora *Indian*, if not the ubiquitousness of the commercial Hindi film, the enthroning of "Bharat Natyam" as the quintessential dance form of India which every young Indian woman must embrace, or the emergence of tandoori chicken as a metonym for Indian cuisine, then to the VHP it is the poignant desecration of Hindu temples in varied landscapes throughout the world.[80] A ruined or discarded temple is the sure sign of a Hindu presence; it is the only living evidence of a diaspora extending to antiquity: it is the reminder that everywhere Hindus, who (in the Hindutvavadi view) knew nothing of the ways of the world and the evil intent of monotheistic religions, have suffered the same fate. Screams one headline on hindunet, "600 Hindu Temples Destroyed/Damaged in Pakistan and Bangladesh!" and from there we jump to another headline drawn from the archives of *Hinduism Today*: "Fiji Temple Burned." For the one mosque destroyed by Hindus in Ayodhya— a destruction that is never fully conceded, since the Hindus chose to repossess what in truth had always been theirs—there were a dozen temples that the Muslims swiftly desecrated in Britain by way of revenge. Who else, the Hindutvavadi asks, writes that history?[81] Etymology—the science of comparative linguistics, itself reborn in the crucible of eighteenth-century theories of race and human origins—and destroyed temples *together* give the Hindutvavadis the universal history they have always desired. "Hindu Kush means Hindu Slaughter," Shrinandan Vyas reminds us in an article on the Internet, for it is in the mountain range of Eastern Afghanistan that goes by the name Hindu Kush that the first, and still unacknowledged, "genocide" of Hindus took place.[82] "Genocide" strikes Hindutvavadis as the apposite term, especially on websites, where the visceral effect is critical, to describe the cruel fate suffered by peaceful Hindus at the hand of Muslim barbarians. There is always the hope that the world will look upon the Hindu as it does upon the Jew, as a specimen of a race that must continually stave off the threat of extinction, and that has more than once been dealt a terrible death. Hindutvavadis deplore the "fact" that the world does not know of the many holocausts perpetrated by the Muslims, and the Kashmir Information Network on the web accords a prominent place on its site to the "AUSCHWITZ IN KASHMIR," highlighting with pictures the "atrocities on Kashmiris by Pakistan-trained terrorists."[83]

I have given a mere inkling of the Hindu histories that dominate on the Internet, and in conclusion it merits reiteration that the very proclivity to argue in the language of the historian shows how far the diasporic proponents of Hindutva have abandoned the language of Hinduism for the epistemological imperatives of modernity and the nation-state. Nothing resonates as strongly as their desire to strip Hinduism of myth, of its ahistoricist sensibilities, and to impose on the understanding of Hinduism and the Indian past alike the structures of a purportedly scientific history. The Hindutva historians have, in all these matters, embraced the methods of their adversaries: thus, nearly every lengthy article pretends to carry with it the paraphernalia of scholarship, and many are prefaced with a summary of the sources marshaled to construct the argument. "All the Encyclopaedias and National Geographic agree," writes Vyas at the outset of his aforementioned piece on the Hindu holocaust, "that the Hindu Kush is a place of Hindu genocide (similar to Dakau [*sic*] and Auschwitz). All the references are given. Please feel free to verify them." Typically, as in the article on "The Destruction of the Hindu Temples by Muslims, Part IV," found on the Satyameva Jayate website, no page numbers are ever furnished, nor are titles of works enumerated; nonetheless, a tone of authority is sought and injected by the note placed at the end: "Works of Arun Shourie, Harsh Narain, Jay Dubashi, and Sita Ram Goel have been used in this article."[84] The mention of "references" imparts a scholarly note to the piece, and the invitation to employ the verifiability hypothesis suggests the detachment of the scientist, the objectivity of the social scientist who has no ambition but the discernment of truth, and the scrupulousness of the investigator. I hasten to add that this is not atypical: the unattributed article, "The Real Akbar, The (not) so Great," is likewise based on a number of sources, though their worthiness as specimens of authoritative scholarship can be construed from the great affection that Hindutva historians have developed for Will Durant. "The world famous historian, Will Durant has written in his Story of Civilisation," writes Rajiv Varma in his Internet article on Muslim atrocities, that " 'the Mohammedan conquest of India was probably the bloodiest story in history.' "[85] The West be damned, but when the occasion demands, the authority of even its mediocre historians is construed as unimpeachable.

From their concerted endeavors to impart a precise historical specificity to the *Mahabharata* and the *Ramayana,* as evidenced by the laborious efforts at reconstructing the chronology of the events depicted in the epics and turning the principal characters into live historical figures who were the Moses, Abraham, Isaac, and Christ of Hinduism,[86] to the onslaught on the generally accepted theory of an Aryan migration to India—an onslaught at first headed, it is no accident, by an Indian aerospace engineer, who is described as valiantly having temporarily set aside his career in the interest of exposing the largest "hoax" in human history[87]—the Hindutvavadis have signified their attachment to historical discourses. The critics of Hindutva who dwell on it as a form of religious fanaticism and fundamentalism, doubtless with political ambitions, may be obfuscating a great deal more than they reveal in their analyses. That is not only because the Hindutvavadis are the least of the Hindus that one is likely to encounter; even their religiosity has something in it of mercantilism and the secular ethos of the marketplace. Historical discourses are preeminently the discourses of the nation,[88] and the Internet, which has something in common with the historical archive, making it intrinsically hospitable to the modernist sensibility of the historian, is poised to become the ground on which the advocates of Hindutva will stage their revisionist histories. Whether cyberspace is Republican is a matter on which I shall defer judgment; but it is poised, alarmingly, to become a Hindutva domain, considering that there are scarcely any websites that offer competing narratives.[89] "*Dharmakshetre, kurukshetre*" ("on the field of dharma, righteousness; on the field of the Kurus, the clan that is said to have given birth to Bharat or India"), says the Bhagavad Gita in its opening line, but today this might well be "*dharmaksetre, cyberksetre.*" If the computer scientist-historian types who inhabit Silicon Valley, and their diasporic brethren, have it their way, Hinduism will become that very "world historical religion" they have craved to see, and Hindutva history will be the most tangible product of the wave of globalization over which they preside from their diasporic vantagepoint.

Postscript: Los Angeles, August 2002

In the few years since this essay was first written and published, a number of phenomena have, it appears to me, conspired to lend renewed urgency to some of my observations and findings. In India, as elsewhere in the world, the Internet has witnessed a remarkable explosion, though some of the loose talk about computers entering every village, which the technocratic and political elites who dream about India's ascendancy to great power status indulge in, is premature and even comical to those aware of the pitiful shortcomings in basic infrastructural facilities throughout the country. Bangalore, and increasingly Hyderabad and Thiruvananthapuram (Trivandrum), may well be home to India's large "manpower" of computer software specialists, many of whom are women, but any other kind of development, such as assured supplies of water and electricity, have been slow to reach these cities. Few urban elites have had time to think of villages; indeed, the village, even while it has ruralized the country's urban landscapes, is rapidly disappearing as the locus of imagination and ethical thinking. But middle-class families in the metropolitan areas, a substantial number of which have some close relative settled in the United States, Britain, or Canada, have found the Internet of incalculable benefit in keeping two generations "connected" across the oceans. What remains "disconnected," or what is disavowed—a more mythic conception of Hinduism, complex traditions of hospitality, a more open reading of the past as well as the future—in the recent synergy on display between North American Hindus and many middle-class and professional Hindus in India itself is less often noticed.

The recent killings in Gujarat, however, provide the most poignant and alarming point of entry into the discussions, around which much of my essay has revolved, on the Indian diaspora, the politics of the Internet in diasporic communities, the Internet as a contested political terrain, and the Internet and the World Wide Web as domains friendly to Hindu militancy. There have been communal riots in India before, and most certainly in Gujarat and its capital, Ahmedabad; but the recent anti-Muslim violence, following the initial perpetration of an attack by a Muslim crowd upon a train carrying Hindu militants,[90] has gone far beyond any previous "riot," and not only because it has claimed 2,000 lives, displaced another 200,000 people, and lasted several months. The vast bulk of the fatalities have been Muslim, and even commentators noted for their restraint agree that a pogrom was instituted against the Muslims, who (in Gujarat, at least) have doubtless been reduced to second-class citizens in the country of their birth. Rarely have communal killings extended so far into the countryside, and just as infrequently have they been so orchestrated, so macabre and theatrical in their demonstrativeness, so indicative of a deep-seated hatred for the Muslim. That all this should have happened in Gujarat has struck some people, even those apprised of the state's recent bloody past and its enrollment, so to speak, in the ranks of the Hindu Right, as surprising and wholly unexpected. Gujarat, after all, has done well for itself: the poverty rate in the state is 22 percent, in comparison to 55 percent in India as a whole, the per capita income in 2000 was twice that of most other states; and economic growth has been steady. Gujarat is one of India's most "developed" states. The cherished theories of those who believe that education and industrialization are calculated to erode religious bigotry, communal passion, and the propensity toward violence lie in tatters. Gujarat is also the land of Mohandas Gandhi—the "Father of the Nation," the greatest son of the soil—and, beyond him, of Narasimha Mehta, the medieval *bhakta* (devotional poet) whose *bhajan* on what makes a person a true Vaishnava, a morally enlightened being, has endeared him to millions across the country over the last few centuries. How, then, could genocide take place in the land of Gandhi?[91]

If Gujarat, one of four Indian states governed by the right wing Bharatiya Janata Party, which advocates Hindu militancy, is unusually prosperous, it has also generated the most affluent diaspora of any Indian community. There are at least 2 million, and perhaps as many as 3 million, Gujaratis living outside India, and they almost certainly account for a greater portion of the 16 to 20 million diasporic Indians than any other community.[92] Perhaps as many as a third of the 1.8 million Indians residing in the United States are Gujaratis, and one has only to scan the community pages of Indian-American newspapers to come to an awareness of the ubiquitousness of the Gujarati presence in Indian diasporic life, extending from the Patel Brothers's grocery stores to the largely Gujarati-dominated jewelry showrooms found in abundance in the little Indias of the large American metropolises. The Gujarati Literary Academy estimated the number of Gujaratis in Britain in 2000 to be "well over half a million,"[93] and Rajdeep Sardesai has suggested that there are 1.7 million Kutchis (from Kutch, a region of Gujarat) overseas, not to mention other Gujaratis, particularly those from Ahmedabad.[94] Yet only the mere skeleton of a tale can be hung on these numbers, for the story of the Gujarati diaspora is doubtless one of the great untold narratives of the last millennium. Gujarati traders were among the most active members of the Indian Ocean trading system, and over time they became renowned for their entrepreneurial spirit, commercial networks, and business acumen. Moreover, as Ashutosh Varshney has recently speculated, "the Gujarati diaspora in the United States, Britain and Africa is fabulously wealthy . . . A lot of the new Gujarati wealth, at home and abroad, has gone to Hindu nationalist organizations."[95] Even in continental Europe, where the presence of Indians is not so marked, Gujaratis have carved out niches for themselves, cornering—to take one instance—the diamond business in Antwerp.

The most obvious questions arising from the above considerations are what relationship the Gujarati diaspora might have had to the anti-Muslim pogrom in Gujarat and, furthermore, what place, if any, the Internet occupies in the interstices of that nexus. In my original essay I was perhaps not sufficiently attentive to the subnational groups that comprise the Indian polity and the Indian diaspora, and consequently failed to reflect on whether certain Indian communities, such as the Gujaratis, are more hospitable—than Bengalis, Malayalis, Tamilians, Punjabis—to Hindu militancy, more inclined to assist in Hinduism's transformation from a religious and mythic language to a historical one that crafts, at the same time, a modernist historical sensibility of injured Hindu subjectivity. What is the political culture of diasporic Gujaratis, and what is their version of Gujarati, Hindu, and Indian culture? Though the violence in Gujarat is attributed by some to the extraordinary political presence of the Hindu Right in that state, and the political leadership of Gujarat has shown every inclination to treat Muslims as though they were hated foreigners, the role of the Gujarati diaspora in abetting the rise of the Hindu Right has not come under sustained scholarly scrutiny. The rise of the BJP to political ascendancy in India in the late 1980s occurred around the time when the Indian community in the United States began to register substantial growth and show increasing self-confidence. Little empirical work has been done on the money trail that is widely alleged to exist between the VHP-America and other organizations committed to Hindu rejuvenation and supremacy in the United States, Britain, and elsewhere, and like organizations in Gujarat and elsewhere in India,[96] but no one doubts that some of the immense wealth generated by overseas Gujaratis has gone to support Hindu militancy in Gujarat.[97]

Whatever the precise financial transactions that bind VHP-America and like organizations to the motherland, Gujarat has also occupied a peculiar iconic place in the transformation of Hinduism to Hindutva. Following independence in 1947, K. M. Munshi, a Gujarati writer and politician with a huge public following, endeavored to have the famous Temple of Somnath rebuilt by the Indian government. Munshi largely introduced the historical novel—a genre that has too often served the interests of those who wish to have historical credibility attached to their narratives without the accountability that the notion of historical truth demands—into the repertoire of Gujarati literature; and, not surprisingly, his historical novel on Somnath was immensely popular. This temple was sacked, with allegedly colossal loss of life, by Mahmud of Ghazni around 1000 C.E. on one of his many raids into India, and its destruction, which British writers did everything to keep etched in Hindu memory, came to be described by some nationalist Hindus as a lasting symbol of Islam's perfidy and the forced submission of Hindus to Muslim rule. It is from Somnath that L. K. Advani, another Gujarati who is the present home minister in the Indian government and the architect of the Hindutva triumph, launched what might justly be described as the contemporary phase of Indian politics in 1989 when he set out on a *rath yatra* (pilgrimage by chariot) to raise awareness among Hindus of historical wrongs said to have been perpetrated upon them by Muslims. The sensibility that he displays is the one most frequently encountered, as I have suggested in my essay, among the mainly middle-class and professional Hindus settled in the United States.

To gauge the strength of the diasporic Gujarati community, it is enough to consider that when a powerful earthquake struck the state in January 2001, wiping out entire towns and villages and leaving behind casualties in excess of 20,000 people, millions of dollars were raised in a few days to aid and rehabilitate victims and the families of the deceased. The mobilization of the Gujarati diaspora was, as many Indians conceded, an extraordinary and inspirational sight to behold. Almost nothing was as effective as the Internet in apprising the worldwide Gujarati community of the news from Gujarat, transmitting appeals for assistance, and collecting money and aid in kind. In 1999, by way of contrast, a supercyclone struck the eastern state of Orissa, killing tens of thousands, immersing nearly half of the impoverished state under water. Yet the tragedy of Orissa barely made the news, and even the government of India, which is responsive to the pressures of ethnic and linguistic groups, reluctantly furnished to the people of Orissa, who are poorly represented in the diaspora, a fraction of the aid that was given to Gujarat.[98] There is an Internet divide, as well, between Gujarat and Orissa: the telecommunications facilities of Orissa are woefully inadequate, and many fewer Oriyas utilized e-mail to relate harrowing tales of life under water. One can only adhere to the view that the Internet is somehow an equalizer if one is prepared to overlook its political economy.

It may be premature to speculate on the precise ways in which the Internet has been brought to bear upon the killings in Gujarat. If the word *riot* had not been less apt where the vast bulk of the killing was perpetrated by members of one community while the victims were largely drawn from another faith, it would not have been an excess to describe Gujarat 2002 as India's first TV riot. Nonetheless, Gujarat's orgy of violence may not inaccurately be described as India's first media killings: independent television stations provided extensive coverage and graphic pictures of arson, looting, and mutilated corpses. There are also reliable reports of the extensive and macabre use of cell phones: hooligans, and even their political bosses, apparently positioned themselves at vital nodal points in Ahmedabad, and by cell phone directed the killers and arsonists to those areas where, in their estimation, the mayhem existed at dangerously *low* levels. There have been reports that Muslims in more affluent communities who found themselves unable to leave their houses for risk to their lives, and whose urgent calls to the police for protection went unheeded, frantically logged on to the Internet in an attempt to reach friends, alert newspapers, and even, as it were, leave behind a record of their desperate will to survive.

Communal violence is indubitably a characteristic aspect of the social and political life of contemporary India, but one of the numerous ways in which Gujarat 2002 stands apart is the deep level of outrage experienced by many Indians, at home and in the diaspora, at the profound violation of all norms of humanity. It would be an enormous stretch to speak of the "emancipatory" possibilities of the Internet at this juncture, but entire websites came up, within days after the massacres began, to document the death and destruction in Gujarat, to help expose the politicians whose patronage gave succor to rapists, murderers, and arsonists, and to energize people to action.[99] It is not unreasonable to suggest that the institution of the pogrom coincided not accidentally with Israel's incursion into the West Bank, and that the advocates of Hindu militancy rightly surmised that events in Palestine would overshadow the slaughter of Muslims in India; and yet, they may well have underestimated the degree to which the Internet can be rendered serviceable as a vehicle for the promotion of human rights and to bring perpetrators of crimes to justice. However inadequate the coverage of anti-Muslim violence in India around the world, diasporic Indians, and their allies in progressive movements across the United States, stumbled upon compelling and irrefutable evidence on the Internet of the carnage in Gujarat even as state officials denied the extent of the violence and, when this line of defense could no longer be sustained, raised the specter of "normalcy."

In less than three months after the killings began in late February, both international organizations—Human Rights Watch and Amnesty International among them—and domestic nongovernmental organizations—had made available on the Internet a dozen or more authoritative reports of the killings, which made it impossible for the governments of Gujarat and India to furnish their own narratives as the only ones that could lay claim to the truth.[100] Moreover, as allegations of ties between Hindu militants in India and significant portions of the large Hindu communities in the United States and Britain began to surface, the Internet became a rallying point for nonresident Indians (NRIs) alarmed at hearing that the violence in Gujarat was being conducted with the active moral and financial assistance of affluent Indians based overseas who themselves did not have to live with the frightful consequences of violence. On the website Rediff.com, which commands the attention of the greater bulk of the Indian diasporic audience, the former director of the Reserve Bank of India, I. G. Patel, himself a NRI Gujarati, was quoted pleading with NRIs that they ought "not to donate money to spread hatred in India, neither to the VHP nor to Islamic fundamentalists. . . . Don't give it to people who propagate violence."[101] Emboldened by the increasing outrage expressed the world over at the events in Gujarat, a coalition of Indian organizations took out an ad in printed newspapers of the diasporic Indian American community and on the Internet warning unsuspecting Indians that their donations were being funneled to extremist organizations: "Did Our Generosity Fund the Carnage in Gujarat?"[102]

As I have, however, been at some pains to argue in this essay, there is ample reason to think that the Internet has not merely been utilized more effectively by Hindutvavadis, but that as a space somewhat akin to the hotel lobby, where stories may be exchanged and rumors are stoked, it has been hospitable to those who wish to argue in the language of scientific history but are not prepared to be subject to those standards of accountability that are generally the norm in academic narratives. Consequently, it comes as no surprise that Gujarat has also been the occasion for a spurt of activity on Hindutva websites, and that the Hindutva presence on the net is taking on the same gargantuan and dispersed characteristics that one associates with Hinduism. The sites I explored in my essay, those of GHEN [Global Hindu Electronic Network] and VHP, among others, have become more ambitious and attentive to contemporary politics, but in the intervening years the Bajrang Dal, a paramilitary organization that prides itself on the defense of the Hindu nation, has since put up a website that is most expressive of the latest phase of Hindu militancy. Thus, at HinduUnity.org, there is no expression of remorse at the killings of Muslims, but rather a paean only to those fifty-eight Hindus whose death in the train at the hands of people whose identity still remains to be determined, apparently prompted Hindus to abandon their meekness and create a climate of total fear. Aggressiveness, a militarized conception of Hindu society, and extreme intolerance of the Muslim are proudly displayed as the three characteristics of a rejuvenated Hinduism. On the home page, viewers are greeted by the icon of a growling tiger, followed by news snippets pointing to Muslim perfidy and the Islamic conspiracy to silence competing faiths. Inflammatory "news" items—"Urgent! Forceful Conversion of Two Minor Hindu Girls to Islam"—are followed by updates on al-Qaeda and Muslim militancy in Kashmir, choice quotations from the Qu'ran that purport to show that Islam can envision only death for "idolaters" (for instance, chapter 9, verse 5), and an impressive array of articles and links that serve no purpose but to persuade Hindus that Islam seeks worldwide domination and thus to encourage Hindus to an aggressive defense of the "motherland."

For North American Hindus, in particular, HinduUnity.org holds out the example of Jewish history as a template for discerning Hindus who wish to comprehend how they might profit from their own brutalized past. Scarcely cognizant of the fact that in Israel the term *holocausts* is never used in the plural, since only "the Holocaust" is recognized, Bajrang Dal activists welcome viewers to the "Hindu Holocaust Museum." Here it is argued that painful as the Jewish Holocaust was, it can be viewed as "an extremely effective trigger for Jewish society to actively go about organising itself, to the extent that it may be argued that the Holocaust has, in fact, been the main trigger for the subsequent consolidation of the Jewish community, and its resultant respect amongst the international community." "Where," the page asks in an evidently anguished and puzzled tone, "is the Hindu Holocaust Museum?" Under this page, Hindus are offered a capsule "History of the Jews," an evident example— and admonishment—to Hindus who seem incapable of uniting themselves even in the cause of self-preservation. And since the very idea of a "Hindu Holocaust" might seem somewhat bizarre to an innocent surfer, the page is graced by a quotation from François Gautier, *Le Figaro*'s correspondent in India over the last three decades: "The massacres perpetrated by Muslims in India are unparalleled in history, bigger than the holocaust of the Jews by the Nazis; or the massacre of the Armenians by the Turks; more extensive even than the slaughter of the South American native populations by the invading Spanish and Portuguese."[103] The Jew, at least, can make something from his suffering: he is able to enlist the discourses of science and history in documenting the past and making it work productively for him, to the point where he can claim a monopoly over suffering, but does the Hindu have a similar will to survival and power? If museums are nearly the temples of advanced polities, does it not behoove Hindus to make a similar spectacle of their oppression under Muslims?

The Jewish example is followed so far that, in a related website, "Welcome to the World of Hindu Holocaust," August 14, the day that marks the vivisection of

India and the creation (from the Hindutva perspective) of the theocratic Muslim state of Pakistan, is designated "Hindu Holocaust Day," and the slogan, "Lest we forget . . ." is splashed across the screen.[104] The "Hindu Holocaust down the Timeline," which opens out to the chamber of horrors—detailed pages on the genocide of Hindus under "medieval Jehadi barbarism," during the partition of India, and under the generals in East Pakistan, to name only three periods of history—need not be enumerated at length: suffice to reiterate the point I first advanced in my essay, that Hindutvavadis are heavily invested in "history" as the authentic sign of the modern. It is the Hindu's own estrangement from his past—an estrangement produced by the confluence of the triumph of the ahistoric mode in Indian thinking, the long years of submission under Muslim rule, and the malicious falsification of history by the British—that makes him rootless and an eternal victim, a pawn rather than a subject of history. Though much has been said in the literature about the Internet as a space for the circulation of rumors and conspiratorial theories, by far the greater consideration that researchers and scholars will have to ponder over is whether the Internet will not lead to a further enthronement of the historical mode of argumentation, and what consequences that may have in shrinking the space of the imaginary in diasporic communities.

In my essay, I had advanced the idea of an Indian/Hindu diaspora that extends far beyond the fifteen to twenty million Hindus living overseas to include those "resident non-Indians," perhaps as many as two hundred million of them, who, though they may make their home in Bangalore, Mumbai, or Delhi, already imagine themselves as part of the North American Hindu community. Sustained perusal of Hindutva literature and websites, in particular, now leads me to advance a yet more radical thesis—namely, that from the Hindutva perspective, nearly the entire Hindu population of some eight hundred million, barring those few millions who are "awakened" to the militant defense of their homeland, displays the characteristics of diasporic people—people living without a true awareness of their past, in exile from history, barely in touch with themselves. The vanguard of true Hindus—the Hindutvavadis who are the footsoldiers of the VHP, the RSS, the Bajrang Dal, the Shiv Sena, the Bharatiya Janata Party, and other similar political and paramilitary organizations, as well as the supporters of Hindu militancy in the purportedly secular societies of the West who are conversant with the critical and indispensable discourses of science, history, and management—are thus charged with shepherding errant Hindus to their new home in the "Hindu Rashtra," the Nation of Hindus. Let us recall what is commonly forgotten: that the notion of the diaspora has, historically speaking, entailed the idea of the return to the homeland. Curiously, those whom we customarily imagine as diasporic Hindus, and especially North American Hindus, are already emblazoned in Hindutva thinking as less diasporic, indeed as comfortably housed in the faith from which their countrymen and countrywomen in India are still largely exiled.

Notes

1. Peter F. Drucker, "Beyond the Information Revolution," *Atlantic Monthly,* October 1999, 47–57. I am grateful to my former research assistant, Ashok Hegde, for his help with library work, and to David Palumbo-Liu, Khachig Tololyan, Rachel Lee, Yossi Shain, and Jim Wilgten for their comments on earlier versions of this paper.

2. As an instance, one might adduce the report of how the homeless in the greater Los Angeles area have taken to the Internet, nursing not only e-commerce ambitions, but creating a new home for themselves. Apparently, according to this report, librarians in Los Angeles and elsewhere report that on some days, as many as 75 percent of the free Internet terminals in public libraries are being used by the homeless. See Greg Miller, "Cyberspace Comes to Skid Row," *Los Angeles Times,* (November 18, 1999), A1, A20–21.

3. *Mondo 2000,* no. 1 (1989): 11. *Mondo 2000* ceased to be in print a few years ago, but similar clichés about the Internet as a radically new space for the articulation of freedom and for humanity's reconnection with the idea of enchantment continue to proliferate down to the present day. We are given assurance that information wants and struggles to be free, that information knows no boundaries or constraints. *Mondo's* disappearance barely a few years after its emergence makes its own point: the web, far from constituting a radical departure from the sociological arrangements of American society, only expands geometrically upon the idea of obsolescence that has been so characteristic a feature of the American polity and economy.

4. Esther Dyson, George Gilder, Jay Keyworth, and Alvin Toffler, "A Magna Carta for the Knowledge Age," *New Perspectives Quarterly* 11, no. 4 (Fall 1994), 28.

5. Ibid.

6. Ibid.

7. Ibid.

8. Ibid., 31–32. Even a cursory reading of the literature leaves one with the inescapable feeling that though the hacker is viewed as a dangerous figure who is liable to crack open the computer files of the Pentagon and compromise the national security of the United States, he is simultaneously a widely admired figure. The daredevil in him taunts not only bureaucrats at the Pentagon, the sleuths of the U.S. Justice Department, and the managers of complex financial and banking systems, but even computer scientists and the software specialists of Silicon Valley. He is the Jesse James and Billy the Kid of the late twentieth century: however regrettable his violation of, and disrespect for, the law, he is that maverick, entrepreneur, and lone ranger who stands forth as an American icon. The political biography of the hacker remains to be written. For a preliminary consideration of "hacktivism," see Amy Harmon, "'Hacktivists' of All Persuasions Take Their Struggle to the Web," *New York Times* (October 31, 1998); a more detailed reading is furnished in Dorothy E. Denning, "Activism, Hacktivism, and Cyberterrorism: The Internet As a Tool for Influencing Foreign Policy," online at <http://www.nautilus.org/info-policy/workshop/papers/denning.html>.

9. José Angel Gurria, from a speech reported by Rodolfo Montes, "Chiapas Is a War of Ink and Internet," *Reforma* April 26, 1995, and quoted in David Ronfeldt, John Arquilla, Graham E. Fuller, and Melissa Fuller, *The Zapatista Social Netwar in Mexico* (Santa Monica: RAND, for the United States Army, 1998), 4.

10. Subcomandte Marcos, cited in Ronfeldt et al., *The Zapatista Social Netwar,* 70. Writing from a perspective wholly sympathetic to the Zapatistas, Harry Cleaver remarked, in a notable study on their deployment of the Internet, that "through their ability to extend their political reach via modern computer networks the Zapatistas have woven a new electronic fabric of struggle to carry their revolution throughout Mexico and around the world." See his "The Zapatistas and the Electronic Fabric of Struggle," online at: <http://www.eco.utexas.edu/faculty/Cleaver/zaps.html>.

11. Ronfeldt et al., *The Zapatista Social Netwar,* 8; see also John Arquilla and David Ronfeldt, *Cyberwar Is Coming!* (Santa Monica: RAND, 1996), reprinted from *Comparative Strategy* 12 (1993): 141–65. For the earliest articulation of Internet warfare, see David Ronfeldt, *Cyberocracy, Cyberspace, and Cyberology: Political Effects of the Information Revolution* (Santa Monica: RAND, 1991).

12. See Ricardo Dominguez, "Digital Zapatismo" (1998), online at <http://www.nyu.edu/projects/wary/DigZap.html>.

13. As is now well known, the term *rhizomes* made its first appearance in Gilles Deleuze and Félix Guattari, *A Thousand Plateaus: Capitalism and Schizophrenia,* trans. Brian Massumi (Minneapolis: University of Minnesota Press, 1987). "Rhizomatic" thinking, which is nonlinear, anarchic, nomadic, deterritorialized, multiplicitous, and so on, is differentiated from "arbolic" thinking, which is linear, hierarchic, sedentary, territorialized, binary, and homogeneous and has characterized the scientific thought of the modern West. It is a commonplace in leftist Internet circles to celebrate the work of Deleuze and Guattari as the theoretical platform for a radical Internet-based insurrectionary democracy: For the most extended Internet expression of these sentiments, see Stefan Wray, "Rhizomes, Nomads, and Resistant Internet Use," (July 7, 1998), online at <http://www.nyu.edu/projects/wray/RhizNom.html>.

14. See Zygmunt Bauman, *Globalization: The Human Consequences* (New York: Columbia University Press, 1998), 88. To speak of Indian elites as finally learning to "live in time" is not to echo the cliched Orientalist expressions of Indians (especially Hindus) as outside time, or the supposed Indian propensity to conceive of time as "cyclical" rather than "linear," but rather to point to the manner in which clock-time has begun to impose its tyranny on a people who have lived with pluralistic conceptions of time. In India, as elsewhere, the American idiom "time is money" has begun to alter the frameworks of social relations. For a brief consideration of the cultural histories of time, see Vinay Lal, "The Politics of Time at the Cusp of the Millennium," *Humanscape* 6, no. 12 (December 1999): 5–12.

15. For an unraveling of the term *franchise* see Vivian Sobchack, "Democratic Franchise and the Electronic Frontier," in Ziauddin Sardar and Jerome R. Ravetz, eds., *Cyberfutures: Culture and Politics on the Information Superhighway* (London: Pluto Press, 1996), 77–89.

16. Ziauddin Sardar, "alt.civilizations.faq: Cyberspace As the Darker Side of the West," in Sardar and Ravetz, eds., *Cyberfutures,* 15.

17. On the distinction between "place" and "space" see Anthony Giddens, *The Consequences of Modernity* (Stanford, CA: Stanford University Press, 1990).

18. Carlos Fuentes, "Chiapas: Latin America's First Post-Communist Rebellion," *New Perspectives Quarterly* 11, no. 2 (spring 1994): 56.

19. For a withering critique of postmodernism's pretensions, see Ziauddin Sardar, *Postmodernism and the Other: The New Imperialism of Western Culture* (London: Pluto Press, 1998).

20. Greg Miller, "Internet Fueled Global Interest in Disruptions," *Los Angeles Times* (December 2, 1999), A24. Mike Dolan, field director for Public Citizens' Global Trade Watch, one of the principal groups that orchestrated the demonstrations against WTO, is reported as saying, "The Internet has become the latest greatest arrow in our quiver of social activism. . . . the Internet benefits us more than the corporate and government elites we're fighting." Among the websites launched to combat the WTO, are <www.seattle99.org>, <www.agitprop.org>, <www.globalizethis.org>, and <www.gatt.org>.

21. David Shenk, *Data Smog: Surviving the Information Glut* (New York: Harper Collins, 1997).

22. Amartya Sen, undoubtedly the world's leading authority on famines, has more than once made the empirical observation that no modern democracy has ever been afflicted by famine. In the course of the last fifty years, the people who have had to face famine have all been victims of authoritarian or despotic regimes, as the examples of the Soviet Union under Josef Stalin, China under Mao Zedong, or contemporary Somalia unequivocally suggest. See Sen, *Poverty and Famines* (Oxford: Clarendon Press, 1981); and Jean Dreze and Amartya Sen, eds., *Hunger and Public Action*, 3 vols. (Oxford: Clarendon Press, 1989).

23. No doubt, as with colonization of untamed territories and what were termed "wastelands," the women will—to put it provocatively—follow men. It can be argued that the Internet might possibly furnish women with a way of bypassing patriarchal institutions and social practices, and enable them to forge their own democratic communities, but as of the moment this is an open question.

24. The 1990 census placed the average household income of Indian Americans at $60,903, above that of Japanese-Americans and Chinese-Americans. I have seen them described as the most affluent ethnic community in the United States; other studies place them below whites and Jews; and yet others describe them as the community with the largest household income. This problem is commonly encountered, since researchers draw upon different databases; but what is transparent is that Indian Americans are well-placed in American society.

25. On the development of the software industry in Bangalore, see Salim Lakha, "Growth of Computer Software Industry in India," *Economic and Political Weekly* (January 6, 1990), John Stremlau, "Bangalore: India's Silicon City," *Monthly Review* (November 1996); Richard Heeks, *India's Software Industry: State Policy, Liberalisation, and Industrial Development* (New Delhi: Sage, 1996); and Monica Prasad, "International Capital on 'Silicon Plateau': Work and Control in India's Computer Industry," *Social Forces* 77, no. 2 (December 1998), 429–52, especially 434–37. A less scholarly, but engaging, account is offered by Richard Rapaport, "Bangalore: Western Technology Giants?" *Wired* 4, no. 2 (February 1996), 109–14, 164–70.

26. In the Hindi version of the joke, Ajit asks Robert to place the hero in "liquid oxygen": liquid won't let him live, and oxygen won't let him die. It doesn't only *sound* absurd—it *is*.

27. For a recent profile of the Indian American community, see Karen Leonard, *The South Asian Americans* (Westport, CT: Greenwood Press, 1997).

28. Ronald Takaki, *Strangers from a Different Shore: A History of Asian Americans* (New York: Penguin, 1989), 294–314.

29. I owe this humorous and not inaccurate formulation to my ethnomusicologist friend Daniel Neuman.

30. John Lancaster, "Activism Boosts India's Fortunes: Politically Vocal Immigrants Help Tilt Policy in Washington," *Washington Post* (October 9, 1999), A1.

31. A message demanding that Warner Brothers issue an apology to Hindus and the film be altered was circulated on the Internet by American Hindus against Defamation (AHAD), a group convened by the Vishwa Hindu Parishad-America, whose activities are discussed below at greater length. AHAD's letter to Warner Brothers on August 3, 1999 stated that "We, American Hindus Against Defamation are baffled, disgusted and annoyed by the use of the *shloka* [verse], and fail to understand your intent and the relevance of its usage." On a subsequent occasion, AHAD warned Warner Brothers that the "billion strong Hindu community around the world" would not remain a "silent spectator to the humiliation of its religious beliefs and scriptures." See the message of August 21, 1999 circulated by Devant, <devant@tstt.net.tt>.

32. The dalits were formerly referred to as "untouchables"; they are the outcasts of the Indian society, the "wretched of the earth" who make their living as scavengers, sweepers, tanners, landless laborers, or pursuing other jobs that most caste Hindus consider polluting.

33. Viji Sundaram, "Diet, Dress Code Enrage Hindu Worshippers," *India-West* (March 31, 1995), A1, A12.
34. It is important to mention this, as some people may argue that American or white Hindus are more likely to adopt the orthodox versions of the faith than Indian Hindus in the United States. White Sikhs, for instance, are known to be more rigidly observant of the symbols and practices of their faith than are Indian Sikhs.
35. R. S. Sharma, *In Defence of "Ancient India."* (New Delhi: People's Publishing House, 1978), 20–21.
36. See Vinay Lal, "The Discourse of History and the Crisis at Ayodhya: Reflections on the Production of Knowledge, Freedom, and the Future of India," *Emergences* 5–6 (1993–94), 4–44.
37. Ashok Singhal, quoted in Vishwa Hindu Parishad of Chicago (VHP), *Seventeenth Annual Calendar* (Chicago: VHP, 1995).
38. One could point to the financial activities of the World Hindu Council, the Vishwa Hindu Parishad (VHP), or the support lavished upon the Hawaii-based newspaper *Hinduism Today,* which is devoted to diasporic Hinduism, by the Hindu Heritage Endowment. See also A. Rogers, "India Seeks Financial Help from Overseas Indians," *Traces World News Digest* 3 (July–September 1998), online at <http://www.transcomm.ox.ac.uk>.
39. *Indian Express,* (January 16, 1993), various city editions; the ad was reprinted in *India-West,* (February 12, 1993). It is heartening to note that a group of people describing themselves as "Indian Citizens in India" placed an ad in the same newspapers (*Indian Express,* January 26, 1993 and *India-West,* February 12, 1993) questioning the political and ethical propriety of nonresident Hindus: "Is it not presumptuous of the Indians who left 'mother Bharat' and caused a severe brain drain to dictate how we Indians, who remained behind should run our country?" There was no ban on Hindutva organizations, but the rumor took on a life of its own—as indeed rumors do.
40. *Indian Express,* January 16, 1993.
41. Federation of Hindu Associations (FHA), *Bhagwan's Call for Dharma Raksha* [including the publication *Hinduism Simplified*] (Diamond Bar, CA: FHA, [1999?]).
42. Ibid.
43. See the letter, protesting the award, by Vinay Lal et al. in *India-West,* (June 23, 1995), 5.
44. See Sudhir Kakar, *The Colours of Violence* (Delhi: Viking, 1995), 197–214, for the analysis of a similar speech by Sadhvi Ritambhara.
45. See Julius Lipner, "Ancient Banyan: An Inquiry into the Meaning of 'Hinduness,'" *Religious Studies* 32 (1996): 109–26. Among observing Hindus, it is widely believed that the water (*jal*) of the Ganga is sacred, and dying persons are often given a sip of this water to provide them solace and ease their passage into the next life. This Ganga jal is sometimes stored in a bottle at home.
46. See Luther P. Gerlach, "Protest Movements and the Construction of Risk," in B. B. Johnson and V. T. Covello, eds., *The Social Construction of Risk* (Boston: D. Reidel, 1987), 115, as cited in Ronfeldt et al., *The Zapatista Social Netwar,* 114.
47. On "swarming" and "flooding," see Ronfeldt, et al., *The Zapatista Social Netwar,* but also Stefan Wray, "Transforming Luddite Resistance into Virtual Luddite Resistance: Weaving a World Wide Web of Electronic Civil Disobedience," (April 7, 1998), online at <http://www.nyu.edu/projects/wray/luddite.html>. Needless to say, 330 million is merely a conventional number, but the concern by diasporic Hindus that this subjects Hinduism to mockery is once again amply witnessed in *Bhagwan's Call for Dharma Raksha* and scores of other like publications. In a section under "Hinduism Simplified," this "problem" of "millions Gods" [*sic*] is described as "lots of misunderstandings," and later, in a portion entitled "What Hinduism Is Not?" it is averred that "Hinduism is not a religion of 330 million Gods. In fact, it is monotheistic polytheism" (n.p.).

48. Arjun Appadurai, "Global Ethnoscapes: Notes and Queries for a Transnational Anthropology," in Richard G. Fox, ed., *Recpaturing Anthropology: Working in the Present* (Santa Fe: School of American Research Publications, 1991), 202.

49. Steven Vertovec, "Three Meanings of 'Diaspora,' Exemplified among South Asian Religions," *Diaspora* 6, no. 3 (1997): 281.

50. All these instances are drawn from the "Library of Hindu History," which can be found online at <http://www.vhp.org/hindu_history>.

51. See <http://www.tezcat.com/~bnaik/chinmaya.html>.

52. See <http://www.bjp.org> and <http://www.rss.org>.

53. "Award Recipient," *India-West* (March 15, 1996), C20.

54. See <http://rbhatnagar.csm.uc.edu:8080/kashmir/html>. Over four dozen articles are linked to the page.

55. See <http://hindunet.org/srh_home/1997_12/0040.html> for an article, reproduced from the *Times of India* (December 22, 1997), by Srichand P. Hinduja entitled "All Indians are Hindus."

56. See <http://rbhatnagar.csm.uc.edu:8080/ramjanmabhoomi.html>.

57. A partial profile of the membership of the RSS and the supporters of Hindutva can be found in Tapan Bose et al., *Khaki Shorts and Saffron Flags,* Tracts for the Times No. 1 (Delhi: Orient Longman, 1993).

58. See Ashis Nandy et al., *Creating a Nationality: The Ramjanmabhumi Movement and Fear of the Self* (Delhi: Oxford University Press, 1995).

59. Narendra Nath Datta (1863–1902), better known as Swami Vivekananda, was the chief disciple of Sri Ramakrishna, a renowned Bengali mystic who is often seen as one of the supreme embodiments of Indian spirituality. Vivekananda established the Ramakrishna Mission, and so introduced not only a new monastic order but also a set of charitable institutions, such as schools and hospitals, that are still active in India today. He took the teachings of Hinduism to the West, propagated a more integral version of the faith, and urged the youth to work toward a "new India." Though his master, Sri Ramakrishna, could become delirious with devotion to Kali, Vivekananda is said to have attached more importance to social work and intellectual discrimination as modes of apprehending the divine.

60. Large statues of Vivekananda have been installed recently in both Trinidad and Chicago.

61. See <http://www.hindunet.org/vivekananda/as_interview>.

62. Ibid.

63. The Vishwa Hindu Parishad of the United States has embraced an expansionist program for the Indian nation-state. One of its recent publications cites, with evident approval, the cherished hope of the Rashtriya Swayamsevak Sangh (RSS) that the "next century will surely [be] the Hindu century," and should this sound implausible, readers are reminded that after the "Mahabharatha War, our culture spread to China, Japan and [the] Americas. The Red Indians of America are the descendants of Hindus who went there some 4000 years ago." These are the words of K. S. Sudharshan, Sat Sarkaryavah (Joint General Secretary) of the RSS, quoted in VHP of Chicago, *Fourteenth Anniversary Calendar* (Chicago: VHP, 1992), 1.

64. See <http://www.hindunet.org/vivekananda/as_interview>.

65. The episode is discussed in Ramachandra Gandhi, *Sita's Kitchen: A Testimony of Faith and Inquiry* (New Delhi: Penguin, 1992), 10. The discussion by Rajni Bakshi, *The Dispute over Swami Vivekananda's Legacy: A Warning and an Opportunity* (Mapusa, Goa: The Other India Press, 1994), is of some use.

66. Swami Vivekananda, "The Future of India," in *Complete Works of Swami Vivekananda,* 8 vols. (Mayavati, India: Advaita Ashram, 1964), 3:289.

67. Ibid.

68. See <http://www.flex.com/~jai/satyamevajayate>.

69. See <http://members.aol.com/_ht_a/Jyotishi/index.html>.

70. "Prophet of Terror and the Religion of Peace—Part I," online at <http://www.flex.com~jai/satyamevajayate/mohwar1.html>. Part III is available at <mohwar3.html>.

71. "The X-Rated Paradise of Islam," online at <http://www.flex.com/~jai/satyamevajayate/heaven.html>.

72. An impressive website, designed from the standpoint of Indian nationalism, is devoted to the 1971 war of "liberation" that led to the defeat of Pakistan and the creation of the new sovereign state of Bangladesh; see <http://www.freeindia.org/1971war>.

73. See the e-mail message by Aditi Chaturvedi, October 17, 1999, available from <devant@tstt.net.tt>, entitled "Undermining Hinduism by Labeling it As Mythology," which begins, "Last month Indian Express inaugurated their new site on Hinduism and contemptuously titled it 'www.hindumythology.com'. The title of course is a not so subtle reflection of the regard that Indian Express has for Hindu beliefs. The implicit suggestion is clearly motivated by a negative approach towards Hinduism. *Obviously many Hindus on the net are not very happy at having their spiritual beliefs termed as 'mythology'* [emphasis added]." I by no means wish to convey the impression that myths do not on occasion create their own oppressions, but secularists and their "fundamentalist" foes are united in their aversion for myth, and it is the consensus behind history as a form of knowledge that has barely been investigated or critiqued.

74. Jawaharlal Nehru, *The Discovery of India* (Calcutta: Signet Press, 1946; reprint Delhi: Oxford University Press/Jawaharlal Nehru Memorial Fund, 1982), 102.

75. Among the more naive of such attempts to furnish Indians with a historical sensibility is Peter van der Veer, *Religious Nationalism: Hindus and Muslims in India* (Berkeley and Los Angeles: University of California Press, 1994); among the more complex efforts to contest the colonial charge that Indians were insensitive to historical thinking is the influential work by Nicholas Dirks, *The Hollow Crown: Ethnohistory of an Indian Kingdom* (Cambridge: Cambridge University Press, 1987; 2d ed., paperback, Ann Arbor: University of Michigan Press, 1992). It is possible to agree with the orientalist reading that Indians did not produce a historical literature; but that cannot be taken as signifying one's consent with the proposition that this was a "lack" as such. The ahistoricity of the Indian sensibility remains one of the most attractive features of Indian civilization.

76. Nehru, *Discovery of India*, 102.

77. "History of Hindu Temples," online at <http://www.vhp.org>.

78. See <http://www.hindunet.org/alt_hindu/1994/msg00658.html>.

79. Rajiv Varma, "The Magnitude of Muslim Atrocities" and "Destruction of Hindu Temples by Aurangzeb," online at <http://www.hindunet.org/hindu_history>.

80. Though there are many Indian cuisines, they have been reduced to north Indian tandoori food in the diaspora; similarly, there are several dance forms—Kathak, Odissi, Bharat Natyam, and Manipuri, among others. Bharat Natyam, literally "the dance of India," reigns supreme among diasporic Indian women (or rather, their parents). Ironically, as much recent scholarship has established, Bharat Natyam, seen in the diaspora as an embodiment of the timeless cultural traditions of an ancient civilization, is not unreasonably described as an "invented tradition," and in its present form it was essentially revived in the early twentieth century. Scholars of the Indian diaspora have not been sufficiently attentive to these kinds of considerations, just as they have studiously ignored the place of the commercial Hindi cinema in the diaspora. Far too much attention has been lavished on Gurinder Chadha, Hanif Kureishi, Mira Nair, and Deepa Mehta, though Indian families show comparatively little interest in their films. Indeed, these films point to an emerging history of the Indian diaspora *as* consumption for advocates of multiculturalism; meanwhile, in Indonesia, Fiji, Mauritius, Canada, Guyana, the United States, and elsewhere, the popular Hindi film continues to provide the Indian population, and often the "locals," with some clues about the mythic structuring of their civilization.

81. See <http://www.hindunet.org/alt.hindu/1994/msg00365.html> (no longer available as of December 2002) and <http://www.spiritweb.org/HinduismToday/94-08-Fiji_Temple_Burned.html>.

82. See <http://www.hindunet.org/hindu_history/modern/hindu_kush.html>.

83. See <http://jammu-kashmir.org/KIN/Atrocities/index.html>.

84. See <http://www.flex.com/~jai/satyamevajayate/temples4.html>.

85. See <http://www.hindunet.org/hindu_history/modern/moghal_atro.html>.

86. The following articles, by Dr. P. V. Vartak and others, in the "Library of Hindu History" are useful: "Mahabharata: A Myth of Reality"; "The Mahabharat Chronology"; "Mahabharat: An Astronomical Proof from the Bhagavat Puraan"; "The Scientific Dating of the Mahabharat War"; and "Astronomical Dating of the Ramayan." All can be found online at <http://www.hindunet.org/hindu_history>. The attempt in each case, wholly unsuccessful, is to provide a firm date for events described in the Ramayana and the Mahabharata. Why this might be important for Hindutvavadis can be understood from the fact that the earliest firm (or nearly firm) dates that can be furnished for ancient Indian history relate to the lives of the Buddha (founder of Buddhism) and Mahavira (founder of Jainism), both of whom signaled their dissent from Hinduism in the sixth century B.C.E. The mythicity of Hinduism was never much of an embarrassment to Hindus until the nineteenth century, and the ascendancy of history, alongside the emergence of the nation-state, has greatly accelerated the process in the period after independence. An engaging perspective on these questions, focusing on the Tamils and Sinhalese in Sri Lanka, is to be found in E. Valentine Daniel, *Charred Lullabies: Chapters in an Anthropology of Violence* (Princeton, NJ: Princeton University Press, 1996); see also Lal, "The Discourse of History," and Vinay Lal, "History and the Possibilities of Emancipation: Some Lessons from India," Historiography of Civilizations; special issues of *Journal of the Indian Council for Philosophical Research*, June 1996, 95–137.

87. Aryan Invasion Theory Links can be found online at <http://www.hindunet.org/hindu_history/ancient/aryan/aryan_link.html>. See also the lengthy article by David Frawley, "The Myth of the Aryan Invasion of India," which claims that the Aryans dispersed from India to the rest of the world, online at <http://www.spiritweb.org/Spirit/myth-of-invasion.html>. Frawley and Keonraad Elst, whose support of Hindutva history and politics is unequivocal, are widely cited in Hindutva histories; for all their nationalism, Hindutvavadis still crave recognition by the white man.

88. Lal, "The Discourse of History," 4–44; Lal, "History and the Possibilities of Emancipation," 95–137; and Vinay Lal, "History and Politics," in Philip Oldenburg and Marshall Bouton, eds., *India Briefing* (New York: M. E. Sharpe for the Asia Society, 1999).

89. My own website, MANAS <http://www.sscnet.ucla.edu/southasia>, provides a comprehensive view of some segments of Indian history and culture, and is epistemologically resistant to the dominant paradigms, since it is animated largely by a civilizational view of India that is deeply informed by Gandhian and neo-Gandhian strains, as well as by a politics that strives for the ecological plurality of knowledges. One other small exception is the Forum of the Indian Left, a New York-based organization, which hosts four or five articles on Indian history on its website; see http://www.foil.org/history. Websites devoted to contemporary politics that offer alternative perspectives are much more numerous.

90. A forensic report, published by the Gujarat state's own laboratory in July 2002, now even makes it possible to question the received account according to which a large Muslim mob set fire to two wagons of a train carrying Hindu militants and their families returning from Ayodhya. For more information on the forensic report, see, online, <http://www.milligazette.com/Archives/15072002/1507200250.htm>.

91. This question is asked in very much the same idiom that people wonder how the culture that produced Beethoven, Bach, Schiller, Schubert, and Goethe could comfortably house Nazism. Apropos this, Benjamin's observation steers us to more

nuanced thinking: "There is no document of civilization which is not at the same time a document of barbarism." See Walter Benjamin, "Theses on the Philosophy of History," in *Illuminations*, ed. Hannah Arendt (New York: Schocken, 1969), 256.

92. The diasporic Gujarati community is serviced by many websites and portals in Gujarati itself—see <Gujarati.indiainfo.com>—but the role of the Internet in keeping the community stitched has not so far been the subject of any English-language scholarly work.

93. See <http://www.gla.org.uk/nxtev.htm>.

94. Rajdeep Sardesai, "The Disaster Divide," available at <www.indian-express.com/ie/daily/20010205/ian05028.html>. A new organization of people of Gujarati origin, the Vishwa Gujarati Samaj, or World Gujarati Association, is utilizing the Internet to link members of the diaspora (see <www.evishwagujarati.net>) and states only that "more than a million persons of Gujarati origin live abroad." See <http://www.tribuneindia.com/2002/20001009/login/main5.htm>.

95. Ashutosh Varshney, "Doomed from Within," *Newsweek* (international edition), March 18, 2002, online at <http://www.umich.edu/~iinet/iisite/media/03-18-02-Newsweek-AVarshney.htm>. Nihal Singh has suggested that "significant characteristics of this [Gujarati] diaspora, grouped under the generic acronym of NRI (Non-resident Indian), have proved hospitable to the seeds planted by the RSS," a paramilitary association that was implicated in the assassination of Mahatma Gandhi in 1948 and has ever since held aloft the banner of Hindu supremacy. See N. Singh, "A Millstone round India's Neck," online at: <http://www.khaleejtimes.co.ae/nihal.htm>.

96. One partial exception is Biju Mathew, "Byte-Sized Nationalism: Mapping the Hindu Right in the United States," *Rethinking Marxism* 12, no. 3 (2000), 108–28, though even here the empirical data is somewhat slim. Gautam Appa, writing of Hindu organizations in Britain, states that "the contribution of these British organizations (VHP UK, HSS) to the work of the Sangh Parivar in India in terms of fund raising is not insignificant. According to the charity commissioner's records, the two main charities associated with VHP (UK) and the HSS [Hindu Swayamsevak Sangh, the international equivalent of the RSS] had collected nearly one million pounds in the last financial year. It is common knowledge that a large chunk of the overt and covert collection ends up in India in the hands of the Sangh Parivar." See Appa, "Gujarat Carnage—the Non Resident Indians (NRI) perspective" (30 May 2002), online at <http://www.onlinevolunteers.org/gujarat/news/articles/appa.htm>.

97. Nor should this be surprising: similar transfers of money on a large scale to the Irish Republican Army (IRA) by Irish Americans until recent years have been heavily documented, and the Tamil insurgency in Sri Lanka is largely fuelled by donations from diasporic Tamilian Sri Lankans. In many respects, from their sophisticated use of the Net to their advocacy of suicide bombings long before the present wave of Palestinian suicide bombings brought this matter to the attention of the world, the Tamil Tigers have established the paradigms for late modernity's insurrectionary warfare.

98. Sardesai, "The Disaster Divide."

99. See, for instance, <http://www.onlinevolunteers.org/gujarat/index.htm> and <http://groups.yahoo.com/group/GujratDevelopment>. Existing websites have added significant sections on Gujarat: see, for instance, <www.sabrang.com>, <www.mnet.fr/aiindex>, and <www.ektaonline.org/cac/index.htm>.

100. Among the more notable of these reports are Human Rights Watch, *We Have No Orders to Save You;* Peoples' Union for Democratic Rights, *Maaro, Kaapo, Baaro: State, Society and Communalism in Gujarat;* and reports by Safdar Hashmi Memorial Trust (SAHMAT), various women's organizations, and the National Human Rights Commission. These reports can be accessed through a number of sites,

principally <www.onlinevolunteeers.org/gujarat/reports/index.htm>. The website of the People's Union for Civil Liberties is also of use; see <www.pucl.org/reports/gujarat-index.htm>.

101. See <www.rediff.com>, archived message of May 13, 2002.

102. See <www.ektaonline.org/cac/actions/gujarat/nriad.htm>.

103. See <www.hinduunity.org>, link under "Hindu Holocaust Museum." Gautier's popularity among Hindus, even in the United States, may be gauged from the fact that he has been on a lecture tour of the United States organized by the Hindu Students Council, the youth wing of the VHP.

104. See <www.geocities.com/hindoo_humanist/>.

5

Reimagining the Community: Information Technology and Web-based Chinese Language Networks in North America

YUAN SHU

As part of the information-centered technological revolution that started in the late twentieth century, the Internet has not only transformed our culture and society in terms of networking, but has also challenged our traditional concepts of identity and community that were geographically conceived and historically constructed. According to the UCLA Internet Report, "Surveying the Digital Future," released in November 2001, "the Internet is now a mainstream activity in American life that continues to spread among people across all age groups, education levels, and incomes."[1] As the Internet expands across North America and around the world, the United States Internet Council, in its 2001 edition of "The State of the Internet Report," announces that the online population has crossed the half billion milestone globally and that online demographics have finally begun to reflect offline realities.[2] What is more interesting in this annual report, however, is its declaration that English speakers have now for the first time lost their dominance in the online world, and represent approximately 45 percent of the total online population. While the United States, European nations, and Japan still lead the Internet in terms of technology and language content, the council further observes, "several other nations such as China, India, and South Korea (have begun) to play larger roles."[3] The latest development of the Internet and the emergence of the three Asian nations as new major players in the IT industry have important political and cultural implications. To begin with, as the Internet continues to facilitate the free flow of information across regional and national boundaries, these three Asian national governments have promoted the technology as a means to integrate their national economies into the global economy and bridge the gap between them and the more advanced countries such as the United States, even though it means that they have to continue to wrestle with issues of authority, jurisdiction, and law enforcement in their traditionally defined nation-states. As a result of their efforts, the Internet and their native language contents on it have now flourished in these nations.[4] Moreover, as the Internet continues to grow at a phenomenal pace, Internet architecture has now expanded to accommodate new multilingual domain names as well as to develop new multicultural top-level domains. What all these changes mean culturally and technologically is that the Internet has finally experienced a transformation from an initial English language-centered and U.S.-dominated environment to the present multipolar, multilingual, and multicultural one, the meaning of which remains to be determined and interpreted by scholars of technology and cultural studies.

At this moment of change that has redefined the function and content of the Internet, how should we reconsider the generalization and speculation made on the Internet and virtual communities that have usually privileged U.S. Internet users, as well as been based primarily on English-language content? How should we assess the role that multilingual content on the Internet has played in prompting new social interactions and cultivating new cultural spaces? In this essay I will examine specifically the function that the Internet and web-based Chinese language networks have performed in informing and shaping Chinese professionals and their transnational communities in the U.S. context. By the term *Chinese professionals* I refer only to the growing number of professionals originally from mainland China, who either (1) come to study and do research in the United States as students and scholars but wind up working in U.S. industries and academic institutions and traveling back and forth between North America and East and Southeast Asia, or (2) are directly recruited by U.S. transnational corporations from mainland China because of their background in the information technology(IT) and their potential capability to open up the supposedly huge Chinese markets for these corporations and businesses. I use the term *transnational communities* to call attention to the emergence of Chinese professionals as a group in the United States, whose legal statuses as naturalized citizens, permanent residents, and H-1B workers, and whose professional interests in both East Asia and North America, have frequently prevented them from fully participating in American public life. Though these professionals cannot articulate their interests and concerns within the parameters of the traditional Asian American identity politics based on the 1960s civil rights movements, they have nevertheless been perceived by the American public as foreigners and Asian Americans interchangeably or both, and have to travel back and forth between East Asia and North America. On the one hand, unlike the traditional working-class immigrants from southern China in the early twentieth century whose life and work revolved around the geopolitical space of Chinatown in the United States, these Chinese professionals hold advanced academic degrees in science and technology, speak functional English, and travel extensively worldwide for professional and business reasons. On the other hand, like the early traditional immigrants in Chinatown in many ways—even though the ethnic enclave itself has recently undergone significant changes and directly attracted transnational capital from Hong Kong and Taiwan[5]—these Chinese professionals remain politically invisible and culturally irrelevant in the dominant American culture and society. The only moment at which they make national headlines is when the few Chinese prodemocracy activists testify in Congressional hearings as victims of communist China and side, ironically, with the most conservative right-wing politicians of the nation. Recently, they catch more attention from the media because they have been singled out by the same batch of the right-wing politicians as potential Chinese communist spies who may someday steal high-tech secrets from U.S. military industries and research institutions and create a potential problem for U.S. national security. In foregrounding the political liability and cultural indifference that these Chinese professionals have been subjected to in American culture and society, I argue that the Internet and the web-based Chinese-language networks have not only served as a medium of communication for these professionals to negotiate their political power and cultural spaces in the United States, but have also cultivated and performed a sense of Chineseness, a cultural imaginary that allows these professionals to achieve what cultural anthropologist Aihwa Ong, in her recent work *Flexible Citizenship*, describes as "flexibility" across national boundaries and "visibility" within a global context.[6]

Information Technology and Web-based Chinese Language Networks

In January 2001, Global Reach, a U.S.-based marketing communications consultancy, noted that the highest concentration of Chinese speakers outside of China is in the United States.[7] While there were only 1.3 million Chinese speakers living in the United States in 1990, the report notices that the number had now reached 2.2 million, with a majority not only owning personal computers but also having Internet access. Indeed, as stated in a similar survey that was conducted by NUA Internet Surveys in February 2001, "almost all Chinese-Americans in the U.S. and (Chinese Canadians in) Canada own a PC and about 60 percent have Internet access."[8] Among these Chinese Americans and Chinese Canadians, the survey concludes, most of them "regularly visit Chinese-language sites—73 percent in the U.S. and 63 percent in Canada."[9]

Though these sources never explain explicitly their research methodology or their definition of "Chinese Americans," their statistics do provide us with a snapshot of Chinese-language Internet users in the United States, which is to say that there are a large number of Chinese speakers in the United States who are comfortable with information technology as well as interested in Chinese-language material. The question, however, is who these Chinese language Internet users are and why they read Chinese language material if they are working and living in the United States. Simply put, what kind of information and services do these Chinese speakers usually expect to get from Chinese-language websites? As the other side of the same coin, who are these providers of Chinese language services in the United States? What are their objectives? Which Chinese speaker groups do they target?

In following these questions, I will examine closely two of the most frequently visited Chinese-language websites among Chinese professionals in the United States in two different periods: Chinese News Digest and Chinese Media Net.[10] While the former network represents an early effort of Chinese students and scholars in the United States to take advantage of information technology and provide Chinese-language services to their communities in the early 1990s, the latter suggests the changing nature of such services that have become more commercial and business-oriented in the wake of the booming economy in China since the late 1990s. I will concentrate on the roles that these two web-based Chinese-language networks have played in informing Chinese professionals and shaping their transnational communities in the United States at different historic junctures.

According to the essay, "The Making of 'China News Digest,'" collaboratively written by its staffers and carried in a special issue celebrating the tenth anniversary of the network on March 6, 1999, Chinese News Digest (CND) as a nonprofit organization was first established by a group of Chinese students and scholars in the United States and Canada on March 6, 1989, in direct response to the political crisis, then brewing in China, that would lead to the Tiananmen Square Massacre on June 4 of that year.[11] It started as an English-language service that had aimed to search for news items related to China on what was then known as Usenet and to deliver them to Chinese students and scholars on campuses across the United States and Canada. In its first month of service, the network had four hundred direct subscribers, most of them being based in Canada. In September 1989, the network not only formally adopted its current name, China News Digest, but also boasted four thousand direct subscribers from the United States and Canada, two listserv accounts, based at Arizona State University in Arizona and Kent State University in Ohio, and a mailing list maintained at the University of Toronto in Canada.

Such a rapid growth of the network and collaboration among Chinese students and scholars on both sides of the U.S.-Canadian border reflected the students' urge to keep themselves informed about the political situation in China as well as the need to communicate among the then estimated eighty thousand students and scholars studying and living across the United States and several thousand in Canada during that period.[12] As they were shocked by the atrocities committed by the Chinese military machine that had always claimed to be the people's liberation army, these students and scholars were very concerned about the political uncertainty in China and the personal safety of the demonstrators. The most urgent question that they confronted at the time, however, was whether or not they should take advantage of the political situation in China to seek political asylum collectively in the United States and Canada. Since such a question would create political and psychological tensions among themselves, CND started offering individual as well as community-related services that included "Introduction to Organizations," "Questions and Answers," and a "Books and Journals Review" in December 1989. While the former two functioned as advising, counseling, and referral services, the latter service enabled these students and scholars to maintain their connection with China and Chinese culture.

In facilitating debates on issues such as Chinese nationalism, survival strategies in American culture and society, and intellectual responsibility of their generations, CND helped the students and scholars to make the psychological transition from identifying themselves with mainland China to considering the alternative of working and staying in the United States and Canada. Moreover, CND also technologically made it possible for the headquarters of the Independent Federation of Chinese Students and Scholars (IFCSS) based in Washington, D.C., to organize and mobilize its local chapters and constituencies on college campuses across the United States. As an organization initially meant to replace the official student associations endorsed by the Chinese embassy in the United States, the IFCSS launched a massive lobbying campaign coordinated by the CND network on both national and local levels, and successfully pressured the first Bush administration (1988–92) to issue an executive order in April 1990 that would allow Chinese nationals to work and stay in the United States temporarily regardless of their legal status. Before the executive order expired in March 1993, CND stepped up its effort to orchestrate a second massive lobbying campaign and helped to convince the U.S. Congress to pass the Chinese Student Protection Act, which would allow 52,425 Chinese students and scholars and their families to adjust legal status and apply for permanent residency in the United States.[13]

As Chinese students and scholars recognized the importance of information technology in developing their political awareness and consolidating their sense of community, they equally realized that the English language had limited their communication ability and failed to convey their sensibilities in Chinese language and culture. On April 5, 1991, CND launched its groundbreaking project—the first online Chinese-language journal, titled *Hua Xia Wen Zhai* (*China Digest*), and started Chinese-language services on Usenet. The Chinese journal featured primarily political critiques of Chinese and American historical events and social issues, such as the Chinese Exclusion Act and its impact upon early Chinese Americans and their communities, McCarthyism and the wave of Chinese students and scholars returning to China in the mid-1950s, as well as the political power struggle in the Chinese communist government and its implications for the future of China. Moreover, the journal also created a section of personal narratives that would enable these students and scholars to articulate their individual senses of cultural dislocation and their nostalgic feelings for the distant homeland.

As the early volunteers landed professional jobs both inside and outside the academy, and new students and scholars continued to come and study in the United States, CND made an important structural change and moved its entire operation to the World Wide Web on June 4, 1994. The new content of CND includes the categories of publications, communities, services, and InfoBase. While it continues to provide daily bilingual news service and publish the weekly Chinese-language journal, CND has also expanded its services to include "Matchmaking Cupid (*yuanyangqiubite*)," "Job Openings (*gongzuojihui*)," "Alumni Associations (*tongxuexiaoyouhui*)," and "Chinese Students and Scholars Associations (*xiaoyuanlianyihui*)" on major college campuses in the United States and around the world.[14] InfoBase, serving as virtual museums and libraries, features topics that include "The Cultural Revolution," "China in 1989," "Chinese Scenery," "Chinese Classic Literature," and "Nanjing Massacre." While "The Cultural Revolution" and "China in 1989" reflect the political interests of the students and scholars as the generations that have been directly affected by these two major events in contemporary Chinese history and culture, "Chinese Scenery" and "Chinese Classic Literature" target a broader audience that has not necessarily visited China but has been interested in China and Chinese culture in a more abstract sense.

In incorporating matchmaking and alumni associations into their services in 1994, the network showed its awareness of the transition that these former students and scholars had experienced legally and professionally as permanent residents and professionals in the United States. While they were building their professional lives and finding their own niches in American culture and society, their interest in Chinese politics and society had declined, but their needs for having their own lives, raising families, and building local communities had surfaced as priorities. Such needs were followed by an increasing concern over the problem of racism in American culture and society and the question of protecting their own civil rights as naturalized citizens and permanent residents. Articulations of these concerns and anxieties, however, were usually not direct inquiries into the fairness of the American political system per se or a matter of familiarizing themselves with the tradition of the civil rights movements in the United States, but were instead personal narratives reflective of their own awkward situations and measuring the impact of these situations upon themselves and their children. In other words, the glass ceiling in the workplace and unfair treatment in their daily lives were often billed as the prices they would have to pay as nonnative speakers of English working and living in their country of adoption and the sacrifice they would have to make for the well-being of their children. As a result, discussion on racism and civil rights usually wound up with some wishful thinking that their children would not have to follow their own paths to work and live as computer programmers in the United States but could choose more respectable and lucrative professions such as those of physicians, attorneys, and business executives. Moreover, since most professionals were more interested in telling their stories of triumph in American culture and society rather than sharing stories of bitterness, that would be construed as personal failure or professional incompetence, victims of institutional racism and individual prejudices usually preferred to remain low in profile in both their online and offline communities, quitting their jobs if they could afford to or simply leaving the United States for China or a third country if they had to.

Since 1995, there have been some significant changes concerning Chinese professionals and their communities in the United States. While many Chinese students and scholars continue to follow their predecessors in their preference to work and live in the United States, there have also emerged a new group of Chinese professionals, H-1B workers, who have been recruited by U.S. transnational corporations directly from China. Though Japan specialist Masao Miyoshi identifies transnational professionals entirely with their transnational corporations in terms of economic interests as well as language ability,[15] I suggest that language and ethnicity still play an important role in shaping these professionals with regard to their personal interests and sensibilities, at least in the case of Chinese transnational professionals that have emerged as a group since 1995. Young and outspoken, these Chinese professionals are not only more proficient in the English language and skilled in information technology compared with those who came to Western countries before 1989, but are also more confident about their own marketability globally and the future of a prosperous China. As a result, they retain their contacts as well as keep up with the latest economic and cultural developments in China. Furthermore, since their professional interests are not necessarily confined to China or the United States, they also look for opportunities in other countries and regions that may vary from Singapore to Australia, from Hong Kong to Japan, and from Switzerland to South Africa. To attract these young professionals and other Chinese speakers in North America and around the world, web-based Chinese-language networks have sprung up in North America since the late 1990s, and among them was Chinese Media Net, a multimedia network that began operations in January 1999.

As noted in its mission statement, Chinese Media Net aims to be an equivalent of CNN for ethnic Chinese in North America and around the world, and thus tries to offer services on various technical, linguistic, and cultural levels.[16] First, it tends to be multimedia in nature, including a Chinese news net, an English news net, a radio news net, a TV news net, a weekly magazine net, a picture news net, and a global newspaper net. Second, it tries to be comprehensive, technically; the Chinese news net alone contains twenty-one news categories, which include important current events, global trends, North American news, Taiwan news, overseas Chinese news, business news, and so on. It not only has its own news agency and journalists to report on current events in North America and China, but has developed partnerships with Reuters, New China News Agency and China News Agency in Beijing, and the Central News Agency based in Taiwan. The news net offers its services twenty-four hours a day, seven days a week, updating news entries and commentaries every few minutes. Third, it is entertaining, carrying martial arts fiction and some controversial books in Chinese, which readers may have difficulty locating locally in their countries of adoption and sojourn. Above all, the network, making good use of the interactive feature of information technology, has created six major discussion forums: everybody's forum, everybody's thoughts and comments, reader's forum, net users report, ball game fans' forum, and documentation of the corrupt officials in mainland China. The last forum not only enables users in China to expose corruption and injustice in the mainland, but it also aims to cultivate a sense of connection among ethnic Chinese around the world, who hope to see an economically strong as well as politically healthy China.

Founded by a group of Chinese journalists and computer professionals based in the United States and Canada, Chinese Media Net has become important in several ways. Equipped with the advanced technologies and operated by the U.S. and Canadian educated professionals, the network aims to compete with the traditional Chinese language media such as newspapers and television based in North America and East Asia, and even to emulate major English-language networks in range and scope in the United States. Moreover, the network targets Chinese-language speakers across regional and national boundaries and endeavors to foster a sense of community based on language, culture, and ethnicity, even though the discussion columns often reveal the fact that their users are primarily Chinese professionals based in North America, West Europe, and mainland China. Occasionally, those who work and stay in Japan, Israel, and South Africa may join the forums by airing their opinions on current world events and pointing out their relevance to ethnic Chinese around the world. Finally, as information technology makes interactivity a reality, the network attempts to bridge political, linguistic, and cultural gaps among Chinese speakers around the world—particularly the gap between those in the United States and those in China. It is ironic to notice, however, that the discussion columns often turn out to be a virtual battleground for mainland Chinese students studying in the United States who promote reunification with Taiwan, and their Taiwanese counterparts who articulate their own desires and anxieties for an independent Taiwan.

Because of its technological capacity and information resources, CMN offers report on the changing culture and society in mainland China, keeps track of the ups and downs of U.S.-China relations and major political and cultural events in the United States, as well as focusing on political freedom in Hong Kong and the military tension between mainland China and Taiwan. The column "News in Focus," which features major current events and facilitates follow-up discussions, reflects concerns and anxieties shared by Chinese professionals in the United States, and in that regard fosters a sense of community that has been conditioned by language and ethnicity. In fact, incidents such as the bombing of the Chinese embassy in Yugoslavia in May 1999, the ongoing Wen Ho Lee case starting in early 1999, and the collision between the U.S. spy plane and the Chinese jet fighter in April 2001 have all generated heated discussion and speculation upon the relations between the United States and China and the future of Chinese professionals and Chinese Americans in the United States. There have not only been angry comments on U.S. imperialism and racism, but also suggestions on how Chinese professionals should help American politicians abandon their Cold War mentality and educate the uninformed American public about a changing China. In fact, when the bombing of the Chinese embassy happened in May 1999, many network users, students and professionals alike, actually organized protests in front of their local courthouses in the United States and around the world and condemned what they had considered as deliberate bashing and provocation of China.[17]

From the emergence of CND to the popularization of CMN, I want to suggest some major features concerning these two Chinese-language networks based in North America. First, as the pioneering Chinese language online network in the United States, CND from the outset had clear political objectives as well as specific readers and communities in mind—that is, the Chinese students and scholars studying and working in the United States and Canada. CMN, on the other hand, had to define and attract its Net users by offering extensive coverage of current events and creating follow-up discussion forums for them to air their positions and opinions. Precisely because of this difference in assessing and targeting Net users, CND tends to be more critical of the Chinese communist regime but less willing to challenge U.S. institutional racism and cultural imperialism, whereas CMN carries a wide range of essays that not only question U.S. domestic and foreign policies but also explore the possibility of reforming the political system in China. In this light, CND has been more reflective of a U.S.-centered environment in which the early Chinese students and scholars as the generations of the Cultural Revolution (from 1966 to 1976) and of Tiananmen Square in 1989 celebrate their presence in the United States and consider themselves victims of the Chinese communist regime. CMN, by contrast, has centered on the recent booming economy in China and catered to the needs of a new generation of Chinese professionals who are outspoken and confident about the future of China as well as eager to see a new China emerging from its historical humiliation imposed by Western powers and Japan since the First Opium War in 1840, and a new China being acknowledged economically and politically by the United States and West Europe.

Transnational Communities: Imagined and Flexible?

If the aforementioned two Chinese-language networks demonstrate different attitudes toward China, how do we understand their respective transnational communities in relation to the Chinese nation-state? Should we consider these transnational communities as being imagined outside the Chinese nation-state by virtue of language, ethnicity, and information technology? Rather than simply evoking Benedict Anderson's critique of nationalism as imagined communities, I argue that information technology and Chinese language networks have reinforced transnational communities by performing "Chineseness" in the sense described by Aihwa Ong in her work *Flexible Citizenship* as a cultural imaginary that would enable ethnic Chinese professionals to negotiate with national governments as well as to maintain their flexibility within the global context. This "Chineseness," argues Ong, serves as an open signifier that acquires its dynamic meanings "in dialectical relation to the practices, beliefs, and structures encountered in the spaces of flows across nations and markets."[18] In employing the term *Chineseness* I do not want to explore the sense of relativity implied by Ong's critique, but instead to investigate the changing meanings of the term that have corresponded to the rise and fall of the Chinese nation-state.

When Anderson introduces the notion of nationalism as an "imagined community" based on his own observation of the formation of the Indonesian nation-state in Southeast Asia, he highlights the function of print technology as an effective medium in disseminating the native language and consolidating the national consciousness, but downplays the significance of the national consciousness in organizing and mobilizing the native people in their political struggle against colonial rule.[19] It is precisely at this point that Partha Chatterjee intervenes in the Western critique of nationalism and introduces the concept of the inner domain of a national culture as an important component of nationalism.[20] Though important in its opposition to Western trivialization of nationalism in the course of the decolonization movement, the concept of the inner domain itself is grounded in some essentialist understanding of native culture, and in that sense fails to recognize the changing nature of native culture in response to colonial rule as well as the dynamics of modernity. As we moved into the information age, not only have the boundaries of the nation-state been questioned, the concept of national consciousness itself has also become suspect. To integrate information technology into his reconstruction of nationalism, Manuel Castells redefines the term as being "more oriented toward the defense of an already institutionalized culture than toward the construction or defense of a state."[21]

Though it is important to discuss the distinction between culture and state, Castells has nevertheless been tempted to salvage the notion of nationalism from its wreckage. In critiquing what she dubs as flexible citizenship, Ong introduces the term *Chineseness* as an alternative notion to nationalism and highlights its dynamic dimension that would encompass the plurality of ethnic Chinese identities across national boundaries and incorporate the diverse factors of gender, class, and sexuality in informing and shaping ethnic Chinese identities and communities. According to Ong, ethnic Chinese in Southeast Asia have never identified themselves with any Chinese nation-state in the first place, but they have always wanted to articulate their own sense of cultural difference and economic accomplishment in terms of abstract Chinese notions such as Confucianism.[22] As Ong maps out this "Chineseness," the term winds up as something between ethnicity and cultural beliefs that have constantly been reconstructed by global capitalism and national government. In my own use of the term, I do not want to rule out the Chinese nation-state as an important element in constituting this "Chineseness," but on the contrary, I examine the ways in which the term has been deployed by Chinese professionals in relation to the Chinese nation-state at different historical junctures and interrogate what this deployment means to the transnational communities in the United States.

When CND started its service in 1989, *huaren* (ethnic Chinese), *zhonghuawenhua* (Chinese culture), and *huaxia* (China proper) were terms conveniently employed by Chinese students and scholars to replace the terms related to the People's Republic of China (PRC) and to exonerate themselves from any negative association with the communist regime in American culture and society. The uses of these terms were also meant to appeal to the overseas Chinese and Chinese American communities in the wake of the political crisis of 1989 so that the students and scholars would get more support from these established communities when they tried to cut off their ties entirely from the Chinese nation-state. The term was most effectively used in the political mobilization of the Chinese students and scholars concerning the protection bill in 1992, when the leaders of the IFCSS tried to convince their communities that they were collective victims as citizens of the People's Republic of China. Only by acquiring permanent residency in the United States and becoming ethnic Chinese in the pure cultural sense of the word could they cherish their dreams of "life, liberty, and the pursuit of happiness." The point of their argument, however, did not lie so much in the protection of the Chinese students and scholars as in its gesture to disassociate themselves from the Chinese nation-state and to reinvent themselves as freedom fighters and competent professionals in U.S. and global contexts.

Meanwhile, the IFCSS also explored the cultural dimension of "Chineseness" that had been manifested in values such as education and meritocracy. In their lobbying activities, the task force of the IFCSS emphasized the uniqueness of Chinese students and scholars in terms of their education levels and potential contribution to the advancement of science and technology in the United States, a strategy that would easily evoke the "model minority" myth surrounding Asian Americans and would likely gain support from both parties in Congress. The subtext was that as Chinese professionals they would not create any welfare problem to the U.S. government, and that the United States would have nothing to lose in granting them permanent residency, a point that would appeal particularly to Republicans. Journalist Susan Lawrence drives the point home by comparing these students and scholars with the refugees from Haiti whose status and future were pending and gloomy at that time. She writes, "As an immigrant group, the students are unusually appealing. The vast majority either hold Ph.D.'s or are studying for them now. Many are skilled scientists—biologists, physicists and engineers. The Haitian refugees may face greater physical danger in their homeland. But, as Cheryl Little, a Miami lawyer who represents the Haitians, notes ruefully, 'the perception is that they are poor, they are uneducated, they are black, they are "undesirables."' [23]

To ensure the passage of the protection bill, the IFCSS played the political and cultural meanings of "Chineseness" right into the anticommunist sentiment prevalent in Congress. During the congressional hearings, one question that had frequently been debated was what would happen to the United States if communist China got all the estimated eighty thousand students and scholars, the majority of whom were holding or studying for Ph.D.s in science and technology. This fear was not entirely groundless considering the fact that when McCarthyism drove back to communist China some two hundred Chinese students and scholars with Ph.D.s in hard science in the mid-1950s, China embraced these returnees, as they provided a unique opportunity to lay down the foundation for higher education and scientific research as well as to build the country's nuclear arsenals in the following decades. Included in this blacklist were distinguished scientists such as Qian Xuesen, "the father of Chinese rockets," and Deng Jiaxian, "the father of Chinese atomic bombs." In light of this history, the legislators perceived the passage of the bill as being crucial to U.S. national security and U.S. global hegemony. At the moment when the IFCSS leaders celebrated the passage of the bill, and the evidence of the very successful involvement of Chinese students and scholars in the U.S. legal and political system, little did they realize that there had been elements of racism and cultural imperialism vested in the anticommunist rhetoric in Congress that would take its toll on the very same Chinese professionals years later.

Though there was no major voice on CND opposing the tactics of the IFCSS, not every Chinese student and scholar bought their argument or took advantage of the legislation to stay in the United States. According to the initial projection of most research and reports there would be 80,000 students and scholars and their immediate families eligible for permanent residency in the United States,[24] but the data collected and released by the U.S. Immigration and Naturalization Service suggested that there were only 26,915 applicants in 1993 and 21,297 applicants in 1994 for permanent residency under the Chinese Student Protection Act, which was effective from April 1993 to April 1994.[25] The total applicants came to 48,212 during that year-long period, a figure that fell far below the projection of 80,000.[26] While there could be different explanations for this discrepancy (i.e., that some students and scholars had already applied for permanent residency under other immigration categories), it did suggest that many students and scholars actually gave up their opportunities to become permanent residents in the United States and left for mainland China and other countries for different reasons. One Ph.D. candidate in material science at Purdue University in Indiana, after his grant proposal on submarine material was rejected allegedly on the basis of his Chinese citizenship, stated explicitly on CND in 1993 that he would never be trusted by the U.S. government as a scientist even though he might become a permanent resident or a naturalized citizen in the future. He concluded that he would rather go back to China than live in a racist country and work as a second-class citizen for the rest of his life. True to his words, he went back to China and started his own high-tech firm in Beijing in 1995, according to the official newspaper of the Chinese government, *The People's Daily*.[27] Moreover, even for those who had become permanent residents, many of them left for China or a third country several years later. In early 1996, ten senior research scientists at Indiana University Medical School in Indianapolis decided to leave their academic positions and started their new careers as a team at a university in Guangzhou, Guangdong province, China.[28]

When CMN began operations as a web-based Chinese language network in January 1999, the profile of Chinese-language speakers in the United States was quite different from that for CND a decade earlier. Not only had there emerged an entire new generation of Chinese professionals in North America and East and Southeast Asia, but the meaning of *Chineseness* itself had also undergone some dramatic changes. As the economy continues to boom in China, the term *Chineseness* has expanded in an economic sense to include the regions of the mainland, Hong Kong, and Taiwan, and resisted political identification with any specific regime even though the governments in all three regions have competed to influence this economic integration according to their own political ideologies and economic models. Because of this economic expansion and prosperity, a new sense of optimism and confidence has widely spread among Chinese professionals. Ironically, this optimism and confidence could easily turn into vulgar nationalism or virtual nationalism, as evidenced in the recent reactions toward the bombing of the Chinese embassy in Yugoslavia in May 1999, when this new economic dimension of *Chineseness* is not honored or understood by Western powers—particularly the United States. As the United States and China are getting increasingly confrontational, this new meaning of the term has finally become a self-reflexive moment for Chinese professionals in North America to reconsider their own positions and their transnational communities in terms of U.S.-China relations.

When the news broke on CMN that U.S.-led North Atlantic Treaty Organization forces had bombed the Chinese embassy in Yugoslavia and killed three Chinese journalists in May 1999, the network immediately became an important source of information and forum for discussion for Chinese professionals as well as Chinese students and scholars in the United States, China, and around the world. Though some net users doubted that NATO had any real motive in doing it deliberately, the majority of the users believed that the Western powers had always intended to bash an emerging powerful China and expressed their outrage that China had been humiliated at its strongest moment since the First Opium War in 1840. As these students and professionals called for investigation and retaliation, their sense of optimism and confidence based on Chinese economy suddenly turned into vulgar nationalism and virtual patriotism. While some student hackers based in China broke into U.S. government websites to post a red flag or a message reading "I'm proud of being Chinese" and others protested in front of the U.S. embassy in Beijing shouting slogans and throwing eggs at the building, Chinese students and professionals in the United States also joined the chorus of protests. On May 11, 1999, sponsored by organizations such as the Chinese Students and Scholars Society at Ohio State University and the Midwest Chinese Science and Culture Association, over a hundred Chinese students and scholars and professionals demonstrated in front of the courthouse in Columbus, Ohio, holding a banner with the words "Peace! Truth! Justice!" and carrying signs that read "Shame On NATO!" "Stop Killing the Innocent," "Violence Breeds Violence!" and "NATO Is the Mistake!"[29]

Before the impact of the bombing was over, a collision between a Chinese jet fighter and a U.S. spy plane took place in April 2001. Chinese professionals in the United States began realizing that there could be a real war between China and the United States and that they as Chinese professionals and Chinese Americans would be particularly vulnerable if caught in the middle. In the discussion forum on CMN in the following weeks, there were heated discussions on the strategies and positions that Chinese professionals should hold in the wake of the crisis. All the participants showed their concerns about the awkwardness that would result if they were caught in a scenario of war between the United States and China. In the second week of the incident, one person predicted pessimistically that the U.S. government would not hesitate in the least to put everybody of Chinese descent into some kind of internment camp, as it had done to Japanese Americans during World War II. Another person countered the prediction by arguing that the U.S. government would not make the same mistake—of violating the U.S. Constitution—twice. As naturalized citizens, the person argued further, Chinese professionals could fight for their civil rights as protected and guaranteed by the First Amendment and would have a strong case if anything like that could happen at all. However, the same person expressed more concern over "patriotism" of individual U.S. citizens who might take things into their own hands, breaking the windows of his house or abusing his kids verbally and physically at public schools. A third person suggested that as Chinese professionals and immigrants they should probably do more in promoting understanding between the Chinese and Americans. A good relation between the United States and China, she argued, would not only benefit people in both countries but would also become crucial to Chinese professionals working and living in the United States, like herself. She concluded by suggesting that people of Chinese descent at the moment should be united in their fight against all sorts of war-monger "hawks" in the U.S. government, the Chinese government, and the Taiwanese government. Discussions like this suggest three things here. First, transnational communities are consolidated in times of crisis, when the professionals feel that their own interest and well-being are at stake. Second, these professionals have always been interested in both U.S. domestic politics and U.S. foreign policies, particularly those that would have a direct impact upon Chinese immigrants and transnational professionals. And third, these professionals usually consider the situations of Chinese Americans in light of U.S.-China relations.

Transnational Communities and Asian American Identity Politics

In their collaborative essay, "Changing of the Guard?" Paul Ong and David Lee examine the transition of the Asian American population from U.S.-born majority to immigrant majority and speculate upon one of the major consequences of this transition as a potential threat to progressive activism, "which has been an important force within Asian American communities."[30] In defining "progressive activism" as the leadership of the "Asian American Movement" between 1965 and 1980 as well as the new group of social service providers and civil rights advocates who "share a liberal or progressive agenda centered on social justice, economic equality, and ethnic/racial pride," the authors ground their perception on two basic assumptions about immigrants.[31] One is that Asian immigrants are more Republican in their political orientation and may not care much about working-class and social justice, an issue that the two authors have addressed at length in their essay. The other assumption is that immigrants are more interested in their home-country politics than those of their country of adoption.

Though there indeed has been a tradition of Asian immigrants engaging in their home-country politics among immigrants since the late nineteenth century,[32] Ong and Lee have failed to address several important questions. First, are progressive activism and immigrant interest always in conflict or in opposition? Is there any common ground that U.S.-born activists and immigrants share? Second, why are immigrants still interested in their home country politics if they are working and living in a new country? To what extent is their home country politics relevant to their experience in their country of adoption? And third, how should U.S.-born Asian Americans educate immigrants about Asian American history, culture, and politics? What can Asian immigrants teach U.S.-born Asian Americans about the specific history, culture, and language of a given Asian nation?

In reconsidering incidents such as the collision of the U.S. spy plane and the Chinese jet fighter and the Wen Ho Lee case, I argue that U.S.-born and Asia-born Asian Americans do share many common interests. In his article "Lee Case Smashes Students' Dreams," Charles Bu, a tenured faculty member in mathematics at Wellesley College who had benefited from the Chinese Student Protection Act, discussed the frustration and sentiment that the Wen Ho Lee case had produced upon Chinese professionals in the United States.[33] Most of them, Bu argued, felt that they could be the next victims of a U.S. politics, which had needed to demonize China as its next major evil empire in lieu of the former Soviet Union. Condemning this right-wing politics as a revival of McCarthyism in the 1950s, Bu warned that this Cold War reasoning could drive many Chinese professionals in high-tech sectors back to China and in that sense self-fulfill the so-called disloyalty of Chinese Americans. Bu concluded by suggesting that he would never let his son study any field related to nuclear technology or defense industry in the future and would call on his Asian and Asian American students on campus to not work for U.S. national labs.

Like Bu, many Chinese professionals do identify with Wen Ho Lee and answer the call from various Asian American organizations to boycott the three major U.S. national labs on weaponry research. As reported on CMN in early 2000, the famous Chinese dissident Fang Lizhi (who sought political asylum in the U.S. embassy in Beijing during the political crisis of 1989, left China under the auspices of the U.S. government, and is currently a professor of physics at the University of Arizona), wrote an open letter to the U.S. Department of Energy, condemning its racial profiling in the Wen Ho Lee case and demanding justice for the Taiwan-born scientist. When his political disciple Wang Dan, a well-known student leader on Tienanmen Square in 1989, was released from a Chinese prison and came to study history at Harvard University in the mid-1990s, Fang was reported to have told Wang not to make too many public appearances or talk about democracy until he had a solid understanding of U.S. politics, history, and culture. Fang's advice was not only meant to protect Wang from political vulnerability, but it also reflected his own concern and experience with the political system and cultural practice in the United States as a prominent Chinese dissident as well as an immigrant scientist. The Wen Ho Lee case was certainly a wake-up call for the former Chinese students and scholars and the more recent Chinese professionals, and it should probably serve as a point that would bridge the gap between what Ong and Lee call "progressive activism" and immigrant concerns if there were any gap in the first place.

In her critique of Asian American identities and politics, Aihwa Ong argues that the strategy of Asian Americans in distancing themselves from transnational communities "discloses an ongoing political vulnerability that merely reifies the ethnic-racial divide between Asian Americans and white Americans."[34] Such a strategy, Ong further suggests, ignores "the objective reality that a majority of Asian Americans are now linked to transnational family networks."[35] The real problem, Ong concludes, is that Asian Americans have bought into an American ideology that "limits the moral claims to social legitimacy of nonwhites."[36] As a cultural anthropologist whose expertise is focused primarily on ethnic Chinese identities in East and Southeast Asia, Ong's critique might not be an accurate description of Asian American reality, but it certainly points out some pitfalls in Asian American identity politics as well as the urgency in theorizing and integrating the transnational professionals and their communities into Asian American identity politics.

As a matter of a fact, since Sau-ling Wong, in a 1995 essay, popularized the notion of a paradigm shift in Asian American studies from the domestic perspective to the transnational one, new scholarship on transnational aspects of Asian American identities and communities has flourished.[37] Now it is time not just for

Chinese professionals to reimagine their communities and negotiate their own political and cultural spaces by applying information technology and Chinese language networks, but a critical moment for U.S.-born Asian Americans to reimagine their own broader community by helping and working together with these professionals and their transnational communities. U.S-born Asian Americans can teach these transnational professionals about Asian American history, culture, and politics, as well as learn from the latter about Asian history, culture, and politics, and their transnational perspectives on issues such as how U.S.-China relations would inform and shape Asian American identities and communities. If U.S.-born Asian Americans do not take the initiative to reach out to these new professionals and transnational communities, then who will?

Notes

This paper was initially presented at the annual conference of the Association for Asian American Studies in Toronto in April 2000. I'm grateful to Sau-ling Wong, who not only inspired me to work on the subject matter in the first place, but has also carefully read my essay at various stages and given me invaluable advice and detailed suggestions for revision.

1. "The UCLA Internet Report: Surveying the Digital Future," online at <http://www.ccp.ucla.edu.>.
2. United States Internet Council, "State of the Internet 2001 Edition," online at <http://www.itta.com/internet2001.exsum.htm>. See also its "State of the Internet 2000," at <http://www.usinternetcouncil.org/>.
3. United States Internet Council, "State of the Internet: USIC's Report on Use and Threats in 1999," online at <http://www.usintenetcouncil.org/papers/stateoftheinternet99.htm>.
4. For the past few years, the Chinese government has tried to crack down on Internet bars and install filters to prevent Chinese Internet users from gaining access to some politically sensitive websites based in the United States. However, most students and professionals in China still have access to these websites by different means. In July 2002, hackers in the United States gathered in New York City and made a manifesto to fight the Chinese government's control of the Internet by all means necessary, which means that they are going to provide free software to Chinese Internet users to circumvent the filters and deactivate the surveillance software. See <http://www.duoweinews.com>.
5. In *Reconstructing Chinatown*, Jan Lin argues that the stereotypical representation of Chinatown simply as a filthy and exotic ethnic enclave in American popular culture is far from being accurate. There are not only discrepancies among businesses and residents in Chinatown these days but also transnational capital involved in Chinatown renovation and development. See Lin, *Reconstructing Chinatown: Ethnic Enclave, Global Change* (Minneapolis: University of Minnesota Press, 1998), 1–22.
6. Aihwa Ong, *Flexible Citizenship: the Cultural Logics of Transnationality* (Durham, NC: Duke University Press, 1999).
7. "Chinese Language Internet Users." Global Reach website, <http://www.glreach.com/>.
8. "CyberAtlas: Chinese-American Lead the Way Online," online at <http://www.nua.ie/surveys/>.
9. Ibid.
10. See the China News Digest website, <http://www.cnd.org/> and <http://www.chinesemedianet.com/AboutUs.html>.
11. Bo Xiong and Gang Yu, "The Making of 'China News Digest,'" online at <http://www.cnd.org/CND-Tech/>.

12. See Jordana Hart and Cheong Chow, "Joy, Envy at Green Cards for Chinese," *Boston Globe*, June 27, 1993, 1. Also see L. A. Chung, "Refuge Program In Response To Tiananmen," *San Francisco Chronicle*, July 2, 1993, A2.

13. Chinese Student Protection Act, online at <http://www.ins.usdoj.gov/graphics/aboutins/annual/fy95/125.htm>. The Chinese Student Protection Act was effective from April 1993 to April 1994. Based on the data from the U.S. Immigration and Naturalization Service, there were 26,915 applicants in 1993 and 21,297 applicants for the adjustment of their legal statuses. There were 4,213 applicants in the year 1995. My understanding is that these applicants in 1995 were mostly spouses and family members of these Chinese students and scholars. For more information, visit the INS website <http://www.ins.usdoj.gov/graphics/ aboutins/annual/fy95/125.htm>.

14. Both the Chinese and English terms used here are the original ones on the website. They are not exact translations.

15. Masao Miyoshi, "A Borderless World? From Colonialism to Transnationalism and the Decline of the Nation-State," *Critical Inquiry* 19 (1993): 739.

16. See the Chinese Media Net website, online at http://www.chinesemedianet.com/AboutUs.html.

17. As reported in the *Columbus Dispatch* on May 11, 1999, there was a protest against the U.S.-led NATO bombing of the Chinese embassy in Yugoslavia staged by Chinese students and professionals in front of the courthouse in Columbus, Ohio. This protest was organized and sponsored by the Chinese Students and Scholars Society, the Midwest Chinese Science and Culture Association, the Ohio Contemporary Chinese School, and the Chinese School Association in the United States. See "Chinese Group Protests NATO Bombing," *Columbus Dispatch*, (May 11, 1999): 1 A. According to CNN on May 12, 1999, there were major protests organized by Chinese students and scholars in Britain, Germany, France, Australia, Japan, South Africa, and other countries around the world.

18. Ong, *Flexible Citizenship*, 24.

19. Benedict Anderson, *Imagined Communities: Reflections on the Origin and Spread of Nationalism*, rev. ed. (New York: Verso, 1991), 46.

20. Partha Chatterjee, *The Nation and Its Fragments: Colonial and Postcolonial Histories* (Princeton, NJ: Princeton University Press, 1993), 9.

21. Manuel Castells, *The Rise of the Network Society*. The Information Age: Economy, Society and Culture Series vol. 1 (Cambridge, MA: Blackwell, 1996), 31.

22. Ong, *Flexible Citizenship*, 40–41.

23. Susan Lawrence, "Chinese Students Hit the Jackpot," *U.S. News and World Report* 115, no. 11 (1993): 38.

24. See Hart and Chow, "Joy," 1.

25. See the INS website at <http://www.ins.usdoj.gov/graphics/aboutins/annual/fy95/125.htm>.

26. See Hart and Chow, "Joy," 1.

27. The official Chinese Communist flagship newspaper *The People's Daily* (overseas edition) gave extraordinary coverage of the Chinese students and scholars who had returned to China during the period of 1990–1995. It was understood as a strategy and gesture to lure these students and scholars in hard science and technology back to China. See *People's Daily*, April 20, 1995, 3.

28. I first heard this story from a friend who had been working at Indiana University Medical School in Indianapolis. The story was reported in the Chinese-language journal *Shenzhouxueren* 2 (1996): 5.

29. See "Chinese Group Protests NATO Bombing," 1A.

30. Paul Ong and David Lee, "Changing of the Guard? The Emerging Immigrant Majority in Asian American Politics," in *Asian Americans and Politics: Perspectives, Experiences, Prospects*, ed. Gordon H. Chang (Stanford, CA: Stanford University Press, 2001), 154.

31. Ibid., 166.
32. Gordon H. Chang, "Asian Americans and Politics: Some Perspectives from History," in Chang, ed., *Asian Americans and Politics*, 30.
33. Charles Bu, "Lee Case Smashes Students' Dreams," *Boston Herald,* September 23, 2000, 13.
34. Ong, *Flexible Citizens,* 180.
35. Ibid.
36. Ibid.
37. Sau-ling C. Wong, "Denationalization Reconsidered: Asian American Cultural Criticism at a Theoretical Crossroads," *Amerasia Journal* 21, nos. 1–2 (1995): 1–27.

6
Laughter in the Rain: Jokes as Membership and Resistance

EMILY NOELLE IGNACIO

"Pinoy Power!!!"

Their voices came booming down the cereal aisle. My teenage cousin Steve and his friends, for whatever reason, decided at that moment to loudly affirm their ethnic identity while running amok through the grocery store, stopping only to offer one another the "Black Power" salute—and to pick out their afternoon snack. While two of them debated between Cap'n Crunch Peanut Butter Flavored cereal and Count Chocula, I asked my cousin what he thought *pinoy* meant.

"You know," he said, "it means we're the baddest Flips around!"

Smiling, I persisted, "Why not just call yourself Asian?"

"Asian?! No way! Pinoys are the baddest Asians there are! We're tough, 'cuz we're BROWN, not like them other geeky ass Asians!" With that, my cousin decided that they should buy and eat the Count Chocula, "'cuz brown is good." I laughed to myself and let my cousin and his friends go about their own business. After all, although I don't recall screaming "Pinoy Power!" at the top of my lungs, I, too, am very proud of my heritage.

What struck me as funny, though, was Steve's inability to articulate what Filipino means (except that we're the "baddest Asians" around) even though it is so important to him. Finding a singular, authentic ethnic identity is important to many Filipino Americans, including, at one point, myself. Yen Le Espiritu found that Filipino Americans feel as if they aren't completely regarded as "Americans" by their non-Filipino counterparts because of their racial characteristics.[1] In addition, the current emphasis on multiculturalism increases many second and younger generation Filipino Americans' curiosities about their heritage.

Many second-generation Filipino Americans believe that to find information about their own culture and identity, it is "best to go to the source"—to first-generation Filipino Americans, or better yet, to Filipinos who reside in the Philippines. This has led many to the Internet, specifically to the soc.culture.filipino newsgroup. In 1996, the estimated number of readers on soc.culture.filipino was twenty thousand, many of whom reside in the Philippines.[2] Thus, on the surface, it appears that second- and later-generation Filipino Americans can easily get information about Filipino identity and culture from this source. However, culture and identity are not static and are constantly being negotiated. Thus, defining Filipino identity is a difficult task. In this article, I show how members of the Filipino diaspora reacted when they realized that there is no singular identity. By following several online debates on the soc.culture.filipino newsgroup, I learned how members of the diaspora negotiated the meaning of Filipino identity with people in the Philippines, and vice versa.

Why the Internet?

When I first started participating on soc.culture.filipino, participants were optimistic about the speed and efficiency of communication via e-mail and newsgroups. With respect to Filipino issues, they hoped to meet other Filipinos worldwide, learn about Filipino history and culture, and find long-lost relatives. All also desired to learn about social and political issues that impacted all Filipinos worldwide. Soc.culture.filipino, in other words, was a virtual homeland to which diasporic Filipinos could return quickly, inexpensively, and frequently.

But why bother with the Internet when transnational links are formed all the time? Rick Bonus, and Madge Bello and Vince Reyes, have shown that diasporic Filipinos in the United States and elsewhere have consistently communicated with friends and family and/or kept up with the news in the homeland via snail-mail letters, telephones, ethnic newspapers, and cable TV.[3] Soc.culture.filipino held the promise of allowing Filipinos worldwide to "come home" and join "the united Filipino community" on a daily basis if desired. In addition, it put people in frequent contact with potentially thousands of other Filipinos that they might otherwise not meet. Although satellite TV companies and the newspapers have numerous subscribers, communication is unidirectional, unlike newsgroups on the Internet.

While I was on the newsgroup, a majority of those that posted resided in the United States and the Philippines; however, by the end, people from Canada, Singapore, Australia, Austria, Sweden, and Greece regularly posted. Although on newsgroups communication is not synchronous, it does provide a lot of information at your doorstep, as well as allowing members to interact with thousands of people around the world through the simple act of typing words on a keyboard. Efficiency and speed constitute "nearness" on the web; thus, in this newsgroup, the Filipino diaspora appeared to converge. As one participant exclaimed, "It's a small world and the Net totally shrinks it!" We had, as Rob Kling and Suzi Iacono warned, believed the hype of the "computer revolution."[4]

The participants' desire to form a community and a strong ethnic identity was often discussed on soc.culture.filipino. The charter document states explicitly that the purpose of soc.culture.filipino is to:

> provide an open discussion on issues concerning the Philippines. This includes the following topics:

—new technology in the Philippines

—"what's happening back home" information and passing this on
to others unable to read news.

PURPOSE: Would like to discuss relevant Filipino issues in a newsgroup
that would single out Filipino culture. Currently, there are several other
nations that have started their newsgroups. . . . I believe that there will
be a consistent flow of news, especially with the state our country is
in presently. This newsgroup may help others to understand what our
culture is really like and not what it is rumored to be.

By separating Filipinos from "others" in the last sentence, the newsgroup's
founder semantically took Filipinos from the periphery to the center. In other
words, it became a place where Filipinos from all over the world could feel as if
they, their culture, their homeland, and ultimately their identity and experience
actually *matter*. Here, the founders reasoned, Filipinos would not necessarily
have to compare themselves with people from other cultures and/or races—
hence their insistence on "singling out" Filipino culture. However, as we know,
identities of people, nations, and cultures are relational. Yet, this utopian notion of a culture is compounded by the contagiousness of the ideology of the
computer revolution. Through the Internet, it is assumed that thousands, even
millions, of Filipinos would converge in this newsgroup, which could, theoretically, mean that we could separate ourselves from others and form a solid,
unified community.

Using the method of instances and a cultural-studies perspective, I analyzed
threads in soc.culture.filipino to understand the process of identity formation.
Before I collected my empirical material, I alerted the newsgroup participants of
my intent. I told them that I was a Filipino American sociologist studying Filipino
identity, and I assured the participants that their responses would be kept con-
fidential and their anonymity preserved. I also encouraged them to e-mail me
if they had any questions and/or wished to tell me their definition of "Filipino"
in private. Because some people checked the newsgroup less frequently than
others and because many new people were joining on a daily basis, I e-mailed
this message once every four weeks to remind the participants of my project.

From 1995 to mid-1997, I logged on to the newsgroup at least once a week to
see how the participants talked about, debated and/or defined Filipino identity.
If anything within the post referred to identity, I saved and printed it. I lurked
and just read the debates most of the time; however, if a person wrote anything
that I felt needed clarification, I posted a response to the whole newsgroup and
entered the discussion. As a participant-observer, my own stories and posts are
included in the empirical material. If something within the discussions made me
rethink my own identity, I either wrote it down in my memos or posted it on the
newsgroup. In two and a half years, I printed and analyzed over two thousand of
the posts. Out of over two thousand posts and more than two hundred threads,

I chose to present fewer than ten threads that contained many of the recurring topics.[5] These threads lasted for weeks or sometimes months and contained the fewest nonconstructive "flames" (heated debates, at times involving insults) and cross-posts.

All names are pseudonyms. Since there are several easily searched archives of Usenet groups (e.g., DejaNews, at <http://www.dejanews.com/>) I did not include exact dates, real names, or the real subject headings of the threads to protect the participants' anonymity. Although the Institutional Review Board designated newsgroups as public spaces at the time I presented my proposal, I still assured the participants of their confidentiality and anonymity. To give readers some sense of context, this study does give the participants' locations, and general time periods for the posts. Although I did not observe many anonymous posters, if I quoted any, I changed their pen names, since finding anonymous posters' "real-life" names *is* currently possible.

For this article, I focused on the use of jokes in the quest for the essence of Filipino culture and identity. In a forum designed to articulate "what Filipino culture really is and not what it is rumored to be," participants of soc.culture.filipino debated hundreds of questions, including.

- Are Filipino values rooted in the Philippines or can they be taught in other parts of the world?
- Do we want to teach our kids Filipino values?
- Do we even know what they are?
- Can Filipinos in the diaspora, especially Filipinos naturalized in the United States, be "as Filipino" as those in the Philippines?
- Or, did they give up their Filipinoness when they became citizens of another country?

Extremely heated debates ensued, with some participants hurling insults at and being hostile toward one another. Toward the end of one particularly difficult discussion (and flame war) about the execution of Flor Contemplacion (a domestic worker in Singapore accused of murdering another domestic helper, Delia Maga, and the son of her employer in 1991), Filipinos on the newsgroup were particularly divisive. This caused one participant to lament, "*What should we believe?! What should we do now?!*"

The answer? We should laugh.

Mourning and Laughter: Using Jokes to Temporarily Deflect Pain

Vicente Rafael has shown that mourning has become something of a common language for Filipinos.[6] When tragedy (such as the execution of Flor Contemplacion) occurs, Filipinos in the diaspora are able to put aside their differences, unite, and form a strong community. In the newsgroup I found this was no exception. Filipinos from all over the world condemned both the Singapore and

Philippine governments for the shabby treatment of overseas contract workers. In addition, massive flame wars between members of soc.culture.filipino and soc.culture.singapore erupted. The March 29, 1995, edition of *Today,* a Philippine newspaper, reported that over two thousand posts regarding the execution were exchanged between the two countries within one week.[7] To place this in context, throughout the three years that I studied soc.culture.filipino, the number of weekly posts never exceeded nine hundred.

Even in the middle of the Flor Contemplacion flame war with soc.culture.singapore, participants of soc.culture.filipino debated with one another. As always, much of the debate centered on loyalty and being a "true" Filipino. For example, participants debated whether those who posted racist remarks against Singaporeans were simply ignorant or were true, loyal Filipinos. In this sense, the degree to which one was defined as Filipino was defined against another Asian ethnic group, the Singaporeans instead of in relation to colonial influences (i.e., Spanish and U.S.) that I describe elsewhere.[8] When some Filipinos berated others for posting racist remarks against the Singaporeans, others defended the latter, claiming that they were only showing loyalty to the motherland.

Debating about the loyalty to the Philippines and the essence of Filipino identity caused the participants great pain. Defining oneself is power; people need an identity for self-recognition and recognition by others.[9] But on this newsgroup, Filipino identity was up for grabs. There were more debates than statements made about Filipino identity in the two years that I was on the newsgroup. As a result, the participants' posts often reflected a sense of anger and despair, because their sense of identity (both individual and group) and their power to define self was challenged constantly.

Because much of the criticism and the dissension were caused by self-defined Filipinos and not by an outside group the pain was even more acute: it's easier to fight an enemy from the outside than from within.[10] As a result, participants often questioned the possibility of defining a "Filipino essence" and achieving "Filipino unity." In the following sections, I show how jokes were used to ease that pain and simultaneously create a sense of community, and thus, a Filipino group identity.

Scholars have shown that humor is often used to ease pain; it is essential to the psychological well-being of people.[11] Michael Mulkay states that jokes offer an "enjoyable release from the restrictions of serious discourse, and also in the sense that it helps them to deal effectively with certain kinds of recurrent interactional difficulty."[12]

In the last two decades, Filipinos have had to deal with intense political corruption, martial law, the assassination of a well-loved expatriate (Senator Benigno Aquino), and the plundering of the country's wealth (the Marcos regime). News of abused overseas contract workers and mail-order brides were made even more apparent with the execution of Flor Contemplacion.[13] Yet with each tragedy a proliferation of jokes erupted.[14]

On the newsgroup, jokes were used as a tool to decrease the tension that arose when various aspects of Filipino identity were debated. Participants used jokes in two ways: to close a heated debate, and, more pointedly, to determine membership within the Filipino community. When debates about Filipino identity became so profuse that people started questioning the very possibility of attaining a group ethnic identity as well as the unification of Filipinos, jokes were offered to show us that we Filipinos *can* and *do* share a common bond.

On many occasions, participants offered jokes to ease their pain from having to debate seemingly endless issues that they felt did not need to be debated in the first place. In addition, they were also used to show us that Filipinos can unify in the face of any disaster. Many participants have argued that using humor to ease pain is *itself* a "Filipino trait." One participant stated,

> Jokes have always been an integral part of the Filipino culture. We are a people who have always been able to laugh at ourselves. This is one of the ways Pinoys are able to face great adversity and hardships. . . . By turning otherwise unfortunate events into something light and funny, we are able to deal with life's hardships easier.

Another participant illustrated the importance of redefining unfortunate events. He recalled that after the assassination of Aquino (expatriate and archenemy of former president Ferdinand Marcos), the collective mood in the Philippines and among members of the Filipino diaspora

> became stale . . . one could really feel it. As if the whole heart and soul of the Filipino people just stopped beating, stopped existing. But right after . . . oh well . . . there was a proliferation of Ninoy Aquino and Rolando Galman (the purported assassin) jokes. . . . Some of which were pretty inane, but some were very sarcastic and true. And funny too.

The pain suffered by members of this newsgroup due to the endless debates about cultural values, the authenticity of Tagalog and other matters seems trivial compared to the above tragedy. But as I stated above, participants believe that "knowing one's culture makes one rich," and dismantling their images of the Filipino culture was confusing and painful. Yet interestingly, many of the most heated debates were temporarily closed through the use of jokes. For example, jokes temporarily ended a debate that centered around the use of the letter *F* in the Philippine language.[15] In this debate, several common beliefs about Tagalog were contested, such as the fact that the traditional Abakada was not wholly constructed by indigenous Filipinos.[16] Thus, those who wanted to ground Filipino identity by finding an authentic Filipino tradition and language lost an important tool. The debate about language incorporated references to assimilation and "colonial mentality," two topics that often were geared more toward diasporic Filipinos, particularly those in the United States, than Filipinos back home. Then one day, a participant posted the following: "As long as we frounounce our f's froferly, I think here's no froblem with that. . . ." At this point, the conversation shifted from a heated debate to a lighthearted conversation as subsequent posts revolved completely around this post. Here is an example of the types of replies to this post

>Iksyusmi,

>

>Did yu jas sey "ep"?? [Excuse me, Did you just say "F"?]
Ang "P" ay ipo-pronawns mo as "PEE"; ang "F" naman "EFF"—Did you get my foint? [You should pronounce "P" as "PEE" and "F" as "EFF"—Did you get my foint?]

Throughout this interchange, it is obvious that the participants knew the difference between P and F, and knew exactly where Ps and Fs should be used, and they were careful to pick words that began with "P" or "F" to make this point. The significance of this particular post lies in their timing, and the use of a topic of much debate in the past (i.e., whether the letter F should be in the official alphabet of the Philippines). It is important to note that the context in which the joke is told is very important. For example, the second person's use of "Filipinized" English ("Did yu jas sey ep?"). The post did not cause a stir at all at this point in time because of the fiery debates that had preceded this letter. Since it was told in a context where participants pointed out that Filipinos do know how to speak English "properly," and was posted after a very lengthy debate about whether F should be in the Filipino language, it was only seen as funny. The transposition of Ps and Fs is not a completely "innocent" gesture. Instead, I argue, it points to something more significant—the imposition of the Tagalog structure over English. This, in addition to some participants' pride in the "Filipino way" of pronouncing English words, are subtle forms of resistance against full assimilation to American culture and colonial mentality.

However, when posts using "Filipinized" English were written after the language debate had long since subsided, another intense and hostile debate erupted, this time regarding the arrogance of Filipinos who critique those who transpose Ps and Fs. What had, months earlier, united the newsgroup community divided it later.

Participants often put naturalized Filipinos in America on the spot because *Filipino* is usually defined against the Filipino-U.S. dichotomy. Because of this, Filipino Americans occupy a marginal space more than other Filipinos in the diaspora. Furthermore, Rafael has shown that *balikbayans* (Filipinos naturalized in the host country who visit the motherland) are viewed with suspicion by Filipinos in the Philippines, as they seem aloof and arrogant, willing to come back home as tourists but not willing to give anything back to the country.[17] Especially when juxtaposed to the image of overseas contract workers, they are perceived to be only sentimental toward, but not really *concerned about,* the homeland.

The "You might be Filipino if. . . ." thread of 1995 was a major thread that began in the midst of debates about Filipino identity, colonial mentality, naturalization and degrees of Filipinoness. This thread began in April, only three weeks after Flor Contemplacion was executed in Singapore, and as members of soc.culture.filipino and soc.culture.singapore declared a cease-fire on the flame war. A Filipino American began the thread, and although Filipinos from around the world contributed to the thread, a majority of the responses came from Filipinos in the United States. I believe the reason for the Filipino American domination in this thread is not merely because they were most likely greater in number. Rather, because much of the discussions revolved around the dubiousness of Filipino Americans' loyalty to the Philippines, Filipino Americans on the newsgroup needed to ground their Filipino identity in *something*. Thus, they created this list of jokes.

Jokes as Genre

Jokes are a specific form of "speech genre." Mikhail Bakhtin has argued that we should not only study their functions in general, but examine *why* particular genres are used at a specific point in time.[18] I believe that the fact the participants began and continued the "You might be Filipino if . . ." genre is a tactical move toward unity. The jokes they put forth did not have to be stated within this particular genre. They could have just sent out stand-alone jokes. In fact, from 1995 to 1996, there were several jokes that were sent independently that, if understood, would determine one's membership as a Filipino as well as demarcate different boundaries around the community. Being able to understand most of these jokes would already establish one's membership in the Filipino community, as they usually contained a reference to a Filipino dish, custom, word, historical event, or stereotype.

The "You might be Filipino if . . ." genre *itself* implies that the goal is the establishment of membership. It is comprised of a list of characteristics or codes that you must comprehend or perform to fit in. The idea is that if you understand the joke you affirm your membership as a Filipino. In addition, if most of these characteristics apply to you, then you are Filipino. Therefore, the use of this particular genre signals both the need for membership and the need for boundary making.

Thus, these lists of jokes were not only put forth to ease pain and create a temporary community, but also to create an identity that addressed the structural relationship between the United States and the Philippines and transcended the American/Filipino dichotomy. This was done not to justify colonial mentality, but to show that the incorporation of colonial words or customs does not necessarily mean that balikbayans have sold out. The incorporation is often resistant in that it mimics the dominant culture, but is distinctly Filipino.

Literature on marginal spaces often includes discussions about hybridity.[19] Bakhtin studied the hybridity within languages, and illustrated how pidgin languages fuse two or more languages together.[20] This is what he terms *organic hybridity*, implying that this "naturally" happens when two or more cultures meet in the "contact zone."[21] Yet according to Bakhtin, there is also another form of hybridity: *intentional hybridity*.[22] This type of hybridity describes the act of appropriating cultural values and norms of the colonial "other" and making them one's own.

This is in contrast to the idea of "colonial mentality," where incorporating "foreign" cultural norms is described as evidence of false consciousness, "selling out," and/or the loss of one's culture. The empowerment of colonized peoples is contingent upon finding the one "true" culture and extrapolating and discarding any elements of the colonial culture. In this dichotomous scenario, either you are "in" or "out" of the circle; this essentializes both cultures, and thus does not make any room for movement in between or the creation of an in-between, or new, space. Filipinos on the newsgroup and outside it are concerned that colonial mentality inhibits the creation of a true Filipino consciousness.[23] Yet, the division between the Philippines and America is not easily discerned.[24]

Another concept, "sly civility" is related to intentional hybridity.[25] Instead of emphasizing the vulnerability of colonized peoples and focusing on their status as "victims," sly civility emphasizes their ability to resist assimilation into the dominant culture by intentionally appropriating the colonists' cultural norms. Therefore, their "civility" is sly because they do not simply mirror the colonial power's culture, but *mimic* or appropriate colonists' culture while simultaneously translating it into their own. They are "almost the same, *but not quite*," a state that irritates the "teacher" and empowers the "student." Frantz Fanon addresses the argument that learning and speaking the colonizers' language indicates a colonial mentality (in his words, "becomes whiter"), an argument echoed by many participants in this newsgroup. He argues, "To speak means to be in a position to use a certain syntax, to grasp the morphology of this or that language, but it means above all to assume a culture, to support the weight of a civilization."[26] However, mastering the colonizer's language is not completely disempowering.[27] Jaune Quick-to-See Smith argues that retaining sentence structure and accents of the "lost" language when speaking the colonizer's language are ways to retain control of one's identity. Mimicking a language allows colonized people to subvert full assimilation and maintain one's culture.[28] Later in this article, I give examples of how the appropriation of the English language is resistance.

Participants who contributed to the list of jokes showed the sly civility of Filipinos and their ability to mimic and appropriate the dominant culture. I have divided these jokes into four categories: (1) sly civility and mimicry, (2) unique pronunciation, (3) novelty, and (4) essentializing behavior. I believe that this especially serves Filipino-American members as these jokes show that incorporating "American" words and customs does not necessarily point to colonial mentality (or as one participant said, "evidence that [we live in a] 'mental colony'"). In this section, I will show that this list of jokes both addresses debates about colonial mentality and transcends the boundaries participants erected between Filipinos in the Philippines and disaporic Filipinos, particularly those in the United States.

Mimicry, Sly Civility, and the Refusal to Assimilate: Taglish As Resistance

Rafael has shown that Taglish has the potential to be a lingua franca for Filipinos in the Philippines.[29] He argues that Taglish is powerful because it both invokes and collapses the hierarchical relationship among English, Spanish, and Tagalog. With respect to the jokes that the participants told, many highlight the appropriation of American English into the Filipino language. Here are some examples of answers to "You might be Filipino if...":

> You refer to the refrigerator as the "ref" or "pridyider" [Frigidaire].
>
> You add an unwarranted "H" to your name, i.e. "Jhun," [Jun (short for "Junior")], "Bhoy," [Boy] "Rhon" [Ron].
>
> You refer to your VCR as a "beytamax" [Betamax].
> You refer to seasonings and all other forms of monosodium glutamate as "Ajinomoto" [Japanese influence is established].

Here we have English words that are given new nicknames ("ref") or new spellings altogether ("beytamax" or "pridyider"). The last joke even reflects the incorporation of a Japanese word into Tagalog, invoking Japanese occupation of the Philippines during World War II. Changing the spelling and creating new nicknames make these English (and Japanese) words Filipino, and in a way reverses the assimilation process and counters accusations of false consciousness and colonial mentality.

Other jokes emphasize a subtle refusal to assimilate through mimicry. It may not be a conscious or violent refusal, but it is a refusal nonetheless. As stated before, mimicry is powerful because being "almost the same, but not quite" points to the failure of teachers, and the silent victory for the subordinate group. The following jokes are examples of mimicry:

> You pronounce F's like P's and P's like F's.
>
> You say "he" when you mean "she" and vice versa.
>
> *Bonus question:* You understand this joke (make sure you read the punch line with a Filipino accent!).
> How many bears were in the car with Goldilocks?
> Four—the momma bear, the poppa bear, the baby bear and the driver [pronounced "dri-bear"].

As stated before, the *P* versus *F* debate refers to the imposition of English letters on the Tagalog (Abakada) alphabet. The "bonus question" refers to the same debate: *V* was not originally part of the Tagalog alphabet; the joke alludes to the substitution of the *B* sound on the *V* words or syllables. And the he/she nondistinction refers to the fact that Tagalog (and other dialects, such as Cebuano), unlike English (the language of the former colonial power) has only one—gender-neutral—pronoun, *siya*.

Though not militant behaviors, these jokes are resistant because the structure of Tagalog is used even when English is spoken. The speakers, in framing these pronunciations within the "You might be Filipino if . . ." genre, show that Filipinos use these pronunciations or structures, not out of ignorance or the inability to speak "proper" English, but presumably because it is the Filipino way of doing things. In so doing, these jokes are examples of mimicry and how Filipinos have kept their heritage despite colonization, and thus show how charges of full assimilation, appropriation, and "colonial mentality" are unfounded.

Unique Pronunciation As Resistance

In a similar vein, some Filipinos on the newsgroup have commented that the particular pronunciation of certain words distinguishes Filipinos from other races and Asian subgroups. This, they argue, should not be a source of shame, but something to celebrate because it sets Filipinos apart from other Asian groups and "Amerikanos" (i.e., white or "whitewashed" Americans). As in the last category, pronouncing English words in a new way is mimicry and resistance, not simply "failed" assimilation. But it differs from the use of Taglish and jokes. Some examples:

> If you pronounce "furniture" as "poor-nit-chyur," you might be a Filipino.
>
> If you say ro-BI-tussin instead of RO-bi-tussin, you might be a Filipino.
>
> If your plural version of the following words ends in 's':
> jewelry
> equipment
> homework
> furniture   then you might be a Filipino.
>
> You are definitely Filipino if the word "Wednesday" has three syllables.
>
> If you say com-`fort-able instead of còm-fort-able, then you might be a Filipino.
>
> If you say in-`ven-tory instead of ìn-ven-tory, then you might be a Filipino.

Note that the pronunciation of "furniture" once again alludes to the *P* and *F* debate; the other words, however, are all English. Unlike Taglish, they are not

English words that are given new Tagalog spellings (i.e., jokes = dyoks); each of these words have corresponding Tagalog words. The difference is largely in the pronunciation. Jaune Quick-to-See Smith has argued that although most Native Americans speak English, they retain use of their "lost" language by using the sentence structure and accents of their languages when speaking English.[30] I argue that the unique pronunciation of the English words listed above is a similar type of resistance against Americanization. These jokes, too, are examples of sly civility and mimicry: English is used, but it is again the "almost the same, *but not quite*" pronunciation that makes it Filipino. As in the section on the imposition of Tagalog sentence structure on English, the participants show that Filipinos use these pronunciations not out of ignorance or inability to speak "properly," but to reflect the Filipino way of doing things. In addition, because they are framed within the "You might be Filipino if . . ." genre, these pronunciations are markers of Filipinoness, and understanding the jokes verify one's membership within the community.

Novelty as Intentional Hybridity

Intentional hybridity—or the creation of new words and new cultural traditions—is the third type of resistance. Here we can see how American things become Filipino:

> You say "comfort room" instead of "bathroom."
> You say "for take out" instead of "to go."
> You "open" or "close" the light.
> You asked for "Colgate" instead of "toothpaste."
> You asked for a "Pentel-pen" or a "ball-pen" instead of just a "pen."
> You refer to the refrigerator as the "ref" or "pridyider."
> You own a Mercedes Benz and you call it "chedeng."[31]
> You say "Kodakan" instead of "take a picture."
> You order a McDonald's instead of a "hamburger" (pronounced ham-boor-jer).
> You say "Cutex" instead of "nail polish."
> You prefer to make acronyms for phrases, such as "OA" for overacting, or "TNT" for, well, you know.
> You say "air con" instead of "a/c" or "air conditioner."
> You have aunts and uncles named "Baby," "Girlie," or "Boy."

Using different English words to refer to common objects and places is not unique to Filipinos; but using this "You might be Filipino if . . ." genre, a person can determine her membership within the community if she either uses these phrases or words or if she at least knows the significance of these substitutions. As in the section on pronunciations, these English words have been Filipinized.

In the third to last joke the reader must know the Filipino definition of the acronym TNT. Though explosive, the definition does not refer to dynamite;

instead it refers to "tago ng tago," or, to put it nicely, a way to extend a friend's visit in your country without wasting governmental officials' time by making them read mounds of official paperwork needed to grant an extension on your friend's visa. In addition, the use of the product name to refer to common objects, I argue, reflects Filipinos' simultaneous love and hatred of Western products. The proliferation of Western, particularly U.S.-based, products in the Philippines serves as a constant reminder of the unequal and codependent U.S./Philippine postcolonial relationship. The love and hatred of their ties to the former colonial power can be found in the language. Through the creation of new nicknames—either by using the product's name as a substitute of the common name, or by merging the product's name with a Tagalog suffix (i.e., Kodakan)–Filipinos have imposed the Tagalog structure over English, and thus made these objects distinctly "Filipino."

The participants also wanted to show that commonly consumed American foods have also been Filipinized:

> You put hot dogs in your spaghetti.

> Your cupboards are full of Spam, Vienna sausage, Ligo, and corned beef, which you refer to as karne norte.

> You fry Spam or hot dogs and eat them with rice.

As we have seen, one of the major focal points was the appropriation of English words, letters, and phrases into Tagalog. Some have argued that "Taglish" is a corruption of Tagalog—among them Teodoro Agoncillo, a nationalist historian, who has labeled Taglish a "bastard language."[32] The national language, Agoncillo and other nationalists argue, should incorporate words from the various dialects spoken in the Philippines, not words from the colonizers. The participants who contributed to these jokes, however, did more than just argue that it was okay to use Taglish. Framing these jokes in the "You might be Filipino if . . ." genre, they showed that Filipinos had successfully taken the language of the colonists, made it Filipino, and effectively socialized this process so that the very *practice* of imposing a Filipino structure on the English language *had become* Filipino. Thus, these jokes both establish membership into the community while demonstrating that intentional hybridity does not necessarily reflect colonial mentality.

Essentializing Behavior

The respondents also attempted to create a feeling of community among all Filipinos in the diaspora through essentializing behaviors. As in the use of unique pronunciations, these behaviors set Filipinos apart from other Asian groups and Amerikanos.

> You have to kiss your relative on the cheek as soon as you enter the room.

> You consistently arrive 30 minutes late for all events.

You point with your lips.
You nod upwards to greet someone.
You eat using your hands—and have it down to a technique.

You put your foot up on your chair and rest your elbow on your knee while eating.

You are perfectly comfortable in a squatting position with your elbows resting on your knees.

You go to a department store and try to bargain the prices.

You put your hands together in front of you as if to make a path and say "Excuse, excuse" when you pass between people or in front of the TV.

None of these behavior examples were contested at the time they were posted, probably because they were a welcome alternative to the flame wars that dominated the newsgroup. Many of the respondents welcomed these references as evidence of the unique behavior of Filipinos. However, taken outside the context, some of these behaviors were characterized as "crass" or particular to a certain class or region. A few weeks after the jokes were posted on the Internet, a Filipino American newspaper, the *Philippine News,* addressed the jokes and condemned the participants who contributed them for belittling Filipinos.

It is interesting to note that class and regional divisions are considered to be majors schisms within the Filipino community at home and abroad.[33] However, in this newsgroup, although the participants talked about regional and class difference, these discussions did not last very long or turn into fiery debates. So, addressing Filipino behaviors that were particular to a certain class or region was not problematic. In other words, at this point in time, in this context, newsgroup members ignored a schism deemed so important in "real life."

Determining the Degree of Filipinoness

Because these defining characteristics were put forth as jokes, they were viewed as nonthreatening, and at the time rarely offended any of the participants. Being a Filipino American myself, I thoroughly enjoyed this thread, and printed out some of the jokes so I could share them with my family. However, it is important to note that these jokes were not considered to be controversial at that particular time because they were put forth by self-defined Filipinos and because they were created at a time when the number of debates about Filipino identity and discussions of Filipino nationalism (with respect to the Flor Contemplacion tragedy) were at an all-time high. If the jokes were created by non-Filipinos or in a different context, it is likely that the participants on the newsgroup would consider the jokes demeaning.[34] In fact, when a self-defined white American male recently posted a thread entitled "You know you're married to a Filipina . . ." a year later, he was burned to a crisp by the newsgroup flames largely because of his position of power. In contrast, when a Filipino-American male posted the same list a few weeks later, only one participant objected and his objection was politely worded.

This list of jokes temporarily diverted the participants' attention away from the Flor Contemplacion execution, the debates about colonial mentality, the daily problems overseas contract workers face, and the "loss" of Filipino women (and Asian women in general) to white males. In this newsgroup, the game was just to add to the jokes. However, a few months later the list of jokes was actually turned into a quiz that people could take to determine their "Filipinoness." Points were accorded as follows:

3 points if you can relate to the following characteristics yourself

2 points if it relates to an immediate family member, i.e. mom or dad or sister/brother

1 point if you know of someone who has the characteristic

At the end, people are to tally their points to see to which category they belong:

259–327 points:
Welcome to America! Judging from your high score, you are an obvious transplant from the Philippines. There's no doubt what your ethnic identity is! You're a Filipino, through and through.

173–258 points:
Congratulations, you've retained most of the Filipino traits and tendencies your family has instilled in you.

151–72:
You have OFT (Obvious Filipino Tendencies.) Go with the flow to reach full Filipino potential. Prepare for assimilation; resistance is futile!

50 and under:
You're white, aren't you?

An interesting move was made here. The jokes, taken out of context, were no longer used as a way for Filipinos in the United States to assert their Filipinoness. Instead, they were taken as Filipino traits and used to separate Filipinos from whites. In other words, the quiz was no longer about *asserting* but *assessing* Filipino identity. And, if you don't have any characteristics, watch out! You might be white(washed).

In sum, when the list of jokes was taken out of the context in which it was generated and made into a "quiz," the way the jokes were used changed. This emphasizes the importance of context in understanding the debates in the newsgroup. When the list of jokes was posted originally, many participants attempted to bridge the Filipino/American gap—hence the proliferation of references to Filipinized English. However, by the time the jokes turned into the quiz, the gap between Filipino and American and the conflation of Filipino and white was once again in the forefront of the debates. As a result, although some of the participants believed the list of jokes showed the common root of all Filipinos, it may be of limited use in other contexts.[35]

Conclusion

When these lists of jokes were generated, none who read the newsgroup publicly disputed anything on it. Instead, most responses were positive. The most active participants on the newsgroup did not publicly complain about the jokes (although some of the jokes could be interpreted as self-deprecating) because they were aware that the jokes started to appear at a time when there were numerous debates and arguments concerning the definition of *Filipino*. Instead, this list of jokes represented a new way of characterizing Filipinos that did not depend on a physical link to the "homeland," nor on the articulation of rigid, "authentic" Filipino cultural values.

However, to those who did not participate in the newsgroup, this list of jokes may have been interpreted less favorably. When someone from the *Philippine News* (a Filipino American newspaper) read the list, he was prompted to denounce the list of jokes as "self-deprecating" and hurtful to the Filipino community. According to Bettye Saar, this is not uncommon. She states that because cultural artifacts (including jokes) are "shared (exhibited), experienced, and relinquished," they are bound to be interpreted in a way that is different from that which the artist intended.[36] Thus, the section above on "essential" Filipino behaviors may be interpreted by Filipinos outside the newsgroup as badly representing Filipino culture. In this way, the list may not have been as liberating as its proponents hoped it would be.

Whether it is liberating or not, of course, depends not only on the context but also on the individuals who read the list. (It should be noted that this list of jokes was recently turned into a book.[37]) However, within the context of this newsgroup, this particular thread provided a positive atmosphere and the promise of unity within diversity.

More important is that this discussion points to something that Internet meeting places can offer that local meeting places cannot: the ability for sustained and efficient dialogue about local and global phenomena, and the possibility for transnational community among multiple members of a diaspora. It is one thing to learn about local and global social, economic, and political issues and their effects on diasporic members. It is another to experience through sustained communication and fierce debates how seemingly remote and "theoretical" issues affect ourselves, those with whom we wish to form a community, and our relationship to these people. The reason for the turn to jokes occurred here because the participants were forced to situate themselves and their local problems within the context of larger, global patterns. For Filipino American members, in particular, the problems participants had with reconciling their ideas about race, gender, colonialism, citizenship, nationalism, and the rigidity and authenticity of cultural boundaries showed them that traditional boundary making and adjudicating of membership based on these traditional categories are a problem. These sustained discussions made the participants (including myself) experience and discover for themselves the power and fallibility of social constructionism. Even though we never articulated it as such, we saw much of our notions of our selves and Filipinoness crumble with each debate and flame war.

Simultaneously, however, we embraced the idea of being able to define ourselves. In many ways, despite the tallying of points at the end of the "game," these jokes represent much more than just membership boundaries. They show us alternative ways of thinking about culture —as an active articulation and enfolding of issues that pertain to ourselves and others in the diaspora. Through these jokes we learned how members of the diaspora turned the impact of colonialism and globalization on its head (albeit temporarily) through the introduction and frequent use of new words like *chedeng*. Though not structurally changing the position of the Philippines and Filipinos in relation to the world, this linguistic turn places Filipinos at the center of cultural creation instead of merely passively taking in outside cultural influences.

Much like hip-hop culture's use of African American urban slang, the use of new Taglish words offers a distinct inside joke for membership. Once commodified, of course, the participants do have a choice whether to bury the word (as the word "def" was literally buried by Rick Rubin, the cofounder of Def Jam records and father figure of hip-hop once it entered dictionaries in the early 1990s) or to keep it.

It may have been possible for these lists of jokes to proliferate and become widespread through more traditional means; indeed, the lists, as noted earlier, were printed in various Filipino newspapers and eventually published in book form. The significance of these lists is that they emerged during some very heated debates that were turning our notions of race, gender, ethnicity, culture, and even nation on their heads. We began to realize the fragility of these concepts and how global economic, political, and social issues affected us simultaneously yet differently as Filipinos living in different areas around the world.[38] It was through this medium, this particular exchange, with its discussions about "unity," that we were able to witness the beginnings of transnational community building, a phenomena often theorized but rarely seen.

Notes

1. Yen Le Espiritu, "The Intersection of Race, Ethnicity, and Class: The Multiple Identities of Second-Generation Filipinos," *Identities* 1, nos. 2–3 (1994): 249–73.

2. Kevin Atkinson, *Usenet Info Center*, (1996), online at <http://sunsite.unc.edu/usenet-i/info>.

3. See Rick Bonus, *Locating Filipino Americans* (Philadelphia: Temple University Press, 2000) and Madge Bello and Vince Reyes, "Filipino Americans and the Marcos Overthrow: The Transformation of Political Consciousness," *Amerasia* 13 (1986–1987): 73–84.

4. Rob Kling and Suzi Iacono, "Computerization Movements and the Mobilization of Support for Computerization," in *Ecologies of Knowledge*, ed. Susan Leigh Star (Albany: State University of New York Press, 1995), 119–53.

5. Some of the recurring topics include the U.S.-Philippine relationship, cultural values, language and colonial mentality, and the construction of "Filipinas." See Emily Noelle Ignacio, "Ain't I a Filipino (Woman)? An Analysis of Authorship/Authority through the Construction of Filipino/a on the Net," *Sociological Quarterly* 41 (2000): 551–72; and Emily Noelle Ignacio, *Building Diaspora: The Formation on the Internet of a Filipino Cultural Community* (New Brunswick, NJ: Rutgers University Press, forthcoming).

6. Vicente L. Rafael, "'Your Grief Is Our Gossip': Overseas Filipinos and Other Spectral Presences," *Public Culture* 9 (1997): 267–91.

7. Romy Alampay, "Forgive But Don't Forget," *Today* (Manila), March 29, 1995, online at <www.today.net.ph>.

8. See Ignacio, *Building Diaspora*.

9. See Craig Calhoun, ed., *Social Theory and the Politics of Identity* (Cambridge, MA: Blackwell Press, 1994); Lucy R. Lippard, *Mixed Blessings: Art in Multicultural America* (New York: Pantheon Books, 1990); and Mary C. Waters, *Ethnic Options: Choosing Identities in America* (Berkeley and Los Angeles: University of California Press, 1990).

10. See Lippard, *Mixed Blessings*.

11. Michael Mulkay, *On Humor* (Oxford: Basil Blackwell, 1988); Rosabeth Moss Kanter, *Men and Women of the Corporation* (New York: Basic Books, 1977); and Roger D. Abrahams and Alan Dundes, "On Elephantasy and Elephanticide," *Psychoanalytic Review* 56 (1969): 225–41.

12. Mulkay, *On Humor*, 153.

13. Benedict Anderson, "Cacique Democracy in the Philippines: Origins and Dreams," in *Discrepant Histories: Translocal Essays on Filipino Cultures*, ed. Vicente L. Rafael (Philadelphia: Temple University Press, 1995), 3–47; Yen Le Espiritu, *Filipino American Lives* (Philadelphia: Temple University Press, 1995); and Rafael, "'Your Grief Is Our Gossip.'"

14. See Rafael, "'Your Grief Is Our Gossip'"; and Rick Bonus, "Homeland Memories and Media: Filipino Images and Imaginations in America," in *Filipino Americans: Transformation and Identity*, ed. Maria P. P. Root (Thousand Oaks, CA: Sage,1997), 208–18.

15. Emily Noelle Ignacio, "Ano ba ang F/Pilipino?: An Analysis of the Negotiation of Filipino (Pilipino?) Identity on the Internet," in *Intersections and Divergences: Contemporary Asian Pacific American Communities*, ed. Linda Trinh Vo and Rick Bonus (Temple University Press, 2002), 89–101.

16. Abakada is the Tagalog alphabet system introduced by Lope K.Santos in 1937. For a history of the construction of Tagalog, see Vicente L. Rafael, *Contracting Colonialism: Translation and Christian Conversion in Tagalog Society Under Early Spanish Rule* (Durham, NC: Duke University Press, 1993).

17. Rafael, "'Your Grief is Our Gossip.'"

18. Mikhail M. Bakhtin, *Speech Genres and Other Late Essays*, trans. Vern W. McGee (Austin: University of Texas Press, 1986).

19. See Gloria Anzaldúa, *Borderlands/LaFrontera: The New Mestiza* (San Francisco: Aunt Lute, 1987); Roger Rouse, "Mexican Migration and the Social Space of Postmodernism," *Diaspora* 1, no.1 (1991): 8–23; and Robert J. C. Young, *Colonial Desire: Hybridity in Theory, Culture and Race* (London: Routledge,1995) for a critique.

20. Mikhail M. Bakhtin, *The Dialogic Imagination*, trans. Caryl Emerson and Michael Holquist (Austin: University of Texas Press, 1981).

21. Mary Louise Pratt, *Imperial Eyes: Travel Writing and Transculturation* (New York: Routledge, 1992).

22. Bakhtin, *The Dialogic Imagination*, 361.

23. See interviews in Espiritu, *Filipino American Lives;* See also Rafael, "'Your Grief is Our Gossip.'"

24. See Ignacio, *Building Diaspora.*

25. Homi K. Bhabha, *The Location of Culture* (New York: Routledge, 1994).

26. Fanon, Frantz. *Black Skin, White Masks* (New York: Grove Press, 1967), 17–18.

27. See Bhabha, *The Location of Culture;* Rafael, *Contracting Colonialism;* and Lippard, *Mixed Blessings.*

28. Jaune Quick-to-See Smith, quoted in Lippard, *Mixed Blessings,* 49.

29. Vicente L. Rafael, "Taglish, or the Phantom Lingua Franca," *Public Culture* 8, no.1 (1995): 101–26.

30. Smith quoted in Lippard, *Mixed Blessings,* 48.

31. *Chedeng* is a nickname for a Mercedes Benz and cannot be translated into English.

32. Teodoro Agoncillo, quoted in Rafael, "Taglish," 109.

33. See Bonus, *Locating Filipino Americans,* for examples.

34. See Lippard, *Mixed Blessings,* on the politics of naming.

35. See Ignacio, *Building Diaspora,* for an extended analysis of those other contexts.

36. Bettye Saar, quoted in Lippard, *Mixed Blessings,* 80.

37. Neni Santa Romana–Cruz, "*You Know You're Filipino If . . .*" (Manila: Tahanan Books, 1997).

38. For further elaborations on this point, see Ignacio, "Ano ba ang F/Pilipino?" and Ignacio, *Building Diaspora.*

7

The Geography of Cyberliterature in Korea

AEJU KIM

Cyberliterature has been called an "avant-garde mode of performance in an age of computers." It is a "new multi-media literature conceived by electronic revolution, reflected and produced by the new digital communications technology."[1] Indeed, these two descriptions provide an accurate definition. Yet, in Korea, it is an avant-garde mode of performance in its infancy. Here, limitations of technology preclude a true hypertext venue where a dynamic flow of textual interaction between writer and reader transforms conventional modes of authorship into plural and borderless texts. Hye-Sil Choi, an outspoken critic, points out that despite the rhetoric, Korean cyberliterature is still primarily dependent on network functions rather than on hypertext.[2] What we have is a body of literature composed on a computer and uploaded onto various literary sites on the Internet; in other words, conventionally written works published in cyberspace. It is in this technical respect that Korean cyberliterature falls short of the true aims and spirit of hypertext.

Although Korean cyberliterature still lacks the interactive technological edge, it is clear that Korean cyberwriters do have a unique literary style distinct from those of conventional writers. Writers such as Sung-Su Lee, Woo-Hyuk Lee, Kyung-Ah Song, Young-Soo Lee, Young-Ha Kim have adopted cyber-conceived subjects, themes, motifs and techniques into their writing. Sung-Su Lee, Woo-Hyuk Lee, and Young-Soo Lee write within fantasy or science-fiction genres, while the writings of Kyung-Ah Song, Young-Ha Kim, and Young-Soo Lee focus on the indeterminacy and nonmateriality of digital texts. These writers, published on the Internet and considered to be on the cutting edge of cyberliterature, have been constrained by technology. But there is another constraint equally compromising to the ethic of a true digital sensitivity, and that is the incentive to publish in print. Clearly print is more lucrative, but even more than money the traditions and psychology of print publishing seem to overshadow the desire for the liberatory textuality of hypertext. Thus, one is led to the realization that, due not only to the constraints of technology but also the reluctance to make a clean break from the conventions of the established literary milieu, Korean cyberliterature has not validated itself as a new literary form.

While applications for hypertext inhabit a technological limbo, the reluctance to embrace cyberideology can perhaps be examined in a more sociopsychological/sociopolitical light. Within contemporary Korean literary circles there is a great tension centered upon the impact of the Internet on literature. Opposing camps are occupied in debate. The opponents of cyberliterature consist mainly of established writers and critics who regard this new literary venue as a charybdis disturbing the pure realm of literature. On the other hand, its proponents—mostly young amateur writers and critics—see cyberwriting as a boon to literature that promises a new paradigm. From either perspective these ongoing discussions are intense, as they lay the groundwork for the viability of cyberliterature in Korea.

The underlying reasons for these intense exchanges stem from a unilateral resistance to this emerging media. The form of resistance suggests it is based on a fear that cybertechnology will encroach upon Korean language and culture, co-opting and dismantling the established hierarchies that regulate Korean literary society. Behind this may loom a more implicit and psychological motivation: the anxiety that the solid textual body may, in a flash, be swirled away and disappear, irretrievably lost in the electronic circuitry. "Corporeal anxiety," termed by N. Katherine Hayles, is defined as a fearful realization that the body is "in jeopardy from a multitude of threats, especially the dematerialization that comes from being translated into digital code."[3] In the period of late capitalism, where information technologies dominate every social sphere, this frightening consciousness is pervasive and heightens the connection between identity and the materiality of published works. Korean cyberwriters, for instance, demonstrate this attachment to the printed book by republishing their online books in print form. This transformation back to the safe terrain of tangible texts reveals a corporeal anxiety over the radical fragility and indeterminacy of electronic texts.

Thus, motivated by potential disruptions to cultural, linguistic, and corporeal identity, the debate over the validity of cyberliterature grows. My argument within this debate comprises two main areas. First, I argue that, notwithstanding its current lack of status as a valid literary genre and the opposition to it, cyberliterature will become a decisive force in shaping the future canon of Korean literature. Evidence for this prediction will be drawn from the sociopolitical terrain of Korean society and its contemporary literature. I will also examine the current underlying anxiety regarding cyberwriting and then speculate on the evolution of cyberliterature by drawing on observations of its ecology and technology to date.

The Debate

From its infancy, when Sung-Su Lee first put his cyber–science fiction novel, *Atlantis Rhapsody,* on the CHOLLIAN net in 1989, Korean cyberliterature has been stymied by convention and constrained within a kind of partial existence.

Before articulating the ongoing contention over cyberliterature, allow me to backtrack and briefly set the stage with a short history of the development of cyberliterature in Korea.

With the opening of the Literature Center on the HITEL net in 1992, information about cyberliterature began to be available to readers. Shortly thereafter, Ger-Il Bok published the first serial science-fiction novel, *Under the Blue Moon*, on the HITEL. Then, in 1993, Woo-Hyuk Lee published *Toemalock* on the "Thriller/Science Fiction" billboard of HITEL net, "scoring" an explosive number of "hits" and winning tremendous popularity among ardent Netizens. When he republished his online book in thirteen printed volumes in 1994, he shocked national literary circles by selling over a million copies. The term "PC communications literature" was first used in 1994 by Seokju Jang in his commentary titled "Revolutionary Switchover of Writing and Reading: PC Communications and the Literature of the Future." Once named, "PC communications literature" took on a more solid form. Critics including Byung-Ik Kim, author of *New Way of Writing and Authenticity of Literature* (1997), and Yong-Uk Lee actively began to state their views on cyberliterature. Lee accelerated the discussion by issuing a quarterly magazine, *Version Up*, the first of its kind on cyberliterature. In addition, he published a critical book of cyberliterature titled *The Challenge of Cyber Literature* (1996). *The Bit Age*, a collection of the best short stories first published on the HITEL Net, featured the work of two cyber writers, Young-Ha Kim and Kyung-Ah Song, and was re-published in print in December 1996. Within academia, a seminal doctoral thesis on cyber literature (2000) and two subsequent dissertations have been presented to date, though the debate promises more scholarly investigation. More recent volumes on cyberliterature include Sunee Lee's anthology *The Theory of Cyber Literature* (2001) and *The Understanding of Cyber Literature* (2001).[4] Though short and lacking volume, cyberliterature's history has nevertheless succeeded in breaking ground for this new genre.

Through its relatively brief history, Korean cyberliterature's role has been confined to that of primary venue for amateur writers. In fact, it has been the only venue and a kind of dead-end street for aspiring writers who choose not to take the established route to prominence. One reason for this has been the lack of active participation by established writers, who seem haunted by existential doubts over the question "Can we really call cyberliterature a valid literature?" and perhaps by the nagging fear of being associated with a low-class art form.

Doubt over the validity of cyberliterature as an authentic art form has exacerbated the debate between conventional literary circles and the cyberinsurgents. Cyberliterature has come under attack, denounced by established writers as unsophisticated and inauthentic and hence a low genre. Byung-Ik Kim describes cyberliterature as being democratic in that it allows easy access to the public.

For the same reasons, however, he claims that by allowing this kind of public access to literature the dignity and integrity of the literary canon may be lost.[5] Woe-Kon Kim also acknowledges both positive and negative aspects of cyber-literature as supporting free, multiple, simultaneous, and mutual interactions while disrupting the uniformity of a literary work, dismantling the sacrosanct identity of the writer and resulting in the degradation of literature.[6] There are, in fact, indisputable factors which justify these criticisms. Deok-Kyu Park, a writer and an advisor for the HITEL Literature Center, notes that "[as] in a computer world where incomplete duplications snatch information from others and demons destroying valuable information are in control, PC Communications literature is full of unqualified emotion and imagination, imitation and mimicry, and absurdity and sensationalism. All of them are without due respect to the existing body of literature. For example, some cyber writers cleverly use exotic and absurd titles to attract visitors, thus gaining a kind of illegitimate prestige through the inflated number of site hits."[7]

Even Park, who maintains a neutral position between established circles and cybercircles, criticizes emergent cyberliterature for its reckless mimicry of other works, its unqualified overflow of emotion and imagination, and its excessive sensationalism and absurdity. But of course these are the very attributes that give it its unique character.

This debate, however, is concerned not only with the visible changes of Korean literature but also with an invisible power struggle within Korean literary circles. These discussions, revealing the Internet's deep and tidal impact on Korean literature and literary society, center on three interrelated points. The first point of contention is whether or not cybermedia is a valid venue for literary endeavor. A second related issue examines the loss of linguistic integrity as a characteristic result of cyberwriting. The third point of dispute looks at how Internet technology subverts hegemonic structures and ultimately shakes the criteria for authorship.

Is the Cyberenvironment a Valid Media for Literature?

Opponents of cybermedia as an environment for literary endeavor rail against electronic language. Holding to the sanctity of print narratives, they maintain that literature must be limited to written words bound in a printed book. Nae-Hee Kang is a traditionalist who believes literature must be confined as a cultural activity based on written words. He sums up the crisis as one of media: "The biggest problem facing literature is found in a weakening in the integrity of the novel. On the other hand, a broader look suggests that the crisis may stem from the transformative environment into which the culture of print and paper has been thrust."[8] Another conservative critic, Jung-Il Dow, also announces that literature is in crisis. Mapping a dichotomy between the analogue and digital ages, he strongly denies that any electronic narratives rendered through binary digits encoded in electromagnetic polarities can be categorized as literary representation. To be credible, literary representations must be mediated through written words. He claims that the loss of written words resulting from Internet technology amounts to nothing less than the death of literature.[9]

Countering this, cyberwriter Ger-Il Bok, posits that "whether loaded in a book a compact disc or a magnetic tape, poetry is poetry and the novel is the novel."[10] He and other proponents of cyberliterature disagree with the traditional and elitist position, proclaiming that the shift of literary media doesn't have to lead to the loss of literariness. They argue that however changed the expressional media is, literary sensibility and imagination survive as they did in the preceding transition from orality to literacy. Furthermore, as literature functions to reflect social reality, they assert that it cannot stand as an exception to the ongoing process of digitalization. According to critic Yong-Uk Lee, there is an urgency to develop a new subversive imagination encompassing the digital age as well as a self-generated theory to cultivate Korean cyberliterature.[11] Bong-Kwan Jeon points out that as digital technology expands into various fields, print media and the creation, reception, and sale of literature are becoming digitalized as well. He adds that the literature of today needs to be understood within a context of culture and aesthetics: "This new consciousness will be based on a multimedia, cooperative approach toward making art. We need to fill cyber space with the world demanded by the cyber space. It will not share the work given to established writers. In cyber space, text artists will work together with artists from other fields of art and that will take root as the digital art of the day."[12]

Is the Cost to Language Too High?

Cyberspace has evolved a truncated style of linguistic and syntactic expression that pervades all forms of Internet discourse, regardless of language or genre. The impact of this can be felt at both the micro- and macrolevels. At the microlevel, digital writing has evolved its own style. Though published in print in *Munhak Dongnae*, a literary magazine, Young-Ha Kim's *A Call* has been touted as quintessential cyberliterature for its characteristic motifs of imaginary personal communications. The following two passages reflect the idea:

> A call?
>
> I picked up the receiver, then pressed the button several times, and hung up. Now a little tough. Now she may fall asleep, so my call may be annoying. . . .
>
> What I did yesterday isn't like me, however I think it over. So just thinking of it makes my heart beat fast. Over my past twenty-eight years, I have never done such a thing. Always, with hesitation at the end, I used to do nothing.[13]

The above two examples illustrate the use of short clauses and a scarcity of rhetorical modifiers, characteristic of digital writing and colloquial speech.

Another characteristic of cyberwriting illustrated here is the use of a significant blank space between paragraphs. These aspects of cyberwriting allow readers to indulge themselves in the aesthetic of momentary lightness and the fluidity of cyberspace. Opponents of cyberliterature criticize these characteristics as contaminating the purity and uniqueness of the traditional Korean literary language. Jong-Dae Lee maintains that the damage is done not simply to the integrity of Korean language but also to our emotional and aesthetic domain, which is fundamentally structured and affected by language. Therefore, an affront to language likewise signifies a deleterious effect upon the culture.[14]

At the macrolevel, these seemingly innocuous breaches of literary tradition take on greater proportions when viewed in the larger realm of politics and culture. The defense against the incursion of cybersyntax is thus informed by and intertwined with extreme patriotism centered around the Korean language. Critics, attentive to the impending globalization of English, fear that the Korean language is being de-Koreanized—reduced, synthesized, and adapted for easy translation into English. They believe cyberwriting plays a pivotal role in this process. Although some Korean writers don't necessarily write their literary works in English, they are conscious of English as the language of globalization and thus have a tendency to simplify their native tongue so that it can be easily translated.

Meanwhile, discussions are underway to make English an official language in Korea, and classes teaching English are ubiquitous even at the kindergarten level. As another indication of the trend to adopt English in some formal capacity, some colleges are accepting new entrants based on TOEFL (Test of English as a Foreign Language) scores alone. In the workplace, demands for English proficiency are formidable. Young job seekers must provide high scores on English proficiency tests to even be considered. Existing employees in the business sectors are scrambling to English-language schools to save their jobs. Clearly the trend is motivated by the pace of globalization and the concomitant spread of English as the universal language. While the inseparability of language and culture has its advantages, it also has disadvantages, especially when played out across the borders of other nation-states. The result, some fear, may be carelessness and disregard for the native tongue. In Korea, critics warn that an uncritical adoption of Western values may slip in quietly alongside its noisy cohort, language. The fear is that this will result in a subtle erosion and rejection of the indigenous culture.

Hae-Jung Hur, a promising female critic, notes that "the loss of mother tongue and culture under the name of globalization is not only a local problem. It predicts a cultural holocaust where all non-English cultures, including ours, will be completely dismembered".[15] It appears that cyberopponents worry over the possibility that Korean language and culture may be ground and swallowed into the totality of what I term "electronic Americanism"—the global phenomenon whereby American culture has been disseminated through the electronic circuits of the Internet, developed by American technology and capital. This notion of dismemberment and disintegration propels the Korean experience of corporeal anxiety wherein language and cultural identity take on a physical presence imperiled now by technology.

Cyberproponents, on the contrary, are favorable toward electronic Americanism and counter that this concern of the conservative agenda is shortsighted. A rejection of electronic Americanism has the dual effect of blocking both Korean cyberaudiences' and foreign audiences' access to Korean literature. Under the premise that necessity is reality, cyberradicals claim that indeed the Korean language must be transformed to keep up with the new literary wave characterized by its simplicity, immediacy, and accessibility. They assert that it is necessary to employ English as a tool for the global dissemination not only of Korean literature but also of Korean historical experience and cultural heritage. This has a philosophical base in the dialectical notion that the instrument of governing often becomes the source of emancipation. As Gwa-Ri Jung notes,

> Indeed, the dynamics of the world are so compelling and complex that an instrument of control does serve as a resource for liberation. The present linguistic environment in which English has become the universal linguistic currency, manifests the influence of Western culture and power. But, if English represents some kind of resource of power and influence, this paradigm shift to globalization will surely broaden the availability of that resource to all native citizens, thereby aggrandizing their potential through the medium of language. Therefore, what is important does not lie in the selection of the instrument but in transforming that instrument to one's own purposes to energize and inspire our own experiences and cultural heritage. In Korea, this transition inevitably leads to arguments over the manner of co-existence between Hangul and English. Thus, we are faced with the dual tasks of making preparation for adopting English and refining Hangul.[16]

Through the use of English as the global language, the forces of globalization can move Korea into the international mainstream. Byung-Ik Kim borrows from John Naisbitt's proposition of "harmonic paradox," which stipulates that when English becomes the second language, people are keenly aware of the importance of their native tongue and feel a strong attachment for their native language. Therefore, the use of English may, in fact, spur efforts to defend and refine Hangul rather than damage and reduce the use of it.[17] But this point remains in contention among the conservative old guard. A look back into Korean history may shed light on reservations surrounding the acceptance of a second language. During the nineteenth century, the Chosun Dynasty maintained a strict policy of seclusion. As early as the late eighteenth century, progressive thinkers including Jae-Ga Park asserted the importance of adopting an open-door policy. He advocated eliminating isolationism and inviting Catholic missionaries in order to learn advanced technologies of the West and promote foreign trade. Moving into the nineteenth century, however, the conservative regime of Daewonkun, the father of King Kojong, strongly defied the demand for an open-door principle by sticking to seclusionism and oppressing Catholicism. As a result, the Chosun Dynasty lost a precious opportunity to rid itself of an absolute monarchy in favor of a modern constitutional monarchy system. It also missed a vital opportunity to open up its doors voluntarily to foreign powers. Consequently, Korea was relegated to the humiliation of opening its doors under the coercive and brutal measures imposed by Japan.[18]

The effects of this remain today in an intransigent backwardness captured in the dubious title accorded Korea: "the Hermit Kingdom." Likewise, a rejection of electronic Americanism may place Korean literature in a similar predicament, causing it to lag behind the tidal wave of globalization. Cyberwriters' radical position presses us to acknowledge the inevitability that some loss at the microlevel of Korean language and culture can lead to greater gains in the worldwide market.

To What Extent Will the Criteria for Authorship Be Undermined?

While the two points of debate mentioned above are concerned with ontological issues of defining literature and identity, the criteria for authorship, which are traditionally based on the requirements of a rigorous contest system, represent an issue that belongs to the system that regulates Korean literary society. The contest system is sponsored by several leading newspapers every spring (*Chosun Daily, Joongang Daily, Dong-a Daily*), and intermittently by literary magazines (*Hyundai Munhak, Changjak and Bipyung, Munhak and Jisung Sa, Munhak Sasang, Munhak Dongnae*). The system is so highly competitive that winners have been instantly elevated to the status of "professional" and have been given the privilege of easy publication and the authority to evaluate other literary works.

The history of the contest system goes back to the early twentieth century, when middle-class writers studying abroad established a new system for determining who could become an author. Their plan situated literature under free competition for commercial purposes. Their intent was to give ordinary people an opportunity to write and put an end to the aristocratic hold on literature whereby only the upper classes of the Chosun Dynasty were able to produce literature without any commercial purpose. In the early 1900's, *Cheong Chun*, a literary magazine, and *Maeil Shinbo*, a newspaper, began the institution of the Korean literary circle by holding a national literary contest. The contest succeeded in raising public interest in literature and produced several notable literary men in those early days. This led to the creation of a type of publishing house in which literary works written by professional writers, recognized through this contest, were printed and distributed nationally.[19] These literary contests produced such professional writers as Yo-Han Ju, Myung-Soon Kim, Yoon-Kyung Kim, and Jung-Whan Bang. The result was the establishment of a modern, capitalistic publishing system and the advent of professional authorship. To put it differently, through this literary contest system, the aristocratic hold of the Chosun Dynasty was replaced by the democratic literary circle.

Ironically, the democratic aims of this system have contributed to the establishment of a new literary hierarchy. The contest system gave rise to strict criteria for authorship and thus drew a firm line between those who met the criteria and those who could not or would not conform to the rigid requirements of the system. The Korean literary circle, formed around those prize-winning writers, was eventually transformed into a closed literary group. Since the 1980s, prize-winning authors in these literary contests sponsored either by newspapers or literary magazines have emerged as the center of power within the official literary circle, leaving those aspiring writers who did not go through the contests marginalized and disenfranchised.

Internet technology precipitates the imminent overthrow of the contest system. In contrast, it offers an accessible space for writing and publishing, making it possible for anyone who wants to be a writer to bypass the rigorous barriers. In this way, the distinction between professional authorship and amateur authorship is blurred. Chan-Jae Woo outlines the losses and gains of the Internet on Korean literature, noting that "opponents criticize it for undermining the established system. They claim that the Internet will bring about a rapid vulgarization of literature and the loss of authorial integrity. On the other hand, proponents applaud the Internet as a step toward the liberation of writing as an art form."[20]

As shown above, the discussion between the two opposing camps reflects the respective losses and gains to Korean literature brought by the impact of the Internet. The debate parallels Korean society, where we can see a dominant and vested old guard stubbornly sticking to tradition and the standards of a rigid and hierarchical system. Meanwhile, argument from the margins clamors for change and threatens to overtake and bypass its opposition. So far, Korean literature has been led by the old guard, which opposes the invasion of Internet technology into literature and guard against its formidable impact. This point can explain why literature seems to remain an area that lags relatively behind the rapid shifts brought about by the computer in other spheres.

The Ecology of Cyberliterature in Korea

Clearly, the development of cyberliterature as a viable genre has been stymied by the fundamentally political nature and thrust of this debate. On the other hand, while cyberliterature may lag behind other uses and users, it is steadily gaining ground. This impetus has been sustained in three principal areas where mechanisms already at work within cybersociety are showing great potential to shape the future of Korean literature. On the basis of these I will venture three predictions: first, that Korean cyberspace will inevitably become a viable and popular venue for all types of literary endeavor; second, that through the revival of traditional subversive Korean popular literature, reborn via the Internet, a new genre of techno-Korean literature will emerge; and third, that the actualization of postmodern theory and thought, through electronic media, will provide a pathway to the next literary paradigm.

While Internet measurement companies such as eIForcast have not tracked the literary uses of the Internet, they do provide figures on the number of Internet users. Using eTForcast data, the Information Culture Center of Korea provides figures on the recent number of Internet users. According to their December 4, 2002 report, the total number of internet users in Korea amount to 26,900,000, which is ranked sixth in the number of Internet users in the world and third in Asia. (First is America, second Japan, third China, fourth Germany, fifth England, and sixth Korea.)[21] Korea is seeing a population explosion of Netizens. Considering these phenomena, is it possible for only literature to escape the mesh of electronic media? Moreover, can we say that literature is performing its proper function to reflect social reality if it looks askance at social change? I think that literature must and will acknowledge the new technology and its dramatic impact in order not to be isolated from real life.

Just as writers will be subsumed by this sociofunctional phenomena, so too will the dynamic tradition of Korean popular literature. Throughout history, Korean popular literature has developed dialogically by absorbing the marginalized into the literary sphere. Three noteworthy Korean popular literatures are the Sasur Sijo of the Chosun Dynasty, the "literature of wrath" in the 1980s, and cyberliterature today. As Yong-UK Lee notes, "Although these three literary periods seemingly have nothing to do with each other, in fact, they share significant features: a radical subversion of the established literature; an inclusive rather than exclusive disposition toward the literary population; and they act as symbol announcing the end of an era."[22]

The disruptive power of Korean popular literature was first recognized in Sasur Sijo, which was formed by dissenting writers disillusioned by the existing exclusive hold on literary endeavor by the ruling classes. It evolved during the late period of the Chosun Dynasty when medieval feudalism had collapsed but modern civil society had not yet fully formed, thus creating a void. During this period of transition, the people who had been alienated from literary circles created a new genre, Sasur Sijo, which had a liberal pattern both in style and theme. Unlike the established Sijo genre, exclusive to the ruling classes, Sasur Sijo was generated by the people and dared to break from the orthodoxies of the established rule. For example, Sasur Sijo writers used Korean language instead of Chinese characters; they defied the traditional rigid pattern of poetry with its restrictions on the length of the first two verses. Furthermore, in contrast to Sijo which restricted its themes to abstract ideas, Sasur Sijo freely absorbed the individual particulars of the common people, including stories of their pathos and love. In his *Modern Korean History Rewritten* (1994), Man-Kil Kang describes the genre's historical significance, noting, "Sasur Sijo got rid of elite consciousness by erasing and rejecting themes of the upper class culture, which had dominated the established Sijo genre. Sasur Sijo freely expressed the ordinary lives and loves of the common people and criticized the harsh realities of everyday life through unreserved metaphor. Sasur Sijo was wholly for the common people and contributed greatly to raising their awareness and social consciousness."[23]

Hence, Sasur Sijo became known as a subversive form of literature expressing the emotion of the common people within their own language. It was a manifestation of mature consciousness of modern civic society which brought about the rapid breakdown of the orders of the medieval feudal system.

In the late 1980s, when Korean people displayed their anger under the pressure of military dictatorship, Korean popular literature again appeared as a form of social activism. People from the working classes and the farming community, who did not have the privilege of professional literary training, employed popular themes and motifs of resistance and pathos in their ordinary lives. From this period a "literature of wrath" was developed. In No-Hae Park's "Dawn of Labor" (1984), an infusion of revolutionary resistance exposes the agonies of workers who try to achieve a humane living while struggling to overcome the dark reality of low wages and long hours of labor in poetry. The literary embodiment of the pathos of ordinary people's lives culminates in Gui-Ja Yang's novel *People in Wonmi Dong* (1987), Soon-Ha Yoo's *Saeng Sung* (1988), and Young-Hyun Kim's *An Evening Primrose* (1989). By expressing the joys and sorrows of ordinary people and the class-consciousness of people marginalized by established institutions, they led Korean popular literature in the late 1980s. Because of their subversive nature, the lives of workers and the defiant class-consciousness of marginalized people had been ignored by the dominant literature until the late 1980s.

In the same context, cyberliterature shares these traditions of Korean popular literature. As many Internet sites show, cyberliterary groups are comprised by the marginal minority and managed mainly by amateur young writers and housewives. These writers, who cannot satisfy the rigid criteria for authorship and are therefore denied space for publishing their writings, are crowding into cyberspace. In fact, most Internet literary sites now include literary circles for housewives, who, in spite of their high level education, cannot qualify for good jobs and do not have the opportunity to express their literary inclinations publicly. A housewives' literary site, "The Community for Those who Love Writing" (http://e-nara.com/jubu.html), provides an electronic cafe for housewives whose writings exhibit a complex matrix at the heart of their ordinary lives. The matrix emerges from a multiple consciousness: a sense of duty as a housewife, the frustration of unfulfilled aspirations and a vague but emergent desire for freedom. The Internet offers them an escape from the matrix of their ordinary world as well as a "room of their own" in which to explore and evolve a literary identity. In this regard, the Internet plays an integral role in satisfying the suppressed talents and aspirations of this marginal group.

Another way cyberliterature functions dialogically between hierarchies of Korean society is in its unique capacity to attract and reflect the imagination and sensibility of the digital age. For instance, the repeated motifs in cyberliterature, computers, PC telegraph, cellular phones, and other audiovisual tools have become the cultural codes of the digital age. In "A Call" by Young-Ha Kim, a cellular phone takes center stage in the intricate narrative by mediating two simulated subjectivities of a caller and the one called. Furthermore, cyberliterature's themes are centered on particular features prevalent in the cybercultural environment, (e.g., false identity, alternation of reality and fantasy, fusion of time, etc.). Kyung-Ah Song's short story "A Book" serves as an illustration of those themes. We read, "Books, a great number of books. I write books, all of which are about my life; forged; copied; torn up; two books in one, the same in the first half of it and different in the second half of it; stylistically different books dealing with the same topic; a book with one deformed page; a book with one misspelled word; a book with a different copy right; a book with a wrong book cover. I will write these books. So nobody would discern which is forged and which one is original."[24]

The above passage illustrates key aspects of the cybernarrative: a simulated text wherein the line between the original and the copy is blurred. This in turn embodies the digital text, in which the possibility of innumerable replication is intrinsic, thereby denying its own completeness and determinacy. This potent fusion of reality and fiction is Jean Baudrillard's core message of simulation, "the generation by models of a real without origin or reality,"[25] which permeates to cyberliterature, including Young-Ha Kim's *A-Call* or Young-Soo Lee's "Under a Sphinx." Thus, by absorbing the marginalized people into the cyberliterary sphere and providing an electronic space for developing digital imaginations, cyberliterature paves the way for a new techno-Korean popular literature.

The revolutionary character of popular literature has been an active force in the deconstruction of the Korean literary canon and the social system that governs it. Sasur Sijo made an intangible contribution to a rapid collapse of medieval feudalism and to the advent of modern civil society. The popular literature of the late 1980s fulfilled its rebellious function to shake up the petit bourgeois of the established literature and open a new literary dimension for the 1990s. Similarly, Korean cyberliterature holds the potential to disintegrate the established literature's rigorous conservatism. This conservatism protects literary standards, the Korean language, and sacrosanct literary materials from being disturbed by Internet technology. With these dynamic traditions Korean cyberliterature is destined to break new ground and explore a new literary paradigm. Thus, by providing a space both for marginalized writers and the development of digital imagination, cyberspace acts as a crucible for a new genre of techno-Korean popular literature.

Techno-Korean popular literature can be said to be a realization of postmodern theory and thought. Korean cyberliterature shares the basic idea of postmodernism that deconstructs the hegemony's hold over those with no power. At the same time, Korean cyberliterature provides us with remarkable examples of the actualization of postmodern theories of text. The "extraordinary convergence" of postmodern theory and electronic textuality noted by many Western and Korean critics prominently appears in Korean cyberliterature.[26]

In his *Hypertext 2.0: The Convergence of Contemporary Critical Theory and Technology* (1992), George P. Landow, noting the convergence of hypertext and literary theory, illustrates that the concept of text proposed by such figureheads as Roland Barthes, Michel Foucault, and Jacques Derrida has been finally actualized through the electronic circuit. Without exception, the three critics, forerunners of postmodernism, capture texts as a completely appropriate concept of hypertext. Barthes defines ideal texts as being open—a space from which no one can assume any decisive meaning—as numerous links of networks interact with each other, without one surpassing another. Like Barthes, Foucault understands texts as nodes on a network consisting of numerous other books, texts, and sentences. Derrida, who frequently uses such symbolic terms of hypertext as *link, web, network,* and *interwoven,* suggests a text composed in "a virtual, dynamic, and lateral manner" not accomplished by the mode of text offered by Plato. Like most other structuralists and poststructuralists, Landow describes text, the world of letters, and the power and status relations they involve in terms shared by the field of computer hypertext.[27] He argues that the terms such as *textuality, interaction, decentralism, multi-languagedness of meaning, open text,* and *intertextuality* are equivalents of hypertexts stemming from "the new economy of reading and writing with electronic virtual, rather than physical, form."[28]

Postmodern theories stirred by poststructuralists and cyberliterature are mentioned by Korean critics as well. Through such notions as the death of the author, the reading of readers, and the uncertainty of texts employed by Derrida and Bakhtin's concept of "multilanguagedness," Korean critics illustrate how these realizations came about through endless generations of meanings through real-time adaptability enabled by two-way communications between an author and his readers.[29]

Internet technology itself provides a means by which writers can track and calculate the number of visitors to their websites; they can then attempt to entice an immediate and dynamic interactivity between author and reader. In addition to the hypothesized interactivity between writer and reader, postmodern conventions of text can be loosely summed up: the death of the author, intertextuality, and the negation of the canon. In fact, these characteristics are realized in cyberliterature. One curious cyberwriter named Djuna provides an enticing example of the manner in which Korean cyberliterature actualizes the postmodern conventions of text. Djuna has not yet clarified his/her/their identity, making its presence known only as an anonymous identifier. Not everyone knows that "Djuna" is the online identity of Young-Soo Lee. Or to put it another way, "Young-Soo Lee" might be thought of as the offline identity of Djuna, creating for these doubles a type of labyrinthine interchangeability. Djuna's recent published collection of short stories, *Tax Exemption Area* (2000), demonstrates the intertextuality of postmodern cyberliterature by including themes alternating between fictionality and reality. These aspects of Djuna provide a case in point of the interactivity and decentering of the literary hegemony. They earmark Djuna as an example of how the electronic media transforms and actualizes postmodern theory. While Djuna is not recognized as a major writer in Korean literary circles, a major literary magazine, *Munhak and Sawhae,* made Djuna a feature writer in its special issue for the fall of 2000. This was a cautious step on the part of an established literary publication. We can see evidence here that cyberliterature is strengthening and expanding postmodern thought beyond its boundaries to create a bridge to the next literary paradigm.

Tentative Conclusion

The disruptive power of Internet technology challenges the consciousness of an age and subverts the established hierarchies underlying our culture. The strength of the Internet to bypass barriers and circumvent hierarchies empowers oppressed housewives and amateur young writers not only to express their literary sensibilities but also to initiate collective action. The ease of Internet access draws both writers and readers to it, only to become indistinguishable from each other as cyberliterary space disrupts those established boundaries that until now marked the terrains of reader, writer, and text so clearly.

This subversive mechanism that undergirds the power of the margins and flows across rigid textual boundaries marks a cyborg politics as articulated in Donna Haraway's "Cyborg Manifesto." Haraway contends that beyond the Western hierarchy of oppressions on which a racist, male-dominant capitalism has been generated, a cyborg—a cybernetic organism—exists as a new powerful icon for networking not only a feminist practice but also any postcolonial praxis. Internet technology is none other than the blessed tool by which the cyborg politics of the margins can assert themselves and explore their political work.

What we must notice here are the double features of the tool and its necessary appropriation. Although the Internet, an incarnation of huge capital and high technology, predicts a new colonialism of electronic Americanism, it exerts at once a reverse effect to decolonize the margins from every oppressive politics. Within this framework, I suggest that it is necessary for Korean literature to appropriate the Internet tool in order to survive in the pervading climate of digital globalization. This strategy for survival is, as Haraway designates, "the power to survive, not on the basis of original innocence, but on the basis of seizing the tools to mark the world that marked [these writers] as other."[30] It alludes that the appropriation of the colonial tool becomes a subversive way to ensure freedom for the margins. Through this strategy of appropriation, Korean literature can interface with other heterogeneous literatures, which may bring about its extension of field. At the same time, within the environment of Internet networking, the inscription of Korean literature into the worldwide literary venue is made possible. This electronic symbiosis paves the way for Korean literature to evolve into a dynamic, syn-/aes-/thetic, global literature.

As a result, the Internet provides a carnivalesque network of possibilities that the reader can activate in many different ways and where heterogeneous genres and literatures can collaborate. For these reasons I have predicted a literary future that transforms present notions of authorship and language. Through cyberspace the subversive traditions crucial to change will be revived and expanded to alter our ways of thinking, and topple the rigid hierarchies that have kept aspiring Korean writers marginalized. This is necessary to form new ideologies in keeping with the imagination and energy of the digital age.

Notes

All Korean references quoted in this paper are originally in Korean and all the translations were provided by the author.

1. The concept of cyberliterature has not yet been fully established in Korea. Most critics do not oppose the view that cyberliterature is an authentic literary activity performance in cyberspace. Chan-Jae Woo, in *Voice of the Other* (Seoul: Munhak Dongnae, 1996), 229, defines cyberliterature as an "avant-garde mode of performance in an age of computers." Another description of cyberliterature, "a new multi-media literature conceived by electronic revolution, reflected and produced by the new digital communications technology," is in Byung-Ik Kim, *New Way of Writing and Authenticity of Literature* (Seoul: Munhak and Jisung Sa, 1997), 63. Yet there are reservations. Both authors maintain that due to the limitations of technology cyberliterature has not yet achieved the status of true hypertext.
2. Hye-Sil Choi, "The Status Quo and Prospect of E-Narrative." In *The Theory of Cyber Literature*, ed. Sunee Lee (Seoul: Wall-In, 2001), 107–26.
3. N. Katherine Hayles, "Corporeal Anxiety in Dictionary of The Khazars: What Books Talk about in the Late Age of Print When They Talk about Losing their Bodies," *Modern Fiction Studies* 43 (1997): 800–820.
4. See HITEL Munhak Gwan, ed., *The Bit Age* (Seoul: Tomato, 1996). See also Yong-UK Lee's dissertation, "The Literary Paradigm of the Informationized Society: A Theoretical Exploration of Cyberism," Han-Nam University, 2000. The two additional dissertations are Jin-Ryang Kim, "A Study on Narrative of the Bulletin Board Fiction in World Wide Web," Hanyang University, 2000; and Chang-Bae Kim, "A Study of the Narrative Character in the Computer Games," Dongguk University, 2001. See also, Sunee Lee, ed. *The Theory of Cyberliterature* (Seoul: Wall-In, 2001), and Sunee Lee, ed., *The Understanding of Cyberliterature* (Seoul: Wall-In, 2001).
5. Byung-Ik Kim, *New Way*, 64.
6. Woe-Kon Kim, "Literary Significance and the Function of Cyber Fiction," in Sunee Lee, ed. *The Theory of Cyber Literature*, 127–45.
7. Deok-Kyu Park, cited in Yong-Uk Lee, *A Challenge of Cyber Literature* (Seoul: Tomato, 1996), 99.
8. Nae-Hee Kang, "Literature in the Digital Age," *Munwha Gwahak*, Spring 1996, 70–79.

9. Jung-Il Dow, "Reading and Experience: Literary Response on the Age of Excessive Information." From United States Information Service Lecture Series. Embassy of the United States of America, Seoul, October 5, 2000.
10. Ger-Il Bok, "Literature in the Age of Electronic Communication," *Munae Joongang,* Fall 1995, 32–37.
11. Yong-Uk Lee, *A Challenge of Cyber Literature,* 188.
12. Bong-Kwan Jeon, "Literature in the Digital Age and the Problem of Its Identity." In Sunee Lee, ed., *The Theory of Cyber Literature,* 279–97.
13. Young-Ha Kim, *A Call* (Seoul: Munhak Dongnae, 1997), 99.
14. Jong-Dac Lee, personal communication with the author.
15. Hae-Jung Hur, personal communication with the author.
16. Gwa-Ri Jung, *The Navel of Civilization* (Seoul: Munhak and Jisung Sa, 1998), 37.
17. Byung-Ik Kim, *New Way,* 289.
18. Man-Kil Kang, *Korean Modern History Rewritten* (Seoul: Changjak and Bipyung, 1994), 177–91.
19. Ki-Sam Hong, "Reflection on the Korea Literary System." Recognition of Korea Literary System Forum I. Korea Literary Critics Association Conference. Chung-Ang Univerity, Seoul, October 17, 2001.
20. Woo, *Voice of the Other,* 236.
21. Online at <www.icc.or.kr/prdesk/it_news/content.asp?num-2519&page-7&st>.
22. Yong-Uk Lee, *A Challenge of Cyber Literature,* 70.
23. Kang, *Korean Modern History Rewritten,* 163.
24. Kyung-Ah Song, *A Book* (Seoul: Mineum Sa, 1996), 34.
25. Jean Baudrillard, "Simulacra and Simulations." In *Selected Writings,* ed. Mark Poster, (Stanford, CA Stanford University Press, 1998), 166–84.
26. Marie-Laure Ryan, "Interactive Drama: Narrative in a Highly Interactive Environment," *Modern Fiction Studies* 43 (1997): 677–707.
27. George P. Landow, *Hypertext 2.0: The Convergence of Contemporary Critical Theory and Technology* (Baltimore: Johns Hopkins University Press, 1992), 3.
28. Ibid., 33.
29. Yong-Uk Lee, *A Challenge of Cyber Literature,* 176–89.
30. Donna Haraway, "A Cyborg Manifesto: Science, Technology, and Socialist-Feminism in the Late Twentieth Century." In *Contemporary Literary Criticism,* ed. Robert Con Davis and Ronald Schleifer, (New York: Longman, 1994).

8

Intercollegiate Web Pedagogy: Possibilities and Limitations of Virtual Asian American Studies

JOHN CHENG
KAREN HAR-YEN CHOW
PAMELA THOMA, WITH
RACHEL C. LEE

Introduction

Rachel C. Lee

> Cyberspace can be a place where ethnic and racial identity are examined, worked through, and reinforced. Cyberspace can provide a powerful coalition building and progressive medium for "minorities" separated from each other by distance and other factors.
> —Beth E. Kolko, Lisa Nakamura, and Gilbert B. Rodman,
> "Race in Cyberspace: An Introduction"

In a project that exemplifies the convergence of the "real life" concerns of Asian Americans and the Internet's potential for building coalitions, Asian American studies faculty at universities on the East Coast and in the Midwest initiated an Electronic Pedagogy Project (EPP) in 1998–99, an experiment in cross-campus, collaborative teaching and "classroom" discussion. In the process, the project also addressed the World Wide Web's "disembodying" potential, exploring issues of racial and gender identity and representation in an actual "virtual" space. Against the dominant practice in cyberspace of taking any mention of "color" as a hostile act,[1] EPP faculty approached information technology (IT) pragmatically as a tool to increase students' awareness of Asian Americans as minority subjects in the U.S. nation-state and to introduce them to Asian American history, culture, and the arts. At the same time, and on a more theoretical level, the EPP ushered in another cybermediated phase of what Sau-ling Cynthia Wong and I, in our introduction to this volume, refer to as Asian America's "virtual panethnicity." Offering a window into this cybercollaboration, the three authors of this essay balance their preproject aims, goals, speculations, and reservations against a postproject evaluation and analysis of their efforts at that intersection of Storrs, Connecticut; Waterville, Maine; and cyber–Asian America. Website and project coordinator John Cheng presents an overview of the project, and faculty participants Karen Chow and Pamela Thoma offer two personal accounts of their initial thoughts and considerations. A final coauthored section collaboratively discusses the unexpected pedagogical challenges this experiment posed for cybermediated instruction and cross-campus Asian American collaboration. It also assesses the benefits and drawbacks of IT to the Asian American pedagogical community given the experiences of the EPP participants.

Overview

John Cheng

The Electronic Pedagogy Project was a collaborative effort undertaken in the spring of 1999 within the East of California (EoC) caucus and network of the Association for Asian American Studies (AAAS). Recognizing the common differences that geography and intellectual perspective produced in their institutional locations, Asian American studies scholars on the East Coast and in the Midwest formed the collaborative network in 1991 to address the concerns and needs of those differences and to develop research programs that explored the intellectual terrain suggested by those same differences.[2] The name East of California represents an intellectual focus more than a geographic accident.[3] Since its inception, the caucus's activities have evolved in response to its changing constituencies, and have included annual conferences involving faculty, administrators, and students; faculty retreats; and several collaborative projects.[4]

The EPP grew out of a discussion at the EoC junior faculty retreat in the spring of 1998 about the pedagogical possibilities offered by emerging information technologies—specifically e-mail, the Internet, and the web. Attendees scheduled to teach Asian American studies courses in the spring of 1999 volunteered to participate in a collaborative pedagogical project that would link their classes and curricula electronically over the Internet. In the end, twelve faculty teaching thirteen classes on eleven campuses in the Midwest and East Coast (with an aggregate of more than two hundred enrolled students) participated in this project.[5]

While participation was voluntary, a range of institutions, faculty, and courses were specifically sought to allow comparisons across their respective differences and conversations bridging those same differences. The majority of institutions were private, small, liberal arts colleges, but several were larger research universities, including two public schools. Geographically, most were in the northeast corridor, but roughly a quarter were from the Midwest. Most faculty members held degrees in English and/or literature; the remainder were scholars in history and the history of consciousness; and one was a trained chemist. Their institutional positions, however, reflected the increasingly interdisciplinary nature of humanities scholarship, as roughly a quarter were located in interdisciplinary department/programs and several others held affiliations within such programs. Courses ranged in size from large lectures to small seminars and in subject from introductory Asian American studies to general disciplinary and interdisciplinary courses—for instance, Asian American literature, women's studies—to special-topics seminars.

Perhaps most significantly, the demographic make-up of students within various participating classes varied. While many of the schools attracted students from across the nation, and often ranging in class background and position, several drew their students locally and regionally. Almost all classes had students from a range of racial backgrounds. Several participating classes had white majorities. Classes with Asian American majorities varied in the ethnic and national backgrounds of their students. Some were predominantly East Asian; others had sizable South and/or Southeast Asian populations. Variations existed as well within those regional subcategorizations: some classes were ethnically mixed; some were largely Korean and Chinese; still others had proportionally large numbers of Hmong. One surprising statistical result of the EPP was that the aggregate of all participating students was more varied and diverse than any single participating class. As Karen Chow and Pamela Thoma relate later, this electronic diversity itself became a desired, modifying presence for several of the instructors participating in the project.

The goal of the project was to use this increased diversity to create a synergetic and syncretic learning experience for students that extended and enriched their classroom experiences. The project itself centered on readings from three common texts: Ginu Kamani's short-story collection *Junglee Girl*, R. Zamora Linmark's novel *Rolling the R's*, and Jeannie Barroga's play *Walls*.[6] Individual faculty chose to assign one or more of these texts for their courses. Schedules and syllabi were arranged so that all faculty teaching one of the common texts taught it in the same week despite differences in their respective semester, trimester, or quarter systems. Students assigned the text were asked to read it within the context of both their specific course and of the larger project. That is, they had class "as usual" with their respective classes and instructors, including discussions and assignments; they then went online to the EPP website to compare their experiences with the experiences of other students who had read the same text,[7] but from their own and (multiply) different perspectives.

The project's website was designed to facilitate and supplement this student interchange. A commercial pedagogical software package, WebCT, provided a single back-end application to provide both an integrated framework for web-content pages and a suite of several commonly used Internet technologies. The site's pages offered a general introduction and context for each text, study guides and questions developed by various participating faculty for their respective courses, a bibliography, and links to other related sites on the web. Internet technologies included an e-mail listserv to facilitate e-mail communication for all project participants; a "calendar" that students and faculty used to schedule online events; a bulletin board for posting messages for one another; and a chat room that allowed participants to be part of up to four separate simultaneous chats (technically, Internet relay chats, or IRCs). The chat rooms differed from the other technologies because they are synchronous rather than asynchronous. This distinction is particularly relevant in its implications for social and cultural practice. With e-mail, the calendar and bulletin board users interact "outside" time: *when* a message is sent (or received), is less relevant than the fact that it has been sent (or received), and the ordered sequence of sending and receiving. In chat rooms, however—now prevalent in "instant messaging" applications—*when* a message is sent and received is crucial, since user interactions are simultaneously sent and received. The same distinction and implications applies to the difference between voicemail and phone conversations: both use the same communications medium, but the one is an asynchronous mode of communication while the other is synchronous.

Perhaps because of this synchronicity and simultaneity or simply its newness to users at the time, the chat room ultimately proved the most engaging and interesting of the website's tools. While participants used other features, it was mostly to arrange and schedule a direct "chat" in one of the chat rooms. For many students, the experience of online chatting was new, challenging, and worth exploring in and of itself. Entering a chat room—by selecting the appropriate button on the chat room webpage—opened a window on their computer screen split into three panes. One listed the log names (real or pseudonymous) of everyone in the room; one displayed the text of what anyone "in" the room "said"; and one provided space for the one chatting to type what he wanted to say.

In addition to the excitement of meeting other students and faculty from the project, participants had to adapt to the cultural environment of the chat room itself. Among other things, these adaptations included negotiating the anonymity implicit behind the mask of log names and remembering to include nonverbal indicators of mood in the purely textual exchanges of the chat itself. One participating class tried an experimental chat in which each person, including the instructor, was named Anonymous in order to explore the social dynamics of this kind of interactive environment. In an event that demonstrated the possibilities that emerging technologies like the web and the Internet offer for pedagogy, the project scheduled an online chat with the author of one of the project texts—Linmark—who was in Manila researching his next novel. The chat was tremendously rich not only because it crossed geography and time, but also because the interactions themselves among students, authors, and faculty were modulated and refracted by the social dynamics that emerged from the chat room. It was these social dynamics—which differed from the dynamics of conventional classrooms—and their implications, not Internet technologies themselves, that the East of California Electronic Pedagogy Project sought to produce and explore.

University of Connecticut

Karen Har-Yen Chow

When John Cheng introduced the idea of using the Internet to link Asian American studies courses from different universities, I thought this held a promising opportunity for my students and me. I was designing a new course, "Asian American Drama," for the spring 1999 semester,[8] and I was curious about integrating this cutting-edge technology-pedagogy project into the course. There were both professional and pedagogical motivations for participating in the EPP. In the process of suggesting and choosing texts, and in e-mail correspondence with the group of instructors who decided to participate, I enjoyed the feeling of being in a teaching community. For Asian American literature scholars, large-group dialogue about our research and pedagogy outside of conferences is rare. Collaboration on this kind of project as a way of engaging more of this dialogue is promising, and would probably be maximized in the summer or winter breaks.

I was eager to incorporate the pedagogy project into the new course I designed. Thus, when we were proposing texts we would agree to collectively teach, I suggested a few plays that I hoped to cover in teaching Asian American drama. Barroga's *Walls* was the only play actually chosen for the pedagogy project. However, I had read an excerpt of Linmark's *Rolling The R's*, and although the text is a novel and not a play, I felt that his first-person narrated chapters could be read as narrative monologue, so I included that work in my syllabus as well.[9] Pedagogically, I was interested in whether students would embrace this opportunity to engage in further dialogue about the issues raised in class through the relative anonymity of the chat rooms. I was also curious about whether the chat room discussion would reinforce or shift the dynamics established in classroom interaction.

As an assistant professor with a joint appointment in the English department and the Asian American Studies Institute at the University of Connecticut, Storrs (UConn), half my teaching course load is devoted to Asian American studies.[10] Consequently, I have taught at least one course on some topic in my field, Asian American literature, every semester since my appointment began in the fall of 1997. Somewhat surprising about the special-topics class "Asian American Drama" that coincided with my participation in the EPP was its lack of Asian American students. Among the seventeen undergraduate students enrolled in my course, the ethnic/gender breakdown consisted of one African American woman, one Latino man, ten white women, and five white men. All but one of the students (a white male) had no prior experience learning about Asian Americans. Most had little personal experience with Asian Americans. This class demography was unusual in my experience at UConn, even though the campus student body is only 5 percent Asian American. Typically, in a class of twenty to thirty, at least five of the students enrolled in my Asian American literature courses are of Asian ethnicity. I later discovered—to my humorous chagrin—that many Asian American students shied away from this course specifically because of the misperception that they would be asked to do dramatic performance in the class.[11] Nevertheless, I set out to make the best of the situation and hoped that if the students had little to no background in Asian American studies they might at least have some interest in being exposed to the texts.

The dynamic for classroom discussion proved challenging, in part because I was the only racially Asian body present for a course that was critically analyzing dramatic representations and performances of Asian bodies. I tried to deal with this situation by stating frankly from the beginning of class that because of the subject matter, we were all going to be personally engaged in ways that would be discomforting, and I encouraged students to ask questions and to challenge me as well as each other. But to my disappointment, class discussion seldom rose above a faltering, timid level. My attempts to contextualize and pose provocative questions and issues were met with little enthusiasm by the majority of the students, and student-led presentations and discussions mostly assumed a superficial critical level and dreary tone. Clearly, the lack of personal connection to the material was a big factor in the students' fear and disinterest. While I had several very engaged, hardworking, and critically sharp students, the majority turned out to be only minimally engaged in discussions and assignments.

What I eventually hoped for even more from the pedagogy project, then, was to expose these students to a virtual "community" of students from other universities who were also taking Asian American studies courses and to offer an alternative means for participation that might engage those students who were too shy to speak in class. I based a significant portion of the course grade (40 percent) on participation, including weekly journal writing and participating in the EoC pedagogy project chats. Yet technological access also proved to be a challenge on the UConn campus. In the spring of 1999 (the time of the EPP), the residence halls and the library did not yet have the many high-speed Internet connections that are present today. In short, there were only a few computer labs with Internet access on campus. Some students thus had difficulty gaining access to the site during the evening hours scheduled for the online chats. Since then, the computer culture at UConn has changed greatly; students now have high-speed Internet access in their dorm rooms, the library computers are all online, and there are additional computer stations at various locations on campus.

An unexpected bonus of the pedagogy project was the usefulness of some of the supplementary resources provided by other participants. In particular, the websites on 1970s culture (provided as context for *Rolling the R's*) were very helpful, as most of these students were either not yet born or were very young during the era in which the book is set. As a result, and for several additional reasons, Linmark's novel became one of the texts that most engaged students in the course. The novel provocatively deals with a young boy's homosexual awakening and struggle with class and racial marginality, framed within an engaging coming-of-age narrative peppered with lively Hawaiian pidgin dialogue. In addition, Linmark's participation in the online chat gave students dialogic access to the author, which made the experience of engaging with the text more personal and less abstract; the papers written and submitted by students on Linmark's novel reflected this greater level of engagement.

Colby College

Pamela Thoma

I was enthusiastic about the EPP because I thought it might enhance and help attract students to the developing curriculum in Asian American studies at Colby College. I decided to participate and synthesize the project into my "Introduction to Asian American Cultures," an interdisciplinary course offered in the American studies program, hoping that the project would give the students a sense of the larger field of Asian American studies and possibly provide connections to Asian American communities outside of Colby College and beyond the geographical context of mid-Maine. Still, I had several reservations about formally using Internet technology in the college classroom and specific questions about using virtual spaces in an Asian American studies course.

Colby is a selective liberal arts college of about 1,700 students located in Waterville, a small city of 16,000 in central Maine, which is a "poor" state with a dwindling industrial base and a population that is largely rural and predominately white; Asian and Pacific Islanders make up less than 1 percent of its population.[12] Colby is more heterogeneous than the state, but even so, only 4 percent of the student body is Asian American and nearly 90 percent of the student body is white. Most students are class privileged and their families typically contribute about half of the "comprehensive fee," which in 2001–02 was $34,290 a year.[13] Beyond the demographic issues that pose specific challenges for teaching Asian American studies at Colby (and that made participating in the EPP compelling), the school's distance from sizable populations of Asian Americans with established networks or coalitions is also significant: Boston, the closest large metropolitan area, is three and a half hours away. Finally, I was concerned about the limitations of my social position as a white person to provide Asian American students with the mentoring and community knowledge that some of them express they need.[14] The EPP potentially offered connections to Asian American communities, an important legacy from the origins of ethnic studies, and I thought it might help students access or learn more about communities not fully established in their immediate social context. Similarly, the EPP might provide a link between our course and the larger field of Asian American studies. This link may have been most attractive to me as a scholar of Asian American studies, but students could also benefit from seeing that the field is an important and respected academic endeavor outside of the "Colby bubble," as it is often called, and they could get a sense of the many directions of Asian American critique and activism.[15]

In the spring of 1999, ten students enrolled in the course; this was a group that by several local measures was unusual, demographically. First, white students were barely in a numerical majority at six (four men, two women). There were three Asian Americans (one Korean American woman and two Chinese American men, one of whom was biracial [Asian/white]), and one African American woman. Another reason this group was atypical was that a community member had joined our course. She was a professor on sabbatical from a nearby community college, white, in her mid-forties, and developing a new course in multicultural literature. Given the diversity of our class and the possibilities of the EPP, I began the semester hoping to shake things up a bit and perhaps locate what Mary Louise Pratt has called a "contact zone," or a border space exploring coalition politics.[16]

"Introduction to Asian American Cultures" opened with discussion and readings exploring the dynamic definitions/constructions of race, ethnicity, identity, and culture in a section titled "Asian American Coalition" and then reviewed Asian American history in a section titled "Early Immigration Policies and Effects."[17] I hoped that the first two sections of the course would provide enough context, history, and exposure to literature so that students would be able to engage in relatively serious discussions in the EPP chat rooms using the basic concepts and issues informing Asian American studies. In the third section, we moved into consideration of "Colonization and Decolonization," which included a discussion of Linmark's *Rolling the R's*. In another section entitled "Post-1965 Asian America," we read Barroga's *Walls*. The course ended with a section on "The Model Minority Myth and Other Violence" in which we watched films and read essays on popular culture/media representation, the L.A. riots of 1992, and domestic violence/battering within Asian American communities. The EPP website made available background materials for both of the project texts, which I incorporated into the class, and writing assignments were coordinated with online chats and texts. But the most formal way in which the EPP became part of the course's requirements was through mandatory participation in at least one multicampus Internet discussion (chat room), an assignment valued at 10 percent of the final grade. Well-equipped computer labs were available to all students, so I was able to assume access and a basic level of proficiency, although the community member in our class had some problems since access wasn't always convenient for her. An additional goal or expectation, then, for participating in the EPP was for the class members (students and myself) to become familiar with cyberspace as a learning tool.

While the EPP appeared to promise Colby students and the "Introduction to Asian American Cultures" course several distinct opportunities, I had reservations about how the demands for Internet technology education seem to justify shifting funding and emphasis away from other areas—humanities education in particular. Further, institutions sometimes seem to use IT education initiatives for the limited purposes of wresting funding from a private sector that attaches conditions, obtaining free or inexpensive student labor for the institution, or training future workers for the global economy. I didn't want my Asian American studies course to become complicit in such projects. And, I wanted to be realistic about and conscious of the kinds of communities created in cyberspace. When early observers who theorized that virtual spaces are more democratic, more egalitarian, and even utopian compared to real spaces (especially with regard to race, gender, and physical ability), I was skeptical that these were entirely neutral or always "safe" spaces. Still—and especially given my interest in the pedagogical possibilities of the contact zone—I saw that potentially at least virtual reality might complicate typically superficial understandings of social identity in real space.[18] Upon beginning the EPP, therefore, I wondered if and how racial and ethnic identities would become legible and how issues of authenticity among various identities would be manifested—how Asian American students, non-Asian students of color, and white students would interact online. I was interested as well in how gender would figure in discussion dynamics. Further, I imagined that a hierarchy could be easily and quickly developed in discussions in which students from certain institutions, especially universities where Asian American studies curriculum is well established, would hold the most authority. While I'm not sure if this dynamic properly constitutes a type of "marginalization" within Asian American studies, I know that assumptions that can accompany the categories *liberal arts college* and *research university* run deep. At the same time, I was concerned as to what extent Colby students would be attentive of and even critical about their own privileges and positions. In short, while I was hopeful, I was also skeptical in certain ways and my goals for the project's effects on the course were shadowed by my doubts.

The Postproject Conversation

John Cheng, Karen Har-Yen Chow, Pamela Thoma, and Rachel C. Lee

After the spring semester of 1999, the three of us involved looked back on the Electronic Pedagogy Project in a postproject e-mail conversation. Our discussion focused on faculty and students' practices in the project to consider what features of Internet technologies had proved the most valuable to our concerns as teachers and how theoretical perspectives and scholarly research on technology and its social dimensions meshed with our own knowledge gleaned from the EPP "classroom." While the general consensus among all the faculty participants was that using IT in the project produced definite pedagogical benefits, our postproject conversation allowed us to reflect more specifically on unexpected and unanticipated results and to weigh benefits against limitations. While we touched on many topics, particularly in discussing the constraints the technologies brought to the project, a common theme emerged: the tension between "purely" technological issues and their embeddedness in social and cultural practice. That is, while in principle Internet technologies appear to facilitate various possibilities and constraints for social practice, in actual practice the social and cultural concerns of the users themselves—which include issues of race, gender, and hierarchical privilege—ultimately determined the manner of those technologies' use. Although the web and e-mail connected all project faculty, for instance, our assumptions about the level of mutual effort in the collaboration fell to individual institutional and professional circumstances and choices about how much to participate, and the more active and interested faculty bore the bulk of the project's work.[19]

In our postproject assessment, three EPP features in particular enhanced our students' discussion of the texts and deepened their knowledge and interest in Asian American history, culture, and the arts. First, the introductory materials on the website complemented course readings and assignments. We found our students benefited from reading the posted materials on Hawaii as context for Linmark's *Rolling the R's*. In addition, links to sites about 1970s popular television and music were useful for helping students to visualize Linmark's references. For discussing Barroga's *Walls*, the various links at the site that dealt with Vietnam War memorials and monuments also proved helpful to students' understanding of the kind of ideological work these structures/artworks do: a number of students reported using these links. The EPP site, along with the viewing of Frieda Mock's documentary *Maya Lin: A Strong, Clear Vision* (in both Pamela's and Karen's classes), awakened students to issues of aesthetics, race, and gender in *Walls* (the title referring in part to the walls of the memorial)— particularly the way in which the ancestry of the monument's female, Asian American architect (Lin) became a not-so-subtle issue with veterans protesting her design's resemblance to an "ugly black scar" on the landscape.

With the exception of the chat room, most of the website's suite of technologies were not used much. The calendar was used primarily as a complement to the chat room, allowing students from different classes and campuses to schedule their chats. The bulletin board was used more inconsistently by students, and while a few instructors used it to communicate, the faculty group as a whole did not adopt its use. A tool for instructors to "track" student site use and record grades was hardly used. In one instance, however, faculty did use the various technologies to work collaboratively. Because Kamani's *Junglee Girl* is a short-story collection, and because individual faculty decided to use different stories in the collection, the project's website and tools—the listserv, content and resource pages, and bulletin boards—allowed instructors to share discussion questions, pedagogical strategies, and approaches across both their campuses and the story collection as a whole. The cross-cutting choices of stories, questions, and discussions produced a synergy in the chat rooms about the book as students compared notes about texts and classes as much as they discussed the works they'd actually read.

Of the technologies the EPP employed, the chat rooms were the most significant in their impact on the courses, especially when that impact was measured in terms of students' increased interest in the texts themselves. All project faculty agreed on the value and potential the chats offered as an alternative "space" for students to discuss the assigned texts in a manner and style with which they were more familiar (i.e., with time for tangents and without the scrutiny of the teacher's gaze). After some discussion, faculty agreed that while faculty could "listen" in to the chat rooms, they were not to be part of the conversations themselves. The additional student voices that the EPP brought to the chat rooms enhanced their already different, electronically mediated environment of textual interaction. Quite tangibly, we noticed an immediate improvement in the depth and variety of ideas in class discussion as well as in written assignments following students' participation in the chats. In Pam's class, students had generated questions about an assigned text in small groups; together the class then chose a few of these questions and posted them on the bulletin board at the site. They had also been assigned a short paper on that same text, to be handed in later that week. When students participated in their first chat room regarding that novel (on March 10), they were in the midst of writing their papers and had actually thought quite a bit about the text. While none of the papers generated by these students explicitly mentioned the site's sources or that chat room, and although the chat was not continued in the class discussion, the students who gathered together "virtually" on March 10 used the occasion as a chance to focus their ideas for the papers they were writing.

The students' practices in the chat rooms, however, contradict theoretical perspectives that emphasize the transformational social effects of technology— its ability to make evanescent "real life" markers of identity such as race and gender. In particular, we take issue with the overly optimistic attitudes of contemporary commentators who celebrate the liberatory possibilities of e-mail, chat rooms, and other new forms of communication on the Internet.[20] In this view, the Internet represents an exceptional opportunity to escape or go beyond conventional—and by implication, *limiting*—social hierarchies, identities, and circumstances in the "real" world. It is assumed that inequalities of race, class, and gender, while politically significant and important, will be dissolved and transcended by the egalitarian nature of "virtual" communication. In our experience with the chat rooms, racial, class, and gender announcements were often evoked textually by speakers to establish what would be more obvious visual, bodily clues in real time and real space.

Claims about the social implications of "new" technologies like the Internet often assume its exceptional nature without referring to or considering comparable precedents. The "anonymity" of e-mail and chat rooms—specifically the lack of physical or visual cues in these electronically mediated forms—is touted for the potential and advantage it offers to public discourse. Rid of superficial markers of social distinction and their potential consequence, people on the Net are free, some have claimed, to converse more openly and honestly. Yet textual anonymity is not new: the anonymity of e-mail and chat rooms resembles, if it is not in fact the same as, the anonymity in "traditional" letters—in today's e-lingo, "snail mail." Indeed, e-mail and much of the "new" communication of the Internet might be seen as but the latest development—enabled by among other things, the widespread increase of literacy and means of delivery—in the last few centuries of a general epistolary culture. In addition, social subjects often resist full anonymity, even when a medium appears to facilitate it. In our students' assigned "chats," we found that the lack of physical and/or visual cues as to a subject's race or gender almost forced them to "fill in" these markers and to adapt various textual techniques to convey that information.

For instance, in the conversations about "ethnicity" and "identity," the discussion edged toward a privileging of "experience" that could have developed into a kind of "hierarchy" in other contexts but that ultimately didn't because of a counterdynamic that sought to avoid overessentializing. During one chatroom conversation, a student began to talk about her personal experiences with race, saying "race exists when you are a kid . . . I could go into sob stories," then stopped herself from generalizing from her experiences, deciding, ". . . but I won't." The tension, indicated by the student initially referring to herself in the second person, was further complicated by the fact that she and another student were both logged into the chat room using the same log name, making it difficult simply to identify who was who. This dynamic to avoid overessentializing experience, we were happy to observe, was a reflection and reinforcement of what many students had discussed in class with their instructors.

One electronic discussion in particular was most successful in heightening student interest in the project texts—namely, the chat in which the author Linmark (or "Zack," as he asked to be called), made a virtual appearance. Many of the participants brought heightened personal expectations—students to meet author, faculty to meet author, author to meet everyone else—in a way that wasn't as orderly or academic as the other chats. We felt that it was certainly exciting to bridge geographical and temporal distances electronically to hear what the author had to say about his work. We recognized, at the same time, that this was really less of a conversation or dialogue among several folks in different communities and in separate Asian American studies classes, than it was a "question and answer" (Q & A) with an author persona. Indeed, in one conversational moment, faculty "listeners" entered into the discussion, speaking despite previous agreements to the contrary, and revealing their own personal experiences with the subject under discussion: Farrah Fawcett's feathered hairstyle in a well-known poster from the 1970s.

Even more unique among the EPP chats, the Linmark Q & A featured one student who addressed the author using "local" idioms favored by people living in the Hawaiian Islands (where the author, himself, grew up). For Karen's class, the actual "real time" unfolding of an exchange in Hawaii's "local" dialect made the pidgin (officially known as Hawaiian Creole English or HCE) seem less alien and foreign.[21] Describing where s/he was from, this student wrote, "brah, I get connections from dis one chick in Wahiawa." The student's method of directing the pidgin only at Linmark (addressing him as "brah" and "cuz") came across as laying some claim of connection to Linmark, in ways that nonlocals (in effect, the rest of the chat group) could not. Moreover, the use of pidgin reiterated the tendency of "virtual" conversants to bring social locational markers into the space of their discussion. Yet, only because of the virtual inclusion of this student from a far reach (physically) from the UConn campus did Karen's class receive a firsthand, spontaneous—though still virtual—experience of the creole "voice." Prior to that exchange, the questions to Linmark and his answers to them had occurred in standard English. In short, the real time "virtual" unfolding of Linmark's and the student's speech made the pidgin seem more immediate to Karen's students than did the exposure to the same pidgin (rendered in the same orthographic conventions) as that displayed in Linmark's printed novel.

In terms of changing the quality of discussions, the electronic forum seemed to allow students within a single, geographically distinct institution to challenge each other in ways they would not face-to-face. For instance, early in the semester of Pamela's class at Colby, an African American female student had challenged a Chinese American male student about his investment in the notion of meritocracy. The two discovered that they were politically quite at odds, and after their initial disagreement had implicitly cut a deal not to challenge each other in class. But, during a discussion session on the site, that agreement was suspended. Thus, information technology allowed Pam's students to challenge each other ideologically in ways they were more hesitant to do, repeatedly, in the classroom. At other times, IT seemed to enable students to engage a topic they were reticent about discussing in the "real space" of the classroom, specifically homosexuality as portrayed in Linmark's *Rolling the R's*. The virtual classrooms/chat rooms, where students could not see faces and hear voices, helped them to talk about looking at and watching (voyeurism was an obvious narrative structure of desire in the text) what some of them considered the sexual promiscuity of the young characters, both gay and straight. In these instances at least, cyberspace seemed to provide a pedagogical contact zone for discussions.

Anonymity, however, was not a simple threshold of increased speaking. For instance, the African American female student in Pamela's class was emboldened to rechallenge her classmate in the multicampus chat, not because of the promise of anonymity, but through her sense that others participating in the project on other campuses (hence, in the chat room) may have shared her critique of meritocracy and were interested in the politics of Asian American critique (of the model minority myth, in this case). So, while the electronic forum allowed students within a single institution to challenge each other in a way that they had tacitly agreed not to do in face-to-face settings, at the same time, overall, the interaction among students across campuses seemed to be limited. Thus, where live exchange had preceded virtual interaction, the medium of the Internet produced surprising, liberalizing effects on students' speech, while in cases where the interaction was all virtual (i.e., in the case of all the cross-campus exchanges), IT could not be assessed to have any transformational effects on student's reticence or nonreticence.

In terms of form, the mode of communication that chat-room technology introduced proved daunting to some students. Participation in this dialogue—or rather, "polylogue"—is disorienting because not only do a number of people "talk" at the same time, every instance of their "speech" is produced as text in a confined computer-screen window, and as the number of voices in the chat increased, some students found it difficult to keep track of who was saying what. Moreover, some of our attempts to institute form—and by extension, formal roles—produced effects that were unintended, indeed, sometimes the opposite of what was intended. During the chats, some participants made it a point to say "hello" to newly logged chat room participants because it seemed polite and also necessary to make the atmosphere "inclusive." In reading the chat room transcripts, however, these "shout-outs" seem disruptive, perhaps another way for the greeter to assert her presence. Thus, while for many of the faculty participants, much of the initial appeal of the EPP's use of Internet technology lay in its ability to distribute information in multiple streams simultaneously—what Mark Poster calls a "many-to-many" network mode of communication[22]—the project participants also encountered pedagogical limits produced by such communication.

Other factors such as lag time between responses, the graphic monotony of scrolling text, and the inability to register silence further apprised us of the limiting contours of Internet technology's putative enhancements to communication. Response lag times made it a challenge to have spontaneous, uninterrupted "conversations" in the chat rooms. The similarity of typeface fonts in the chat room software also tended to blunt the diversity and distinctiveness of its voices, making conversations appear less like dialogue and more like one singular scrolling text that would linger on the page until it fell off the top edge of the screen. We agreed it would be interesting to try a chat where participants could choose their own distinctive font (or alternatively, color), something that is now both available and prevalent among users of commercial "instant messaging" chat applications like AOL Instant Messenger.[23]

Silences also register differently within these virtual contexts. Learning to "read" differently on the Internet is complicated enough, but because silences make themselves present by their absence—they are, in a sense, unrepresentable textually and semiotically—they needed to be read even yet more differently. Given how poorly people typically read silences in "real life" conversations and interactions—including instructors' reading of student silence in the classroom—or in printed texts, we suspect that grappling with "e-silence" is both a pedagogical issue and Internet research problem that we have only just begun to contemplate.[24] Like all communicative media, chat-room dynamics benefit and appeal to some but turn others off. Some instructors observed that a few usually reticent students in the classroom engaged actively in the chats, and one normally active class participant maintained unusual silence in the chat. (He later admitted that he felt disoriented by the rapid threads and never felt comfortable jumping into the stream of text.)

Despite these several limiting factors, the EPP's use of Internet technology did, in our opinion, work toward the project's main goals. In retrospect, we expected from the outset of the project that the EPP network would increase the heterogeneity of our aggregate student body and that such magnified diversity would be an unquestionable pedagogical positive. When "live" classrooms were unusually monochromatic or where Asian Americans were entirely absent (as in Karen's course), the chat rooms' greater diversity was a definitive benefit. However, for those IRL classrooms that already had a mixture of students, the aggregate diversity of the EPP as a whole was less important pedagogically than demonstrating "mass"—showing geographically isolated students the reality of a critical assemblage in Asian American studies that extended beyond the parameters of any particular university. In other words, the texts and issues under discussion on the Net were endowed with a greater legitimacy as students saw more people engaging those subjects. A further legitimizing effect, one that went to the Asian American studies project on the whole, resulted from students' seeing how many schools offer courses in this area as well as the variety of courses/texts offered. The vigorous pace of the online chat with Linmark also confirmed for students the significant interest in the field and its political projects. Indeed, in a fitting twist, this critical mass was demonstrated, not in the virtual space of the Internet, but by the material effect of thirteen Asian American classes collectively adopting common texts at the same time. Project faculty were reawakened to the critical mass of Asian American studies when the EPP produced a shortage of books at Kaya Press, publisher of Linmark's *Rolling the R's*.

Finally, a word on the public and private facets of the EPP chat rooms and our analysis of them. In conceiving the project, we had several partially conflicting conceptions of the kind of "public" space we hoped ideally to achieve. On the one hand, we wanted to allow students the "freedom" to explore the chat rooms in order to talk to each other—emphasizing the importance for faculty not to enter student chats. On the other hand, we assigned the project to students, giving them instructions or guidelines, and perhaps implicitly, interpellated roles as "student" and "teacher" that participants may have brought with them into the chats. Further complicating matters were the capabilities that the software we used in the project offered for monitoring student chats and activities—like all Internet "communications" technologies. Because the software produced, as a matter of routine operation, records of every affirmative action and speech act, student chats and interactions could be used, after the fact, for purposes beyond class pedagogy. We were acutely aware of this issue in our postproject conversation for the obvious reason that in writing about the EPP we were pursuing such a purpose.

At the nexus of these issues were the chat-room logs—records that noted when someone entered and left the chat room as well as the transcript of the chats themselves. Everyone in the EPP agreed that the logs would not be released for general public dissemination.[25] We explained to students before the project began that the chats were going to be logged and that we weren't going to release them to anyone outside the project. As the project coordinator, John turned down requests from other East of California faculty outside the EPP who wanted to see them for their own curiosity and interest. Aware of such privacy issues, we tried in our initial postproject exchanges to be vague or generic about students in our discussions of the chats. We realized, however, that we still needed to be specific in our examples and discussed the alternative of changing personal names, schools, and other relevant identifying information for particular students—an ironic alternative given our intellectual focus on issues of markers of identification within a "virtual" world. We agreed that it was appropriate to use chat logs during our conversation and in writing our summaries, if simply to double-check our memories and accounts.

Conclusion

John Cheng, Karen Har-Yen Chow, Pamela Thoma, and Rachel C. Lee

The main benefit of Internet technology for students in the Electronic Pedagogy Project lay in its expansion of routes of knowledge prompted in the classroom and the methods favored there: a reliance on the benefit of exchange between different readers about their various responses, and hence different approaches, to the text. It is less clear, however, whether the EPP proved a forum for the Asian American studies faculty-participants themselves to reflect explicitly about their pedagogical methods or even to question whether they did have a common aim or pedagogical approach. Posting resources and sharing discussion questions provided one means of exposure to other faculty members' pedagogical styles and strategies; however, the possible comparative analysis of pedagogical method and aim was only implicit in the project. Thus, for some instructors, this seminal project proved confusing on the very topic of pedagogy, precisely because the lack of a clear unified vision of—or space to hammer out—what a common pedagogical project would be across disciplinary emphases (as opposed to what the EPP did emphasize as its point of commonality, a shared pedagogical tool).

Nevertheless, on balance, the EPP produced tangible benefits in its willingness to capitalize upon the capacities of the Internet to collapse geographic distances. Many project participants were the only people at their institution with a certain specialization (e.g., Asian American literature, history, etc.), so the EPP provided a welcome chance to connect to an intellectual community on a more regular basis than that of sporadic conferences. Moreover, the project revealed and destabilized the presumption that Asian American students are the primary population taking Asian American studies courses—or, to put it in a different way—that Asian American studies is *for* Asian American students, an argument made by administrators who limit or underfund such studies on campuses where there are few Asian American students. It was not at all evident that most of the students participating in the chats were Asian American; nor was it evident that the majority of students participating in the project courses were Asian American.

Our postproject conversation raised as many issues and questions as it addressed. Situating the EPP and the Internet in a broader historical perspective allowed us to see technology and social dynamics and circumstances as interrelated in the way they shape emergent forms of communication. Whether or not they are truly liberatory, Internet chats and e-mail discussions force us to read our own thoughts as texts. In the more interactive environment of the chat room, we have to "publicize" our interpretations of texts and are privy more quickly—perhaps too quickly—to others' responses to those interpretations. Does this aspect of chatting raise our stakes in our identity and make the replication of "real life" hierarchies and differences in the virtual world difficult to avoid? Perhaps preventing hierarchies from emerging in the virtual world may not be any more possible or impossible than preventing them in the real world. Still, the important aspect of critical pedagogy is to teach our students to be aware of the existence of hierarchies, how they emerge, and how they benefit some and not others. What they choose to do with these lessons is a more difficult issue, but the EPP was our (initial) attempt to consider the implications of emergent information technologies for pedagogy seriously and critically. One final question and issue with respect to the EPP and our postproject conversations is whether the issues of textuality, its modes of address, and complex social dynamics will become irrelevant in the future with the development of new Internet technologies that provide for audiovisual communication. Such developments will require further critical consideration; such is the nature of critical pedagogy.

Notes

1. Lisa Nakamura, "Race in/for Cyberspace: Identity Tourism and Racial Passing on the Internet," *Works and Days 25/26,* 13, nos. 1–2 (1995): 181–93.
2. The caucus/network's stated goals are (1) to institutionalize Asian American Studies; (2) to develop regional-specific research and publications; and (3) to provide mutual support to individuals and programs.
3. Gary Y. Okihiro and Lee C. Lee, eds., *East of California: New Perspectives in Asian American Studies* (Ithaca, NY: Asian American Studies Program of Cornell University, 1992).
4. The East of California network also sponsored a multicampus project, "Transforming the Centers," about issues of marginalization within the research and teaching of Asian American Studies.
5. Participating faculty, courses, and campuses included Patricia E. Chu, English 47a: "Introduction to Asian American Literature," Brandeis University; Robert Lee, Brown University; Nancy Cho, English 235: "Asian American Literature," Carleton College; Pamela Thoma, American Studies 277: "Introduction to Asian American Cultures,"

Colby College; Patricia P. Chu, English 187: "Asian American Literature," George Washington University; Janet Carlson, Comparative North American Studies 45: "Living on the Edge: The Asian American Experience," Macalester College; Shilpa Davé, English 185: "Alienation, Isolation, and Difference," Oberlin College; Nayan Shah, History 267: "Asian American History," State University of New York, Binghamton; Frank Ken Saragosa, English 67: "(Asian) Ethnicity and (Hetero) Sexual Normativity," Swarthmore College; Karen Har-Yen Chow, English 278W: "Introduction To Asian American Drama," University of Connecticut, Storrs; Elena Tajima Creef, Women's Studies 312: "Feminist Inquiry," Wellesley College; Elena Tajima Creef, Women's Studies 249: "Asian American Women in Film and Video," Wellesley College; Yoon Sun Lee, English 284, "New Literatures: The Literature of Asian America," Wellesley College. John Cheng, from George Mason University, was originally to be a participating faculty member as well as project coordinator, but went on leave for spring 1999 and did not teach the scheduled class; he did, however, serve as project coordinator.

6. Ginu Kamani, *Junglee Girl* (San Francisco: Aunt Lute Books, 1995); R. Zamora Linmark, *Rolling the R's* (New York: Kaya Press, 1995); Jeannie Barroga, *Walls,* in *Unbroken Thread: An Anthology of Plays by Asian American Women,* ed. Roberta Uno (Boston: University of Massachusetts Press, 1993), 201–60.

7. See <http://eoc.gmu.edu/EP/epindex.html>. The web site's entry page and links to online syllabi still exist, but the link to the WebCT tools and content pages no longer works because the site was removed from the George Mason University servers.

8. See <http://eoc.gmu.edu/EP/kc-syll.html> for the syllabus.

9. I structured the course readings mainly around Asian American plays, critical interpretations of some of these works, and Ronald Hayman's "How to Read a Play," a handbook on reading drama (New York: Grove Press, 1977). When possible, I showed videos depicting productions (*The Wash, M. Butterfly*) as well as the documentary *Slaying the Dragon* (about images of Asians in Hollywood) and Frieda Mock's documentary on Maya Lin, *A Strong Clear Vision,* as context for and counterpoint to Barroga's play. See Michael Toshiyuki Uno, dir., *The Wash* (Academy Entertainment, 1989); David Cronenberg, dir., *M. Butterfly* (Warner Productions, 1993); Deborah Gee, dir., *Slaying The Dragon* (San Francisco: Cross Current Media, dist. National Asian Telecommunications Association, 1987); Freida Lee Mock, dir., *Maya Lin: A Strong, Clear Vision* (American Film Foundation, 1994). Josephine Lee, *Performing Asian America: Race and Ethnicity on the Contemporary Stage* (Philadephia: Temple University Press, 1997) was also an assigned text.

10. The history of the creation of both the Asian American Studies Institute (the academic unit) as well as the Asian American Cultural Center (cultural and educational programming and student services resource unit) is a classic and compelling narrative of how student- and faculty-led struggles and demands resulted in these units' presence at UConn. A seminal moment for Asian American political awareness on campus was a racially motivated attack against a group of eight Asian American undergraduates by two white football players on December 3, 1987. Faculty members Paul Bock and Peter Luh galvanized a hunger strike on campus and persuaded the administration to respond strongly to the situation. The result was the formation of the Asian American Institute and the Asian American Cultural Center, both of which began operating in 1993.

11. The Asian American student population grew very rapidly in the 1980s—increasing from 1.7 percent of the campus population in 1983 to 4.42 percent in the spring of 1994, and now stands at 5.0 percent in 2000. Statistics for UConn's student enrollment may be accessed at: <http://vm.uconn.edu/~wwwoir/choosex.html>. According to these reports, the spring 1999 total university enrollment (including the Storrs, Hartford, Waterbury, Stamford, and Torrington campuses) stood at 20,372 full- and part-time undergraduate and graduate students. The total number of students at the flagship

Storrs campus and law school was 17,256. The breakdown by ethnicity was: "Non-Resident Aliens" 980 (5.6 percent); "Black" 823 (4.7 percent); "Native American" 53 (0.3 percent); "Asian American" 843 (5.0 percent); "White" 13,854 (80.3 percent). ("Non-Resident Aliens" include many international students from Asia.)

12. Maine ranks thirty sixth among all states for annual personal income level, at $20,366 (online at <http://www.bea.doc.gov/bea/regional/data>), and the state is 97.6 percent white with only a 0.72 percent Asian and Pacific Islander population (at <http://www.census.gov/population/estimates/state>).

13. Colby's demographics should not be too closely correlated to the state's, since students come from all over the United States and the world—only 11 percent of the student body is from Maine. In 1999, the student body was 5 percent Asian American, 3 percent Black, 2 percent Hispanic, less than 1 percent Native American, and slightly less than 90 percent white. Following disturbing national trends, Colby is not "need blind," and there are very few "full" scholarships. While I do not want to suggest a homogenous student body at Colby, it is true that most students are relatively economically privileged. Unless otherwise noted, all categories, statistics, and figures on Colby College were provided by Stephen Collins, Director of Communications for Colby College. See also the college's, website, <http://www.colby.edu/college/about>.

14. There are a few Asian American faculty at Colby, but they do more than their fair share of mentoring, and I do not feel comfortable referring students to them on a regular basis. Such practices can be exploitative and essentialist and may imply that mentoring can only be effective between individuals who share similar social positions, whether defined by race, gender, sexuality, or some other category; I am also skeptical about the prevailing notion of role modeling, which seems to be based on a simple homology and identification between developing subject and positive model. Nevertheless, I appreciate students' needs and think connections with Asian American faculty and community members are crucially important.

15. Asian American Studies curriculum at Colby was demanded by students, many of whom were involved in the early 1990s in Students of Color United For Change, a coalition of progressive students of color and white students, and some of whom formed an active Asian American Student Association. "Introduction to Asian American Cultures" has been taught, consistently though not annually—thanks to the ongoing interest of students and the general support of faculty—since 1996, when I first began teaching at Colby in a joint appointment in American studies and women's studies. Students who take this course often already have interests in African American studies, comparative American ethnic studies, and women's studies. Yet most of the students typically start with little specific knowledge of Asian American Studies as a field, and—like their peers across the nation—students of Asian ancestry are often ambivalent about identifying as "Asian American."

16. For a discussion of the contact zone, the classroom, and the community, see Mary Louise Pratt, "Arts of the Contact Zone," *Profession* 91 (1991): 33–40. For commentary, see also Richard E. Miller, "Fault Lines in the Contact Zone," in *College English* 56, no. 4 (1994): 389–408, and Joseph Harris, "Negotiating the Contact Zone," *Journal of Basic Writing* 14, no. 1 (1995): 27–42.

17. See <http://eoc.gmu.edu/EP/pt-syll.html> for the syllabus.

18. For a discussion of the sensationalist scapegoating of the Internet and how focusing on its dangers is one more way not to deal with more threatening social problems, see Emily Toth's cogent review of Katherine Tarbox's *Katie.com* (New York: Dutton, 2000), "On the Screen Where You Live," *Women's Review of Books* 18, no. 1 (2000): 4–5. Recent discussions of race, gender, and cyberspace complicate the most utopic observations, though many remain hopeful of the potential for resistance that the Internet may hold. A discussion of the possibilities cyberspace offers, if society exploits them, for the disruption of racial schemas can be found in Jerry Kang, "Cyber-Race," *Harvard*

Law Review 113 (2000): 1130–1208. See also Wendy Harcourt, ed., *Women@Internet: Creating New Cultures in Cyberspace* (London: Zed Books, 1999); and Marc A. Smith and Peter Kollock, eds., *Communities in Cyberspace* (New York: Routledge, 1999).

19. The EPP provided the means for instructors of Asian American studies to collaborate cross-campus and, theoretically, to capitalize on efficiencies of the division of labor. However, in practice, Internet technology did not produce a spontaneous collaboration among faculty but shifted much of the labor to the project coordinator and webmaster, John Cheng. In terms of sharing teaching materials, faculty who contributed the intro- ductory materials for each text did so individually, with no guarantee of reciprocity.

20. Mark Poster, for instance, argues for the nonhierarchical possibilities of "network" modes of communication such as the Internet that differ from those of "broadcast" modes of communication like radio or television. See Poster, "Virtual Ethnicity: Tribal Identity in an Age of Global Communications," in *Cybersociety 2.0: Revisiting Computer- Mediated Communication and Community,* ed. Steven G. Jones (Thousand Oaks, CA: Sage, 1998): 184–211.

21. For an in-depth analysis of Internet use and Hawaiian language revitalization, see Mark Warschauer, "Language, Identity, and the Internet," in *Race in Cyberspace,* ed. Beth E. Kolko, Lisa Nakamura, and Gilbert B. Rodman (New York: Routledge, 2000), 151–170.

22. Poster, "Virtual Ethnicity," 190.

23. This point had particular implications for the notion of "anonymous" chats. The issue that possible differences in typeface and color raised wasn't so much about anonymity— having a voice without recourse to a specific individual's identity—as the possibility and need to distinguish generally between individual voices.

24. One of us shared the fact that students admitted to her that their classroom silence is not always indicative of lack of interest or boredom, but that sometimes the way she phrased questions made them too complex for students to address immediately.

25. Use of chat—and other Internet—logs is considered research on "human" subjects and bears consideration of the ethical issues involved. See the American Association for the Advancement of Science website on ethical and legal aspects of human subjects research in cyberspace, at <http://www.aaas.org/spp/dspp/sfrl/ projects/intres/main.htm>.

3
Gender, Sexuality, and Kinship through the Integrated Circuit

9

Filipina.com: Wives, Workers, and Whores on the Cyberfrontier

VERNADETTE V. GONZALEZ
ROBYN MAGALIT RODRIGUEZ

Three different images of Asia and the Internet frame this introduction. The first is of two young, hip, androgynous Asians who grace the cover of the July-September 2000 special edition of *Newsweek International*. They boast a cyborg aesthetic, complete with red-streaked hair, futuristic microfiber clothing, and metallic makeup. These representatives of the "New Asia" stand against a traditional dragon backdrop like modern technocrats emerging from an oriental chrysalis. The accompanying articles boost the idea of this new modern, liberal subject. As leaders of the "quiet revolution", their technology of "liberation" is the Internet.[1] In the "New Economy" section, several articles raise the prospects of "liberat[ion] by the internet,"[2] and the Internet's "revolutionary" potential to create a "commercial democracy."[3] One particular writer suggests that, "Out there in cyberspace the old Asia of paternalism, cozy insider deals and murky transactions is fading. Meritocracy rules."[4] This *Newsweek* issue celebrates the cultural and economic revolution that the Internet promises, implying that technology will succeed where communism failed to deliver. Finally, democracy (and the logic of capitalism) has broken down the last bastion of the East. For the "New Asian Woman" in particular, the Internet heralds a "new world of possibilities" in information technology-led economies, signifying progress from Oriental patriarchies and traditional, circumscribed, gender roles.[5] The profiles of several Asian women prominent in their fields testify to the role that the Internet has had in their success. The celebrated androgyny on the front cover testifies to how gender is both ostensibly unmarked and unremarkable, the playing field is leveled in cyberspace.

Ironically, on the inside page of the special edition, a Singapore Airlines ad—the second image—contradicts the notion of a departure from old patriarchies. Two Asian female flight attendants, dressed in exotic native costume, smile while serving a white businessman in a suit and hover around his luxuriously appointed first-class seat, evoking long-established logics of colonial service. The color scheme is "old world," with rich but muted colors suggesting tradition, old money, and the comforts of wealth. This ad calls attention to an important dissonance in the celebratory discourses of cyberspace, epitomized by the triumphalist *Newsweek* issue. Against and alongside an emerging vision of a rejuvenated, modernized, and competitive Asia, a different reality exists—one cut by class, race, and gender lines in ways that echo old colonialisms and that bring to mind emergent imperialisms in the age of globalization.

However, while Asian women in general continue to function as markers of sexualized difference in virtual and material realities, we argue that the bodies of Filipinas haunt this dawning Asian "cyberdemocracy" in a historically specific way.[6] Typing *Filipina* on virtually any Internet search engine yields the third image—the following sites at a "100% match": "Filipina 4 Love"; "Filipina Ladies" (an Internet introduction service); "A Filipina Bride: Mail Order Brides Dating Personals" (which offers a low-priced, professional service); "FILIPINA LADY—Who is She?" (a pen-pal service); and "Erotic explicit filipina pussy pictures" (which speaks for itself). Following these choices are a grouping of sites from "Hearts of Asia" (another mail-order bride/introduction-service site) conveniently arranged by age group. While occasionally a search like this can yield a personal website by or about a Filipina that is not about mail-order brides, pornographic representations, or questionable pen-pal services, the overwhelming character of the results center around the "1st Lady-FREE" introductions to "pre-screened Filipinas" model. This is a particularly gendered phenomenon: typing *Filipino* yields links on culture, the Philippines as a nation, food, and entertainment of the more innocuous type. Filipino men are not a hypervisible commodity to be traded on the Internet (even as they, too, make up a significant number of the labor exported by the Philippine state). *Filipina*, in this case, becomes a marker of sexual difference that has historical roots.

It is clear that *Newsweek*'s construction of the "New Asian Woman" does not take into account the thousands of websites that depend on the continuing availability of the "backward" Filipina woman as both the antithesis *and* enabler of this very modern, financially independent and technologically savvy Asian capitalist.[7] Information and communications technologies exacerbate intra-Asian and imperialist histories of exploitation in the present, creating a specificity of experience that begs for a critical rethinking of the Internet as a revolutionary technology. The exotic and serviceable bodies advertised in the Singapore Airlines ad as well as numerous websites provide material and discursive counterpoints to the *Newsweek* cover, complicating the Internet's claim as the harbinger of the ultimate "quiet revolution" and the emergent tool for "first world" and "third world" feminists.

Without a doubt, the lightning-fast information superhighway is becoming *the* critical source of global information today. This democratic informationalism claims to transcend and obliterate all borders—embodied, national, and global. For its users, the Internet is a vast repository of knowledge and truth, democratizing information, and, ultimately, political and economic power. Its newest members, such as the New Asian capitalists featured in the *Newsweek* special issue, extol the new economic and political enfranchisement that the Internet offers: "From Tokyo to Katmandu, the Net is spawning opportunities and a sense of individualism. It may even help bridge the rich-poor divide."[8] However, the dissonance between Newsweek's "New Asian Woman" and Filipina realities (virtual or otherwise) raises critical questions about this touted "new world of possibilities" as well as the rhetoric of liberation and neoliberalism that cloaks it. We are forced to ask, whose and which revolutions are enabled by the Internet, and which Asian women do neoliberal discourses celebrate? More important, how does the Internet embody a rhetoric of triumphant individualism and equal opportunity even as it heightens the locally felt unevenness of globalization? What are the continuities and discontinuities between the ideologies and technologies of American monopoly capitalism and American imperialism from the turn of the twentieth century and the rise of the "New Asia" at the turn of the twenty-first? In a medium celebrated for transcending difference and borders in the ether of cyberspace, how is it that instead difference both enables and is exacerbated through the exoticized visualizations of third world bodies?[9]

In order to trouble the supposed democratic and liberatory narratives of information and technology, we look specifically at how humans develop and use technology. The ways in which search engines participate in creating and reinforcing racial and sexual logics has serious ramifications for meaning-making for particular bodies on the Internet. We analyze websites that circulate Filipinas in ways reminiscent of colonial and global histories in order to further understand how signifying practices in cyberspace flesh out the set of logics by which Filipinas are constrained. The specific sites/sights of Filipina bodies track a counterdiscourse that problematizes the "innocent" notions of a cyberdemocracy and questions Information and Communications Technology's (ICTs') claims to transparency. Trafficking in women has intensified globally with the advent of telecommunications technology,[10] and while Filipinas are not the sole commodity in this traffic, they represent unique sites where histories of U.S. and Asian imperialisms, militarisms, and capitalisms coalesce.

We reconsider the limitations and possibilities of the Internet for a postcolonial third-world feminist politics in light of the violence committed against Filipina women (and others) in its circuits. Representations of Filipinas like those that proliferate in cyberspace reveal the linkages between technologies and ideologies of "progress" and "development" and different forms of imperialism and "scattered hegemonies";[11] the complex politics of representation and commodification in the age of flexible accumulation;[12] and the limits of concepts like "democracy" and "individualism" when one is marked as Filipina in cyberspace. What alternative questions and theoretical frameworks need to be imagined in this less than revolutionary landscape?

Filipina Bodies on the Cyberfrontier

We turn to the site of Filipinas on the cyberfrontier because they embody the difference that enables and haunts capitalist circuits. Filipinas, as they circulate on the Internet, unravel capitalism's democratic myth. Our critique of neoliberal cyberdemocracy rests on the Filipina body for several reasons.

First, the Philippines continues to function under de facto if not de jure, American imperialism. The history of U.S. colonialism in the Philippines established the "rest and recreation" industry on a large scale for its military troops stationed there. In its present anti-terrorist reincarnation, U.S. militarization of the Philippines slips comfortably into long-established infrastructures and cultures of imperialism. As Cynthia Enloe argues, the masculinity and morale of the "martial races" must be supported by domestic feminine troops.[13]

Framing the discourses of cyberspace through the manifest destiny of the American frontier is nothing new. Ziauddin Sardar's provocative and sometimes problematic analysis of the colonial roots of technological modernity argues that the frontiers of cyberspace are "set to follow the patterns of the old West."[14] Similarly, as Jeff Ow notes, early scholarship on the liberating potential of community on the Internet, such as Howard Rheingold's *The Virtual Community: Homesteading on the Electronic Frontier,* deployed romantic views of pioneering on the American West that once again reify the emptiness of the territories to be occupied.[15] In the case of the Philippines as a U.S. colony, however, an analysis of frontier discourse must include a discussion of its sexual and racial politics.[16] The liminal space of the frontier was the threshold upon which a European man, perhaps overcivilized (and thus effeminate) could regain his manhood and claim his American cultural identity by taming the savage lands (and people) of the New World and beyond.

For Filipinas, American militarization in the Asia Pacific (to "protect" its territories) has meant efficient interpellation into the military industrial and ideological apparatus as sex workers. The specificity of the Philippines as an American frontier—one that had and has tragic consequences for Filipinas living in that border zone—must be tied to the ways in which the Philippines functions as an outpost of difference on the cyberfrontier. As U.S. "wards," Filipinas have served and continue to serve as bodies of pleasure and labor.[17] For Filipinas who circulate as global domestics, entertainers, wives, and otherwise, this has meant an ongoing national and cultural marking and marketing as historically circulated consumer items. Following Rolando Tolentino, we suggest that the ways in which Filipinas circulate in cyberspace is symptomatic of U.S.-Philippine neocolonial relations.[18] The circuits of cyberspace disseminate a concealed politics of power and desire that underpins what Renato Rosaldo calls "imperialist nostalgia."[19]

Circuits of multinationalism, militarism, and transnationalism, symptomatic of U.S.-Philippine colonial and neocolonial relations, continue to enmesh representations and realities of Filipina bodies in global capitalism's networks of desire and consumption. Filipinas circulate as particular commodities—of labor and pleasure—within Asian networks, marking historical and emerging intra-Asian national hierarchies. *Newsweek*'s "New Asia" elides the ways in which communications technologies like the Internet discursively and materially discipline Filipina bodies in multiple, historically familiar ways. This regulation of

Filipina bodies is perpetuated for the flexible accumulation of the Philippine state and global capital, and for the pleasure of and consumption by prospective husbands (in Europe and the United States) and middle class women (in Asia's Tiger economies, as well as in the Philippines itself).

Second, as Neferti Tadiar argues, Filipina bodies "become sites for the construction of and contestation over the nation abroad."[20] With technology that can virtually tour the ends of the earth in a matter of seconds, one can explore and shape the contours of the Filipina body and the Philippine state. On the Internet, representations of Filipinas become synonymous with the Philippines as a nation-state. Searching the Internet for *Philippines* and specific Philippine localities, for instance, obtains mail-order bride and domestic-worker agencies as well as sex sites. Using the search engine Infoseek we searched for *Cebu* and found (with an 84 percent match) mail-order bride agencies like "A Cebu Bride" specializing in women from a particular locality. Even on mail-order bride sites that do not explicitly focus on Filipina women from particular regions, one can, as in www.holton.com/filipina, pick a woman by city. Boundaries are necessarily staked on the Internet, and Filipina women's bodies act as markers for national and regional borders. Particular localities are evoked on the Internet to elicit specific kinds of consumption and desire that are predicated on reified difference.

Third, the Philippines' foreign capital-dependent economic program, which promotes the expansion of export production and the tourism industry, requires the production of difference and the disciplining (both "violently" and "benevolently") of Filipinas as "cheap" and "docile" workers on the one hand, and "beautiful" and "generous" embodiments of the nation on the other. While the Philippine state must regulate its national borders in order to discipline Filipina labor (its most profitable export) as it moves in and out of these borders, these very same borders continue to be salient in the ether of cyberspace. Neoliberal development in the Philippines means that "modes of labor regulation extend beyond the capitalist workplace per se to domestic units and to capitalist nation-states—the latter engaging in discursive inscription and control."[21] The Philippine state, in order to promote tourism, celebrates Filipina women's beauty by hosting Miss Universe pageants in order to establish itself as an exotic destination and a land of beautiful women.[22] As labor export has outpaced tourism and export production as the country's top source of foreign exchange, the Philippine state has deployed nationalist narratives as a means of containing Filipina migrant workers while simultaneously requiring their mobility.

Last, representations of Filipinas in cyberspace have real, material consequences. While constructed and imaginary, they no less constitute and are constituted by lived social relations. In cyberspace, the ideologies and technologies of racialization and sexualization materialize on the Filipina body. Donna Haraway argues that "communications technolog[ies] . . . are the crucial tools recrafting our bodies. These tools embody and enforce new social relations for women worldwide."[23] Following Haraway, we argue that the Internet is a crucial tool of globalization, sedimenting and enforcing particular and familiar meanings on Filipina bodies. What "Filipina" signifies, and how Filipina bodies circulate on the Internet problematizes the ways in which capital functions and represents itself. Filipinas signify "outposts" of difference on the cyberfrontier, embodying the very difference that neoliberal democratic discourses reject or nominally accept. At the same time that Filipinas stand for the "other" on the cyberfrontier, representations of Filipinas that litter the Internet rely on prefigured, already constituted notions of Filipinas that erase important differences among them. Filipinas embody continuing histories of violent imperialisms. Images of Filipinas on the Internet sustain old imperial fictions, fantasies, and imaginaries that shape desires for relaxation, wives, prostitutes and ultimately domestics and low-wage workers.[24] As Lisa Nakamura states, in this modality, cyberspace "reinforces a post-body ideology which reproduces the assumption of the old one."[25] Filipina bodies functioned—then and now—as repositories of difference. We insist on calling attention to difference in order to reveal how individualism and democracy on the Internet are in fact ideologies of power that conceal the unevenness of "real" life. The "si(gh)ting" of Filipinas has real-life impacts, discursively legitimizing, normalizing, and naturalizing the diasporic Filipina body as domestic, prostitute, whore, for sale.

Marxist theorist Henri Lefebvre's work on the creation of "abstract space" is a useful detour here because he reiterates that "capital and capitalism 'influence' practical matters relating to space."[26] We draw from Lefebvre's method, which aims to find a syntax of space that would "expose the actual production of space."[27] Because "(social) space is a (social) product," Lefebvre claims that there must be a process of abstraction that conceals the social relations embedded in space.[28] He argues that capitalism and neocapitalism have produced abstract space, which includes the "world of commodities," its "logic" and its worldwide strategies.[29] From Lefebvre we argue that the ways Filipinas are "searched" on Internet search engines are particularly problematic as the images that circulate in cyberspace are passed off as "information" and "knowledge"—abstracted from uneven social relations. Andrew Herman and John H. Sloop likewise argue that "utopian dreams of bodily transcendence" must be rewritten and reworked in order to expose the networks of corporate capitalism as well as the histories of colonialism and imperialism that underwrite the development of technology.[30] Indeed, the ways search engines function are neither objective nor transparent. The information that is at the fingertips of the user has already been filtered through several layers of inequity.

Technologics

Cyberspace, created by new and expanding communications technologies, cannot be abstracted from the social and material relations in which it is embedded. The Internet is still the domain of the first world. The basic technological infrastructure that enables the creation of search engines and the enormous databases they must support are owned and located mainly in the United States and a very few European nations. With the American deregulation of ICTs in 1996, the concentration of ownership in this industry has increased. Even now, with the rest of the world supposedly becoming wired, the United States and Europe still control how information is delivered on a simple search like "Filipina." Meaning making is not a democratic process.[31]

Ironically, the origins of information and communications technologies—the rational tools of progress and capitalism—are mired in the anxieties of the Cold War. The offspring of ARPANET, a communications network first developed by the U.S. Department of Defense, the Internet today is still an American-dominated medium, even as it is a "World Wide Web."[32] As the progeny of Cold War paranoia and surveillance ideologies, it is implicated in the spread of capitalist democracy against the encroachments of communism. *Newsweek's* "New Asia" illustrates how ICTs are imbricated in a self-consciously "progressive" colonizing project that looks to the third world as a frontier. "Technologic" has made the "less-developed" countries of the third world objects of various interventions "by uncompromisingly reducing poverty to a technical problem, and by promising technical solutions to the sufferings of powerless and oppressed people."[33]

While technologic is used as a means of justifying intervention, technology itself is an intervention. Development experts promote the expansion of new technologies (production, communication, etc.) that also serve as a kind of "moral force" enabling the spread of modernist ideals.[34] The easy access to information furthers the aims of neoliberalism, as rational economic actors are enabled to make (more) rational economic choices. Information technology unleashes the liberating forces of the (more perfect) market. What difference may have threatened, informationalism can overcome. The "free trade" of commodities that developmentalism sought to secure, enforced by institutions like the World Trade Organization in partnership with global capital and third world states, has become more efficiently facilitated with the Internet.

Ultimately, then, information technology is about the surveillance of new subjects and the creation of new markets. Coco Fusco points out that "the political and economic implications of its centrality to globalization are elided by the repeated fetishization of new technologies as the primary agent of democracy."[35] Following Fusco, we argue that information and communication technology is not merely about knowledge and democratizing information exchange but also about the consolidation of a cash nexus for globalizing capital. Scholars such as Fusco and Olu Oguibe have long argued that the digital divide breaks down on familiar global lines. As Fusco notes, "The digital revolution has provided the technology that has reorganized what used to be known as the third world, making those territories into low end markets and low wage labor pools for multinational corporations."[36] New technologies, imbricated in capitalism, thrive on difference.

While the Internet's exponential growth in the past ten years has made information technology a priority in developed and developing countries' economies, what has resulted instead of technological progress is a second "brain drain." The Philippines today provides a large bulk of the global information technology (IT) workforce, and technology-driven degree programs are multiplying at a rapid rate, creating a new batch of exportable workers to ease the nation's perennial financial straits. Their English proficiency, a colonial legacy, is seen as a "comparative advantage" in the global information technology (IT) market. In August 2001, President Gloria Macapagal-Arroyo declared in her State of the Nation address that information technology is the "foundation of the Philippines' future economic development." However, the fact that Filipinos might be making a mark in the IT workforce has not made an impact on the meanings attached to Filipina bodies on the Internet for the simple reason that the IT workers are cyberspace's wage laborers and not its owners.

"Information" on the Internet is never objective or exhaustive. The creation of a world of information to be searched is predicated on critical exclusions and inequities. For those of us who have access to the Net, the immediacy of information retrieved allows us to believe that *all* the information "out there" is at *our* fingertips. However, "even the largest of the search engines, Inktomi, has indexed only about half the web."[37] Also, and most important, this indexed information is always already mediated on several levels.

The process of creating "objective " information is deeply subjective. Several kinds of search-engine companies exist to index the information available on the web. These companies first create "universes" of webpages that their search engines "crawl" and from which they retrieve particular kinds of search requests. The "directory style" search engine utilizes a clearly subjective process for reviewing, registering, and indexing websites to include in its "universe." This is dependent on human editors, who hand-index information.

One of the more popular search engines, Yahoo!, is not really a search engine at all, but rather "a team of editors [who] index the Internet." Yahoo! creates its universe from individually submitted forms that contain information about the site.[38] The second kind of search engine (that of Google, Alta Vista, or Excite) uses computer-generated algorithms. These function according to the "personality" of the particular search-engine company, which decides how to organize searches and create a hierarchy of information. For instance, Google's link-based search algorithm prioritizes websites according to the number of sites to which it is linked. Others are linguistically based, with search results depending on the number of search words on particular sites. In either case, a certain kind of cultural capital is necessary in order to create a website that will appear at the top of a search result: "Some people will do almost anything to receive a top ranking from a heavily used search engine ... [because] the first response in a search will bring more viewers, more business."[39] These techniques include pages that repeat a key word many times in "invisible type" (that is, using the same color as the color of the page) so that the search engine ranks a certain website as more relevant, and therefore, higher on the search results list.[40]

The complex algorithms that enable the completion of a particular search are created by human programmers who are shaped by the social relations in which they live. The recent spate in hiring of linguists, psychologists and sociologists by Silicon Valley is no accident.[41] Technology is becoming more and more aware that it needs language and behavioral analysts in order to predict market behavior and consumer choices. One particular website consulting company, Cyber Eyes, advertises: "Convert Your Website Into An Energized Matrix Of Keyword Power Phrases Which Search Engines Will LOVE!" One of its consultants advertises the fact that he is a "wordsmith, with a B.A. in Classical English literature . . . a published writer, poet and fiction author" who has the requisite skill "when it comes to squeezing keywords into short sentences to maximize keyword density."[42]

Ultimately, "information" is not free. While each search engine is run differently, website applicants who wish to be registered on a particular search engine database must pay. As Michael Specter writes, "The most direct way to get your Website to the top of a search—and the most pernicious—is to pay for it."[43] In fact, companies can bid on certain key words, such as "travel" or "sex" paying a search engine like GoTo a certain amount for every person who clicks on their sites. For profit-based popular sites, this is a bargain. For others, such as nonprofit websites like Gabriela (a Philippine-based alliance of progressive women's organizations), this means that it must compete with Gabriella (a popular porn site). Deadlock Design, a website promotion/consulting company affiliated with Cyber Eyes boasts that it can "handle everything for you . . . build your site . . . promote it . . . and add sophisticated interactive systems if that's your pleasure" all for the low price of $499 for preparation and submission (to search engine companies) and $125 per month for maintenance.[44] Market forces come into play when websites that can afford to pay for promotions services (such as for-profit mail-order sites) appear near the top of a search list for "Filipina," as opposed to a young New York–based lesbian Pinay writer such as Bamboo Girl.

The linking of *Filipina* to *sex, mail-order bride,* or *domestic* is no accident. It is shaped by those who have the capital to hire or buy them, as key words can be purchased. In businesses that concentrate on analyzing keyword power and strategy, keyword reports are sold to interested companies who want to maximize their market value.[45] As Deadlock Designs states, "With zillions of people and sites coming online, the engines and directories simply want to cull out the Lightweights, to make room for Heavyweights. This is all very simple: Survival of the Fittest."[46] Thus, while Filipinos are presently becoming a visible presence in the lower and middle rungs of the global IT industry, Filipinas continue to travel the circuits of the web as flesh for sale.

Wives, Workers, and Whores

Search engines change the Filipina into cyberscript, change and conflating her body into "sex/worker"—rendering her into a universal code. The results of a search using *Filipina* illustrate the ways in which cyberspace erases and conflates difference. Examining websites of Filipina mail-order bride companies and domestic-helper agencies demonstrates the interchangeability of Filipina identities on the Internet. On these websites, Filipinas are commodities displayed, processed, and sold (sometimes returned) to particular kinds of consumers. Specific visualizations render Asian women, and, we argue, Filipinas in particular, as "the most immediately conjurable" embodiment of "garment worker," "factory girl," or "G.I. prostitute." This Asian working body is simultaneously erased of historical and material specificities, then exported and circulated as a specular signifier of broader socioeconomic formations such as "the global assembly line," the "export processing zone," "military prostitution," and/or "sex/tourism."[47] Filipinas in cyberspace are the site at which these various identities are conflated. In websites for pen pals, brides, and domestics, we note a significant similarity in the ways Filipinas are represented.

The "Filipina Penpal" site invites the "browser" to "meet beautiful women from the Philippines, Manila and Cebu."[48] On the main menu, "Filipina Penpal" offers the user the opportunity to view "sincere and marriage minded" women by age group: 18-22, 23-25, 26-34, and 35 and up. Further, it offers information on and services for immigration and visas, including a direct link to the U.S. Immigration and Naturalization Service, as well as detailed information on INS regulations pertaining to "mail order brides." It also provides travel tips, links to the best airfares, and a dollar converter to make the consumer's transaction efficient and easy. When one clicks on an age group to see the women, head shots of women are arranged catalog style and are identified by name. One can choose a woman's picture that lists further details about her, such as her age, height, and weight and a short description. Women are variously described as "loyal," "sincere," and "quiet." To purchase the pen-pal service, checks or money orders are sent, appropriately enough, to a postal address at "Colonial Station" in Massachusetts. Note once again that this site is purportedly for "pen pals."

At "A Filipina Bride," (www.afilipinabride.com), one can order online with Visa, MasterCard and even American Express (never having to leave home). On this site, pages of women can be browsed by age group.[49] In this case, however, women are identified by first name and last initial only and are assigned an identification number. Addresses are ordered by inputting a particular identification number on the online order form. As in "Filipina Penpal," a woman's vital statistics are available: age, height, and weight. Here, at least, women can describe themselves in a brief sentence. While it is arguable just how much room for self-statement a prospective bride has on this site, we suggest that whatever self-statement, allowed is highly circumscribed by market forces. "A Filipina Bride," however, is not exclusively focused on Filipinas. It also features women from throughout Africa, Latin America, and Eastern Europe, encouraging the user to "Click Here Now! Do It!" (fast, while supplies last). What is significant, though, is the way that this particular site stands for the traffic of other women, and not just Filipinas, while using "Filipina" as its signifier for spouses that can be purchased. In this way, "Filipina" becomes a universal icon for the mail-order bride industry.

Like "A Filipina Bride" and "Filipina Penpal," potential domestic helpers can be browsed by age group with the added feature of browsing by body build (e.g., small, medium, large or tall). In "Maids on Line," selecting "on-line services" from the main menu leads to a site that depicts a map of the Philippines and Indonesia.[50] Women's faces color the map. One can click on these faces to get detailed information on the women themselves, or click onto the designated icons to view video presentations about the countries. The women's photographs are arranged onscreen almost exactly like the online catalogs for mail-order brides. Head shots, and sometimes full body shots, are shown. The women are identified by ID number, sometimes by name. Their age, height, and weight follow. In addition to those basic statistics, information on their religion and educational background is included.

Our point in reviewing the websites above is to highlight the strikingly similar ways in which Filipina women are sited/sighted on websites devoted to providing different services. A search for *foreign domestic helper, Filipina domestic* or *domestic helper* also pulled up mail-order bride sites. Under *Filipina domestic,* websites like the ones described above were found, but some also featured specific women, drawn from "pen pal" or "introductory" services, who identified themselves as domestic workers, in countries outside of the Philippines. What these websites and searches actually suggest is that Filipina bodies are si(gh)ted as simultaneously bodies of pleasure and consumption, as well as bodies for labor. Filipina women's bodies are important for their corporeality (age, height, weight) and the desires their corporeal bodies can fulfill—as good wives and diligent domestic-helpers. Search engines and webmasters, as well as the services themselves, often conflate these categories. Filipinas are closely inspected and ultimately processed for their desirability in a way analogous to American slave auctions. Mail-order bride and domestic-helper sites ultimately promise deliverance for Filipinas while guaranteeing "love" for prospective husbands and help to middle-class women. The benevolence of love or a job belies the commodification of Filipina women's bodies and the ways in which these visualizations rob Filipinas of subjectivity. While some of these sites offer space for women to speak for themselves, it is rarely outside of the parameters set by businesses catering to their customers' desires.[51]

Further, in the course of studying different websites, we found instances not only where Filipina bodies are interchangeable, but, indeed, where *Filipina* becomes a kind of universal signifier for other women's bodies. On the "Filipina Bride" webpage, for example, *Filipina* becomes the signifier for multinational women. At the same time, however, Filipinas remain distinct. At this site, catalogs of "beautiful Filipina women" and "beautiful women of all nations" are separate. In another example, a sex site entitled "Filipina Fantasies," Filipina bodies are noticeably absent.[52] Only one picture of a Filipina in a bikini is pictured while pornographic pictures of white women crowd the page. While the site boasts of "uncensored Filipina sex action" including photo galleries, chat rooms, sex stories, and movie clips—they cannot be accessed by a nonpaying surfer. What is accessible are film clips of Japanese pornography, or nude pictures of Pamela Anderson—not Filipinas. This was also true of "Filipina Hardcore," a site linked to "Filipina Fantasies."[53]

As the Philippines continue to export thousands of Filipinas to work as domestics, entertainers, and low-wage service workers throughout Asia, it becomes clear that Filipinas render specific purposes in the bodies they occupy. The circulation of Filipina workers' bodies is not innocent or natural. They are disciplined as "sincere," "loyal," and "quiet," which invariably translates into "docile" and "cheap"—a boon to the struggling Philippine state and the profit-seeking multinational corporation. Filipina women are fixed in cyberspace to be sighted and known by ostensibly first-world or "modern" users for their pleasure and consumption. A Filipina in cyberspace "speaks" to the desires, fantasies and imaginations her viewer is thought to have; her self-narrations are prescreened for her consumer.

Parting Words: Agency and Its Discontents

The question with which we struggle now is, given the ways in which Filipina women are circulated as icons and offspring of an unholy alliance between militarism and capitalism on the Internet, how can this same technology offer subversive potentials to undo histories of exploitation today?

Many scholars have written about the ways in which ICTs have failed to live up to their liberatory promise, particularly for the subaltern body politic. Some argue that the Internet's claims to leave the body behind are specious, particularly for women and people of color who have access to these technologies.[54] Critiques also point out the ways in which the Internet is run in the interests of capital.[55] Others look to the ways that "different" unruly bodies are absorbed and commodified by capitalism in ways that render them benign and yet irreducibly "other." Lisa Nakamura argues that Internet corporate discourses of a "postethnic America" claim to eradicate race and "the rest of it," even as difference itself is used to boost a product's marketability.[56] Jennifer González similarly argues that a different kind of tourism occurs where Internet consumers of avatar sites surf racial and gendered identities unlike their own, reinforcing already accepted racial and sexual stereotypes through an interpellative process of "cyberpassing."[57]

On the other hand, we must also seriously contend with research that has found its way into a cautious but optimistic view of these same technologies.

Many scholars have written about the potential that ICTs have for reframing and rearticulating a more complex and self-reflexive subaltern feminist politics. Marisa Belausteguigotia Rius, Kekula P. Bray Crawford, and Alloo Fatma have noted the effects and potentials of the Internet for third- and fourth-world feminist struggles.[58] Mimi Nguyen chooses to forgo visibility in her website altogether, rejecting cyberspace's "offer of abstraction," which insinuates that "it's [her Asian female] body—and not the cultural logic that organizes and disciplines [her] body—which checks [her] access into allegedly democratic publics."[59]

Arturo Escobar argues that linked with a critical concept of local place, a "political ecology of cyberculture" can be a useful tool for "a defence of places out of which gender and ecological relations might emerge transformed."[60] Donna Haraway's now classic essay on cyborgs, as well as her responses to critics of that essay, attempt to find modalities of agency through the "monstrous self" created by the hybridity of women and technology.[61] For Haraway, cyborg politics provide a way to disrupt the universal code that commodifies certain bodies more readily than others. In Haraway and Escobar's views of the subversive potential of IC technologies, technology and science itself are not demonized, but rather reclaimed from the site of virtuality where "the illegitimate offspring of militarism and patriarchal capitalism" reside.[62] In this sense, Filipina cyberbodies can both reproduce as well as haunt reality. To the extent that these visual bodies haunt flickering screens (and hence, global imaginaries), they illustrate the violence of reification as wives, workers, and whores. However, we must note that the potential heteroglossia that their bodies signify is rarely enunciated—it is more often than not concealed, transformed, and disarmed in the service of capital. Their potentially transformative heteroglossia is abstracted in the process of production and consumption. For Filipinas, the fictions that litter the Internet are representations crafted by discursive strategies perfected by global capital and the Philippine state in "real life"—rarely from Filipinas themselves. The Filipina self-representations that we have found are highly circumscribed by the constructions of particular websites, but, more important, by the webs of power in which they are enmeshed.

There's no denying that Filipina women exercise agency in a variety of different forms and forums such as Gabriela, the New People's Army, various nongovernmental organizations and cooperatives, and so on. Isis International, an Asian-based women's group, suggests that the lack of access and training for women in impoverished nations continues to pose a big hurdle for notions of democracy through connectivity, even as there are slow gains being made.[63] Gabriela, an alliance of progressive Filipina women's organizations that targets, among other issues, the global trafficking of women, has established itself online but is also highly aware of the ways in which the technology it is using to disseminate information is the same one that eases the trafficking of women.

What we also found, however, is that technology is quick to adapt and circumscribe the ways in which information is sought out. As we mentioned earlier, looking up *Gabriella* instead of *Gabriela* on the Internet ironically brings up a site devoted to pornography rather than the website for the largest alliance of Filipina women's organizations globally. Even *Pinay*, a popular catchword for ostensibly politically conscious Filipinas in the United States, has been appropriated as a synonym for *Filipina* on the Internet. Typing in *Pinay* brings up, along with websites on Pinay music and personal websites, sites such "Sexiest Pinay Celebrities," "White Pinay Lover Messages," and "The Pinay Pleasures Webring."[64] Intriguingly juxtaposed to the *Pinay Webring*, which targets "aLL The PiNaY GiRLz oR GuYz WhO WaNNa ShOw THiEr PiNa(o)Y PriDe ThROuGh ThIer HomEPagEz," the Pinay *Pleasures* Webring promises "some of the finest Filipina ladies on the Net."[65] Even common misspellings of *Filipina* or *Philippines* are accounted for. While there is more space for Pinays in their personal web pages who are "RePrEsEnTiN' To ThA FuLLeSt" [sic], we are uneasy with the prospects of agency or subversion in this space.[66]

While we agree with Haraway and Escobar that the Internet's social space is at once the site of hegemony and counterhegemony, we continue to have reservations about the possibilities of "contradiction" in this space when it is clear that any eruptions of violence are usually aimed at Filipina women's bodies.[67] Instead, we find that the internet eases the processing of Filipina bodies into the circuits of capital.[68] With search results like these, do scholars located in the first world need to reassess our definitions of agency even as we must necessarily keep the slippery power relationships on the Internet in view? What are the possibilities and alternatives of representation in a medium that insists on abstract identities even as it reifies certain bodies as "specular delicacies" and commodities for the consumption of the first world?

Performativity of identities, a potentially powerful process, is unavailable to most Filipinas who are being reified as "visual treats." There is little heterogeneity regarding the kinds of identities preconstituted for Filipinas on the Net, which is not to say that it does not exist in other media and other spaces.[69] For example, Pinays on ostensibly non- mail-order, pen-pal, or domestic-worker sites identify themselves with similar markers of femininity, such as "lil" (little), "swyt" (sweet), "QT" (cutie), and "enchanting." While this could be read as self-affirming play with language, this self-infantilization reveals the tenuousness of agency when even scripts for self-representation are caught in capitalistic and neoliberal webs of power. Neoliberalism assures the opportunity for free, individual self-statement, even as capitalism curtails the language available for this statement. Upon entering the realm of cyberrepresentation, Filipinas are often inadequately represented and shuttled into pregiven representational categories constructed for them by an inadequate language. The key search words used to inscribe/describe Filipina identity on the Internet are more often that not, frozen in their meanings. Search engines, tools used to categorize, the Filipina, are more readily constructed to pull up certain definitions that center around her reified body.

We argue, that while representations of Filipinas in cyberspace leave room for incisive political critique, cyberspace as it exists in its first world–centered, class-biased incarnation is a limited space of agency for Filipinas and other women who are passed around in global capitalism's circuits of desire. It may in fact not be the critical space for the exercise of agency and resistance—at least on the part of Filipinas who are being trafficked in various ways. At best, it allows them a space for survival and out of the depressing economic situation in the Philippines—which is, in itself, a liberating move for many. On the other hand, it circulates and disciplines them as particular commodities. Thus, the cyberfrontier as "democratic" becomes important for us to critique especially when the Internet is being celebrated as the new space for transnational solidarity and struggle by some and "commercial democracy" by others. While it does provide the mechanism for the fast transfer of information, we must question how women's solidarities and alliances are forged in this space, which abstracts Filipinas from their historical and material specificities. On the other hand, dismissing its usefulness to scholars and activists alike would be foolish. For many Filipino/a activists and scholars, the Internet is a substantial resource for research, networking, and coalition building. Our objectives in this paper, however, have been to dismantle the celebration of this final, abstract frontier and to critique the interlinked aspects of race, gender, class and sexuality as they play out, and are lived through, particular disenfranchised bodies.

Further, as we enter the twenty-first century, we believe that the reemergence of colonizing discourses of progress that have cropped up with the expansion of internet technologies must force us to take pause. There is a danger in these discourses, particularly as scholars are swept up in their so-called liberatory promise. There are critical parallels, and we would argue, critical linkages between technologies of imperialism in the last century and today's technologies of globalization. Even while there are important differences between the colonialism of old and globalization today, we believe it is necessary to draw out the connections that continue to enable the logic of capitalism as it changes over time—if only to create responsive and responsible strategies of resistance. In order to be able to flesh out the nuances for a viable and informed critical politics of feminism on the Internet, feminists who have access to and enjoy its services need to take into account the place of Filipina and other "othered" bodies in this abstract and abstracting space.

Notes

1. Dorinda Elliot, "Asia's Big Bang," *Newsweek International,* July–September 2000, 8.
2. George Wehrfritz, "Liberated by the Internet," *Newsweek International,* July–September 2000, 14.

3. Kiyoshi Nishikawa, "Power to the People," *Newsweek International,* July–September 2000, 20.

4. Elliot, "Asia's Big Bang," 11.

5. Barbara Koh, "Rise of the Asian Woman," *Newsweek International,* July–September 2000, 36.

6. In this paper we use the term *Filipina* to refer to women of Philippine descent in the diaspora.

7. See Evelyn Nakano Glenn, "From Servitude to Service Work: Historical Continuities in the Racial Division of Paid Reproductive Labor," *Signs: Journal of Women in Culture and Society* 18, no. 1 (1992): 1–43; Lisa Lowe, *Immigrant Acts: On Asian American Cultural Politics* (Durham, NC: Duke University Press, 1996); Laura Hyun Yi Kang, "Si(gh)ting Asian/American Women As Transnational Labor," *Positions* 5, no. 2 (1997): 403–38; Neferti Tadiar, "Domestic Bodies of the Philippines," *Sojourn* 12, no. 2 (1997): 153–91.

8. Wehrfritz, "Liberated by the Internet," 14.

9. We think in particular of the ad campaigns for companies like Hewlett-Packard, whose motto of "e-inclusion" is illustrated by a picture of unspecified, yet rural and "traditional" third-world women on its website who now, ostensible, have access and can be counted in modernity's census. Another example is the cover of the October 1999 *Silicon Valley Tech Week,* which depicts a crouched African man in a loincloth, holding a bow and arrow in one hand and a cellular phone in the other. The accompanying article discusses how wireless technology is enabling the entrance of the third world into cyberspace (although it does not discuss who exactly embodies the third-world party being celebrated). For a discussion on exoticized visualizations and "difference," see Judith Williamson, "Woman Is an Island: Femininity and Colonization," in *Studies in Entertainment,* ed. Tania Modleski (Bloomington: Indiana University Press, 1986); Cynthia Enloe, *Bananas, Beaches and Bases: Making Feminist Sense of International Politics* (Berkeley and Los Angeles University of California Press, 1989); and Lisa Nakamura, "Where Do You Want to Go Today? Cybernetic Tourism, the Internet, and Transnationality," in *Race in Cyberspace,* ed. Beth E. Kolko, Lisa Nakamura, and Gilbert B. Rodman (New York: Routledge, 2000), 15–26.

10. Donna Hughes, "The Internet and the Global Prostitution Industry," in *CyberFeminism: Connectivity, Critique and Creativity,* ed. Susan Hawthorne and Renate Klein (North Melbourne: Spinifex Press, 1999), 157–84.

11. Inderpal Grewal and Caren Kaplan, *Scattered Hegemonies: Postmodernity and Transnational Feminist Politics* (Minneapolis: University of Minnesota Press, 1994). See also M. Jacqui Alexander and Chandra Talpade Mohanty, *Feminist Geneaologies, Colonial Legacies, Democratic Futures* (New York: Routledge, 1997).

12. See David Harvey, *The Condition of Post-Modernity* (Cambridge: Blackwell, 1990); Aihwa Ong, *Spirits of Resistance and Capitalist Discipline: Factory Women in Malaysia* (New York: State University of New York Press, 1987); and Lowe, *Immigrant Acts.*

13. Cynthia Enloe, "Martial Races and Ladies' Drinks," paper presented at the Inaugural Lecture for the Center for the Study of Race and Gender, University of California, Berkeley 2002.

14. Ziauddin Sardar, "alt.civilizations.faq: Cyberspace as the Darker Side of the West," in *Cyberfutures: Culture and Politics of the Information Superhighway,* ed. Ziauddin Sardar and Jerome R. Ravetz (New York: New York University Press, 1996), 22.

15. Jeff Ow, "The Revenge of the Yellowfaced Cyborg Terminator: The Rape of Digital Geishas and the Colonization of Cyber Coolies in 3d Realm's *Shadow Warrior,*" in *Race in Cyberspace,* ed. Beth E. Kolko, Lisa Nakamura, and Gilbert B. Rodman (New York: Routledge, 2000), 51–68.

16. While pronouncing itself a democracy and offering itself up as a model of representative government for the rest of the world, the United States proceeded, in the War of 1898, to

violently "acquire" the territories "ceded" by Spain. The Philippines, along with Cuba and Puerto Rico, were one of the first American colonies. On these foreign islands, fantasies of frontier manliness and a civilizing mission could take place, even as thousands of native bodies were raped, maimed, and killed during the course of "pacification" and "benevolent assimilation." See Kristin Hoganson, *Fighting for American Manhood: How Gender Politics Provoked the Spanish-American and Philippine-American Wars* (New Haven, CT: Yale University Press, 2000); and Stuart Creighton Miller, *"Benevolent Assimilation": The American Conquest of the Philippines, 1899–1903* (New Haven, CT: Yale University Press, 1982). Not coincidentally, the same players who populate Frederick Jackson Turner's paean to the Western frontier appear in the American subjugation of the Philippines. Cowboys and the rugged Western pioneer remade their beleaguered identities on the "empty" islands across the Pacific Ocean. See Hoganson, *Fighting for American Manhood;* Gail Bederman, *Manliness and Civilization: A Cultural History of Gender and Race in the United States, 1880–1917* (Chicago: University of Chicago Press, 1995); Theodore Roosevelt, *Theodore Roosevelt: An American Mind*, ed. Mario R. DiNunzio (New York: St. Martin's Press, 1994). The United States, in the Spanish- and Philippine-American wars, established itself as the emerging global enforcer of liberal democracy. Lisa Lowe argues that it is through these wars in Asia that the United States further attempted to resolve the constant contradictions that haunted democracy and capitalism (Lowe, *Immigrant Acts*). The Philippines provided a space for the vanishing American frontier, bringing opportunities for militarism, economic expansion, and, ultimately, domestic political stability in the United States. As Amy Kaplan points out, the colonial project galvanized American nation formation by exporting its domestic conflicts, bringing together the rugged individual and industrial capital in a unifying imperial adventure; (see Kaplan, "'Left Alone with America': The Absence of Empire in the Study of American Culture," in *Cultures of United States Imperialism*, ed. Amy Kaplan and Donald E. Pease (Durham, NC: Duke University Press, 1993). On Philippine shores, then, two seemingly contradictory ideologies are wedded through the creation of an "other" to be colonized.

17. See Enloe, *Bananas, Beaches, and Bases;* Venny Villapando, "The Business of Selling Mail-Order Brides," in *Making Waves: An Anthology of Writings by and about Asian American Women*, ed. Asian Women United of California (Boston: Beacon Press,1989), 318–26; Rebecca Villones, "Women in the Silicon Valley," in Asian Women United of California, eds., *Making Waves*, 172–76; Nicole Constable, *Maid to Order in Hong Kong: Stories of Filipina Workers* (Ithaca, NY: Cornell University Press, 1997); Elizabeth Uy Eviota, *The Political Economy of Gender: Women and the Sexual Division of Labor in the Philippines* (London: Zed Books, 1992); Sylvia Chant and Cathy McIlwaine, *Women of a Lesser Cost: Female Labor, Foreign Exchange, and Philippine Development* (London: Pluto Press, 1995); Rhacel Salazar Parreñas, "Filipina Women: Your Global Servants," in *Manuel Ocampo: Heridas de la Lengua*, ed. Pilar Perez (Santa Monica: Smart Art Press, 1997), 72–74; and Robyn Rodriguez, "Embodied Resistances, Contested Sexualities and Alternative Nationalisms: Perspectives on Philippines International Migration," unpublished paper, 1998.

18. Rolando Tolentino, "Bodies, Letters, Catalogs: Filipinas in Transnational Space," *Social Text* 14 (1996): 49–74.

19. Renato Rosaldo, *Culture and Truth: The Remaking of Social Analysis* (Boston: Beacon Press, 1993).

20. Neferti Tadiar, "Domestic Bodies of the Philippines," *Sojourn* 12, no. 2 (1997): 153–91. See also Emily Noelle Ignacio, "Ain't I a Filipino (Woman)? An Analysis of Authorship/Authority Through the Construction of 'Filipina' on the Net," *Sociological Quarterly* 41, no. 4 (2000): 551–72.

21. Aihwa Ong and Donald Nonini, eds., *Ungrounded Empires* (New York: Routledge, 1997), 10.

22. See Linda Richter, *The Politics of Tourism in Asia* (Honolulu: University of Hawaii Press, 1989); and Walden Bello and Robin Broad, "The International Monetary Fund in the Philippines," in *The Philippines Reader*, ed. David Schirmer and Stephen Rosskamm Shalom (Boston: South End Press, 1987), 261–67.

23. Donna Haraway, *Simians, Cyborgs and Women: The Reinvention of Nature* (New York: Routledge, 1991), 595.

24. See Kang, "Si(gh)ting Asian/American Women As Transnational Labor;" Enloe, *Bananas, Beaches, and Bases*; and Ignacio, "Ain't I a Filipino (Woman)?"

25. Lisa Nakamura, "After-Images of Identity: Gender, Technology and Identity Politics," paper presented at The Discipline and Deviance: Gender, Technology and Machines Conference, Duke University, October 2–3, 1998.

26. Henri Lefebvre, *The Production of Space*, trans. Donald Nicolson-Smith (Oxford: Blackwell Publishers, 1991), 9.

27. Ibid., 16.

28. Ibid., 26.

29. Ibid., 36, 53.

30. Andrew Herman and John H. Sloop, "'Red Alert!' Rhetorics of the World Wide Web and 'Friction Free' Capitalism," in *The World Wide Web and Contemporary Cultural Theory: Magic, Metaphor, Power*, ed. Andrew Herman and Thomas Swiss (New York and London: Routledge, 2000), 86.

31. Discourses on Filipinas in the West circulating in circuits other than cyberspace are constituted by and constitutive of representations of Filipina bodies on the Internet. In the early 1990s, to cite a popular culture example, a *Frasier* episode on NBC featured a segment entitled, "Quick, get Manila on the Phone." Niles, Frasier's brother, enters the scene announcing that his wife had spent $20,000 on a facelift. His father retorts that with that kind of money, Niles "could have bought a brand-new wife from the Philippines." The *Frasier* episode epitomizes the dynamics of international power that contribute to popular notions and images of Filipinas that are exacerbated by the fact that the West literally owns the hardware of communications technologies.

32. Martin Dodge and Rob Kitchin, *Mapping Cyberspace* (New York: Routledge, 2000), and Susan Hawthorne and Renate Klein, "Introduction: Cyberfeminism," in Hawthorne and Klein, eds., *Cyberfeminism*.

33. James Ferguson, *The Anti-Politics Machine* (Minneapolis: University of Minnesota Press, 1994), 256.

34. Arturo Escobar, *Encountering Development* (Princeton, NJ: Princeton University Press, 1995).

35. Coco Fusco, "At Your Service: Latinas in the Global Information Network." Keynote lecture for the 1998 conference of the Inter-Society for Electronic Arts, online at <htttp://www.hkw.de/forum/forum1/doc/text/fusco-isea98.html>.

36. Fusco, "At Your Service." See also Olu Oguibe, "Forsaken Geographies: Cyberspace and the New World," paper presented at the Fifth International Cyberspace Conference, Madrid, June 1996, online at <http://eng.hss.cmu.edu/internet/oguibe/>.

37. Michael Specter, "Search and Deploy: The Race to Build a Better Search Engine," *New Yorker*, May 29, 2000, 90.

38. Ibid., 90.

39. Ibid., 88, 90.

40. See Specter, "Search and Deploy," as well as the Cyber Eyes webpage, <http://www.meta-tags.com>, which gives advice regarding website promotion as well as offering professional services for a fee.

41. Thanks to Inderpal Grewal, who pointed this trend out to us.

42. See the Cyber Eyes webpage, <http://www.meta-tags.com>.

43. Specter, "Search and Deploy," 91.

44. See the Cyber Eyes webpage, <http://www.meta-tags.com>.

45. See the Wordtracker website, <http://www.wordtracker.com>.

46. See the Cyber Eyes webpage, <http://www.meta-tags.com>.

47. Kang, "Si(gh)ting Asian/American Women As Transnational Labor," 202.

48. See the Filipina Penpal website, <http://www.filipinapenpal.com>.

49. See the Filipina Bride website, <http://www.afilipinabride.com>.

50. See Maids Online, <http://www.maids-online.com.sg>.

51. At "Filipina Penpal" for example, a woman can apply to have her picture (for free no less) on the website. Required to answer a questionnaire, she must sign an agreement that commits her to responding to all of her suitors even if she decides she does not want to write to them. Failure to do so would threaten her presence on the website and ultimately, her chances of meeting men. Only once she agrees to sign the agreement can she use the back of the application to describe herself in more detail.

52. See the Filipina Fantasies website, <http://www.filipinafantasies.com>.

53. See the Filipina Hardcore website, <http://www.filipinahardcore.com>.

54. Alecia Wolf, "Exposing the Great Equalizer: Demythologizing Internet Equity," in *Cyberghetto or Cybertopia? Race, Class and Gender on the Internet*, ed. Bosah Ebo (Westport, CT: Praeger, 1998), 15–32; Meta G. Carstarphen and Jacqueline Johnson Lambaise, "Domination and Democracy in Cyberspace: Reports From the Majority Media and Ethnic/Gender Margins," in Ebo, ed., *Cyberghetto or Cybertopia?* 121–35; and Nina Wakeford, "Gender and the Landscapes of Computing in an Internet Café," *in The Gendered Cyborg: A Reader*, ed. Gill Kirkup, Linda Janes, Kath Woodward, and Fiona Hovenden (London and New York: Routledge, 2000), 291–304.

55. Vivian Sobchack, "Democratic Franchise and the Electronic Frontier," in Sardar and Ravetz, eds. *Cyberfutures*, 77–89; Robert McChesney, "So Much for the Magic of Technology and the Free Market: The World Wide Web and the Corporate Media System," in Herman and Swiss, eds., *The World Wide Web and Contemporary Cultural Theory*, 5–35; Granville Williams, "Selling Off Cyberspace," in *Access Denied In the Information Age*, ed. Stephen Lax (New York: Palgrave, 2001), 178–98.

56. Lisa Nakamura, "'Where Do You Want to Go Today?' Cybernetic Tourism, the Internet, and Transnationality," in Kolko, Nakamura, and Rodman, eds., *Race in Cyberspace*, 15–17.

57. Jennifer González, "The Appended Subject: Race and Identity As Digital Assemblage," in Kolko, Nakamura, and Rodman, eds., *Race In Cyberspace*, 29.

58. Alloo Fatma, "Information Technology and Cyberculture," in *Women@Internet*, ed. Wendy Harcourt (New York: St. Martin's Press, 1999), 156–61; Marisa Belausteguigoitia Rius, "Crossing Borders: From Crystal Slippers to Tennis Shoes," in Harcourt, ed. *Women@Internet*, 23–30; and Kekula P. Bray-Crawford, "The Ho'okele Netwarriors in the Liquid Continent," in Harcourt, ed., *Women@Internet*, 162–73.

59. Mimi Nguyen, "Tales of an Asiatic Geek Girl: *Slant* from Paper to Pixels," in *Technicolor: Race, Technology, and Everyday Life*, ed. Alondra Nelson and Thuy Linh N. Tu with Alicia Headlam Hines (New York: New York University Press, 2001), 177–90.

60. Arturo Escobar, "Gender, Place and Networks: A Political Ecology of Cyberculture," in Harcourt, ed., *Women@Internet*, 53.

61. Donna Haraway, "A Cyborg Manifesto: Science, Technology, and Socialist Feminism in the Late Twentieth Century," in *Simians, Cyborgs and Women: The Reinvention of Nature* (New York: Routledge, 1991), 154; Donna Haraway, "The Promises of Monsters: A Regenerative Politics for Inappropriate/d Others," in *Cultural Studies*, ed. Lawrence Grossberg, Cary Nelson, and Paula A. Treichler (New York: Routledge, 1991), 295–337.

62. Haraway, "A Cyborg Manifesto," 154.

63. Rhona Bautista, "Staking Their Claim: Women, Electronic Networking, and Training In Asia," in Harcourt, ed., *Women@Internet*, 173–83.

64. For these sites, see <http://pinaycelebs.fsn.net>, <http://www.egroups.com/list/white_pinay_lover>, and <http://lavendar.fortunecity.com/poiter/28/index.html>.

65. See <http://lavendar.fortunecity.com/poiter/28/index.html>.

66. See <http://come.to/lilpinay76>.

67. Because of the legal and material disadvantages that face them abroad, Filipina women are subject to multiply patriarchies: the execution of Flor Contemplacion, a Filipina domestic, by the Singaporean government in 1995 is only one well-known example.

68. In searches for *foreign domestic helper* and *domestic helper*, sites operating in countries like Canada, Hong Kong, and Singapore offering placement services for Filipina domestic helpers were found. The Canadian site listed Canadian immigration regulations for domestic helpers with a special note on the specific educational requirements for Filipina, Chinese, and Hong Kong women. Meanwhile, a hospital website in Hong Kong advertises a "Domestic Helper Check" that includes a chest X-ray, pregnancy test, urine test, a stool test, an HIV test, and a doctor's consultation.

69. See for instance, Jane Margold's work on consumer narratives, which argues for Filipina domestics' construction of memory and identity as consumers even as they are exploited as workers in Hong Kong; Margold, "Pictured Selves: Photos and Videotapes by Domestic Workers in Hong Kong," paper delivered at the Sixth International Philippine Studies Conference, Manila, July 10–14, 2000.

10
Will the Real Indian Woman Log-On? Diaspora, Gender, and Comportment

LINTA VARGHESE

When I first encountered Meera, she was being charged as the following: "a foul-mouthed but temple-going woman, an openly bisexual/lesbian woman...a downright slutty woman." It was the first posting of a thread titled "Bring Back the Stigma," written by Anu, who felt compelled to post excerpts from an article by Donna Rice of the same title. The message was to serve as

> an antidote to some of the immodest trash Meera has posted in this newsgroup. If Meera's intelligent (if misguided) and powerfully persuasive writing style has skewed your sense of what is right and what is wrong, what is acceptable and what is not, and who is a slut and who is not, perhaps this will help deskew it.[1]

The excerpted article begins with an image of a teenage boy probing a *Penthouse* magazine. The author claims that looking at the pictures is "nothing more than a healthy curiosity about sex." However, "if he leafs through *Penthouse* without feeling furtive, something has gone wrong: his parents have failed to instill in him the values of modesty and self-restraint that are the bedrock of middle-class life." According to Rice, the best way to ensure the feeling of shame is through stigmatization, thus "while tolerating deviance, we can still stigmatize it." Anu's posting is not only an opprobrium against Meera and other Indian women who have "exploded on arrival in this more liberal society" but also of the other newsgroup members who tolerate or encourage them through their views and positions.

Although the bulk of the posting revolved around "immodest and trashy" behavior by newsgroup members, the questions in the closing paragraph provide the real source of Anu's concern. Ending his own words and introducing Rice's article, he writes,

> Makes you wonder what Indian culture and values are all about, anyways. Do these people really represent Indian women, or are they really Indian-born American women? Why do they lurk around these Indian

newsgroups? Is it because they haven't received as much acceptance as they would like from the white American community they have been trying to meld into?

I locate Anu's statements and questions in dynamic debates concerning what it means to be *really* Indian in the United States. As can be seen from the leading statement, what "Indian culture and values are about" is heavily negotiated. The same statement shows that, to some, just claiming Indian heritage is not enough to claim Indian identity. In this formula, *India* is a "hyperreal" term that "refer[s] to certain figures of imagination whose geographical referents remain somewhat indeterminate. As [a] figure of the imaginary [it is], of course, subject to contestation."[2] The targeting of Meera and a few other women on the Usenet newsgroup alt.culture.us.asian-indian for immodest and slutty behavior indicates that gendered and sexualized nature of 'true' belonging to the Indian community.

Using Bring Back the Stigma and two other threads, Sangria Night! and Meera and Priya—READ THIS, this essay analyzes discussions of dating, marriage, and sexual behavior on alt.culture.us.asian-indian to examine constructions of women's diasporic Indian identity in the United States. In these negotiations, women's sexual comportment becomes one site where group boundaries are erected. By looking at both at a specific member of the group and larger group replies, I seek to "gauge the processes of subject constitution in the articulation of individual with master narratives."[3]

Notes on Anthropological Net Surfing

Gathering information on the "textual construction" of gender and community poses a number of predicaments for traditional methods of anthropological fieldwork.[4] Anthropologist Arturo Escobar states that cyberculture "concern[s] what anthropology is about: the story of life as it has been lived and is being lived at this very moment." Under suggested inquiries, Escobar writes, "How can these practices [those generated around/by computers] and domains be studied ethnographically in various social, regional, and ethnic settings? What established anthropological concepts and methods would be appropriate to the study of cyberculture? Which would have to be modified? How, for instance, will notions of community, fieldwork, the body, nature, vision, the subject, identity, and writing be transformed by the new technologies?"[5] As solicited by Escobar, using the Internet as a site for field work opens up numerous challenges to what have become entrenched methods of anthropological work.

Going out to do field work is a rite of passage marking the transition from anthropologist-in-training to anthropologist. This passage is important because "fieldwork...helps define anthropology as a discipline in both senses of the word, constructing a space of possibilities while at the same time drawing the lines that confine that space."[6] Further, "'fieldwork' is a form of dwelling which legitimizes knowledge production by the familiarity that the fieldworker gains with the ways of life of a group of people."[7]

The hallmark of anthropological methodology has become participant observation. In this formula the "truths of anthropology are grounded in the *experience* of the participant observer."[8] But how does one do participant observation in a site that is purely textual? What the Internet precludes, and participant observation depends on, is the ability to visually observe what is occurring. Observation of actions is crucial to the authority of experience since, as Joan Scott writes, "when experience is taken as the origin of knowledge, the *vision* of the individual subject (the person who had the experience or the historian [or anthropologist] who recounts it) becomes the bedrock of evidence on which explanation is built."[9]

The limitations of the Internet makes it a productive site to question both the anthropologist's and subject's "authority of experience."[10] In many disciplines and areas of study, experience has come to be a transparent category explaining and authorizing knowledge. In this belief, "experience [is] treated as an objective category in discourse."[11] Rather than rely on this notion of experience, I use the notion that experience is "not the origin of our explanation, not the authoritative ... evidence that grounds what is known, but rather that which we seek to explain, that about which knowledge is produced."[12] In other words, experience and subjectivities need to be seen as a process rather than stable categories.

What the Internet allows is outside the purview of traditional notions of participant observation. Internet research makes painfully clear the careful and contested construction of an individual identity. The constructed experiences of the subject cannot be verified or observed, and the only experience of observation the anthropologist has is watching the scrolling text.

As with the rejection of the transparency of experience, I also reject the transparency of language. I read language as outlined by Joan Scott, who notes that this kind of reading "would not assume a direct correspondence between words and things, nor confine itself to single meanings, nor aim for the resolution of contradiction. It would not render process as linear, nor rest explanation on simple correlations or single variables. Rather it would grant to 'the literary' an integral, even irreducible, status of its own. To grant such status is not to make 'the literary' foundational, but to open new possibilities for analyzing discursive productions of social and political reality as complex, contradictory processes."[13] To Scott's approach I would add recognizing the temporality of speech. This allows us to "gain another lens on the constitution of subjectivity" through "the partiality of identity" expressed at different moments.[14]

The newsgroup presents an interesting space in which to view temporality. How do you read temporality when constant reference to "what you said earlier" is possible? Indeed, pieces of threads that were missing from my files were easily accessible through Internet archives that document all postings on most newsgroups. I have attended to this project by understanding each thread to be a different conversation—temporally and from a participant stand point.[15] This allows each thread to function as an ongoing but distinct set of interactions through which people change their minds, pause to think through issues, and play with different positions. Foregrounding my project in terms of subject production, not unification, helped keep the importance of temporality in focus.

My project, the reading of textually created identities, seeks not to translate or explain the practices of the participants. Rather, I seek to understand in one specific instance, located in a larger set of ongoing debates in the Indian-American community, the ways a gendered subject is produced both personally and through interactions with participants in a space inhabited mainly by men. Thus although I do not take what is posted as the truth about participants' lives, I do understand the postings to be indicative of desires, stereotypes, and events that concern the actors.

Meera's postings usually consist of opinion pieces and short stories. The content of the postings cover a wide range of topics from musings on how attractive she finds Indian men ("Sexy Indian Men") to the need of nonresident Indians to pressure the Indian government to ensure that tribal land and ways of life are protected ("Towards a Sustainable Society"). Although only one thread discussed in this paper is authored by Meera, her presence on the newsgroup is a major point of discussion. Her mode of interaction with the newsgroup is to post and generally stay out of the ensuing debate. Her ability to spark discussion and refusal to participate places her in a very influential position in that although she does not constantly engage the topics discussed, she very often affects what these topics are. This prompted Rajesh, a member who finds Meera's position un-Indian, to state,

> "You have to understand the unique position that Meera is in. Her intelligence and writing skills give her the power to sway a lot of minds. She is one of the most intelligent and among the best writers on this forum. A lot of people revere her. This gives her enormous peer power. A lot of people are going to think 'if it is OK for Meera then it must be OK for me too.'"

Many of the short stories Meera post begin with the disclaimer "All characters in this short story are fictitious." "Sangria Night!" however, begins with the statement, "Some characters are fictitious :)." Exactly which ones is never confirmed. Yet due to the name of the main character, Heera, being only one letter apart from the name Meera, other newsgroup members assumed that the story was a retelling of Meera's sexual escapades. The story is quite long for a newsgroup posting—six pages total—and filled with explicit sexual descriptions.

As the title of the story indicates (or at least to me it did), "Sangria Night!" is fashioned after steamy, pulp "true romance" stories from women's magazines. The story begins with the line "Heera just finished flirting with the last of the single men in the room." After a description of the party and the dancing Heera just finished, the story relates a pick-up scene between her and David, the "only forty year old" white man at the party. After a series of exchanges such as

> David: Can I get you a drink? You look like you need something to cool you.
> Heera: Tell me. . . . was I the best?
> David: Yes, you were. You don't need me to say that. You had every guy here salivating over you.
> Heera: Didn't that make you jealous? You didn't dance much. You can't keep up with the guys, uh?

David returns with a drink, a "Sangria—cheap and sweet but with the right amount of kick to it." After some more banter, the couple leaves the party and Heera convinces David to drive to San Diego. End of part 1.

Part 2 opens on the road with Heera "cruising at 75." Eventually the couple end up in the parking lot of a Motel 6, but do not have a sexual encounter. Rather, David resists Heera's advances and then, fed up, loses his temper and becomes violent, regrets his aggressiveness and apologizes. Heera accepts his apology and they drive off, only to have David put his welcomed hand up her skirt and say "sangria may be cheap and make us groggy but it is sweet and irresistible."

Negative responses to the story revolve around the construction of Indian women as "aggressive" and "fast" sexual beings. All these replies ask what the point of the story was and then go on to ask, as does Sudhir, if it is

> to show that an Indian woman can be sexually aggressive? If that was the case, do you think she (Heera) would've acted in such a manner if it was an Indian guy with her, as opposed to Dave [sic], the typical sexually receptive anglo [sic] guy?

In a similar vein, Pluto83 asks,

> [W]hat is the message (or theme) of this story and how significant is it to this newsgroup? Are you trying to say that Indian women are getting "fast"? It is everyone's freedom (including the fictional Heera and real life Meera) to do and say what they please. But, what about the basic ethics and morality that Indian society was built on? . . . I have found Indian women in the US to have high moral and ethical standards, strong family ties and a will to excel.

Through a number of assumptions, binaries of women's chasteness/fastness and their sexual behavior with Indian/non-Indian men are set up, with the former representing authentic sexual practices of Indian women. Both responses point to the potential changing sexual behavior of Indian women and attempt to delegitimize it in different ways. Sudhir's claim that it is the presence of the "typical sexually receptive anglo guy" that allows Heera's sexually aggressive behavior places her actions outside the realm of a true Indian woman's demeanor. In addition, it is interracial sexual encounters that permit this conduct. Sudhir's placement of Anglo men's always-ready sexual behavior as antithetical to Indian men's restrained sexual behavior draws a distinction not only between the sexual behavior of Indian women and men, but also that of Indians and non-Indians.

Pluto83's question, "[A]re you trying to say that Indian women are getting 'fast?'" rests on the claim that previously Indian women were not "fast." Given that Indian identity is seen to rest on a specific set of behaviors, in this instance women's sexual behavior, continuity between putative comportment in India and in the United States is crucial. However, continuities do not necessarily need to be traced back and are often created to "respond to different crisis."[16] Thus, if Indian women are getting fast, a crisis that undermines the "basic Indian ethics and morality" and destroys the foundation of Indian society is at hand.

Although posted two weeks apart, "Bring Back the Stigma" can be read as a response to "Sangria Night!" in that the former thread is directly chastising postings by Meera that some members find too sexual for proper Indian women. In addition, "Sangria Night!" centers around sexual/romantic relationships between Indian women and non-Indian men.

As noted by Floya Anthias and Nira Yuval-Davis, cultural boundaries are "organized around rules relating to sexuality, marriage and the family, and a true member will perform these roles properly."[17] The singling out of Meera and a few other women as "slutty" and thus not truly Indian by some members on the newsgroup reveals anxiety produced by the crossing, and thus threatens the cultural boundaries erected.

The main tactic to quell fast women such as Meera is to show how far from Indian culture they have gone. "Bring Back the Stigma" is a post that sought to contain and ultimately subdue the crisis presented by stories such as "Sangria Night!" Discussions spinning "Bring Back the Stigma" carried on for two weeks garnering 190 responses to the original post. Unfortunately, the original point of discussion, Meera's improper sexual behavior and the need to stigmatize it, gradually gives way to a long discussion of the misogyny or lack of it on the television series *Seinfeld*. However, there are a number of responses that defended the "right" of Meera and others to behave how they want (many based on the rhetoric of "in America there is diversity and freedom to be what we want" and a number that defend the pogrom outlined by the original post). It is the latter type of posts that I will address here. The discourse of stigmatization forwarded by both Anu and Donna Rice is a method of "shaming" people who are viewed as deviating from the norm. In this case, as seen from Anu's opprobrium and the examples of deviance Rice uses, both authors are advocating a method to curb what they view as improper sexual behavior. Anu positions women as the symbols of "honour of family and community." In this position "exclusive control of her sexuality by the legitimate 'owner' is the practical aspect of the notion of honour."[18] Supporters of stigmatization placed the "extremist moral standards" of Meera in the realm of the family through references to parental authority, brotherly guidance and the need for suitable wives.

When Anu is asked by Nirav, another male participant, why he is so concerned about a few outspoken Indian women on the Net when there are "far more of the outright profane and unreasoned articles from Indian men to worry about," he answers,

> I am not going to marry any of those men, but I do plan to marry an Indian woman. That's the reason I am concerned about the moral values, precedents and standards that are being set on this forum. If Meera convinces other Indian women that it is OK to be slutty then that affects me directly.

However, potential husbands are not the only legitimate owners of women's sexuality and the familial (dis)honor it carries with it; parents and brothers are also official keepers. Answering the same posting by Nirav, Manoj comes to Anu's defense and Meera's offense. His response, however, implicitly accuses newsgroup members who support or are indifferent to Meera of being so only because she is not under their direction. Thus, he writes,

> Think about what you would do if your own sister said some of the things Meera has said on this forum. Would you just shut up and accept it as the norm? If Meera were my sister I would give her a swift kick in the butt. That should straighten her ass out. I wouldn't let my sister destroy herself like this. Unfortunately for her, Meera is not my sister.

> What is probably even more shocking to you Americans is that I consider being there for my sister as my duty. I will be there (and my parents too) to guide her through any turbulence that she faces in her youth due to immaturity.

In the justifications of why and how Meera should be stigmatized a family emerges: wife, husband, parents, sister and brother. In the family order, part of a brother's inherent duty is to ensure that his sister makes it through "turbulence" that youth may offer for the family, and patriarchal control exercised through the family is one means to keep the sanctity of the nation intact. In addition, family in the Indian American context carries special ties to the nation, for "the national cultural distinction that Indians abroad tend to idealize most is the strength of their family relationships and the extent to which individuals define themselves in terms of their families."[19] Indeed, Manoj uses "American" to refer to those newsgroup members who have disavowed belief in appropriate functions of the Indian family.

The national boundary replicated symbolically in the family can also be imperiled through marriage and sexual encounters with members of other nations. In an exchange began by Samarth (a man) to Priya Kumar-Peters (a married woman) in the thread "Meera and Priya—READ THIS," he types "this is a newsgroup of Indians and . . . introspection . . . about some of their issues. *Your* outside perspective should be qualified." Although Priya is a very common name for an Indian woman, and Kumar, the first part of her hyphenated surname, a regional caste name, Samarth addresses her as *Mrs.* Peters, the last name of her non-Indian husband. In response, Priya vehemently defends her Indian identity with the statement

> I am Indian, from Bangalore, but have lived in the US for most of my life. I am Indian, first and foremost. I follow all the customs that my parents do (they were born and raised in India) and I go to temple regularly. I believe in my culture and am proud of it.

In his reply, Samarth not only changes the address to *Ms.* Priya Kumar Peters, but states he assumed her to be an outsider partially due to her last name. Transgressing proper rules of marriage, Priya's marital choice precluded and replaced her Indian identity. In a rejoinder to Priya and Samarth's exchange, another newsgroup member, Raj writes, "for us, all desi [Indian] girls are ours, and the thought of a 'foreign' chap violating what 'is ours' really irks."

Discussions on the newsgroup regarding "intercultural" dating and marriage invariably draw responses of territoriality, using such terminology as "rightfully ours," "rights," "betrayed," and so on. Negative responses to general queries regarding opinions of "intercultural" dating are steered towards relationships between Indian women and non-Indian men. Indeed, a thread titled "I am a Scientist, a Sex Scientist" in which a male member of the newsgroup recounts his multicultural sexual exploits of the past weekend garnered reproaches around safe sex and honesty with sexual partners, but no rhetoric of proper sexual behavior for Indian men.

The two threads, "Bring Back the Stigma" and "Meera and Priya—READ THIS" bring the importance of appropriate families into view. A challenge or rupture in the family poses the same threat to the nation as the family is projected onto the nation. Any notion of a nation is implicitly based on family through ideas of genealogy. From founding fathers, to the mothers and sisters men of the nation need to protect, to the inheritance of culture, the family is not only "the nation in microcosm"; it also "act[s] as the means to turn social processes into natural, instinctive ones."[20] Thus, it is only natural that Indians, regardless of where they find themselves, possess and enact a specific set of cultural practices.

However, as seen from the threads, this view is heavily challenged. Though this sexist and oppressive vision of what it was to be an Indian woman was often the loudest, Meera's presence on the newsgroup provided a space for alternative visions of being an Indian women. Meera often presented various constructions of herself in response to the context at the moment.

Acknowledging her multiple approaches to hostile men, Meera writes, "sometimes you walk away, sometimes you just smile coyly, sometimes you argue calmly, sometimes you shout and sometimes you kick the guy where it hurts most." Meera writes about women's desire vis à vis its sameness to men's sexuality, its complete opposition to men's sexuality and within the discourse of passive, feminine women who want to be "charmed . . . and wooed by a gorgeous man."

Feminist theorist Chela Sandoval refers to this shifting of tactics as appropriate to the situation of "differential consciousness."[21] Meera is a self-identified feminist and, using Sandoval's theory, can be understood as deploying differential consciousness. In exchanges where she feels the tone was sexist, Meera consistently makes reference to her beliefs in feminism and the oppressive nature of patriarchal society. Most of her posts make an intervention into an ongoing, male-dominated set of debates, discussed both explicitly and implicitly, about the comportment of "real" Indian women in the United States.[22] Her constant referral to her own gender, desire, and sexuality vis-à-vis male attempts to control these positions challenge the notion of the public sphere as abstract, radically democratic and ungendered. Further, her highly controversial visibility, with her persistent highlighting of her position as a woman, both enable and disrupt discussions of female comportment carried out mainly by male participants.

While Meera and other women on the newsgroup vigorously challenge the conceptions of an ideal Indian woman being created on the newsgroup, they rarely place either their responses or the creation of the ideal in the larger framework of "national" identity. The concluding posts to "Bring Back the Stigma"—"Makes you wonder what Indian culture and values are all about, anyways" and "Do these people really represent Indian women, or are they really Indian-born American women?"—are ideal entry points to theorize the role of women in the creation of a diasporic national identity.

Diasporic Women's Question

During the nationalist struggle against colonialism in India, debates that emerged around the position of women in postindependence India were often referred to as the "women's question."[23] The centrality of this history to my argument does not rest on the equation of all nationalisms and productions of gender with what is understood to be an "Indian" space. Rather, the "woman question" is a useful framework to examine a gendered female subject vis-à-vis national culture. Both the original and diasporic "woman question" asks what space women should occupy in a nationalist economy. In addition, the answers to both questions depend on the ability of women to reproduce a true, pure, Indian culture.

Framing my analysis in terms of the "woman question" explodes the myth of an ungendered subject, as the question's very articulation rests on the different roles and positions women and men occupy. In this fragment of the diasporic "woman question," Indian women's sexual behavior is one site at which true national culture is produced. Thus, heteronormative chastity and modesty in sexual behavior marks not only women from men,[24] but also "true" Indian women from Western women—whether of Indian descent or not. The creation of a standard, true Indian woman generates a "category [that] is understood as representing a set of values or dispositions [which] becomes normative in character and, hence exclusionary in principle."[25]

Although some writings on diaspora advance that diaspora challenges the nation-state.[26] I would argue that the nation provides the most prominent trope of cohesive identity, even in the diaspora. On alt.culture.us.asian-indian, debates over what and who is and isn't "Indian" are also debates that seek to create an authentic Indian identity discernible outside of India. In this process, the nation, or rather, conceptions of the nation of India, are the boundaries that define us and our identity from those of others.[27] Thus, one cannot adequately examine the gendered nature of diasporic belonging without examining the "construction of the notion and nation of India" in Indian-American diasporic negotiations and contestations.[28]

Amarpal Dhaliwal's insightful pairing of "notion" and "nation" forces an examination of these two separate, but intrinsically related, ideas of India utilized in the process of cultural homogenization. The notion of India, always dependent on the nation of India as a reference, constructs "India" as the home of a true, shared identity. However, it is the notion of India as a coherent cultural identity, not a return to the nation, that is the goal of homogenization. Away from the physical space of Indian culture and susceptible to other influences, the claim to Indian ancestry or familial ties in India is no longer an adequate measure of who is *truly* Indian. "Indian" identity is no longer based on national citizenship but on proper cultural behavior. In this formula the issue "is not just 'being Indian' in some natural and self-evident way . . . , but 'cultivating Indian-ness' self consciously for certain reasons."[29]

Although the discourse of an authentic Indian culture gives primacy to the Indian nation-state, the United States and what is understood to be "American culture" is equally important. In a thought-provoking essay titled "Is the Ethnic 'Authentic' in the Diaspora?" R. Radhakrishnan writes, "In the diasporan context of the United States, ethnicity is often forced to take on the discourse of authenticity just to protect and maintain its space and history. . . . It becomes difficult to determine if the drive toward authenticity comes from within the group as a spontaneous self-affirming act, or if authenticity is nothing but a paranoid reaction to the 'naturalness' of dominant groups."[30] In this instance the United States must be recognized as a "diaspora space," "the intersectionality of diaspora, border, and dis/location as a point of confluence of economic, political, cultural and psychic process."[31] This space "is 'inhabited' not only by those who have migrated and their descendants but equally by those who are constructed and represented as indigenous. In other words, the concept of *diaspora space* (as opposed to that of diaspora) includes the entanglement of genealogies of dispersion with those of 'staying put.'"[32] Creating a coherent Indian identity in the United States is predicated upon the situation in which immigrants find themselves. This is a situation that forces coherence through identifying immigrants first and foremost as members of another nation without recognizing the intranational differences of the "originary site."

In the "diaspora space" of the United States, the Indian diasporan is interpellated as an Indian national subject from the moment she begins the process of movement. American immigration law locates both potential and successful immigrants as subjects of another nation—in this case, as Indian citizens. This process wipes out divisions present in India such as ethnicity/language, religion, and class and caste, among others, presenting the space for a coherent national subject with an accompanying national culture. What exactly comprises the national culture is highly contested. The ongoing debates over Indian authenticity illustrate the internal search by segments of the Indian-American community to delimit boundaries and define what it means to be Indian. In this shift, *Indian* is no longer a national identity but a coherent cultural identity.

The danger of losing our true Indian identity through contact and possible assimilation requires us to be forever vigilant of both our own behavior and that of others who claim Indianness without acting it out. In "diaspora space," Indian culture becomes "recently *traditionalized*,"[33] and roots "become portable accessories profusely re-imagined and remade."[34]

Although Radhakrishnan's essay opens up a number of issues for diasporic Indians in America—the relationship to both the home and new country for different generations, why there is a need to invoke authenticity, how we "know" about India—he does not address how gendered positions are placed in the pursuit of Indianness. Rather the group players in his essay split along generational and ethnic lines. However, since "women serve as the visible markers of national homogeneity,"[35] any examination of nationalism or the recreation of a national culture that elides gender is an incomplete examination.[36]

Conclusion

Through excerpts from "Bring Back the Stigma," "Sangria Night!" and "Meera and Priya—READ THIS", I have attempted to read how diasporic Indian women are deployed in the construction of Indianness in the United States. In an attempt to differentiate Indian women from American ones, the sexual behavior of the former comes to represent the juncture at which this difference emerges. Neither national citizenship nor ties to India guarantee Indianness in the "diaspora space" of the United States. Though dependent on the nation-state of India, true Indianness is established through cultural behavior. What composes a true Indian woman is not stagnant, however. Contested by both women and men, the cultural boundaries erected through notions of women's sexual comportment are continually dismantled as women like Meera and Priya demand inclusion and challenge the "'imagined' constructs in and through which 'women' emerge as subjects" in the Indian diaspora.[37]

In these discussions, ties to the notion and nation of India rest on cultural and not solely territorial ideas of affiliation. Thus, *Indian* is understood to be a cohesive culture that has the potential to unify all persons identified as "Indian." In this construct, cultural identity is defined "in terms of one, shared culture, as sort of collective 'one true self,' hiding inside the many other, more superficial or artificially imposed 'selves,' which people with a shared history and ancestry hold in common."[38]

Like some of the newsgroup members, my original urge was to look for a coherent, seamless subject. Searching through the archives of the newsgroup, I though I could piece together certain postings from Meera to create a unified subject without contradiction or ambiguity. However, posting and staying out of the debates proved to be a tactic that encouraged uncertainty about the subject, Meera. Unable to visually verify her "authentic" existence, both the anthropologist and newsgroup members were forced to rely on reading the narratives she created of herself. That these narratives did not allow for complete unification of the subject should not be seen as an obstruction to sound anthropological method, but rather as a productive point.

Meera's identity was under such suspicion that she did agree to meet another member in person who then reported to the newsgroup that she is an Indian woman. A question of this project in its inception was how I could know if the people posting, claiming to be Indians, really were Indian. Again, both instances demand verification of a category—in this case, Indian. What the Internet allows is a production of the subject through textual reading that calls attention to processes that create a category. Rather than attempting to smooth out points of ambiguity and contradiction, a focus on those moments will give insight into the productive spaces where experience, identity, and contestation are made.

Notes

For their comments and criticisms of earlier drafts of this essay, I thank Kamala Visweswaran, Ted Gordon and Junaid Rana. I am also grateful to Rachel Lee and Sau-ling Wong. I am also grateful to the anonymous reviewers at Routledge.

1. All posts are from the newsgroup alt.culture.us.asian-indian.
2. Dipesh Chakrabarty, "Postcoloniality and the Artiface of History: Who Speaks for "Indian" Pasts?" *Representations* 37 (1992): 1.
3. Kamala Visweswaran, *Fictions of Feminist Ethnography* (Minneapolis: University of Minnesota Press, 1994), 50.
4. Amit S. Rai, "India On-Line: Electronic Bulletin Boards and the Construction of a Diasporic Hindu Identity," *Diaspora* 4 (1995): 42.
5. Arturo Escobar, "Welcome to Cyberia: Notes on the Anthropology of Cyberculture," *Current Anthropology* 35 (1994): 214.
6. Akhil Gupta and James Ferguson, "Discipline and Practice: The 'Field' As Site, Method, and Location in Anthropology," in *Anthropological Locations: Boundaries and Grounds*

of a Field Science, ed. Akhil Gupta and James Ferguson (Berkeley and Los Angeles: University of California Press, 1997), 2.

7. Ibid., 39.

8. Ibid., 18.

9. Joan Scott, "The Evidence of Experience," in *The Lesbian and Gay Studies Reader,* ed. Henry Abelove, Michèle Aina Barale, and David M. Halperin (New York: Routledge, 1993), 339.

10. Scott, "Evidence," 339.

11. Julie Stephans, "Feminist Fiction: A Critique of the Category 'Non-Western Women' in Feminist Writings on India," in *Subaltern Studies 6,* ed. Ranajit Guha (Delhi: Oxford University Press, 1989), 24–25.

12. Scott, "Evidence," 401.

13. Ibid.

14. Visweswaran, *Fictions,* 50.

15. This approach also produces a set of problems, however. Since the functioning of newsgroups does not allow for synchronic exchange, the ability to closely read a message and reply to specific points often takes the thread on a series of twists and turns. In addition, new threads often emerge that are precipitated by a previous one.

16. KumKum Sangari and Sudesh Vaid, "Recasting Women: An Introduction," in *Recasting Women: Essays in Colonial History,* ed. KumKum Sangari and Sudesh Vaid (New Delhi: Kali for Women Press, 1989), 17.

17. Floya Anthias and Nira Yuval-Davis, *Women-Nation-State* (London: Macmillan, 1992), 113.

18. Purshottam Agrawal, "Surat, Sarvarkar and Draupadi: Legitimizing Rape As a Political Weapon," in *Women of the Hindu Right,* ed. T. Saran and Urvashi Bhutalia (New Delhi: Kali for Women Press, 1995), 38.

19. Arvind Rajagopal, "Transnational Networks and Hindu Nationalism," *Bulletin of Concerned Asian Scholars* 3 (1997): 54.

20. Paul Gilroy, *"There Ain't No Black in the Union Jack": The Cultural Politics of Race and Nation* (Chicago: University of Chicago Press, 1987), 43.

21. In this tactic, "power can be thought of as mobile—not nomadic but rather cinematographic: a kinetic motion that maneuvers, poetically transfigures, and orchestrates while demanding alienation, perversion, and reformation in both spectators and practitioners...it permits functioning within yet beyond the demands of dominant ideology." Chela Sandoval, "U.S. Third World Feminism: The Theory and Methods of Oppositional Consciousness in the Postmodern World," *Genders* 10 (1991): 3.

22. I do not wish to give the idea that femininity was the only issue discussed in the newsgroup. Indeed, discussions ranged from how to extend a visa to non-Indian-specific subjects such as the latest movies.

23. For a full discussion of the woman question in India, see Chakrabarty, "Postcolonial Artiface"; Partha Chatterjee, *The Nation and Its Fragments: Colonial and Postcolonial Histories* (Princeton, NJ: Princeton University Press, 1992); and Sangari and Vaid, *Recasting Women.*

24. Although bisexuality emerges once, in Anu's opprobriums that open this essay, women's non-Indian sexual behavior tends to be marked around promiscuity, premarital sex and sexual relations with non-Indian men, all actions that do not preclude the reintegration of the actor into normative heterosexual relationships. For a discussion that "queers" the diaspora, see Gayatri Gopinath, "Nostalgia, Desire, Diaspora: South Asian Sexualities in Motion," *Positions* 5 (1997): 467–89.

25. Judith Butler, *Gender Trouble: Feminism and the Subversion of Identity* (New York: Routledge, 1990), 325.

26. James Clifford, "Diasporas," *Cultural Anthropology* 9, no. 3 (1994): 302–38; Amarpal Dhaliwal, "Reading Diaspora: Self-Representational Practices and the Politics of

Reception," *Socialist Review* 24, no. 4 (1994): 13–24; and Paul Gilroy, *The Black Atlantic: Modernity and Double Consciousness* (Cambridge, MA: Harvard University Press, 1993).

27. This is not to claim that these differences are erased or ignored. Rather, they come to be something that is contained in the larger supra identity named Indian.

28. Dhaliwal, "Reading Diaspora," 19. At the time of my research (1997) religious inflections of a true Indian identity were rarely, if ever discussed, in the newsgroup. While mention of a Hindu God or going to temple were used to assert true Indian identity, religious distinctions—in terms of who was and wasn't truly Indian—were not common. On the other hand, the absence of overt references to Hindu culture may also signal that there was an unsaid understanding that Indian culture *was* Hindu culture. However, I do not want to force this reading. For a good example of how communal ideologies may function implicitly in Indian diasporic culture through Hindutva, see Gayatri Gopinath, "'Bombay, U.K., Yuba City': Bhangra Music and the Engendering of Diaspora," *Diaspora* 4 (1995): 303–21; and the special issue on Hindutva, *Ethnic and Racial Studies* 23 (2000). See also Vinay Lal, "North American Hindus, the Sense of History, and the Politics of Internet Diasporism," in this volume.

29. R. Radhakrishnan, "Is the Ethnic 'Authentic' in the Diaspora?" in *The State of Asian-America: Activism and Resistance in the 1990s*, ed. Karin Aguilar-San Juan (Boston: South End Press, 1994), 225.

30. Ibid., 229.

31. Avtar Brah, *Cartographies of Diaspora: Contesting Identities* (New York: Routledge, 1996), 181.

32. Ibid.

33. Brackette Williams, *Stains on My Name, War in My Veins: The Politics of Cultural Struggle* (Durham, NC: Duke University Press, 1991), 10.

34. Rajagopal, "Transnational Networks," 46.

35. Ann McClintock, *Imperial Leather: Race, Gender and Sexuality in the Colonial Contest* (New York: Routledge, 1995), 365. See also Anthias and Yuval-Davis, Women—Nation—State.

36. Two anthologies that examine this issue through both academic and personal narratives are Women of South Asian Descent Collective, ed., *Our Feet Walk the Sky: Women of the South Asian Diaspora* (San Francisco: Aunt Lute Books, 1993) and Shamita Das Dasgupta, ed., *A Patchwork Shawl: Chronicles of South Asian Women in America* (New Brunswick, NJ: Rutgers University Press, 1998).

37. Rajeswari Sunder Rajan, *Real and Imagined Women: Gender, Culture and Postcolonialism* (New York: Routledge, 1993), 10.

38. Stuart Hall, "Cultural Identity and Diaspora," in *Colonial Discourse and Postcolonial Theory*, ed. I. Chrisman and P. Williams (New York: Columbia University Press, 1994), 393.

11

The Revenge of the Yellowfaced Cyborg Terminator: The Rape of Digital Geishas and the Colonization of Cyber-Coolies in 3D Realms' *Shadow Warrior*

JEFFREY A. OW

> *Listen. Understand. That Terminator is out there. It can't be reasoned with, it can't be bargained with ... it feels no pity or remorse or fear ... and it absolutely will not stop. Ever. Until you are dead.*
>
> —*The Terminator*, 1984

In the Orwellian prophesied year 1984, a foreboding *The Terminator* propelled Arnold Schwarzenegger to superstardom. Super Mario soldiers began their Asian invasion in 1986, as the 8-bit video game console implanted Nintendo narratives within the minds of red-blooded American youth. Yet neither by movie nor game, constructed neither of masculine metal nor transnational marketing, Donna Haraway's seminal "Cyborg Manifesto: Science, Technology and Socialist Feminism in the 1980s," crafted in 1985, heralded the age of the (academic) cyborg.[1] Writing in the temporal center of an American Reaganism, where technology-laden militarized buildups resurrected binary paradigms of good and evil, Haraway built a theoretical cyborg capable of navigating the domestic Evil Empire. She explained,

> Cyborg imagery can help express two crucial arguments in this essay: first the production of universal, totalizing theory is a major mistake that misses most of reality, probably always, but certainly now; and second, taking responsibility for the social relations of science and technology means refusing an anti-science metaphysics, a demonology of technology, and so means embracing the skilful task of reconstructing the boundaries of daily life, in partial connection with others, in communication with all of our parts.[2]

Haraway asserts that cyborgs are not born, but constructed by the hands of others, and as a result are neither entirely innocent nor guilty of their actions. The constructs fracture existing myths of a naturalized "universal womanhood" averse to science and technology by embracing a hybridized politic of shifting boundaries In her words,

> Cyborg politics is the struggle for language and the struggle against perfect communication, against the one code that translates all meaning perfectly, the central dogma of phallogocentrism. That is why cyborg politics insist on noise and advocate pollution, rejoicing in the illegitimate effusions of animal and machine.[3]

Despite Haraway's call for a complex feminist project, her work has often been reduced to the closing, "I would rather be a cyborg than a goddess," by many second-generation cyborg works.[4] These works celebrate the freedom that technology affords women with the newly developed spaces in computer mediated communications—gender bending, lesbian e-mail lists, playful NetSex liaisons within multi-user-dimension (MUD) chatrooms, and other social investigations focusing upon the importance of identity on the Internet.[5] Nowhere is this celebration more apparent than within the following quote taken from a biographical article on Haraway from *Wired* magazine online: "Feminists around the world have seized on this possibility. Cyberfeminism—not a term Haraway uses—is based on the idea that, in conjunction with technology, it's possible to construct your identity, your sexuality, even your gender, just as you please."[6]

Why would Haraway not use the term *cyberfeminism* in this manner? While her manifesto indeed embraces the feminist implementations of technology, it also critically questions "devastating assumptions of master narratives deeply indebted to racism and colonialism" located within Euro-American feminism to marginalize the bodies and thoughts of women of color.[7] Chela Sandoval observes that cyborg politics "run parallel to those of U.S. third world feminist criticism," stressing oppositional consciousness to hegemonic feminisms.[8] She further realizes that Haraway's position as an established white feminist theorist gives her a racialized authority to be listened to within intellectual communities, commenting, "when uttered through the lips of a feminist theorist of color, [similar theories] can be indicted and even dismissed as 'undermining the movement' or as 'an example of separatist politics.'"[9]

In further revisions of her manifesto, Haraway first refines her analysis to better include issues of race and later begins to examine issues of masculinity. In "Cyborgs at Large: Interview with Donna Haraway," she admitted that problematic usage of "we" in "We are all cyborgs," which did not embrace impoverished women, often Third World women with little choice but to serve as workers in electronic sweatshops.[10] As a corrective, she suggests an expanded "family of displaced figures, of which the cyborg is one," yet of which men are none.[11]

Believing men to possess unbelievable amounts of privilege, she wanted to avoid any avenue for a masculinist response in her work.[12]

Haraway finally recognized the dangers of the male cyborg warrior in 1995 in "Cyborgs and Symbionts: Living Together in the New World Order," an order dominated by this very same male cyborg warrior: the Terminator. She explained, "the Terminator is much more than the morphed body of a virile film star in the 1990s: the Terminator is the sign of the beast on the face of postmodern culture, the sign of the Sacred Image of the Same."[13] Unlike her female-gendered cyborg, which utilizes her hybridity to negotiate dangerous superstructures, the "male" cyborg continues to march on preestablished pathways of colonization, domination, and destruction through his militarized versions of video games and Nintendo wars.

Nowhere is the terror of the male cyborg more apparent than in 3D Realms' 1997 IBM-PC computer action game, *Shadow Warrior*, where yet another male monster rampages through a city, raping, colonizing, *terminating* all within his path. Yet this monster is not the muscle-bound Aryan Schwarzenegger cyborg, but instead wears the digital makeup made famous by fellow monsters Warner Orland, who played Charlie Chan, David Carradine of *Kung Fu* fame, and Jonathan Pryce, the Engineer in *Miss Saigon*: yellowface. Yes, the tale I will tell is *The Revenge of the Yellowfaced Cyborg Terminator!* (Insert anguished scream here!) This Yellowfaced Cyborg Terminator, amalgam of middle-class white man and digital ninja, revels in the material hybridity between human and machine, using this positionality to reinscribe master narratives based on racism and colonialism.

While this Terminator may represent the apocalyptic future as viewed in its namesake movie, my Yellowfaced Cyborg Terminator possesses strange hybridizations that potentialize fatal flaws. Similar to common notions of race-neutral "cyberfeminism," Yellowfaced Cyborg Terminators perceive and revel in the material hybridity between human and machine, but they utilize this celebrated space to assert common narratives of racial domination, sexual abuse, and capitalist consumption. Yet the Yellowfaced Cyborg Terminator little realizes the changing contours of cyberspace—the significant role of Asian-owned transnational corporations, the growing role of female gamers, and the need to remain technologically competitive on the electronic entertainment marketplace—and this rigidity suggests his growing obsolescence.

My interest in the naming and the racializing of one masculine Terminator that has been "yellowfaced" stems from a recent controversy surrounding *Shadow Warrior*, which will center this discussion of its digital terrorization of the Asian body. After the release of a demonstration version of the game, Elliot Chin, columnist for *Computer Gaming World* magazine, castigated the games' creators for producing "a game that is patently offensive in its racial humor and, even worse, shows great ignorance about its very own subject matter: East Asia and ninjas."[14] Proud of its ability to ignite conflict, 3D Realms continued to promote its racist and sexist agendas, expressing their distaste of "politically correct" wars against multiculturalists, explaining their product is only a parody/homage of seventies chop-socky movies, and essentializing their argument to, "If this game offends you or anyone, go play another game. We won't mind."[15]

As an Asian male cyborg in my own right, I choose to play my own intellectual game with the *Shadow Warrior* controversy, acknowledging the perverse pleasures of weaving an oppositional read of the controversy, creating much more horrid creatures of the game designers and gaming public than the digital entities on the computer screen. In each level of my game, the Yellowfaced Cyborg Terminator morphs into different entities, from the individual gamer, to company representatives, ending with the corporate entities. Level 1 examines the battle of cultural representation between Yellowfaced Cyborg Terminator gamers and its critics. Within this level, I will unmask the Yellowfaced Cyborg Terminator from his ascribed position as a postmodern parody to reveal his true identity as a white male, middle class cultural colonizer. In Level 2, the contestants grow larger, as the Yellowfaced Cyborg Terminator, in the embodiment of 3D Realms, battles its Pacific Rim opponents over domination in the video game marketplace within the arena of global capitalism. Here I will *terminate* the Terminator by exposing his powerlessness when facing a larger, Japanese popular cultural juggernaut that understands the pulse of the international popular economy much better. Each level will examine how the Yellowfaced Cyborg Terminator aspires to amalgamate aspects of Oriental aesthetics and Asian power to be Asian/Oriental, but they neither know nor care how to pursue an authentic path. It is unwilling to truly transform itself, but it only wears the digital skin to become superficially Oriental. Digitized Yellowface, the new makeup of the Millennium.

Level 1—The Fantasies of White Male Cyborgs

> *Guy (interviewer)—Although I think it's a wise marketing move to position Lo Wang as having an eclectic Asian background, there has been some questions as to whether Lo Wang is Chinese or Japanese? Your thoughts?*
>
> *George Broussard—Our thoughts are "who cares"? ;) We intentionally mixed the nationalities, not out of ignorance, but because we knew it would generate mass amounts of flames and email debates online. We just wanted to give people something to talk about ;) in the end Lo Wang is who you want him to be, and since "you" sort of become him in the game, we think it's good to have a fuzzy background, so you can assume his role more easily.*[16]

In the spirit of propagating a "virtual reality," George Broussard asserts that the malleability of Asian ethnicity surrounding the main character in *Shadow*

Warrior allows the video gamer added comfort within a digital body. The digital body with which one can interface and become is that of Lo Wang, a racist and misogynist Yellowfaced Cyborg Terminator, on his solitary quest to rape, pillage, and claim the Asian continent, leaving nothing but carnage. Or, as the Yellowfaced Cyborg Terminator prefers to read himself, as a "wacky blend of all things Asian."[17] In this level, I closely examine how the hybrid Yellowfaced Cyborg Terminator of Lo Wang as gamer, plays the roles of movie star, tourist, and colonizer, unsuccessfully negotiating through these contradictory perspectives.

As Lo Wang, the gamer situates himself within a flimsy plot that has little bearing on the action of the game. Lo Wang's background is that of a former henchman for a Japanese conglomerate, Zilla Enterprises, who, as "a man of honor," resigns from the company upon discovery of a "demonic scheme to rule Japan, using creatures summoned from the dark side."[18] Master Zilla subsequently sends his loyal henchman to Lo Wang's studio in an assassination attempt, and thus the game begins, unfolding like many other "one-man-versus-corrupt-capitalists" narratives such as *Blade Runner* and *RoboCop*.[19]

Within the four-level demonstration game offered for free on the Internet, two levels occur in a techno-Tokyo, designed and populated with anachronistic and geographically displaced beings.[20] Bamboo sliding doors open to allow access to the Bullet Train station, revealing hordes of bare-chested yellow ninjas hefting Uzis and throwing stars in the company of green kamikaze coolies carrying explosives, all waiting to die by Lo Wang's sword, Uzis, or nuclear weaponry. If injured, the gamer searches for fortune cookies to refresh his health levels. In frustration, Elliott Chin castigates the ignorance of 3D Realms, arguing that *Shadow Warrior* is "a game that caters to the stereotypes of Americans as to what a Japanese adventure should be . . . but 3D Realms can't even get their own stereotypes right."[21]

The 3D Realms official response, written in an open letter distributed on the Internet claims,

> We designed the game this way on purpose. In fact, we thought that our mixing of Asian cultures was so outright obvious that no one could possibly mistakenly think it was done from ignorance . . . We are having fun with the whole Asian culture, and we blatantly mixed up all the elements and cultures to make a fun game.[22]

In another statement, George Broussard of 3D Realms clarifies, "Our intent was not to make a racist game, but a parody of all the bad kung-fu movies of the 60's–80's. We wanted to make a 'fun' game that didn't take itself too seriously."[23] Rather than interrogating each sentence he utters, I choose to construct and examine an amalgamation of his statements, "We are having fun with the whole Asian culture . . . Lo Wang is who you want him to be . . . a parody of bad kung-fu movies." According to this statement, the gamer should enjoy the game as an "Asian" actor, but I argue that he ultimately finds more enjoyment as a tourist/colonizer/rapist Terminator cyborg...in yellowface, of course.

The digitized yellowfacing of the Yellowfaced Cyborg Terminator gamer as an actor is both subtle and overt. Lo Wang is rendered virtually bodiless in the game. Unlike many video games where the gamer controls the character—for instance, Pac Man—from the third person perspective, directing the small, iconic character through the maze, avoiding ghosts and eating dots, *Shadow Warrior* is a three-dimensional game (actually, to be technical, 2.5D) from the first-person perspective. That is, the computer screen represents both the gamer's line of vision and body, with only weapon-carrying limbs exposed "in view." Thus, the gamer does not see his appearance in the game, enabling, as Broussard explained in this section's epigraph, the gamer to imagine himself as anyone he prefers. Thus, the gamer could *potentially* assume the role of the bald, goa-teed Lo Wang depicted on the product box, a white warrior from a James Clavell novel, or himself transported into a mythical Asian society. Preferably, Broussard suggests the gamer take an Oriental filmic role. Thus, wearing the body of Lo Wang, the gamer can pretend to be a chop-socky martial artist like Bruce Lee when he kills an enemy with his bare fists, pretend to be slick gangster extraordinaire Chow Yun Fat when he mows down screaming hoards with two fisted Uzi gunplay, pretend to be faithful student Caine of Kung Fu conversing with Master Leep high on the mountaintop.

Yet sound effects confine the gamer to act as the inscribed character of Lo Wang rather than any other imaginary characters. As the gamer interacts with the virtual world, certain canned digitized quotes will emanate from the computer speakers. Voice actor "John Galt" (an eerie pseudonym perhaps referring to Ayn Rand's "superman" character in *Atlas Shrugged*), an expert at the stereotypical pidgin-English inflection spoken by all yellowfaced performers, gives Lo Wang the voice to shout such profanity as the phallocentric "Who wanta some Wang?" and "Howza that for kung fu fighting, you chickenshit?" Clearly, any type of "honor" afforded to Lo Wang's characterization in the plot blurb is forsaken for childish, bawdy humor geared for giggling adolescent guys.

Thus, the gamer is forced to view the game in the constricted parody script written by Broussard and company. As a movie parody of Asian films, the game fails miserably. While many of the Asian movies popular in the United States focus on heavy action and light plots, the action invariably emphasizes intricate choreography. Both well-produced and "bad" kung-fu movies showcase awesome physical flexibility, speed, and artistry in the performer's martial arts skills. Through many innovative film techniques, director John Woo transformed gory gunfights into an art form, inspiring such upstart filmmakers as Quentin Tarantino to follow in his path. In contrast, having Lo Wang throw open bamboo doors, throw down a nuclear bomb, throw forward the phrase, "Just like Hiroshima," parodies a wise cracking Arnold Schwarzenegger Terminator flick rather than anything typifying an "Asian" film aesthetic. The Lo Wang wisecracks prevail so heavily within the game that they eliminate any suspenseful moments, neutralizing the immersive action that should be the central selling point.

Whereas the advancement through the levels can be read as the ascribed plot progression of the heroic story of a just Asian warrior battling the hoards of corporate demons, the journey of the Yellowfaced Cyborg Terminator can also be read as a colonizing narrative where conquest and exploration, rather than upholding justice, become the primary goals. Mary Fuller and Henry Jenkins trace the threads of colonial domination in the more simplistic, linear games on Nintendo home console based video games, comparing the games to the journals of New World explorers. They state,

> We want to argue that the *movement* [italics mine] in space that the rescue plot seems to motivate is itself the point, the topic, and the goal and this shift in emphasis from narrativity to geography produces features that make Nintendo and New World narratives in some ways strikingly similar to each other and different from many other kinds of texts.[24]

They explain that character development in many video games consists of the acquisition of advanced weaponry and pointed avoidance of life-depleting dangers rather than this psychological development. The experiential enjoyment the gamers receives is not from plot twists, but from their own constructed narrative of exploration. The onscreen character serves as a vehicle in the exploration of different levels of this visibly complex virtual world. Only after the complete exploration of one level, finding all the secret passages and hidden weapons, will the gamer complete his preestablished goal, opening the gilded door with the jeweled key, for example, to see what world the next level will bring.

This exploration narrative connects well with the popularity of American tourism in Asia. Christopher Connery examines a subgenre in literature he coins "the Japanese Wanderjahre," where "young American men go to Japan for a year or two and either find themselves or muse on the confusion of life reflected in the odd juxtapositions that surround them."[25] Yet since the importing of Japanese anime and Hong Kong gangster flicks continues to influence "American" popular culture, and Oriental porn and Asian mail order brides are readily available on the Internet, does one really need to travel to Asia for an enlightenment that can be achieved through virtual vacations?

Playing *Shadow Warrior* becomes an escape from white middle-class (sub)urban drudgeries to exotic Asian worlds where racialized problems of cultures clashing is subsumed by a canned plot. Within this fictional Tokyo, the Yellowfaced Cyborg Terminator is indeed the target of Master Zilla's Oriental minions, yet he is not the *gaijin* white foreigner victimized by inquisitive, reproachful stares as he walks down the street, because he possesses digital skin that hides his whiteness (as well as his high-tech weaponry). With this perfect disguise, the gamer battles through the train station, terminating all the Orientals within, not fearing that any one enemy alive will further advance Zilla's domination of the world, but so he can leisurely eye the detail of this gaming world—riding the bullet train, climbing Mt. Fuji, enjoying Japanese bathhouses and bathing beauties. His only true interaction with this culture is to appreciate it before he destroys it. Realistically rendered Buddhist statues can be demolished with a well-placed bazooka blast, while Pachinko machines can be slashed to release yen.

To rearticulate in ghastly detail words all too familiar, the Yellowfaced Cyborg Terminator commits genocide in a territory in order to enjoy the goods available there, while native bodies lie bloodied. When bored with the current territory, he will travel to the New World/Next Level to once again violently wrest that area away from the natives.

A specific example brings this colonizing narrative into focus. 3D Realms situates all female characters nude in contrived conditions, such as bathing underneath a waterfall in the midst of a battlefield or sitting on a toilet in Master Leep's temple. The limited interactivity of the game allows the gamer two options. Firstly, he can "talk" by pressing the key that denotes "action," resulting in lewd questions and comments are hardwired into the game: "Those real tits?" "Ha ha! You go poo poo! I leave room." Susan Clerc notes that "boys online [on computer discussion boards] seem to have an obsession with actresses' breasts and their compulsion for discussing them in public," what she calls the "big tits" thread; the games comments cater to this crowd.[26] Beyond verbally molesting the female characters, the gamer is compelled to kill these stationary women in "self-defense," which is actually a thinly veiled reactionary response to liberated women. After Lo Wang's lewd comment, the woman replies with a dismissive comment of her own, "You jerk," accompanied by her own machine gun, which rattles off a burst of bullets. Thus, under the guise of self-defense, Lo Wang can execute the Asian woman who just spurned his advances with a few bullets cast in her direction, and walk away with a giggle as the woman explodes with a shriek into a mist of blood.

The constraints of the game forces the gamer into the role of the cold-blooded colonizer, who rapes, pillages, and kills like a digitized reenactment of the My Lai massacre. Passing off any type of problematics as entertainment, the Yellowfaced Cyborg Terminator does not care to interpret these meanings. If anything, because of the controversy, the Yellowfaced Cyborg Terminator revels in the carnage, playing the game as a political statement for anti-intellectualism. Fred Snyder, in a letter to the editor of *Computer Gaming World* in response to the controversy, states, "If I seek cultural education, I'll see *Farewell My Concubine* again. If I want to play an ultraviolent computer game, I will do so without regard for any bruised egos on the part of those who might associate themselves with the game's subject matter."[27] Alas, Snyder expects to be educated from a movie, in contrast to a parody of a movie, never realizing that both products are both representations of a culture, and whether authentic or not, would always be in question.

Level 2—Corporate Warfare: The Battle of the Big Bosses

> All in all, *Shadow Warrior* will not be getting my (and this half
> of the world's) support.
>
> —Rick Ong, Singapore[28]

Despite the bravado 3D Realms assumes in the cultural wars they instigate, their mantra, "if you don't like it, don't buy it," may become their death-knell if they choose to incorporate the phrase in their international marketing strategy. The video gaming industry is a highly competitive and profitable global industry and should not be taken with such a cavalier attitude. Although the origin of the video game began in the United States, Japanese manufacturers dominate the console unit and coin-operated marketplaces globally. Can the Yellowfaced Cyborg Terminator survive with a strategy that denigrates the Asian market? This level will examine the marketplace for video games, both domestically and internationally, again from a colonizing paradigm. Only here, it is the virtual dragons of the Orient that impinge on the assumed territory of the Yellowfaced Cyborg Terminator.

In "alt.civilizations.faq: Cyberspace As the Darker Side of the West," Ziauddin Sardar exposes the vocabulary describing cyberspace as one fraught with colonialist overtones, revealing another Western advancement toward claims of new spaces. Comparable to *Star Trek's* Captain James T. Kirk's argument of space as the "final frontier," Sardar notes that the Internet has been likened by media voices to an electronic frontier. Quoting from a British magazine he explains that it is "one of those mythical places, like the American West or the African Interior, that excites the passions of explorers and carpetbaggers in equal measures."[29] The full title of Howard Rheingold's book, *The Virtual Community: Homesteading on the Electronic Frontier*, further reflects the romantic aspect of civilizing this space. Yet these romantic views of colonization are, of course, those of the privileged colonizer who invokes manifest destiny in their unconscious, or uncaring possession of spaces.

The continuous modernization of this Internet frontier can be seen further in Vice President Al Gore's popularization of the Internet as the "information superhighway." Steven G. Jones parallels this analogy with the federal highway system, in which former Senator Al Gore Sr. played an instrumental role. Both were designed to facilitate transport of militarized operations, and any benefits the citizenry may enjoy are secondary. Furthermore, although the highway metaphor is viewed as one that connects communities, highways often disrupt and disperse the communities through and over which they are built—namely, communities of color.[30] Yet it is this elision of race that is ignored, whether passively or actively, within this modernization/civilizing utopian paradigm. Julian Bleecker finds that race takes a formidable presence as racial tension in dystopic films like *Blade Runner* and *Demolition Man*, yet a close analysis of the utopian city simulation, *Sim City 2000,* reveals "raceless" urban uprisings blamed instead on "high heat, high crime, and high unemployment, all desperate allusions to life in the inner-city ghetto. Through the disaggregation of race, the gamer can construct a more 'benign' narrative justification while the specter of a racial context remains implicit."[31]

Metaphors of colonization prevail in video games. A casual perusal of the January 1998 issue of *Computer Gaming World* magazine, self-proclaimed as "the #1 Computer Game Magazine," reveals the popularity of "Strategy/Wargames" as the magazine reviews eleven new games, with titles such as *Age of Empires*, *Conquest Earth*, and *Prelude to Waterloo*. Running second are "Action" games, with seven reviews, including a lackluster review of *Shadow Warrior*, while only one "Puzzle" game made it to the review board. In the same issue, the magazine hails "Sid Meier's *Civilization* [as the] #1-rated game of all time," as an "indescribably addictive world conquest/exploration game."[32]

Haraway describes how the potential and real alliances between the military and gaming companies represent her Terminator cyborg of male colonization and domination:

> The Terminator is the self-sufficient, self-generated Tool in all of its infinite but self-identical variations. It can be the transfused blood fraternity of information machine and human warrior in the cyber-enhanced airforce cockpit, those pilot projects for the equally—or maybe more— profitable cyborg theme parks and virtual reality arcades to follow in the great technology transfer game from military practices to the civilian economy that has characterized cyborg worlds.[33]

Sardar also finds the relationship between computer wargames and actual warfare unsurprising, due to the military origins of the computer, both hardware- and software-related. He argues that the defense industry invests in the entertainment arena to reap further profits from its technology, originally built for war: "Once the military has opened up the new frontier, the settlers can move in to play their games, to explore, colonise, and exploit the new territory taking us back to mythic times when there were other worlds (Islam, China, India, Africa, America) with resources beyond imagination and riches without limits."[34] Yet two stark examples show that technology is coming of age beyond its military origins—the privatization of war works both ways. At the request of the U.S. Army, video game manufacturer, Atari, converted the popular *Battlezone* video arcade game into a computerized military tank simulator. More frightening, the U.S. Marine Corps reprogrammed an inexpensive popular computer game, *Doom II* (originally retailing for fifty dollars), to serve as a Marine infantry training simulation.[35] Have video games advanced to the point that they are accurate simulators of war?

While patterns of Western colonizing narratives of the Terminator deserve continued reflection, colonization should not be pinned on Western civilization exclusively. Although Japan may no longer send air combat troops over the Pacific, their cars, consumer electronics, and media icons have infiltrated every corner of the earth. No longer does Santa bring Lionel Train Sets and Cabbage Patch Kids to the excited children in the Western world. Instead, video game consoles named Sega, Sony, and Nintendo top Christmas lists, with Bandai Tamogotchi "virtual pets" as stocking stuffers. Even the hot-rodding Asian American teenagers of the Silicon and San Gabriel Valleys dream of four-banging' four-cylinder Acura Integras rather than the V-8 Chevys and Mustangs of 1950s Milwaukee *Happy Days* lore.

Christopher Connery chronicles the rise (and decline) of a "Pacific Rim Discourse," noting an equivalent relationship between Asian and America sounding suspiciously cyborgian: "Its world is an interpenetrating complex of interrelationships with no center: neither the center of a hegemonic power nor the imagined fulcrum of a 'balance of power.' "[36] Based partially upon the rise of an economically strong Japan and an economically weakening America, this discourse examines the exchanging and punctured absorption of culture. According to Connery, his idea of the Pacific Rim Discourse weakens in the late 1980s, and he notes how another period of economic uncertainty in the United States resulting in Japan bashing. If these two aspects signal the decline of his discourse, I would argue that the decline began in the early 1980s, with the murder of the Chinese American engineer in Detroit, Vincent Chin, by two unemployed autoworkers looking (mistakenly) for a Japanese scapegoat. Instead, I propose that material products and culture continue to be amalgamated into the cyborg consciousness of America, always creating disruptions, but nevertheless continuing unabatedly.

Super Mario, a portly Italian plumber, and Hello Kitty, a white cat with no mouth have much more in common with a certain black mouse than the red color of their overalls/blouse/shorts. All three are squeaky-clean childhood icons, seen internationally on cartoons, video games, clothing, lunchboxes, and practically any other product with a merchandizing license. Yet of these three, only Mickey Mouse is not a Japanese immigrant. Nintendo's flagship icon, Super Mario, appears on over 120 million video game cartridges worldwide, with the best-selling game of all time, *Super Mario Bros. 3*, grossing $500 million.[37] With Nintendo wielding this amount of popularity and monetary power, Fuller and Jenkins carefully remind readers that the belief that cultural imperialism only flows in an Eastern direction has its Orientalized flaws. They note Japan's ability to manipulate, repackage, and resell aspects of Western culture, and subsequently ask,

Does Nintendo's recycling of the myth of the American New World, combined with its own indigenous myths of global conquest and empire building, represent Asia's absorption of our national imaginary, or does it participate in a dialogic relationship with the West, an intermixing of different cultural traditions that insures their broader circulation and consumption? In this new rediscovery of the New World, who is the colonizer and who the colonist?[38]

In the past decade, America has bristled at the Japanese purchases of culturally American icons, such as the Pebble Beach golf course and the Seattle Mariners baseball team, but recent American commercials for Japanese products reflect a definite, if not Orientalized, Asian association. Sega game commercials of the past ended with a figure in their commercial, a teenager or video game character for example, shouting "Sega" in a brash, masculine onomatopoetic form, yet current Sony Playstation commercials end with a feminine enunciation of "Playstation" pronounced with a distinctly Japanese accent. A Japanese man and his dog recently hawked Nissan trucks nationwide in a country that demonized Asian Americans fifteen years previously. And despite the destabilization of the Asian economy in the late 1990s, Colonel Sanders has still been seen shilling Japanese video-game inspired Pokémon beanie toys with his buckets of Kentucky Fried Chicken![39]

Given the hegemonic power that Nintendo, Sony and Sega have in the international gaming community, the Yellowfaced Cyborg Terminator named 3D Realms finds itself in a problematic position. While it may (rightly) believe that its IBM-PC based game will sell well to the primarily American and European markets that own IBM-PCs, can it successfully market, let alone license, *Shadow Warrior* in its entirety to the strictly regulated, yet more profitable, video-game console industry? A $150 video-game console is ten times less expensive than a $1500 midrange computer, and thus a much more affordable present purchased by lower and middle class families acquiesce to their whining children.

Despite its "bad boy" position, 3D Realms has indeed already compromised its reactionary vision upon its recent release of *Duke Nukem 3D* for the Nintendo console. Gone are the demeaning female strippers in a bawdy nightclub, replaced by an inoffensive warehouse. No longer is the gamer forced to kill the women trapped in cocoon casing; here they can be rescued.[40] Yet the content of *Shadow Warrior* is not as easily correctable. Can they fix a game whose central selling aspect and peddle it to overwhelmingly Asian-owned multinational companies that sell products to a large Asian market? These questions would not have to be answered if 3D Realms actively considered the Asian market, rather than using Asian products as gags.

On the other hand, *Shadow Warrior* might indeed gain approval by the Japanese companies. First, according to Sandra Buckley, pornography and other fetishizations are more openly accepted in Japan, so the parodic nature of *Shadow Warrior* could be profitable if marketed to those specific subcultures.[41] Yet Nintendo markets itself as a family-oriented company, like Disney, and closely regulates and rates its licensees to prevent parental/consumer backlash over inappropriate products. Second, and more important, the transnational entities of the video-game manufacturers may permit 3D Realms to produce an offensive *Shadow Warrior* to sell primarily to the American and European markets, as Masao Miyoshi asserts that true multinational/transnational corporations show little allegiance to their originating country and will eschew "morals" in lieu of hefty profits.[42] Yet the fear of this particular Yellowfaced Cyborg Terminator marching through a worldwide marketplace can be junked. Despite the controversial publicity surrounding the game, consumer data obtained from software marketing firm PCData reveals that, unlike its predecessor *Duke Nukem 3D*, *Shadow Warrior* failed to sell. During its first year of availability, never once did it become a monthly top-20-selling game. No consoles game manufacturer has opted to translate *Shadow Warrior*, and the 3D Realms website does not indicate any further activity with the game. Did Lo Wang, *Shadow Warrior*, and 3D Realms die a dishonorable death?

Endgame

Because of the construction of the Yellowfaced Cyborg Terminator and the accompanied milieu in *Shadow Warrior*, female cyborgs and cyborgs of color can create few, if any sensible narratives in a game built around their destruction. Yet, ultimately, 3D Realms will not profit much from *Shadow Warrior* because of its reliance on gimmickry to cover its technological obsolescence. Game manufacturer Id Software created the first widely popular first-person perspective shooter, *Doom* (1993), and continues to lead the industry with *Quake* (1996) and *Quake II* (1997). Their games showcase more advanced graphics and gameplay within the same genre in which 3D Realms publishes titles. Furthermore, Id pays careful attention to the needs of their consumer base. A growing number of women "cyborgs" play the militaristic *Quake* (an essentially "plotless" game where a soldier runs through a beautifully Gothic world, shooting demonic creatures), enough to warrant the inclusion of nonstereotypical gender and ethnicity choices for the militaristic main character in *Quake II*. 3D Realms' decision to be, in the words of its head, Scott Miller, "a controversial company by choice," one that doesn't "shrink away from issues that would send PC-anal companies running with their tails tucked between their legs," suggests that their market is primarily the white, middle-class conservative male who enjoys demeaning portrayals of women and people of color.[43] 3D Realms sells controversy, not gaming content, and will fail to reach the prosperous levels of Nintendo or Id if the company fails to expand its market beyond the Yellowfaced Cyborg Terminators.

The Yellowfaced Cyborg Terminator, trapped behind the seemingly contradictory bars of cultural appreciation and cultural imperialism, marches disjointedly on colonial paths well worn by the steps of men before him. Yet a motley crew of other cyborg renegades threatens the ways of the white imperialist: Asian American keyboard critics, female Quakers, and a Super Mario hegemony. Unlike the faceless enemy hordes in *Shadow Warrior*, this heterogeneous group can divide and conquer their yellowfaced enemy, dismantling the cyborg mind and body, rendering their forms of racism, sexism, and colonialism obsolete. Like a bad movie, *Shadow Warrior* has been all but forgotten within the fast-paced gaming community, left to linger in the ghettoized bargain software bins. That is, until a new entity picks up these discarded vestiges, reworks them to incorporate into a newer, nigh-invincible cyborg to resume the race for world conquest. Will the Yellowfaced Cyborg Terminator rise again?

Cyborg Suicide: An Epilogue (2002)

In reviewing this essay since its inception in 1997, I am struck by many events that trouble my previous conception of the Yellowfaced Cyborg Terminator. In the five years since, the American technoscape escaped the empty threats of Y2K computer glitches at the turn of the atomic clock, yet nevertheless is now suffering a technological meltdown for other reasons. With the wave of Adam Smith's "invisible hand," dot-com capitalism vanished. Enron, the bankrupted energy mogul, left California in the dark before pulling its own plug based on nefarious business deals. And as passenger planes fall from the skies, destroying American symbols of capitalism and militarism, we have to wonder if we are witnessing the suicide of the American cyborg. Are "our" mechanical hands effectively strangling our human necks?

My original identification of the Yellowfaced Cyborg Terminator focused on the consumer marketplace, pointing toward cocky software developers and their adolescent-minded users who donned Asian disguises during their digital quest for economic domination and sexual pleasure. American-based manufacturers continue to fail cloning their own masculinist yellowfaced cyborgs, as their creations stagger through the marketplace, due in part to the power of the finicky consumer. American corporate behemoth Microsoft jumped into the Japanese-dominated console videogame market with the launching of its X-Box game system, yet its sales still linger in the shadows of Sony's Playstation 2, especially in Asia. Despite the high global box-office receipts, many critics and science fiction fans savagely critique the terrible writing and wooden acting in *Star Wars, Episode II: Attack of the Clones.* George Lucas's fifth retread of Akira Kurosawa's samurai films continue showcasing orientalized stereotypes, replete with a "brown horde" of Maori soldiers masquerading in white storm-trooper outfits, an unnecessary massacre of an entire village of dehumanized sand people, and of course, even more Yoda-speak, this time with Kung-Fu fighting! Even clothing manufacturer Abercrombie and Fitch marketed T-shirts emblazoned with tired "oriental laundryman" stereotypes in an attempt to curry dollars out of the pockets of the plastic masses of fraternity boys, only to be rebuffed by angry Asian American consumers boycotting this representation.

On the military front, American supersoldiers continually place themselves dangerously in check when playing war games with East Asian adversaries due to an array of tactical technical miscalculations. Over the past few years, the United States military has mistakenly(?) bombed the Chinese embassy in Yugoslavia, clipped a Chinese fighter pilot with a spy plane, run into a Japanese fishing boat with a nuclear attack submarine, and, of course, accused Taiwanese American nuclear physicist Wen Ho Lee of stealing military secrets. Nevertheless, due to the events of September 11, 2001, the military continues to invest in destructive technological "solutions" rather than more humane diplomatic discourse. Thus, the death of the cyborg terminator has been widely exaggerated.

However, in the Haraway tradition, many rebellious cyborgs have arisen within the past five years, violently shattering the status quo with their master's tools. The year 1999 marked a rash of school shootings by white middle-class students, headlined by Eric Harris and Dylan Klebold at Columbine High School in Littleton, Colorado. The two students obtained easily accessible weaponry to wreak havoc with the school system, enacting their vengeance against people they hated. Damaging computer viruses hit worldwide networks in 2000, with the infamous "Love Bug" virus suspectedly crafted by some students in a small technical college in the Philippines. And, of course, little more needs to be articulated about men reportedly armed with the technologies of box cutters and jet-pilot training. The disparate army of disaffected cyborg soldiers, albeit wearing masculine garb rather than feminist wrap, speak a politics of destruction to puncture holes in the gleam of corporate and governmental hegemonic facades.

Where my original identification was admittedly a pleasurable academic exercise, I do wonder what concrete effects my work, along with other cultural analyses of technology, truly has in the "real world." To what extent do our published observations become policy interventions? Is it possible for scholars to keep up with the information overload that Tim Jordan defines as the "spiral of technopower?"[44]

David Harvey and Manuel Castells propose such paradigms as "time-space compression" and "the network society" to describe how technology restructures and affects sociality.[45] No longer does a letter addressed to California from New York take weeks to travel via the Pony Express, when the technology of the telegraph, telephone, overnight couriers, fax, e-mail, and satellite transmissions can transmit information across the globe instantaneously. This technology enables both intellectual and manual labor to be decentralized and parceled across many minds and bodies.

While unstated, it is precisely the decentralization and redundancy of productive labor that propels the maxim of the high-tech industry: Moore's Law. Gordon Moore, a founder of Intel Corporation, observed that each new computer chip doubled its capacity every eighteen months, facilitating an exponential growth in computer capability. However, unlike the "natural" exponential reproductive growth of amoebas or rabbits, the doubling of chip capacity relies on the large capital investments to pay for advanced equipment and the numerous skilled and unskilled workers toiling hundred of thousands of hours to make such advances.

Intellectual cultural production in the university may not work as quickly, however, because the networks of thinkers lack the resources. While academics access some technologic tools through electronic archives, databases, and e-mail communications with others, the production of scholarship and the technology of writing severely limit the pace. Cultural studies researchers often examine an already produced yet thought-provoking product or event, chewing through their analysis primarily on their own. After painfully ascribing the analysis, the scholar must market her work to academic publishers as an article or manuscript, one publisher at a time. In the time that the work gains approval, editing, and eventual publishing, the corporate industries of technology and entertainment hire many more minds and bodies to produce more advanced computer games and films, even incorporating planned obsolescence into their products. Thus, when cultural studies papers written about *Blade Runner,* multiuser domains, and *Shadow Warrior* hit the shelves, the "cutting edge" of the technology and cultural industries has moved on, leaving many of the antiquated products in the computerized trashbins of the consumers.

May I propose my own corollary to Moore's Law? Because of the exponential growth of technology combined with the linear lag of academic production, traditionally published cultural studies pieces regarding technology run high risks of obsolescence at the moment of publication, appearing simultaneously on the "new book" shelves and the remainder tables.

Can academics prove my corollary wrong? What can be done to alleviate the widening gaps based on space-time compression and the technopower spiral?

Academics who study technology need to understand the industry more intimately, beyond that of an end user. Like the stereotypical high-tech nerd (or the oriental spy), the academic needs to be attuned to the trade journals, business pages, and inside information to keep track of all the corporate moves. In addition, academics cannot rely on the "traditional" processes of the academy to disseminate their thoughts. While scholars can press for changes in the academic publishing worlds as well as the tenure process, we can also publish our works in other venues that engage others more quickly, taking advantage of print periodicals or online journals with much quicker turn-around time. Finally, perhaps we all need to don our cyborgian battle armor, ready our ability to analyze on the fly, throw caution to the wind, attack bravely, and hope we can exploit the "chink" in our enemy's armor.

Notes

A hearty thank you to editors Rachel Lee and Sau-ling Wong, who granted approval of my "special edition" of this previously published article with an additional epilogue. Special appreciation goes to Wendy Hui Kyong Chun, Susana Gallardo, Beth Kolko, Lisa Nakamura, Mimi Nguyen, Greta Niu, Masha Raskolnikov, Gil Rodman, Laura Verallo Rowell, and Ann Wilson, all who greatly assisted the thinking during the original inception of the Yellowfaced Cyborg Terminator.

1. Reprinted in Donna Haraway, *Simians, Cyborgs, and Women,* (New York: Routledge, 1991).
2. Ibid., 181.
3. Ibid., 176.
4. Ibid., 181.

5. Quotation from Haraway, *Simians*, 181. See Nina Wakeford, "Sexualized Bodies in Cyberspace" in *Beyond the Book: Theory, Culture, and the Politics of Cyberspace*, ed. Warren Chernaik, Marilyn Deegan, and Andrew Gibson (Oxford: University of London, 1996); Shannon McRae, "Coming Apart at the Seams: Sex, Text and the Virtual Body," in *Wired_Women: Gender and New Realities in Cyberspace*, ed. Lynn Cherny and Elizabeth Reba Weise (Seattle: Seal Press, 1996); and Anne Balsamo, *Technologies of the Gendered Body*, (Durham, NC: Duke University Press, 1996) for these specific examples of cyberfeminism.

6. Hari Kunzru, "You are Cyborg," *Wired* 5.02 (February 1997) n.p. Online at <http://wwww.wired.com/wired/5.02/features/ffharaway.html>.

7. Haraway, *Simians*, 1; emphasis added.

8. Chela Sandoval, "New Sciences: Cyborg Feminism and the Methodology of the Oppressed," in *The Cyborg Handbook*, ed. Chris Hables Gray (New York: Routledge, 1995), 412.

9. Ibid., 411.

10. Constance Penley and Andrew Ross, "Cyborgs at Large: Interview with Donna Haraway," in *Technoculture*, ed. Penley and Ross (Minneapolis: University of Minnesota Press, 1991), 12.

11. Ibid., 13.

12. Surprisingly, she admitted in this interview published six years after her manifesto, "This really is the first time [she had] to imagine that line being read by people—not just male people—in a masculine subject position." Ibid., 19.

13. Donna Haraway, "Cyborgs and Symbionts: Living Together in the New World Order," in *The Cyborg Handbook*, ed. Chris Hables Gray (New York: Routledge, 1995), xiv.

14. Elliot Chin, "3D Realms' Folly: Shadow Warrior's Ignorant Stereotypes are too Offensive to Stomach," *Computer Gaming World* 157 (August 1997), 221.

15. Scott Miller and George Broussard, "An open letter to Elliott Chin, 'Action' columnist of *Computer Gaming World*," June 30, 1997, *PC World Online*, at <http://www.pcworld.com/annex/games/articles/game_beat/jul97/beat071697b. html>.

16. Guy Smiley, "Exclusive Interview with SW creator, George Broussard" June 4, 1997, *The Shuriken Times*, online at <http://www.shadowwarrior.com/times.html>.

17. Scott Miller, "Plan file," August 26, 1997, online at *Quakefinger*, <http://finger.planetquake.com/plan.asp?userid=scottm&id=1413>.

18. "Shadow Warrior v1.1 On-Disk Technical Support Manual," *Shadow Warrior Game*, 3D Realms, May 26, 1997.

19. Irony prevails as 3D Realms takes the company line of berating and belittling the individual critics who have issues with their own attempts at gaming domination.

20. Software manufacturers often offer abbreviated "demos" or time-limited "shareware" versions of their products for consumer sampling. My *Shadow Warrior* analysis is based on this four-level demo game, and ongoing debate and research in computer trade magazines and Internet webpages. Thus, none of this author's dollars have been exchanged with 3D Realms!

21. Chin, "3D Realms' Folly," 222.

22. Miller and Broussard, "Open Letter."

23. George Broussard, "Plan file," September 7, 1997, online at *Quakefinger*, <http://finger.planetquake.com/plan.asp?userid=georgeb&id=4720>.

24. Mary Fuller and Henry Jenkins, "Nintendo and New World Travel Writing: A Dialogue," in *Cybersociety: Computer-Mediated Communications and Community*, ed. Steven G. Jones (Thousand Oaks, CA: Sage, 1995), 58.

25. Christopher Connery, "Pacific Rim Discourse: The U.S. Global Imaginary in the Late Cold War Years," *Boundary 2*, 21.1 (1994): 49.

26. Susan Clerc, "Estrogen Brigades and 'Big Tits' Threads: Media Fandom Online and Off," in *Wired_Women: Gender and New Realities in Cyberspace*, ed. Lynn Cherny and Elizabeth Reba Weise (Seattle: Seal Press, 1996), 82.

27. Fred Snyder, "Letters to the Editor," *Computer Gaming World* 159 (October 1997): 30.

28. Rick Ong, "Letters to the Editor," *Computer Gaming World* 159 (October 1997): 30.

29. Ziauddin Sardar, "alt.civilizations.faq: Cyberspace As the Darker Side of the West," in *Cyberfutures: Culture and Politics on the Information Superhighway*, ed. Ziauddin Sardar and Jerome R. Ravetz (New York: New York University Press, 1996), 17.

30. Steven G. Jones, "Understanding Community in the Information Age," in *Cybersociety: Computer-Mediated Communications and Community*, ed. Steven G. Jones (Thousand Oaks, CA: Sage, 1995), 10–11.

31. Julian Bleecker, "Urban Crises: Past, Present, and Virtual," *Socialist Review* 24, 1 – 2 (1995), 210.

32. "Hall of Fame," *Computer Gaming World* 162 (January 1998): 370.

33. Haraway, "Cyborgs and Symbionts," xv.

34. Sardar, "alt.civilizations.feq," 21.

35. Rob Riddell, "Doom Goes to War," *Wired* 5.04 (April 1997): n.p. Online at <http://www.hotwired.com/collections/future_of_war/5.04_doom1.html>.

36. Connery, "Pacific Rim Discourse," 32.

37. J. C. Herz, *Joystick Nation* (New York: Little, Brown, 1997), 133, 21.

38. Fuller and Jenkins, "Nintendo," 71–72.

39. "Pokémon World News Story," 1 Online at *Pokémon World*, <http://www.pokemon.com/news/nw-kfc.html>.

40. Duke Ferris, "7 Dirty words you can't say on a website: Duke Nukem 64 Review," December 1997: Online at *Game Revolution*, <http://www.game-revolution.com/games/n64/duke.htm>.

41. Sandra Buckley, "'Penguin in Bondage': A Graphic Tale of Japanese Comic Books," in *Technoculture*, ed. Constance Penley and Andrew Ross (Minneapolis: University of Minnesota Press, 1991), 12.

42. Masao Miyoshi, "A Borderless World? From Colonialism to Transnationalism and the Decline of the Nation-State," *Critical Inquiry*, 19.4 (summer 1993), 726–51.

43. Miller, "Plan file."

44. Jordan refers to the spiral of technopower as "the constant promise that a vital piece of information or a vibrant place of virtual life are just out there, slightly beyond our reach, often drives those in online life further into the embrace of information." Tim Jordan, *Cyberpower : the Culture and Politics of Cyberspace and the Internet* (New York: Routledge, 1999), 119.

45. See David Harvey, *The Condition of Postmodernity: An Enquiry into the Origins of Cultural Change* (Cambridge, MA: Blackwell, 1989), and Manuel Castells, *The Rise of the Network Society* (Cambridge, MA.: Blackwell, 1996).

12

Good Politics, Great Porn: Untangling Race, Sex, and Technology in Asian American Cultural Productions

THUY LINH NGUYEN TU

Introduction

According to the journalist John Tierney, throughout history, sex and the erotic have always had "a peculiarly creative impact on communications technologies," sometimes a driving force in its innovation, but virtually always one its first and most successful uses.[1] The VCR, which was saved from sure extinction in its early days by the sales of pornographic videos, is a shining example.[2] But similar stories can be told about print, photography, television, and film—all technologies whose commercial success and everyday popularity were bolstered by their close affinities to this "most enduring killer app."[3] And it is a mutually beneficial relationship, helping not just technology but the sex industry as well. As the scholar Brian McNair has put it, "No account of the pornography industry can neglect to mention the close connection between the spread of sexually explicit material in capitalist societies and the invention of new forms of information dissemination."[4]

Given this history, it should not come as much of a surprise that every month approximately 31.3 million people, or 36 percent of everyone online, visits an adult website—a figure that has remained constant throughout the history of the web.[5] Or that each year Internet pornography contributes to the U.S. economy approximately two billion dollars—roughly 10 percent of the total amount of money spent online.[6] The phenomenal success of the online adult industry is the result, however, of not just the web's high-speed connections and its promise of anonymity, but of something much more low-tech: the presence of Asian bodies. For in this multibillion-dollar business, Asian porn sites are, according to some statistics, pulling in 25 to 30 percent of its revenue.[7] While it is difficult to judge the accuracy of any estimates given the notoriously capricious nature of the industry—sites rise and collapse in the course of just weeks—those involved in the trade are sure of Asian porn's popularity. SexTracker, a company that provides data about online pornography for webmasters (to help "maximize their profits"), shows that nearly all adult portals offer Asian porn. Tellingly, in its lineup of "elite" links, SexTracker lists 1008 sites showcasing "Asians," as compared to merely 69 for "Blonds."[8] These figures suggest that if we accept McNair's formulation about the integral link between sex and technology,[9] we must also acknowledge the ways that racial ideologies operate in this network, or, to use his terms, account for the close connection between sexually explicit material, the invention of new forms of information dissemination, and the commodification and sexualization of racialized bodies.

The ubiquity of these sites confirms what cyberskeptics have always suspected: that despite corporate promises of a disembodied technofuture, bodies still matter very much in cyberspace. Quite early on, the theorist Sandy Stone showed us that while we could not strictly see the body in cyberspace, it was there nonetheless, existing in the "descriptive codes that 'embody' expectations of appearance."[10] On pornographic sites, the body, as real as it can be, is in fact what is being offered; its gender and race are not only legible, but the main draw. What it sells is not just flesh—digital or "real"—but much more precisely the underlying histories and myths that such bodies invoke. Asian porn sites trade on long standing (certainly predigital) and relatively unimaginative assumptions about Asian women: that they are exotic and hold limitless sexual knowledge, yet docile and eager to please. Hardly a product of the web alone, they produce, reflect, recycle, and make easily available those fantasies already existing in the social world.

In a strange reversal of fortunes, Asian women's invisibility in most cultural arenas has been amply replaced by their hypervisibility in this new virtual arena, and in the old industrial arena that supports it; for Asian women's overwhelming presence here is matched only by their numbers in the related industry of microelectronics production, where they and Latinas comprise 60–80 percent of the workforce.[11] So perhaps it bears repeating, even at this late date, that rather than erasing lines of difference altogether, the information revolution has in some important ways actually reinscribed lines that distinguish bodies from each other, virtually and materially. As many theorists have already noted, one of the distinct features of technologically enabled global restructuring of capital is its ability to profit not through homogenization but through differentiation of specific resources and markets, regions and nations, that permit the recruitment of a flexible workforce whose difference can be exploited to both increase productivity and decrease wages.[12] In this quest for differentiation, the "oriental girl" is singled out as particularly suited for the "feminized" work of high-tech production and, if the number of porn sites are any indication, sexual stimulation.

While it is difficult to assert that Asian women in these industries have ever had much access to spaces of creative expression, digital or otherwise, it is possible to imagine that the technologies they make offer new tools for speaking back to the representational regimes that sustains their social position. It is possible to see these technologies as unfaithful to their origins and as enabling a whole range of creative and political possibilities, as providing opportunities to create imaginative narratives that can be brought to bear creatively upon the social itself.[13] And Asian American artists, activists, and entrepreneurs have seized on this. Grabbing onto available technologies and using Asian women's prominence in the adult industry as a point of departure, they have found new opportunities to play with, comment on, and even profit from the tangle of race, sex, and technology. Perhaps the most direct come from people like Mimi Miyagi, publisher of *Oriental Dolls* magazine, who recently bought two servers so that she and her fellow models could "sell their own photos and films [and] . . . make the money instead of the video companies."[14] The strategy is an old but effective one: wrestle the modes of production from porn's power elite and put it in the hands of the workers themselves. But, as Donald Suggs has reported, the aim here is to please, not politicize. Like most of the industry in which she toils, Miyagi is indifferent to racial critiques of her work: after all, as she says, stereotypes about Asian women attract a lot of men.[15]

Others less directly involved with the industry have sought different goals, attempting not to claim control over the mode of production, but to interfere with the process of consumption. Mimi Nguyen was among the first. When Nguyen initially began using the web in the mid-1990s, she quickly discovered that her searches for Asian women would inevitably land her at sites like "Anal Asians," "Singapore Sluts," and "Filipina Fantasies."[16] Frustrated, she created "Exoticize This," a site for Asian American feminist resources, to document the "the amazing women that aren't to be found, it seems, anywhere on the web."[17] Now folks looking for pornography are sometimes sent inadvertently to her site. This happy coincidence, which must be quite confusing and disquieting to accidental visitors, is precisely what artists like Prema Murthy, Kristina Wong, and Greg Pak have tried to encourage. Armed with a type of "hacker knowledge," they have sought to "interrupt, upset, and redirect the smooth flow of structured communications that dictates their positions in the social networks of exchange," and that, not coincidentally, makes pornography profitable.[18] In doing so, they have imaginatively reorganized ideas about what may be the "proper" place, spatially and socially, for Asian Americans.

I

Neither the adult industry's technosavvy nor its insatiable desire for "Asian digiflesh" was lost on the artist and performer Prema Murthy. A few years ago she "was searching for interesting art sites that were up-to-speed on the technology and found that it was the porn industry that was way ahead of everybody. They were using the newest [and easiest] software . . . and making money at it as well."[19] Indeed, as researchers have since confirmed, it was adult entrepreneurs who streamed in images, sounds, and videos even before artists and designers, and it was they who, through online sales mechanisms like monthly use fees and pay-per-view, managed to turn cyberspace into a marketplace. This discovery became the inspiration for *Bindigirl*, a digital art installation come "tongue in cheek amateur porn site." Part website, part performance, *Bindigirl* was, as Murthy put it, her "ironic response to the fascination with Asian female bodies and the ways technology facilitates such voyeurism."[20]

Bindi made her debut in 1998 on the web art warehouse Thing.net.[21] At first glance, the site looks quite like any other adult portal, with its boldly posted adult-content warnings and its various legal disclaimers. Upon closer inspection, however, the viewer notices that the usual under-twenty-one prohibitions are surprisingly matched with cautionary quotes from the *Kama Sutra*, like "Women are hardly known in their true light," and may "extract from [men] all the wealth that they possess." A red Bindi dot guards the entrance to the site. Once visitors enter, they are greeted by a hot pink lotus flower, and introduced to Murthy in the character of Bindi, who is entirely nude except for strategically placed digital Bindi dots. Animated images of Bindi frantically loop through the screen, superimposed with texts, also from the *Kama Sutra,* offeing advice on how to be a successful courtesan. The courtesan, it is urged, must "do everything to [a man's] satisfaction"; must not "act too freely"; must "adapt her tastes and actions to his liking"; and, most crucially, must always "remain silent."

Audiences navigate the site through the use of a remote control, choosing from options like: "Love Chat," a comic, fictional dialogue between Bindi and an impotent admirer ("My measurements are 36, 24, 36"); "Bio," Bindi's meditations on her life ("Its so lonely in here"); or "Harem," a photo portfolio of other South Asian women sporting nothing but red dots. Avid fans whose interests extend beyond visual stimulation were invited to join Bindi's interactive "performances." Every Wednesday evening, for a small fee of five dollars per month and a free download of CU-SeeMe software,[22] audiences could actually speak with her. To own a little piece of Bindi, however, cost much more; prices for the "Exotic souvenirs"—Bindi's socks, panties, and even her sacred dots ("All editions worn, signed, and numbered by Bindigirl")—ran from $50 to $150.

There is no doubt that Bindi and her fellow models are seductive—coyly revealing, and eminently sexual. There is also no doubt that they understand something about the art of the courtesan. And yet there is something uneasy about this sexuality. All the images of Bindi, particularly the animations at the beginning of the site, are violently cropped and confined in small circles. While Bindi herself is quite physically exposed, the composition creates an impression of contraction rather than of expansion. Throughout the site, there is an obvious tension between the images' voyeuristic allure and the way that they undoubtedly produce a feeling of claustrophobia. And the juxtaposition of images that would be at home on any adult site (excepting the Bindi dots, of course) with protofeminist quotes from Indian religious texts, like "Women are the perfection of wisdom," certainly solicits some contradictory readings. There is power and freedom in Bindi's sexuality, but there also seems to be resentment that her sexuality is the only thing we can see. Here Murthy makes a fine distinction: her critique is not against Asian women's sexuality—which is at once powerful and mysterious—but against the desire to see Asian women as *only* sexual.[23]

This overwhelming feeling of constraint, visually produced by the restrictive composition, seems to echo Bindi's complaints. In her biography Bindi asks the viewer pointedly, "What is the reason for my existence? Why am I confined to this space? Who and what do I need to get out of here—to go beyond my boundaries? At first I thought technology would save me, arm me with weapons. Then I turned to religion. But both have let me down. They continue to keep me confined in my "proper" place."[24] "Place," the scholar Dolores Hayden reminds us, " is one of the trickiest words in the English language, a suitcase so overfilled one can never shut the lid." It carries the resonance of both "location" and "position in a social hierarchy." According to Hayden, the idea of place has historically had both spatial and political meanings; phrases like "knowing one's place" or "a woman's place" still carry the weight of both.[25] Such double meanings are clearly at play in Bindi's lament; she feels restricted, partly by the boundaries of the screen, but certainly also by those of the social world. And, surprisingly, it is technology and religion—social creations usually lauded for their ability to extend humans' physical and mental limitations—that have confined her to her place.

As Murthy explains, Bindi is an avatar, but in more than just one sense of the word. She is both "an alias in the virtual world" and "a play on the word which in Hindi means the incarnation of a deity or the embodiment of an archetype."[26] In both the technological and religious sense, Bindi exists only in the abstract, in an idealized form that is unburdened by the complexities of daily life. But to her, this abstractness, often heralded as one of the web's most powerful new advantages, looks very much like an old and familiar trick. It smacks of the colonialist feint, where representations are used precisely to deny the complex subjecthood of the colonized population.[27] It hints of the (U.S.) Constitutional ruse, where a system of abstract citizenship recognized and conferred advantages only to white property-owning males. Hardly liberating, abstractness is for Bindi less a hope than a demand, a condition foisted on her by both technology and religion.

Though, as Bindi admits, neither religion nor technologies can help her to "go beyond [her] boundaries," she does not passively accept her digital predicament. Bindi knows she's being watched and she asks for something in return. In part, that something is the five-dollar monthly membership fee and the price of merchandise on the site, and in part it is something much more costly.

By stealing from the porn's profit-making model—albeit much more modestly—*Bindigirl* is not only mocking its use of Asian women, but also actually extracting revenue from that relationship. The fees are small but significant, both as a matter of good irony and as a pragmatic response to the market conditions for digital art. While web art has recently gained a certain amount of institutional legitimacy, as indicated by its showcase in major exhibitions in recent years,[28] there is still much debate about what precisely it is and how it fits into the art economy. More specifically, there are still questions about how to reward digital artists for creating works that, unlike traditional art objects, are widely accessible, highly reproducible, and do not easily fit into a traditional museum or gallery system. Murthy's pay-per-view approach, popularized by pornography, is one model being taken up by other artists beleaguered in their search for monetary compensation.[29]

But these fees are nominal compared to Bindi's real demands: for the audience to recognize their complicity in her plight. When viewers tuned into Bindi's Wednesday night "performances," they saw Murthy (as Bindi) in her studio working on the computer, sleeping, painting her toenails, putting oil in her hair, and carrying out other entirely mundane activities. There were no overt acts of seduction, only the site of a woman typing code. This provoked participants to raise questions about what they were actually watching. Was it real? Live? Video? What was this "performance"—which was no performance at all—supposed to mean?

Murthy's use of CU-SeeMe, a low-tech video conferencing software originally designed for distance learning, holds the key to these questions. In Murthy's own work and in her collaborations with the performance art collective Fakeshop, the use of CU-SeeMe is central to her aesthetic practice. The software appeals to Murthy and other artists because its two-way transmission makes it an ideal interactive tool; with CU-SeeMe, the artwork is never created solely by the artists, but by their interactions with the audience. As she put it, "[It is like] the surrealist game where someone would draw something, fold the paper and someone would add to it unknowingly and it would create this work of art. We were using chat in the same way."[30] With this device, artists could potentially draw on the millions of people already online to create a unique collaborative work.

CU-SeeMe's only requirement is that exchanges be mutual, or that users must transmit images in order to receive them.[31] As a result, those watching Bindi on Wednesday nights were forced to also put themselves on display; the real performance, of course, was their participation. This demand for reciprocality fundamentally challenges the producer-to-consumer relationship made profitable by online pornography. In fact, it is presumably this two-way exchange that has kept sexually explicit CU-SeeMe content from winning much of a following; after all, most consumers want to be sexually gratified without reciprocation—without the burden of having to, themselves, gratify.[32] By insisting that her viewers participate in the performance, Murthy forces them to contribute to the creation of the narrative, and along the way to recognize their own implications in it. She makes very visible the often hidden connections between the consumer and what he consumes. As Murthy says, the idea is that "the responsibility is on the viewer," a sensibility that is noticeably absent from the porn industry.[33]

Bindigirl is meant to provoke art audiences to think about questions of representation, commodification, technology, and even Murthy herself. "By placing the project in an art context," she explains, "I hope to get people to ask if I'm making a comment or just using my girlish wiles to get some attention."[34] The intentional circulation of the project within an art context (first the online art "warehouse," then a museum) is significant. In these circles, audiences are generally primed to detect subtle ironies, and to expect that things may not be as they appear. As such, the project can successfully play with the gray areas, and can perhaps destabilize the dichotomies that have historically constrained Asian women's lives—traditional versus modern, goddess versus whore, proper versus improper. These are Murthy's limited goals. She accepts "the fact that my work is made mainly for an art audience and that effective activism targets a more widespread mainstream audience, an audience that I may not necessarily want to engage with in all my projects."[35] The aim here is neither to present a truer version of Asian women's sexuality, nor to convert wayward sexual consumers. While the piece is highly politicized, its political possibilities are self-consciously limited.

II

When Kristina Wong launched her own Asian porn spoof, she was far more adamant about her activist intentions. Hoping to lure in more than just art enthusiasts, Wong deliberately linked her site to "nasty clubs and chat rooms," and coyly advertised it as a legitimate service.[36] Soon patrons of Asian porn would find themselves haplessly diverted to BigBadChineseMama.com, where, in place of lovely lotus blossoms they would find "not so exotic Asians," who ask, in mocking irony, "aren't I the most delicate thing you have ever seen?"[37] The idea, as Wong puts it, was to "subvert the expectations of a nasty guy in search of petite naked Asian bodies by showing him [their] full ugliness."[38]

Wong's low-tech subversion—achieved simply by cutting and pasting metatags from adult websites—obstructs the passive consumption of porn by "intruding on the intruder" and injecting "noise into the signal as it passes from transmitter to receiver."[39] This, as Mark Dery defines it, is the work of a culture jammer, the "part artistic terrorist, part vernacular critic," who is "ever mindful of the fun to be had in the joyful demolition of oppressive ideologies."[40] As such, Wong belongs among a long list of pranksters, hackers, and saboteurs who, if only for a moment, have managed to derail the smooth flow of media.[41] But these types of practices belong not to activists alone. It was, after all, the pornography industry that perfected the art of "page-jacking"—the scam whereby an extra bit of coding is attached to copies of popular webpages in order to reroute surfers to adult pages. The practice had become so common that the FCC began a full investigation in 1999.[42] Wong's use of the tactic here is effective and appropriate—a clever allusion to both media activism and adult entrepreneurialism.

One can imagine that customers detoured to Wong's site were less than satisfied with what they found. Like *Bindigirl*, *BigBadChineseMama* also features a photo gallery, but hardly the kind to entice. "The Harem of Angst," which doubles as a faux mail-order bride catalog, displays no lithesome lasses, just photographs of angry Asian women sent to Wong from all over the world. Bearing names like "Phuc Yu" and "Madame Bootiefly," these women are obvious in their contempt; the photos reveal very little skin, few sweet smiles, and no pretense of seduction. In addition to the catalog, the site also carries a guide to "Frequently Un-asked Questions" about Asian brides ("Will my bride make an easy adjustment from her Asian Culture to the liberal American lifestyle?"); a response to Arthur Golden, "Memoirs of An Anti-Geisha" ("I have gigantic size $9\frac{1}{2}$ feet, crater zits . . . and a loud mouth"); a "Manifesto"; a comments page; helpful links; and, of course, souvenirs (T-shirts and stickers).

BigBadChineseMama is "webgrrrlism" at its finest, a blend of amusing journal entries, memoirs, and pranks, combined with frequent spurts of poststructuralist deconstruction. It is self consciously antislick: hastily scanned images, unedited prose, and low-tech coding give it the do-it-yourself feel common to most traditional "zines". And, perhaps most notably, it is funny—an effect that is not without purpose. Wong's intent here is to use wit and irony as a political tool; indeed, as her manifesto states, the site is in large part an effort to give "the revolution a sense of humor," and to make political work "fun."[43]

In this endeavor Wong might find a willing accomplice in the independent filmmaker, Greg Pak, whose digital short, *Asian Pride Porn!* is a hilarious send up of the adult industry.[44] The film, starring playwright David Henry Hwang, is a faux infomercial for a healthier alternative to popular porn films: a XXX video titled *Asian Pride Porn!* Purchasing pornography is bad enough, Hwang confesses, "I don't need guilt over the sexual oppression of women of color and anger about the absence-slash-emasculation of the Asian male in the American media" to add to it. Having found *Asian Pride Porn!,* he can now pass up clichéd titles like *Oriental Blossoms* (found at 555-ME-So-HORNY), for a collection of "positive images of confident Asian American men and women caught on tape."

With this collection of politically correct porn, viewers can stick with *Asian Pride Porn!* where they are sure to catch satisfying sex between a yuppie Asian woman and a virile Asian man, or they can choose from a variety of other empowering titles, including: "*Princess Mononookie, Anna and the Kink,* and *Whole Lotta Hapa: the Eurasian Man-Meat Special.*" To ensure confidentiality, each film comes discreetly marked "Chinese Voter Registration Turnout in Sacramento Municipal Elections, 1972–1976, Volume 4"—appropriate packaging for videos that, Hwang boasts, can actually take consumers "from onanism . . . to activism."

"Sex films are *the* most successful films online," says Pak, "so I knew there would be an immediate audience for *Asian Pride Porn!*" Having "figured out that sex and jokes are what people use the Internet for," he decided to make a product that would cater to what they wanted, but would also send out "a little subversive message."[45] The tactic worked: *Asian Pride Porn!* drew in a record audience. When the film debuted, Pak, who had never drawn a large audience for his short comedic films, found himself on the all-time top 10 list of the popular film website, Atom Films, and on the cover of *Time Magazine Asia*'s feature on digital filmmakers.[46]

Explains Pak of the spoof, "I figure I can bitch and moan about representations of Asian men and women, or I can make fun of it."[47] In much of his work, and certainly apparent in this film, Pak has consciously inserted himself within a broader tradition of artists who have used humor as a form of social commentary. And like other political humorists, Pak's skills lie in his linguistic ingenuity. Shot in the style of a typical pornographic video, the movie makes up for what it lacks in aesthetic sophistication with its verbal jokes, plays on words, and visual gags. The film's biggest payoff, however, comes from its use of what the scholar John Lowe calls "the most basic kind of comedy, that of incongruity."[48] Pak plays on this by casting Hwang, a figure of "high" literary art as the promoter of very "low" consumer goods, and by overloading the film with unlikely juxtapositions: onanism and activism, pornography and empowerment, and so on. This incongruity allows him to get laughs, but much more seriously, to throw into question the constructed nature of social arrangements. It makes it possible to contest the traditional high/low divide, and perhaps to imagine a new relationship between art and the masses. And, most important, it makes it possible to see racial and sexual politics as social constructions that can be played with, reorganized, and even laughed at.

None of this can be achieved, however, without a little creativity and a number of risks. "The typical polemic will only play to a certain audience," says Pak, but using humor may be a more strategic way of dealing with a broader audience, an audience that surely would not suffer through fist-raising lectures on the politics of representation.[49] Many of the viewers of *Asian Pride Porn!* it turned out, were misguided surfers who accidentally stumbled onto it looking for porn. How would they receive such a film? Are there not risks of misreadings when it bears such striking aesthetic resemblance—the camera angle, the texture of the images—to real porn? Says Pak, "They may get off on it, they may feel really cheated, or they may just find it funny. But, they may also think about stuff they wouldn't necessarily think about. I can't control how people interpret my work. I can only make it interesting enough for them to give it some thought."[50] Reiterating Murthy's sentiment, Pak argues that he is willing to take these risks since controlling the audience is neither possible nor really desirable.

In this Pak and Murthy differ from Wong, who seems much less interested in leaving her work open to interpretation; indeed, she is quite obvious and utterly unapologetic about her distaste for Asian porn consumers (whom she appears to assume are all white men). There are very few ambiguities in *BigBadChineseMama*—no beautiful bodies to look at, no double entendres to mislead. The T-shirts and stickers she sells on this site have less to do with questioning commodification than with spreading the word about the project. There is little room here for embracing Asian women's sexuality or the various and complex ways that she may deploy it for her own gains.

There are limits, as Sau-ling Wong has said, to art that depends solely on an oppositional stance: "stereotype-busting is not, in itself, a sufficient raison d'etre for artistic creation."[51] Certainly, Kristina Wong's project betrays these limits— lacking in both an aesthetic and critical subtlety, it fails to be truly provocative. But her aggressive style is well suited to her purpose, which, in spite of all the jokes, is to express an acutely felt anger. Some of it is personal, as when Wong writes about being taunted because of her big feet. But much of it responds to the "deeply embedded [sic] anger and frustration" that Wong says are "realities in our communities."[52] This collective anger pervades the various testimonies and images. At times it comes off a little heavy-handed, as when women are shown quite literally kicking down white boys in a fit of rage. Often, though, it is a poignant reflection on the lived experiences of racism and sexism, and on the possibility of speaking out against those forces.

The anger comes across clearly to visitors, who insist that Wong should "get the chip off [her] shoulders," or admonish that "[her] anger may give [her] a loud voice, but it does not mean anyone wants to listen." These, along with enraged exhortations that the project is "complete garbage," "racist and bigoted," "offensive" and no more than simply a "lesbo case of sour grapes," are stored on the site.[53] Wong holds onto these responses, despite the strain on her server space, because they send a much-needed message to Asian Americans: "Look at the people we're up against. We need to stop insulating ourselves."[54] At least part of her anger is directed at her own communities, whose apathy, inaction, or—worse—armchair criticism has, she charges, done little for the cause of social change. The challenge for Asian Americans, according to Wong, is to move outside their own networks to where their rants about "the Man" can actually be heard by him.

The web is one such space. Both Wong and Pak are convinced that the Internet is a very viable—and much needed—place for politicized art, a space where they can be assured they are not just preaching to the converted. Tapping into this site of public dialogue allows them to more effectively target their activism. Explains Pak, "I've gone on panels and Asian American circuits and spoken the good line about issues of identity and representation, but ultimately *Asian Pride Porn!* might be more effective in getting the message out."[55] And, equally important, web projects, relatively inexpensive and easy to produce, make it possible for artists to experiment with new narratives and images. This is no small advantage, particularly for those facing the perennial challenge of how to make, as Pak put it, "good politics *and* great porn."

Conclusion

In her keynote address to the 1998 conference of the Inter-Society for Electronic Arts, the cultural theorist Coco Fusco asked, "How can technologies that are promoted as the means for dissecting the physical world, of extending our physical and mental capacities, and of creating an imaginative realm beyond the social be brought to bear imaginatively upon the social itself? Is there a way to intertwine reality and fiction that does something other than convey that life looks more like a movie or that we would prefer to live in one?"[56] The artists and activists discussed here seem to have implicitly and in varying ways offered their answers.

The fascination with Asian bodies, in flesh and pixels, has everything to do with the representational histories and political ideologies that pervade the social world and, by extension, permeate cyberspace. By refusing the role of the passive consumer—indeed, refusing the smooth flow between production and consumption—the artists here have forced renewed public dialogue about these histories. While these types of dissident cultural creations remain on the margins of the porn industry, hardly posing a threat to its proliferation or profits, they do serve an important political function. These creations, like the Asian American artistic productions that preceded them, can "subvert white society's expectations of Asian American's proper place and stimulate the creation of heteroglossic Asian American culture."[57]

Creative works like these, however, are politically tricky, playing as they do with the easily misunderstood tools of humor and irony. Here they are made even trickier by the uncomfortable fact that they rely, both symbolically and materially, on the exploitation of Asian women—on their overrepresentation in the factories and on the screen. But while these artistic productions may not alter most Asian women's lives, they can challenge the representational order that dictates their position. They can break open the seamless flow of information that presents women's historical conditions as historical necessities. As these artists have shown, if there is in fact a productive way to intertwine reality and fiction, it cannot be accomplished by giving up what little technical knowledge they have in order to avoid complicity.[58] There is still too much to be done.

Notes

1. John Tierney, "Porn, the Low-Slung Engine of Progress," *New York Times*, January 9, 1994, H1.
2. When the VCR was introduced in 1979, sales of pornographic videos accounted for more than 75 percent of its market.
3. Tierney, "Porn, the Low-Slung Engine of Progress"; "Killer app" refers to a computer software application.
4. Brian McNair, *Mediated Sex: Pornography and Postmodern Culture* (London: Arnold Press, 1996), 115–16.
5. Study on online adult entertainment market conducted by Jupiter Media Metrix (an online marketing consulting firm), online at: <www.mediametrix.com>.
6. Frederick Lane, *Obscene Profits: The Entrepreneurs of Pornography in the Information Age* (New York: Routledge, 2000), 70.
7. Estimate received from the CyberAngels Network, a child pornography watchdog organization.
8. See <www.sextracker.com>. It is interesting to note that Asian porn seems most popular among the online market, taking up a proportionally greater share than it does in print or video. The reasons for this are as yet unclear.

9. Claudia Springer presents a similar thesis in her study of technology and the erotic; see Springer, *Electronic Eros: Bodies and Desire in the Postindustrial Age* (Austin: University of Texas Press, 1996).

10. Allucquere Rosanne Stone, "Will the Real Body Please Stand Up? Boundary Stories about Virtual Cultures," in *Cyberspace: First Steps,* ed. Michael Benedikt (Cambridge, MA: MIT Press, 1991), 102–03.

11. For an examination of the racial and gender composition of the microelectronics industry see Aihwa Ong, *Spirits of Resistance and Capitalist Discipline: Factory Women in Malaysia* (Albany: State University of New York Press, 1987); Maria Mies, *Patriarchy and Accumulation on a World Scale: Women in the International Division of Labour* (London: Zed, 1986); Karen J. Hossfeld, "Their Logic against Them": Contradiction in Sex, Race, and Class in Silicon Valley," in *Women Workers and Global Restructuring,* ed. Kathryn Ward (Ithaca, NY: Cornell University Press, 1990).

12. See, for example, Manuel Castells, *The Rise of the Network Society* (Oxford: Blackwell, 1996).

13. I borrow this formulation from cultural theorist Coco Fusco, who argues that bringing the creative realm to bear on the social is a central challenge for cultural producers in the information age; see Fusco, "At Your Service: Latinas in the Global Information Network," keynote address, 1998 conference of the Inter-Society for Electronic Arts 1998, later published as: "At Your Service: Latina Performance in Global Culture," in *Reverberations: Tactics of Resistance, Forms of Agency inn Trans/cultural Practices* ed. Jean Fisher (Maastricht: Jan Van Eyck Akademie, 2000).

14. Donald Suggs, "Hard Corps: A New Generation of People of Color Penetrates Porn's Mainstream," *The Village Voice,* October 21, 1997, 39.

15. Suggs, "Hard Corps," 39.

16. This situation has changed somewhat due to screening technologies used on most web browsers and due to an increase in work by and about Asian women on the web.

17. "Original Statement," September, 1997, "Exoticize This!" online at <http:// members.aol.com/critchicks/original.html>.

18. This term comes from Andrew's Ross's essay "Hacking Away at the Counterculture," in which he broadens the understanding of "hacking" to include all activities, "no matter how inexpert," that can tamper with the flows of information. See Ross, "Hacking Away at the Counter Culture," in *Technoculture,* ed. Constance Penley and Andrew Ross (Minneapolis: University of Minnesota Press, 1991), 124.

19. Prema Murthy, interview with Eric Baudelaire, June 3, 1999, online at <http:// rhizome.org/ print.rhiz?1459>.

20. Prema Murthy, interview with the author, January 21, 2001.

21. *Bindigirl* is now housed at the Walker Art Center in Minneapolis, but can also be found in The Thing's online archives at <http://www.thing.net/~bindigirl>.

22. CU-SeeMe (see you, see me) is a video conferencing software originally developed at Cornell University. It allows users to send and receive moving video images and sounds in a small-screen format through a simple video camera and video card capture.

23. Notes Murthy, "I have always seen sexuality as a source of power for women which in earlier feminist agendas has not always been the case. There is something very seductive and empowering in allowing others to see you as a sexual being but at the same time it can be constraining if what people see does not move beyond that." Prema Murthy, interview with Ricardo Dominguez, December 10, 1996, online at <http://www.thing.net/~rdom/ decrev96.02.html>.

24. See <http://www.thing.net/~bindigrl/bio/biotext.html>

25. Dolores Hayden, *The Power of Place: Urban Landscapes As Public History* (Cambridge, MA: MIT Press, 1995), 15–16.

26. Murthy interview with Bandclare.

27. See: Homi K. Bhaba "The Other Question: Difference, Discrimination and Discourse of Colonialism," in *The Location of Culture* (New York: Routledge, 1994).

28. The *Bitstreams* exhibit at the Whitney Museum of American Art and the *010101* exhibit at the San Francisco Museum of Modern Art were the first significant shows featuring digital arts in a major arts institution. Digital art was included in the Whitney Biennial for the first time in 2000.

29. Journalist Mathew Mirapaul argues that the pay-per-view model, first used by artists like Murthy, is catching on in digital-art circles; see Mirapaul, "Pricing of Computer Artwork Continues to Evolve," *Austin American-Statesman*, Weekly Business Review, May 29, 1999, 1.

30. Prema Murthy, interview with Josephine Bosma, January 25, 2001, online at <nettime-l@bbs.thing.net>.

31. Though it is possible to use CU-SeeMe as a voyeur, most adult reflectors discourage this by not allowing users to receive images without also transmitting them. The software is specifically designed to detect if a user is broadcasting or simply "lurking."

32. Other factors that may have contributed to its lack of commercial activity include the relatively small number of users, the technical challenges of using the device, and somewhat erratic video quality. See Frederick Lane, *Obscene Profits*, 249–51.

33. Murthy interview with the author.

34. Ibid.

35. Ibid.

36. Wong bought several ads in the personals sections of the *New Times* in Los Angeles.

37. See <http://www.BigBadChineseMama.com>.

38. See <http://www.BigBadChineseMama.com/manifesto.html>.

39. Mark Dery, "Culture Jamming: Hacking, Slashing, and Snipping in the Empire of Signs," online at <http://web.nwe.ufl.edu/~mlaffey/cultjam2.html>.

40. Ibid.

41. Well-known culture jammers include the group Processed World Collective, the magazine *Adbusters,* and the art collective ArTMark.

42. Leslie Miller, "Unsuspecting Web Users Get 'Page-Jacked' into Porn Sites," *USA Today,* September 23, 1999, 3A.

43. See <http://www.BigBadChineseMama.com/manifesto.html>.

44. *Asian Pride Porn!* dir. Greg Pak, 1999, 3 minutes, miniDV, color. Pak has just recently finished a similar spoof called *All Amateur Ecstasy:* "Three women experience the most earth-shattering climaxes of their lives—with a twist. Warning: Film contains no nudity, but involves adult themes. Not for kids and probably not something you should watch at work!" *All Amateur Ecstasy,* dir. Greg Pak, 2001, 2 minutes, miniDV color.

45. Greg Pak, interview with the author, November 22, 2000.

46. See <www.atomfilms.com>. See also *Time Magazine Asia* 156, no. 22 (2000).

47. Pak interview with the author.

48. John Lowe, "Theories of Ethnic Humor: How to Enter, Laughing" *American Quarterly* 38.3 (1986): 439–60.

49. Pak interview with the author.

50. Ibid.

51. Sau-ling Cynthia Wong, *Reading Asian American Literature: From Necessity to Extravagance* (Princeton, NJ: Princeton University Press, 1993), 211.

52. See <http://www.BigBadChineseMama.com/fuq.html>.

53. See "Kim Strikes Back," <wysiwyg://10/http://www.BigBadChineseMama.com/kimbacktalk.html>.

54. Kristina Wong, interview with Logan Hill, unedited transcript, May 12, 2001.

55. Pak, interview with the author.

56. Fusco, "At Your Service."

57. Sau-Ling Cynthia Wong, *Reading Asian American Literature*, 210.

58. I draw this from Andrew Ross, who writes that "we cannot afford to give up what technoliteracy we have acquired in deference to the vulgar faith that tells us it is always acquired in complicity, and is thus contaminated by the poison of instrumental rationality, or because we hear, often from the same quarters, that acquired technical competence simply glorifies the inhuman work ethic." Ross, "Hacking Away at the Counter Culture," 132.

13

Queer Cyborgs and New Mutants: Race, Sexuality, and Prosthetic Sociality in Digital Space

MIMI NGUYEN

Long ago I learned my lessons from the comic books. I learned that mutant bodies were powerful but vulnerable bodies; vulnerable because such powers made one a target for social control, prejudice, enmity, and evildoers seeking recruits, vulnerable because these energies threaten to overcome and eclipse the fragile vessel of the body. In 1980 the Marvel universe introduced the superhero team called the New Mutants, a multicultural crew of misfit teens led by an ascetically thin Vietnamese refugee Xi'an Coy Manh, the daughter of a South Vietnamese colonel with an evil twin (and also mutant) brother and a criminal ganglord uncle. Recruited by Professor Xavier for his New England School for Gifted Youngsters and called Karma in her X incarnation, she was a grim and conscientious figure, able to seize control of other people's minds and bodies—a fortuitous alteration of her genetic code in the aftermath of her mother's exposure to mutagenic chemical defoliants used during the war. The luckless subjects of her power would become extensions of her will and her senses—prosthetic mannequins speaking in her voice, attacking their fellows with their physical strength or armor where she had little of both. Though she could possess several subjects simultaneously, her control would be fragmented and sometimes awkward, distributed among the hosts. In many ways, it was a curious power that left her vulnerable to physical threat and harm. Her own flesh was not protected by any aspect of her power, and she was forced to find some discrete corner or shield herself with the bodies of her more physically powerful team members. And the experience drained her; often she would eventually collapse from the exhaustion of controlling another's mind and body. If she remained in possession of her subject for too long, she would begin to leak into the subject, or the subject into her—and her distinct personality and memories would be melded with those of the host. Nine issues into the series Karma had been captured by an enemy called the Shadow King and disappeared, only to reappear herself possessed by his disembodied spirit and of monstrously large proportions, having lost both her psychic strength and bodily control.

When I was young I sought to develop my own psionic strengths, hoping perhaps my mother, too, had been exposed to the same chemical substances. This did not seem wholly unreasonable; after all, like Coy Manh I had relatives in the former South Vietnamese army, a brother with definite potential for evildoing, and an enduring sense of being a categorical mistake. Like the mutant teenagers that populated the Marvel universe, I felt my birthright was to exist "outside" the normative social body of central Minnesota. I reasoned that this awkward, preadolescent exterior—garbed in mismatched, secondhand clothes and thick eyeglasses—would serve me well as a secret identity for the while; but my real self (which would arrive with puberty, as it did in the comic books) would be eruptive, powerful, and wield a mastery of my body and my surroundings that I didn't yet possess. No revelations were forthcoming, however, and after a while I consoled myself with the assurance that there were dangers I would never be then forced to face, so frighteningly realized by Karma's own possession and loss of self.

For years the appeal of comic-books faded away, and punk rock had come and gone as my chosen venue for social mutancy. But in a Boston comic-book shop, between sessions at an MIT conference on race and digital space, I discovered an old back issue of the New Mutants series, with a cover featuring a possessed Karma as an enormous puppetmaster, dangling and jerking her chosen avatars (her former New Mutants team members) at the ends of their strings. Because story arcs in comic books are ruled by fateful coincidence and constant resurrection, I recognized this encounter for what it was—a fortuitous link between the mutant in my imaginary and the cyborg in my work. It made sense: both Karma and the cyberspatial body represent popular cultural visions of the intersection between organic bodies and technologies, and the powers and dangers involved in the transgression. The mutant body and the cyborg body act as metaphors, representations of social structures and cultural systems in a seemingly new, complex, and contradictory configuration. She is an image of our notions about body and bodies in a moment of transformation, creating the imaginary spaces that the mutant/cyborg inhabits and posing new human possibilities and problematics.

In this essay I examine representations and images of the mutant/cyborg subject in feminist and queer science fictions; even progressive cyborgs need to be resituated within the material and ideological conditions of their origins to make sense of their political motives and possibilities. With comic book in hand, the following group of commentaries traces this intersection and transgression in science fiction and cyberspatial culture through two very queer concerns: our prostheses and our mobility. From the Greek, *prostithensis* means "to add"— *pros*, "in proximity," and *tithensis*, "to place"—a word, a part to something else. The prosthesis—a human-machine encounter enhancing movement, function, or activity—is often conceptualized as the interface allowing increasing freedom, mobility, and speed. As such, a prosthesis connotes several meanings: an artificial part replacing what has been irrevocably lost; an addition to the principal body enhancing movement, function, or activity; the intimate interpenetration of the biological with the mechanical. But the prosthetic subject describes both the incorporation of these meanings and a particular kind of doubling—the worker whose mechanized labor is assisted by robotic arms or machinery; the abstract citizen who, desiring the protection of the state, gives up the particularity of her body; the comic book avatar, a mutant who temporarily possesses the bodies and minds of others; the lesbian or transgendered subject, equipped with a harness and a dildo, resignifying the phallus and sexual meanings and practices; and the virtuality of a material body in digital space, interpenetrated by informational patterns and protruding machinery (keyboard, mouse, monitor). As technologies of the self, prostheses are both literal and discursive in the digital imaginary. They are a means of habitation and transformation, a human-machine mixture engaged as a site of contest over meanings—of the self and the nonself, of the strange and the familiar, of the parameters of mobility and its limits. At this interface the body is at stake—where it begins or ends, what it means, what is replaceable (and what is not), what its limits might be, what dangers may lurk in the encounter.

Locating my inquiry at the intersection of the imagination and material reality, I begin with the New Mutant Karma to interrogate the premises of what I call the "recombinant liberal subject" of cyberspatial fantasy—an abstract, sovereign subject released from social location. It is this capacity for inclusivity, attributed to the imagined neutrality of the cyborg in cyberspaces, that allows feminist and queer theorists to reimagine a radical subjectivity that celebrates fluidity and mobility. I then focus on feminist and queer interventions in science fictions and queer practices that seek to disrupt the "straight" taxonomy of sex/gender/desire, with profound consequences for representations of race and the cyborg subject. At this juncture I ask, What effects do our prostheses—whether figured as abstract personae in a global public or fantastical bodies of mixture and masquerade, as projective fantasies of control or sliding, shifting walls of invisibility—have upon subjectivity and social relations? What are the implications of feminist and queer conceptualizations of digital space and prosthetic sociality for the examination of race, not in isolation, but in critical, complex, and contradictory articulation with gender and sexuality? Is there a vanishing point at which, as Karma so powerfully worries with her fiction, the body ever really disappears?

"Your Mind—Your Body—Belong to Karma!"

While a minor character in the Marvel pantheon, Karma is massively traumatized: she grew up during the war in Vietnam as bombers and bullets flew overhead; her parents were imprisoned in a reeducation camp until she freed them with her powers; their escape on an overcrowded fishing boat was violently marked by the attack of Thai pirates; too weak from hunger to use her powers, she was forced to watch while the pirates murdered her father and raped the women, including her mother; her mother then died the day the survivors were rescued by the U.S. Navy; responsible for herself and her young siblings Leong and Nga, she moved to New York City where her ex-general, secret crimelord uncle kidnapped Leong and Nga in an effort to force her cooperation in his schemes. Originally gathered to fight "evil mutants" who (of course) sought to subjugate humanity, these teenage New Mutants are nonetheless viewed with fear and suspicion by the nonmutant population. Flanked by her teammates, Karma is an admittedly odd figure; often she holds her head in her hands, the only outward indication of the use of her powers. (The others erupt into black masses of solar energy, transform into animals, project spirit forms, or burst out at breakneck speed.) In the comics her powers are visually rendered as a kind of boundary-breaking psychic ray—it extends multihued (but usually in shades of fuchsia) from her furrowed brow to envelop her usually unwilling but violent opponents, traversing panels to intervene in other spaces. In the fashion of all comic-book characters, who are given both to lengthy exposition and statements of the obvious, she might declare, "Your day is done, villain! Your mind—your body—belong to *Karma!*"

Taken as a kind of evidence—and because comic books often wage battles across titles and temporalities—Karma can be read as a warning about the dangers of prostheses and possession, self-transformation and the boundaries of limitless mobility. For decades, both cyberpunk and corporate science fictions (and the intersection of both) predicted anarchic affairs between automaton and autonomy, negotiating the possible achievement of total liberty from the body (or derisively, the meat) or regulation. These fictions produced a cybernetic fantasy of the recombinant liberal subject—an abstract, sovereign subject reconstituted by the interpenetration of the virtual-systems interface with liberal humanist discourse, the transcendent figure of the technological sublime. That is, because both textual and graphical virtual interfaces make possible the decoupling of public persona from the materiality of the body, digital space can be made to sanction a body politic in which subject formation is understood as divorced from assigned or ascribed characteristics or social location. The appearance of the skin, the distribution and texture of hair, the bone structure of features, the contours of the body, the quality of grooming, the coterminous interplay of surfaces—the visual apprehension of race, gender, class, sexuality, and the like falls apart. To the extent that liberalism deems these to be constraints undermining autonomy and utopian subjectivity, digital space promises their removal through the absence or mitigation of presence.

But the figure of Karma substantiates the dangers of abstraction. Her powers might be said to mirror the powers of the recombinant liberal subject in digital space, enabling an escape from the flesh and the possession of other bodies, but the hope that this genetic cyborg can be read as an autonomous social agent is circumscribed.[1] The history of this cyborg is continuously apprehended in the present: the source of her powers, her ability to possess other bodies and minds, can be traced to a series of technological interventions in the war and to her DNA.[2] The history of Karma, but also of Xi'an Coy Manh (her "secret identity"), is thus embedded in the historical reality of the biochemical weaponry of the U.S. military-industrial complex, and necessarily references a disturbing past of neocolonialism and medical experimentation. She is a cyborg whose creation could have easily resulted in physical deformity or damage—as it did for others whose exposure to the chemical defoliants did not end so fortuitously—and yet she is nonetheless a freak. She is a cyborg *because* she is Vietnamese. Her adventures are constant reminders of this past—she joins the New Mutants and acts as Professor Xavier's secretary so that she might continue to provide for her siblings, who somehow contrive to be kidnapped again and again by various villains, including their uncle. As a "new mutant," she displays the arrogance of the war's engineers not on the surfaces of her body but from *within*, projecting these properties of possession and control onto others. As a New Mutant, her powers mirror the conditions of her creation. Against the utopian technological discourse in which the body is rendered inconsequential and immaterial, her *particular* body in all its permutations is the instrument of (and not the impediment to) her powers.

And far from being an abstract subjection position ensuring autonomy and mobility, the "new mutant" reinscribes the difference and the social powers that the recombinant liberal subject disavows. Her genetic mutation does not allow Karma unusual access to freedoms. On the contrary, because of the dangers and risks that accompany her powers, she must demand discipline from her prosthesis. As a cyborg, Karma must pass for human or risk being the object of fear and hostility, but to do so she must deny the history of her genetic mutation in an attempt to approximate the ideal (nonmutant) or be marked (by the *X*) as an "illegitimate" human being. The trauma of passing is realized in the "secret identity," which is *not* the mutant superhero but *the persona of normalcy*. This secret identity—and its recombinant liberal counterpart in digital space—implicates the social powers that produce, situate, and constrain legitimate/illegitimate subjects. This subject who suppresses is provided a kind of prophylaxis, to borrow from Lauren Berlant—a prosthetic status as abstract "person" that disguises her particularity.[3] But the impossibility of this disembodiment erupts repeatedly. While Karma may pass for human, she cannot otherwise pass as other than Asian; the consequences of the first kind of passing may bear upon the second, in which her body is already marked as "foreign" in the West, and vice versa. The objectification of the Vietnamese by the U.S. military as "mere gooks" during the intervention—and thus justifying the usage of napalm and biochemical defoliants—suggests that the hope to pass for human is precarious and a historical contingency. For the body that is understood as too much body—too much sex, too much skin, too much history—the ideal of the unmarked liberal subject is violence.

But the mobility attributed to the recombinant liberal subject is not limited to abstraction; in the release of the body from social powers, the ability to wear a body that does not reflect or refer to the physical appearance of the user/performer is perhaps the most popular aspect of science fictions. And when superpowers fail to manifest, digital space provides. The emergence of the cybernetic interface has posed an incipient and significant challenge to some essentialisms as cyborg subjects generate new bodies and design new selves in the choosing and fusing of new parts in a potentially endless process of consumption and self-invention; the prosthesis of digital space enables a mobility that promises both autonomy and inclusivity. But however transgressive (and some avatars might be within certain parameters), these are choices that may simultaneously participate in the reconstruction of a recombinant liberal subject—continuously accumulating surplus (material and cultural) capital in late modernity. Such modes of cross-identification and cybernetic drag are coded as safe or entertaining, divorced from social consequence or political conditions. Even as "warranting" (the process of making the physical body legible) becomes problematic in digital space, the corporeal codes or tokens of "identity tourism" or cross-identification can still be fetishized, and the relations of power that produce and circulate such narratives about specific bodies are concealed, made invisible in electronic environments. These codes do not require the physical body that authorizes them into digital space to match, to be *warranted*, but they invoke bodies nonetheless, and in very specific ways.

This may easily become the occasion for (a desire for) escape, a wish for a post-body future in which one might enjoy the exoticism of otherness or dodge complicity by inhabiting that space of difference. Indeed, the fantasy of becoming "other" (or some approximation of her) is a feature of modern commodity culture and contributes to the apprehension of mobility for the liberal subject. The contemporary spectacle of multiculturalism appropriates racial and national otherness for use in a range of fantasies of identification. Lisa Nakamura describes this as "identity tourism"; writing of the Lambda MOO environment, she observes that "Asian-ness is co-opted as a 'passing' fancy, an identity-prosthesis that signifies sex, the exotic, passivity when female, and anachronistic dreams of combat in its male manifestation."[4] In these user-built environments, Nakamura suggests that the transgender and transracial "identity tourist" who occupies the space of the "other" is engaged in a fantasy of social control. The popular avatars that Nakamura discusses—the samurai, ninja, or mail-order bride—are deeply implicated as codes in contemporary anxieties about gendered labor and transnational capital. That many of the persons who adopt the identity of an "Asian Doll" in electronic environments are, as Nakamura surmises, white men, would then suggest that the performance of transracial and transgender performance does not necessarily disrupt social (or geopolitical) relations *between* specific bodies; digital space allows for the nonmimetic act to be ideologically contained by the abstraction of virtual reality. Released from an empirical referent, the digitized token is circulated as "play" and severed from the sociopolitical and ideological processes that produce it. Nonetheless, these codes reference a body politic and frameworks of cultural intelligibility that, in this case, spectacularize already hypervisible bodies.

To what degree, then, does the autonomy of the recombinant liberal subject depend upon the suppression of other subjects, throwaway cyborgs used as servants, laborers, or toys? Maintaining multiple subjectivities drains Karma, and she is always in fear of losing control of her prosthesis, or worse, abusing its capacity. Her twin brother Tran developed similar abilities, and enjoyed the power over others. Having both saved and spared his life on numerous occasions she was forced to absorb the essence of her evil twin (effectively killing him) when he threatened innocents (having possessed Spiderman) under the guiding criminal thumb of their ex-general uncle. And when possessed by a mind more powerful than her own after a raging battle of wills, Karma grows enormous, gorging to satisfy the appetites of the Shadow King, the disembodied mind of an Egyptian crimelord once trapped in the astral plane who inhabits her body for his own vicarious purposes, fulfilling fantasies of consumption, disguise, and desire. In the throes of this possession, she traps her former team members— who had thought her dead—and pits them against one another in a gladiator-style battle for an audience of the international elite. Always a risk when using other bodies as a personality, she is submerged in the appropriation of *her* physical form; the Shadow King even dresses her physical body like a geisha in an enormous kimono and top-knot. Possessed, she becomes her own enemy; could the dangers of inhabiting other bodies be more obvious?

The Queer Appeal of Cyborgs

Because of this fluidity, this mobility, feminist and queer appropriations of science fictions are rewriting gender and sexuality in cyberspaces, fashioning pervert avatars in drag and powerful cyborg selves in a space perceived as boundaryless. If digital space makes possible a Cartesian abstraction or the commoditization of the flesh, it also suggests that there is no necessary mimetic or expressive relation of psychical identifications to physical bodies. Digital space represents a situation in which the interiority of subjectivity is no longer easily located on the subject's flesh, potentially disrupting the (presumption of an) expressive relationship between embodiment and social identity. The image in digital space does not necessarily refer to an actually existing object/subject or body; the virtual medium is a medium for discontinuity. The detachment of public personae from the physical location/material of the body can have the effect often attributed to drag or transgender identifications, denaturalizing gender norms and making possible the articulation of a plurality of sexual subjectivities.

It is at this juncture of theory and technology that many feminist and queer scholars have engaged cybernetic politics as a space of identity play and gender reconstruction.[5] A *Wired* editorial extols the virtues of cyberfeminism "based on the idea that, in conjunction with technology, it's possible to construct your identity, your sexuality, even your gender, just as you please."[6] Others argue that "[a]ll the things that separate people, all the supposedly immutable facts of gender and geography, don't matter quite so much when we're all in the machine together."[7] Thus, digital space is hailed as a liberatory space, disrupting the social determinism of the body from the identifications of the self, allowing for sex play/gender fuck transcending the unidirectional implication of "sexual orientation" and gender norms. This radical potential is often identified with the gender trouble instigated by Judith Butler—that is, that gender does not constitute a metaphysics of presence, that a particular gender is not inherent to a particular sexed body, and that sex and gender do not thus exist in a one-to-one expressive relation to each other, that sex itself is a gendered construct.[8] The appeal of drag as a metaphor for subversion in digital space is located in the act of cross-identification and *self-conscious* performance. Utilizing various modes of performance, drag is theorized as the revelation of the prosthetic nature of gender. Rather than a "bad copy," drag is the disclosure of *no* original, of the fabrication of gender as essence through the repetition of its expectations and signifying systems by the "wrong" sex.[9] Both drag and digital space make possible the nonmimetic mapping of bodies, dislocating embodiment from social identity or self. Both imagine new ways of making subjects—including cyborgs as drag queens or genderqueer rebels—seemingly free of social imperatives. Drawing upon Butler's arguments, feminist and queer scholars like Thomas Foster, Allucquere Roseanne (Sandy) Stone, Cynthia Fuchs and many others have argued that the cyborg offers an imaginative site for radical potential because "nothing in a cyborg body is essential."[10] This crucial recognition—that nothing in a body, cyborg or not, is essential—does not, however, null the body.

As such, feminist and queer science fictions do negotiate the body in digital space in complex ways. In Melissa Scott's novel *Trouble and Her Friends*, a group of gay and lesbian computer hackers have been implanted with "brainworms," neural-electrical connections that allow them to directly interface their nervous systems with cybernetic networks—the now-familiar prosthetic capacity for "jacking in" in cyberpunk science fiction.[11] Of them the main protagonist India Carless, a white lesbian hacker (with a suggestively "colorful" name), abandons the shadow world of brainworms, dollie slots, and hacking ICE (Intrusive Countermeasures Electronic) when an electronic surveillance act is passed by the U.S. Congress (notably, against an international treaty). She is compelled to return to the networks when someone adopts her former code name—Trouble—to wreak havoc. The specter of government regulation inspires a crisis of identity for her circle of friends, who are also faced with the choice to "go straight, moving out of the shadows into the bright lights of the legal world, the legal nets."[12] The dangers of "going straight" are clear—whether assimilation into the mainstream of computer technicians and system operators, legally bound to follow a set of rules and conventions, or assimilation into the mainstream of heteronormativity and "wholesome" values. In contrast, digital space represents for the characters a space of liberation as queer individuals whose mobility is constrained and regulated in "real life"—it is a place where "a woman could easily be as hard and tough as any man,"[13] where their skills are the measure of their worth, not their sexualities. Nevertheless there is prejudice in the world of hackers too, including a kind of corporeal disgust for those hackers who've had the "brainworm" implanted. At one point Trouble speculates that "maybe that was why the serious netwalkers, the original inhabitants of the nets, hated the brainworm: not so much because it gave a different value, a new meaning, to the skills of the body, but because it meant taking that risk, over and above the risk of the worm itself. Maybe that was why it was almost always the underclasses, the women, the people of color, the gay people, the ones who were already stigmatized as being vulnerable, available, trapped by the body, who took the risk of the wire."[14] The novel groups women, queers, and people of color as a category of individuals willing to take more risks with the body because this "stigmatized" body has not been historically available as a vehicle for liberal subjectivity. The hope of "escaping" these social constraints (and acts of violence) is articulated in this novel as a possibility located in the antiessentialist ether of digital space; but this imagined capacity for radical inclusion, attributed to the prosthetic sociality afforded by cyberspace, treads dangerous ground. This is a queer cyborg subjectivity enabled by a purported universality in which digital space facilitates not only an escape from social location but also the reappropriation of the queer cyborg as a recombinant liberal subject. Whether in the replication of a universal antagonism (binary gender), in statements of solidarity or in the hope for gender and/or sexual insurrection, these accounts are often characterized by a critical lack of attention to examining the boundaries drawn around gender and/or sexuality as a social category to the exclusion of other vectors of analysis.

Nor is the transgender subject necessarily any more suited to resolving this dilemma. Sandy Stone suggests that in cyberspace, "the transgendered body is the natural body. The nets are spaces of transformation, identity factories in which bodies are meaning machines, and transgender—identity as performance, as play, as wrench in the smooth gears of the social apparatus of vision—is the ground state."[15] While aptly articulating the challenge to gender expressivity that digital space and virtuality may pose, the seeming elevation of a singular or "natural" subject/body should give us pause, as should the seeming reduction of identity to performance and play. Having dismantled the mythology of a natural woman located in biological or psychic substance in both patriarchal and feminist discourse, or the universality of "queer" as a signifier for fluid and mobile sexual or intellectual practices, can the substitution of another body—however self-consciously constructed—as a universal subject provide a new paradigm for future identification? Where is the agency of this body located? Is it in the act of passing among other nonmimetic bodies? Is the transracial body *also* a natural body? And in considering this last question, to what extent can digital drag acts and the queer challenges these pose to traditional relations between sex and gender ideologically and politically occlude—if not contain—an emergent discourse (and conflict) with transracial performance?

In these science fictions mutant bodies and cyborg bodies are analogized as minoritarian bodies, subjected and subjugated, but the limits of this analogy are striking. Moreover, these "stigmatized" bodies are differently disciplined through sometimes conflicting and sometimes collaborating operations and structures; the work of intervening in these operations and structures must account for these different modalities of social subjection. In one problematic instance, the blurred boundaries of human-machine have inspired allusions to Gloria Anzaldúa's work to describe deracinated cyborg subjects with a gendered and racialized geopolitical vocabulary; for instance, the iconography of the borderland and mestiza in Sandy Stone's theoretical project is used to describe *all* agents participating in electronic virtual communities.[16] The representation of the mestiza as a privileged figure transcending racial and ethnic boundaries—or those boundaries between physical and virtual space—is also the problematic relocation of a specific configuration of history, gender, race, sexuality, and nation. What are the consequences of theorizing the cyborg as mestiza for the actually existing (racial) mestiza? For the mestiza who works in the *maquiladoras* (factories) of multinational electronics industries, the mestiza who is "in the machine," but in a radically different relation? What are the consequences of equalizing the imaginative gap between physical and virtual space with the juridical sociopolitical division of the U.S.-Mexican border? To what extent does the particularity of race (or racialized gender) as a social or subjective force disappear in order to extend the metaphor of hybridity? Far from allowing a neutral or transgressive subject position of liberty or autonomy, this powerful fantasy of the hybrid cyborg subject can function as a technology for seeming to become "other" while allowing for the reassertion of the agency and fluidity of the liberal self. The argument that "bodies don't matter here" might be another kind of prosthesis in and of itself—the deliberate disdain of a tangled materiality for a uniformly prophylactic body, encased in hard plastic and disguised as a safe sociality because in digital space, *everybody has one*. It is a queer erasure indeed.

Overkill

Just where does the science fiction end and the cyborg possibilities begin? Feminist and queer fictions of digital space and technological transformations of the body blur the boundaries in the search for a utopian space, simultaneously producing and contesting the political terms of liberalism. In particular, the novel *Nearly Roadkill: An Infobahn Erotic Adventure* uses practices of gender play to conceptualize virtual reality and digital space in a curious blend of liberal humanism and postmodern queer theory.[17] Transgender theorist Kate Bornstein and Caitlin Sullivan's collaborative work explicitly probes the possibilities for transgendered performances in contemporary cybernetic technologies (which are also suggested by Bornstein in her nonfiction "guide" to sexual subversion, *The Gender Workbook*),[18] while demonstrating the limits of the drag/transgender metaphor for digital embodiment. Set in the near future, the central characters, Winc and Scratch, are ordinary users (i.e., not hackers) who enjoy the performance of a host of differently sexed and gendered identities in chat rooms, message boards, and instantaneous private exchanges. In the course of their online flirtations and flings in various textually rendered bodies, they examine the nonmimesis of gender, sex, and desire and fall in love. They do not reveal their physical bodies to either the readers or each other until halfway through the novel, at which point we learn that Winc is a male-to-female transsexual whose gender identity remains fluid and unfounded and Scratch is a butch lesbian. Notably their whiteness, unlike their complicated negotiations with gender and sexuality, is invisible and implied in the absence of explicit racial markers. During the course of the novel Winc and Scratch inadvertently become rebel icons for a larger community of users, having refused both to mimetically reproduce themselves in their online gender and sexual performances and to register their "real" identities with the U.S. government. Corporations have pressured the government to pursue this program of registration as a mutual venture of the public and private sectors, making it possible to gather demographic data and to tailor advertisements and strategies of surveillance for individual users based on the given information. Against the enthusiastic endorsement of actual cyberlibertarians like R. U. Sirius—for whom "commerce is the ocean that information swims in"[19] —these fictional queer agents are seeking an escape from the commoditization of being and compulsory consumption. Against the "natural" order of the corporation (made "natural" through sheer ubiquity) in digital spaces, Winc and Scratch seek to resist the field of invisibility cloaking the corporate logo and capital through which the contemporary social body travels.[20]

Winc and Scratch are postmodern queer hero(in)es, and their virtual and actual acts of performance and "becoming" are clearly meant to be read as modes of transgressive mobility and fluidity, colored with the liberation of desire. While the state and transnational capital are located as nodes of power creating and regulating gendered citizen consumers, digital space is envisioned as an untamed and radically decentered expanse in danger from commercial colonization. They are the ultimate, technologically enhanced drag performers, imaginatively speeding through digital guises and urban spaces eluding captures of all kinds. And while themes of anticorporate resistance are not new to science fiction, it is rare that such resistance is spearheaded by a queer couple who simply want to fuck however they chose. The valence of choice becomes the pivotal antagonism of the novel: between government/corporation and the individual, assigned gender and gender fluidity, regulation, and liberty.

Perhaps nowhere is the extent of virtual systems' premise of unfettered mobility more evident than in an appeal for democratic liberal pluralism, made later in the novel as the characters discuss the implications of their rebellion. Weighing their options, Winc and Scratch argue that digital space is where "anyone who can't speak up because they were always afraid of being put in their place" is granted the freedom to do so—to speak out, to act up.[21] But while Winc and Scratch imagine that anybody—female, black, Latino, "Asians getting off the boat in California," gay, lesbian—can live more freely in digital space, "there is almost no consideration of how this technology might be used by blacks, Latinos, or Asians, despite their inclusion in the list of social subjects who might share [their] attitude toward the Internet."[22] The implications of this conversation are otherwise ignored. How might these other subjects—who are hardly a homogeneous bunch—access, use, and interpret the mobility offered by digital space? And would this necessarily entail a *desire to escape location or engage in identity play*, and if so, could we be assured that the meanings attached to these acts would be the same, or familiar to Winc and Scratch?

What is also not acknowledged is that at least some of these "others" are subjects of an abject modernity, encompassing vulnerable (biological) bodies, militarized borders, and microchip assembly lines.[23] As such, the recombinant liberal subject can be read as an autonomous social agent *on the condition* of the making of other kinds of cyborgs, highly gendered and racialized workers mechanized and merged as interchangeable parts, widgets in a different order of machinic-organic assemblage. So while the question of race and transracial performance is always already implicated in the electronic environment—whether figured as invisible labor or identity play—it is overwhelmed by the spectacular and celebratory narrative of gender and sexual cross-identifications in the novel. When race *is* invoked it is always problematically aligned as a category either parallel to gender or altogether alien.

In the midst of an online dialogue about gender uncertainty and the context of ambiguity while occupying one of her online personae, Leila, Scratch muses, "There's this civil rights march in my neighborhood once a year. All of us, black and white, march in it. Suddenly people smile at me who wouldn't give me the time of day otherwise. The colors of our skin don't matter then, because it's *that* day, that march." Assuming "Leila" is black, and unaware that she is a persona animated by Scratch, Winc replies, "I hadn't even considered your race. Ouch." "Exactly. You probably assumed I was white, right?" Scratch then "wearily" replies, "It's OK, it happens all the time. One of the cool things for black folks online is they are assumed to be white, too. Not that they want to be white, but they're assumed to be 'in the club,' without having to prove credentials at the door."[24]

This brief passage juxtaposes a field of racial discourses in complicated and sometimes contradictory ways. In the first instance the force of racism is located in the alleged fixity of visual knowledge. Its apparent counterstrategy is situated in the technologically enhanced ability to pass, extended by digital space to all persons of color. Passing here is construed as transgressive because it traverses boundaries of social identity, and because it exposes the categories as arbitrary. Yet passing is not a secured set of political effects or meanings, but instead encompasses a range of exercises and radically different implications for different subjects seeking to pass through different and uneven relations of power. The ability to pass is interpreted here as a deliberate strategy to reap certain benefits and avoid harassment, though the privileged body (white, male, heterosexual) retains its social power as the neutral body. In appropriating the rhetoric of disembodied abstraction, the asymmetry of corporeality ascribing universalism to some bodies and particularism to others is problematically reproduced in digital space. As a counterstrategy, passing in this instance depends upon the silence and invisibility of the minoritarian subject even as "the humiliating positivity of the particular" is attached to her body. Because this prosthetic of abstraction—facilitating the claim to legitimacy and mobility—is a relative privilege, the reproduction of the "bodiless citizen" of liberal humanism as a transcendent cyborg position in virtual systems is a clear danger, permitting the black body only an incorporeal participation in the dominant cultural body. Even as liberty is imagined as effortless mobility, it sets the terms of prosthetic sociality and places limits upon marked subjects who have no previous claim to abstraction. The presence of race is a disruption in a space that claims an asymmetrical neutrality. Oddly enough, Scratch, whose transgendered performances deliberately inspire anxiety, does not ask the obvious question, Why not be disruptive?

The answer—or *her* answer—is contained within the same conversation. Raised in this passage is the assurance that racial difference is easily surmounted—that in the visual absence of epidermis or because of an assumed political solidarity, race as an organizing principle and/or disruption disappears and "the colors of our skin don't matter." Scratch, feigning fatigue and passing as black, reiterates the sovereignty of the recombinant liberal subject—the "cool thing" about online sociality is that it allows "black folks" to adopt the prosthetic of whiteness.Here again race is imagined as *only* a superficial visual regime, and racism is abstracted from its historicity in ideological apparatus and social relations. However, even as Scratch asserts that cyberspace allows black people to pass as white, she herself passes as black by signifying race at all. The social transgression of her genderfuck is aligned with her passing, functioning to position transgender drag on an expressive level approximating that of racial otherness. The theoretical celebration of blurred boundaries and pluralism masks the act of appropriation here, disguised as empathy or the denaturalization of racial categories. The passage thus performs the elision of whiteness as transparency—and not necessarily as an effect or privilege of power—even while positing gender as functionally and politically "the same" as race, *even while* reductively assigning race a merely visual affect/effect and the positivity of particularity. These moves position the two kinds of racial drag in lopsided and slippery opposition; for while the prosthesis of neutral whiteness allows black people to passively participate as abstract individuals, Scratch's own transracial performance functions, like her drag, as self-conscious transgression. Thus, the structural and discursive distinction between the black subject who passes as white and the white subject who passes as black is not disavowed but *reconstituted* in an unfolding power play, displaced by the drag metaphor, in which the white subject reasserts her agency (and appropriation) as privilege and her "special" knowledge (about civil rights, the suffering of African Americans, etc.) as authority.

When Winc and Scratch do finally interact face to face, Scratch admits to a seemingly endless desire to occupy multiple personae, a desire that she is uniquely able to fulfill online, in which she juxtaposes racial identity with animal: "I wish I were black because I hate my skin and probably next week being a wolf would be even better."[25] For her, both blackness and animalness signify escape from the felt abjection of inhabiting her particular body—and their juxtaposition has an imperial archive that is obscured in the "play" of the virtual interface. Such fantasies of identifying with and knowing "others" through a proximity, or, in the case of digital space, *approximation* of the "other," reify a racial being while simultaneously establishing a normative (e.g., white) self against which racial otherness is performed as radical difference. For Scratch, that radical distance from her sense of self can best be articulated as blackness or animalness in a romantic appeal to a state of being prefigured as more real, more authentic, more primal, perhaps—an appeal that has a lengthy history in colonial and imperial relations. As a queer subject whose mobility is deemed her weapon, her willingness to occupy blackness is represented as an empathic, rather than preemptive, identification. This fantasy of redemptive identification appropriates/approximates the (imagined) experiences of racial or national otherness while depoliticizing the social powers that produce them. This racial difference is fixed in order for Scratch to imagine herself as a transgressive subject, redefined by her consumption of this otherness in which blackness becomes a fetish-object *through which she comes to know her self.*[26] The list of "Latinos, Asians, et cetera" cited elsewhere in the novel as a multicultural vision of digital potential is nominally fulfilled by Scratch's appropriation of *all* difference as her drag and/or her desire.

In a novel that otherwise celebrates digital space as the denaturalization of gendered and sexual norms and the proliferation of multiplicity, race is both mythologized as radical difference ("I want to be black because I don't want to be me") and radical similarity ("I can pass for black because color doesn't matter here"). Winc and Scratch are queer agents whose universality (as rebels, as countercultural heroes) reanimates the production of an abstract, sovereign subject that is instrumentalized in a liberal humanist discourse of digital space.[27] Their protests and play are limited to the language of individual rights and the promise of mobility, and freedom is defined as individual license and couched in the rhetoric of "choice." It is an emancipatory project that reproduces the liberal cyborg subject as the ideal condition of personhood, with a twist. If the transgender body is the *natural* body in the cybernetic interface because its nonmimetic logic is universalized, then transgender *in this instance* becomes the neutral subject position that secures liberty and autonomy, and digital space is the field of fantasy in which particularities are rendered equivalent, even while racial positivity (especially when articulated as nonwhiteness) continues to figure (if sometimes inadvertently) as surplus, difference, or disruption. Resting on the liberal premise of equality, the antiessentialism of cross- or transgender identification in digital space can thus subsume and mask the differential reception and meanings of racial or transracial identification. That race, gender, and sexuality are simultaneous modalities of social subjection does not mean that they operate analogously, or that the technologies of their regulation or the strategies for their transgression and destabilization will be commensurate. This queer practice cannot destabilize racial categories as a scientific concept, biological or metaphysical essence, or even as a system of classification simply by refusing to acknowledge its borders; and this queer cyborg subject may designate a flexible space that accommodates various and fluctuating positions, but its ambiguity also creates a space of ahistoricity, of social forces and cultural asymmetries once again rendered invisible.

Can this queer cyborg subject conceptualize an avatar that isn't an escape? After all, as a young girl I was inclined toward revenge—feelings of betrayal aside, this was not an identification with abstract bodilessness. There was no small part of me that sought to recuperate my body, this ill-fit, awkward thing, through the exercise of my hoped-for mutant powers. As such, Karma might provide an alternate route of the politicization of the queer cyborg subject. It is significant that as a New Mutant she wears a uniform, but not a mask; in refusing to do so, she deliberately forsakes her "secret identity," the abstract prosthesis of normalcy, passing, or identity play. So rather than imagine escape, we might imagine disruption, like Karma reading the histories of our mutant/cyborg/queer bodies into the matrix to indict the social powers and material conditions that produced the regulatory apparatus of deviance and normalcy.

Re-Membering Our Cyborg Bodies

"I sold my first harness yesterday!" Karyn tells me, quite excitedly, in a downtown Oakland restaurant where, I am almost sure, such words have never before been uttered. An attractive, heterosexual Chinese American woman with a penchant for black metal (black-colored pieces of metal) and longhaired Nordic types, Karyn stirs her soup as she's relating her "firsts"—first vibrator, first dildo, first harness sold. I think to myself that I've never seen anybody get so excited about their retail job, and wonder if the glow of selling sex toys—even for a women-owned collective business—will fade in time. Jokingly, I ask her to differentiate one harness from another, and she launches into a lecture—still fresh in her mind—given to her just the day before. I get dizzy with the wide array of choices available on the market and my mind starts wandering into theory, as it often does when not corralled, and I begin to speculate about the reach of consumer capitalism and the liberation offered by the commodity, and, Oh dear, should I be thinking these things while Karyn explains the difference between silicone and rubber?

I remind her to let me know where and how the products she sells are manufactured, again.

I tell this story because before I rediscovered the comics, I began thinking through digital space by way of the dildo (so often accompanied by the harness), which I had been thinking about in terms of historicity, multiple modes of production, and material relations. Sexuality is implicated in the spatial dynamics and the economies of late capitalism, producing and organizing desire; and the merger of the multibillion-dollar sex industry with plastics technologies inspired bold entrepreneurship in the realm of prosthetic parts, the imaginative stuff that stocks the shelves of the above-mentioned, internationally renowned feminist sex shop. In this context, the figure of the dildo in lesbian theorizing occupies a prominent location in sexual subversion, skewering notions of an authentic lesbian sexuality and "[turning] techno-culture's semiotic regime of simulation and the political economy of consumer culture back against the naturalization of masculinist hegemony."[28] As poststructuralist feminist and queer scholars have argued, conflating a representation (a dildo) with reality (a penis) is problematic; the dildo is not a penis, nor does it necessarily refer to a "real" penis. The mass-produced dildo does however expose the penis as itself only a representation or a failed imitation of the phantasmatic phallus, a copy of a copy of that infamous seat (or staff) of patriarchal power.[29] The site of the dildo, then, is open to multiple modes of inquiry—its mass production as a commodity in transnational capital, its meaning production as an erotic object of queer sexuality and (to invoke the cyborg in the dildo) the resulting interface of automaton and autonomy. As a technology/toy, the dildo (with or without the stabilizing harness) enables a fluidity and mobility of sexual practices and meanings. Still, as Heather Findlay observes, "lesbians with uncooperative sexual tastes still market and purchase politically incorrect dildos that are shaped like penises and named after mythological patriarchs, as in the 'Adam I' or the 'Jupiter II.'"[30] Clearly there is more to be disentangled than cords, buckles, or loose limbs—if the representation is not equivalent to the reality, then what does it mean, and why?

In the electronic environment, the disavowal of the material flesh on a visual register is partnered by a simultaneous preoccupation with the digital reconfiguration of bodily pleasures, the virtual striptease of concealment and exposure in parts. Something about sex lends itself to prostheses, the body capable of incor-porating a wide range of attachments, physical *or* psychic, and as such something about cyberspace lends itself to sex, an appended metaphor for artificial bodies, the technological imaginary and mediated sociality, or what Howard Rheingold calls "teledildonics."[31] Imagining a technology that will allow users to map their physical bodies onto virtual images and translate movements in digital space into sensual stimuli, the possibilities—wiring virtual hand to physical crotch—again suggest the breakdown of the mimetic relationship between material flesh and electronic prosthesis. But as I have argued, all bodies in electronic space are prosthetic—involving technological extensions or reinventions of the body and its senses. Thus, digital space is often theorized as the penultimate *play* space, where "asymmetrical power relationships [become] part of a much larger and more diverse erotic and experimental toolkit,"[32] and an eroticized technology will offer "pleasures of corporeality that render meaningless the arbitrary di-visions of animal, spirit, and machine."[33] An entire economy of longing and desire is organized around this impasse of presence and absence, embodiment and abstraction; clearly, erotic electronic technologies *depend* upon the signs of difference to establish the parameters of interfacial fantasy and subsequent transgression. But such that digital space and all its prostheses are sites of contest (like the dildo), we cannot assume that the fact that digital space makes pos-sible this more diverse "erotic toolkit" that the form that follows is necessarily subversive. The relevant inquiry would thus be, If *prostheses* does not reference a "real," organic body, what does it *mean* in digital space? Do our prostheses emerge fully formed and innocent into circuits of desire, without memory? Do they necessarily circumvent the referentiality of bodies or produce new tangles?

Several years ago, browsing Good Vibrations in San Francisco, I stumbled over a African-American History Month display. On a low-standing table cov-ered in kente cloth sat propped-up porn videos featuring black performers, "black erotica" novels and how-to guides, and a veined black rubber dildo, com-plete with testicles, modeled on black porn star Sean Williams's penis. Though on some level this collection was "merely" an exhibition of the goods and commodi-ties available for purchase in this worker-run collective—an organization that is explicit in its sex-radical feminist politics—its display was provocative.[34] Michel Foucault warns that sexuality is not simply a stubborn drive or animal instinct adverse to control; sexuality is endowed with "the greatest instrumentality" in relations of power, the affective quality of historical circumstances and haunting absences.[35] Again, the notion of "instrumentality" is double-edged; Karyn tells me that the "realistic" black dildo is immensely popular, as Alycee J. Lane also attests— "What does it mean when white hegemony extends to the production of dildos?" —during her own foray into sex-shop bins.[36] When approached simply, prosthetic bodies (and parts) are assumed to be autonomous objects/subjects possessing meanings independent of the particular circumstances of their pro-duction or reception. The black dildo is simply molded, tinted rubber on the shelf on the sex shop, and in digital space all bodies are *just* bodies because they are deliberate fictions in the absence of physical verification—we lack evidence, or the evidence of bodies (or body parts) is disassembled. And though the virtual avatar or the rubber dildo does not necessarily refer to an original or factual reality, the significance of the prosthesis still is produced through a contest of meaning that refers to a body politic. There is a politics embedded in the production, circulation, and consumption of sex toys beyond the dominant and often reductive discourses of deviancy or liberation.

I bring up the dildo in the midst of comic-book characters and science fictions in order to make two points about the material production of these (fantasies of) prostheses and the constructedness of all our images and realities. I began this inquiry with a question: What are the implications for mutant cyborg futures for Karma, whose powers to possess are the "reap what you sow" result of the systematic destruction of the war in Southeast Asia, and whose body inspires suspicions (traitor, gook, foreigner, freak) of all kinds? And from Karma's body to others like hers, not so "lucky," who stayed or immigrated, too: What are the implications for transgression when the bodies of Asian and Asian immigrant women workers (in sweatshops and factories of varying working conditions) provide the labor for the production of dildos and circuit boards, those instruments of identity play, mobility, and freedom? How do we account for the "other" social forces in the exploration of sexual and gender plurality—like the gendered economies of service labor, and other kinds of desire (for money, for food, for power)? We have the "new mutant" produced from the conjuncture of U.S. militarisms and economic imperatives and the "new cyborg" produced from the same. Their prosthetic existence, technologically enhanced by the technologies of war and mass production, implicates the racial geographies of transnational capital, globalization, and postcolonialism. Clearly, the hope that we might elude the naturalized order of the corporation (and the state) in digital space or queer sex play—as Winc and Scratch seek to do—is itself implicated in the technology.

Importantly, these realities of free trade zones and biochemical defoliants, sexual deviance and racial pathology, dildos and motherboards, are apprehended as meaningful through images and representations. We cannot retreat to "essence" or "experience" as an antidote to the fictions of hypersexual black men or limitless cyborg desire. While there is a physical world external to language, no order of meaning exists in itself in a thing called "reality." Without assigning meaning to the black dildo in the feminist sex shop, I would argue that it is impossible to transcend the politics of the prosthesis/signifier; to invoke Jacques Derrida, we are forced to take a detour through signs. What does it mean that an eight-inch "monster" dildo, complete with veins and testicles, is named "The Beast" and only comes in black?[37] Is it possible to consider the reference to animalistic fervor, paired with an exclusive hue, without recognizing and grappling with the troubling historical allusion to a vilified black male sexuality?[38] Having invested bodies with the power and knowledge relations of discipline, management and constraint, these various representations do not reveal or conceal their empirical referents; they *constitute* them. The prosthetic, without referencing a real (flesh) body, can still approximate a (symbolic) body politic and sometimes a troubled or troubling one, and in addition to the obvious body politic of its material production. That is, the absence of a material referent—never mind Sean Williams, or the fact that Karma is a fictional character, or the commodity fetish that "disappears" laboring bodies—does not occlude the prosthesis as a site of meaning or historical citation. The hope that a return to the "real"—of bodies, of experiences, of social relations—will act as an antidote to these representations and fictions ignores the fact that the image, the prosthetic, *is* a social relation. While there is no *particular* black person who is necessarily immobilized in this particular citation by a feminist collective for the purposes of a "celebratory" display, *blackness* is domesticated as an image and a subject position. So too are the bodies of labor and war, whose gendered Asianness is defined by "nimble fingers" or the "mere gook rule." As such, avatars and dildos are meaningful codes formed in relation to an "outside," with social forces implicated in their exchange. To insist on the historical and relational grounds of meaning is to resist divorcing the fetish object from its productive conditions—in this circumstance, the total abstraction of the prosthetic from social relations (the black dildo means nothing, and is produced invisibly) or in the uncritical reiteration of stereotype (the Black Buck, for instance).

While the resignification of bodies, of names, of parts, is politically compelling, we cannot sever this project from its structuring conditions—those that gave rise to the need to imagine resistance, or from the site of contest, in which it must produce its meaning. To make sense of our prostheses, analytically and politically, or to imagine how we might assign new meanings, we are forced to resituate them within the conditions of their construction or manufacture, and in the context and circumstances of their usage. We must therefore attend critically to what kinds of subjects digital space produces at this interface of the automaton and autonomy, the machinic and the human. What seemingly new articulations are given form and what might these occlude, or displace? What are the possibilities and what are the limitations of resignifying—a body, a practice, a name, a prosthesis? Consider the dildo in the harness as a metaphor, imbued with layers of meaning and performance. A prosthesis molded and painted by an assembly line of orderly machines and ordered immigrant women workers, a copy of a copy of the imaginary phallus, a sly subversion of masculinist prerogative, and a web of straps connoting the constraining, the taming of the nonhuman, animal or abject. Silicone, rubber, plastic or leather, vinyl, D-rings or clasps, the contradictory connotation of this amalgam of technologies/toys is a desire realized through both control and abandon, confinement and release, possessor and possessed. As such, is it any surprise that the prosthesis (the image or representation) may easily become the location of both sexual *and* racial "terror and desire,"[39] of control and the promise of freedom?

These comments return us to the hopes of progressive discourses of digital space, and the transracial identifications of queer agents like Scratch, who seek to bridge the imaginative gap between self and other by adopting a prosthesis that may harness an image in the attempt to "free" it by claiming a loving identification with radical difference while eliding the circuits of power. Her approach to blackness—as radical similarity and radical difference—indicates her knowledge of a difference that is subsequently disavowed: it is there but it is not. Her fetish produces the desire to encompass and consume difference while renouncing it, or more problematically, seeking to resolve that difference in its consumption. Reading the classic Freudian account in which the (heterosexual) fetishist's object allays the absence of a relation between the sexes, Findlay similarly suggests that "the black dildo fetish can 'make acceptable' a specifically racial lack—the lack, that is, under white hegemony of a relation between the races.... [T]he big black dildo allows whites to carry on a relation with blacks that is, in reality, no relation at all."[40]

All these fears and fantasies of floating, unattached prostheses are deeply implicated in each other, and what is often unremarked is the *political power* of their fictions, their thick historicity haunting the "positive" space of our prosthetic sociality. If we are not after all separate from our machines, it seems that our machines now embody our most radically symbolic activity—representing ourselves to ourselves, or in the often violent, always vexed interface of social relations.

The Future of Cyborgs and Mutants

What digital space could then mean for our politics is both problematic and profound. What had previously been established as separate domains (the virtual and the real) are mutually informed processes of signification; and our prostheses are not just symbolic but instead symptomatic of our contemporary contradictions. The fetish of digital space, of the body released from history or mimesis or materiality, manifests for progressive discourses both the hope for liberation from prior meaning and the desire to become the instrument of resolution. Digital space, as a redemptive technology of new life forms, may reproduce a modernizing or progressive idealism that reiterates the limits of transgression in the *political* coding of race (as difference) as disruptive. The cyborg may designate an elastic and progressive space that accommodates multiple and fluctuating positions, including social misfits, drag queens and kings, and transgendered rebels, but its ambiguity must not resubordinate the subjects (recalling Winc and Scratch's list of Latinos, Asians, etc.) for whom such claims are made by erasing the historicity of those social forces and relations of power that generated the desire to be "free" in the first place.

The progressive, feminist, and queer discourses of digital space examined here are limited in scope—in defining freedom as license, liberation as choice, and identity as self-fashioned. They adhere to liberal democratic models of subjectivity and publicity premised on the imagined absence of social forces and the micro- and macropolitics of power. The fact of incoherence—of signs and signifiers mismatched, of bodies disappeared or made anew (or seemingly so), of social identity detached from material flesh—does not necessarily signal the disruption of a more hegemonic reality, and such incoherence can be easily accommodated by equally fluid rearticulations of power.[41] A more useful approach to digital space would necessarily find ways to discuss the production of signs and circuit boards simultaneously, study the material and ideological labor of the technological imaginary, and examine the differential ways in which the blurring of flesh machine manifests across free trade zones and troublesome histories of colonial fantasy.[42] To otherwise affirm an antiessentialist subject while asserting a unified subjectivity through the valence of the transcendent cyborg, endlessly shifting and ambiguous but somehow outside of social forces or relations of power and capital, is a posture of erasure and danger.

And because her name, after all, invokes return and reprisal, I want to look to Karma one last time for a guiding lesson about agency, control, and the ambivalent instrumentality of our prostheses. As a "new mutant" she is a marginal being whose existence poses a question and a threat to the normative social body and to the status quo of human relations, but not simply because of her powers—these cannot be isolated from the historical conditions of her creation as a Vietnamese mutant subject. While her psychic powers disallow a reductive conflation of body with subjectivity, or a necessary expressive relation between interiority and exteriority, she grounds the play of self and nonself in a nuanced contest of social forces and circuits of power. No matter how powerful her prosthesis, her marginalized body is vulnerable; rather than allow for total mobility, her mutant superpowers—literally and figuratively marked with an *X* for excess, for exclusion, for ex-human—illustrate the dangers of reproducing an abstract subject through the discourses of antiessentialism or liberal humanism. So while the celebration of porosity between mind and body in discourses of technological mobility would pose a subject who is able to transcend the flesh, Karma's creation as a mutant subject and its constitutive conditions must be *looked at* rather than *looked through*. Last spotted as a pinkhaired lesbian film student, she defected from superhero-dom because she could no longer abide by the comic book universe of binarisms, which allowed little room for contradiction or complexity. Mobility and fluidity are not the apex of freedoms, as Karma learns the hard way (the only way in the comic books), and there are consequences and dangers involved in the prosthesis. After all, the possibilities and limitations of her prosthetic abilities make Karma a more critical queer cyborg subject *in her Vietnamese-ness*, distinct not because of an essence but because of the epistemic and corporeal violence involved in the production of her existence, because of the contours of her historically specific biotechnological transformation from human girl to *something more.*

But even if no cyborg is ever born innocent—like Karma, born of a neocolonial encounter and possessed of a comparable power to occupy other bodies—this does not mean we may not simultaneously take *some* pleasure in our cyborgs and yet interrogate the conditions of their existence, as science or fiction. Against a nostalgic discourse of authentic selves or organic interaction, of natural bodies and traditional communities, what might instead be revealed in digital space is the constructedness of all selves, interaction, bodies, and communities; what must be attended to are the structures and relations that produce different kinds of subjects in position with different kinds of technologies.[43] While the cyborg bodies we create to navigate these new spaces will not resolve the material realities or social contradictions of their manufacture, they provide a rich assemblage of myths, legends, fears, fantasies, codes, and tools with which to interrogate which bodies matter and why. In doing so we might be better equipped to imagine or even achieve alliances among mutants and cyborgs alike.

Notes

1. The term *genetic cyborg* is also used by Mark Oehlert in his essay, "From Captain America to Wolverine: Cyborgs in Comic Books, Alternative Images of Cybernetic Heroes and Villains," in *The Cyborg Handbook,* ed. Chris Hables Gray (New York: Routledge, 1995), 219–32.

2. Among the original New Mutants, Xi'an Coy Manh is the only member who might be read as a symptom of modernity's violence. The others—a wary Cherokee woman able to manifest images from others' mind as spirit forms; a naive Appalachian boy who becomes a flying, invulnerable human cannonball; an insecure Scottish human-wolf shapeshifter; and a black Brazilian boy who inexplicably draws upon the sun to become a roiling energy mass—are simply mutants with no particular explanation for their abilities.

3. Lauren Berlant, "National Brands, National Body: Imitation of Life" in *The Phantom Public Sphere,* ed. Bruce Robbins (Minneapolis: University of Minnesota Press, 1993), 176.

4. Lisa Nakamura, "Race in/for Cyberspace: Identity Tourism and Racial Passing on the Internet," in *The Cybercultures Reader,* ed. David Bell and Barbara M. Kennedy (New York: Routledge, 2000), 718. Lauren Berlant identifies this code crossing as "borrowing the corporeal logic of an other, or a fantasy of that logic, and adopting it like a prosthesis"; see Berlant, "National Brands," 200.

5. Alternately, cyberfeminist theorist Sadie Plant has argued that the electronic environment provides a pre-oedipal space that reflects a "feminine subjectivity" of weaving and webs, destroying patriarchal control: "[A]t the peak of his triumph, the culmination of his machinic erections, man confronts the system he built for his own protection and finds it is female and dangerous"; see Plant, "On the Matrix: Cyberfeminist Simulations," in Bell and Kennedy, eds., *The Cybercultures Reader,* 335.

6. Hari Kunzu, quoted in Jeff Ow, "The Revenge of the Yellowfaced Cyborg: The Rape of Digital Geishas and the Colonization of Cyber-Coolies in 3D Realms' *Shadow Warrior,*" in *Race and Cyberspace,* ed. Beth E. Kolko, Lisa Nakamura, and Gilbert B. Rodman (New York: Routledge, 2000), 52.

7. Shannon McRae, "Coming Apart at the Seams: Sex, Text, and the Virtual Body," in

Wired_Women: Gender and New Realities in Cyberspace, ed. Lynn Cherny and Elizabeth Reba Weise (Seattle: Seal Press, 1996), 262.

8. See Judith Bulter, *Bodies That Matter: On the Discursive Limits of 'Sex'* (New York: Routledge, 1993), and Judith Butler, *Gender Trouble: Feminism and the Subversion of Identity* (New York: Routledge, 1990).

9. The fact that such gestures may be performed by the "wrong" sex suggests that there is no "right" or "wrong" body for any given gender identity; moreover, that the argument for "nature" is actually a political one, the normalization of social control and its violence. Against what Butler calls a "metaphysics of substance," or the articulation of gender as a coherent essence located within the sexed body, gender is instead revealed as a historical affect of a regulatory heterosexual matrix—or in effect, a technology of the self revealed as prosthetic. It would be a mistake to conflate performativity (as a modality of power as discourse or expressivity) with performance (as a deliberate display) in characterizing acts of cross-identification.

10. Cynthia Fuchs, "'Death is Irrevelant': Cyborgs, Reproduction, and the Future of Male Hysteria," in Gray, ed., *The Cyborg Handbook*, 283.

11. Melissa Scott, *Trouble and Her Friends* (New York: Tor Books, 1994). Thomas Foster makes a similar argument in his essay "'Trapped by the Body?' Telepresence Technologies and Transgendered Performance in Feminist and Lesbian Rewritings of Cyberpunk Fiction," in Bell and Kennedy, eds., *The Cybercultures Reader*, 439–59.

12. Scott, *Trouble*, 33–34.

13. Ibid., 210.

14. Ibid., 128–29.

15. Sandy Stone, *The War of Desire and Technology at the Close of the Mechanical Age* (Cambridge, MA: MIT Press, 1995), 180.

16. Sandy Stone, "Will the Real Body Please Stand Up? Boundary Stories about Virtual Cultures," in Bell and Kennedy, eds., *The Cybercultures Reader*, 524.

17. Kate Bornstein and Caitlin Sullivan, *Nearly Roadkill: An Infobahn Erotic Adventure* (New York: High Risk Books, 1996).

18. Kate Bornstein, *My Gender Workbook* (New York: Routledge, 1998).

19. R. U. Sirius, quoted in Vivian Sobchack, "New Age Mutant Ninja Hackers: Reading Mondo 2000" in *Flame Wars: The Discourse of Cyberculture*, ed. Mark Dery (Durham, NC: Duke University Press, 1994), 27.

20. Their cyberspatial maneuverings and their constant travel in the "real world" to escape detection and capture echo the blurred impermanence—and its anarchic, nomadic possibilities—suggested by Sandy Stone: "[S]ome people are getting harder to track. Not by getting physically shifty, but by dissolving, by fragmenting—by being many persons in many places simultaneously, . . . by refusing to be one thing, by *choosing* to be many things"; see Stone, "Split Subjects, Not Atoms, or, How I Fell In Love With My Prosthesis," in Bell and Kennedy, eds., *The Cybercultures Reader*, 400.

21. Bornstein and Sullivan, *Nearly Roadkill*, 135.

22. Foster, "Trapped?" 452.

23. As Coco Fusco notes, the so-called digital revolution has "reorganized what used to be known as the Third World, making those territories into low-end markets and low-wage labor pools for multinational corporations" (Coco Fusco, "At Your Service: Latinas in the Global Information Network" (1998) online at <http://www.hkw.de/forum/forum1/doc/text/fusco-isea98.html>.

24. Bornstein and Sullivan, *Nearly Roadkill*, 74.

25. Ibid., 195.

26. In an incisive interrogation of cross-racial empathy, Sara Ahmed notes that "[blackness] become[s] a means through which [a woman] can know herself (as black), by providing what is lacking in her self. Passing for black is a technique of knowledge insofar as it

remains tied to the narrativization of the white female subject's knowledge of herself through her sympathetic incorporation of others (by assuming an image of blackness, it becomes known as that which is lacking in the white self)"; see Ahmed, *Strange Encounters: Embodied Others in Post-Coloniality* (New York: Routledge, 2000), 133.

27. In describing digital space as nomadic and themselves as guerillas, their "adherence to modernist myths of extreme dislocation and refusal of 'home' ground" can replicate the "appropriation of the margins by the center in the name of a supposedly radical theoretical practice." Caren Kaplan, "The Politics of Location as Transnational Feminist Practice," in *Scattered Hegemonies: Postmodernity and Transnational Feminist Practices*, ed. Caren Kaplan and Inderpal Grewal (Minneapolis: University of Minnesota Press, 1994), 146.

28. Cathy Griggers, "Lesbian Bodies in the Age of (Post)Mechanical Reproduction," in *The Lesbian Postmodern*, ed. Laura Doan (New York: Columbia University Press, 1994), 121.

29. Ibid., 118–34; and Heather Findlay, "Freud's 'Fetishism' and the Lesbian Dildo Debates," in *Out in Culture: Gay, Lesbian, and Queer Essays on Popular Culture*, ed. Corey K. Creekmur and Alexander Doty (Durham, NC: Duke University Press, 1995), 328–42.

30. Findlay, "Freud's 'Fetishism,'" 332.

31. Howard Rheingold, *Virtual Reality* (New York: Summit, 1991), 350.

32. Stone, "Split Subjects," 397.

33. McRae, "Coming Apart," 262.

34. In a series of coincidences, I'd been reading *A Red Record* by Ida B. Wells in a graduate seminar and following the trial that eventually convicted the first of the white supremacist men who had brutally murdered black Texan James Byrd Jr. I remember listening to the reports from the courthouse that February; a Pacifica Public Radio journalist had described the damage done to Byrd's body, seen in autopsy photographs, noting the mutilation of his genitals. And in a contemporaneous letter to a sex-advice columnist that I had read, a white woman narrated her arousal watching *Amistad*, visions of buff, black men in chains triggering an erotic fantasy of bondage and domination. She did not understand why her black boyfriend would not reenact those scenes and wanted to know how she might convince him.

35. Michel Foucault, *The History of Sexuality: An Introduction*, trans. Robert Hurley (New York: Vintage, 1990), 103.

36. Alycee J. Lane, quoted in Findlay, "Freud's 'Fetishism,'" 335.

37. The blurb in the Toys in Babeland catalog reads, "If your favorite refrain is 'More, please,' you're sure to keep this hefty, realistic rubber model at the top of your toy pile. Tipping the scales at an impressive 8″ long and 2 ¼″ in diameter, you can even use this monster in a harness... that accommodates a dildo with balls, and use extra-tight ring.... Available in black only"; online at <http://www.babeland.com>. Thanks to Madeline Neighly for alerting me to this product.

38. In a related prosthetic phenomenon we might consider the older cousin of digital space, the telephone, as an extension of the body barreling through fiberoptic cable, and never more obviously than when sex is exchanged. Highly efficient coders and skilled programmers of desire, phone sex workers by necessity must draw upon a widely recognizable range of social codes in order to invoke erotic modalities of desire: taste, touch, smell, and so on. These social codes and verbal cues mobilize certain expectations about the bodies being exchanged in the token; and desire requires no physically present body to draw upon the ensemble of social forces that sustain dense meaning from code.

39. Findlay, "Freud's 'Fetishism,'" 334.

40. Ibid., 335.

41. In an earlier essay, I noted that "virtual harassers" to my Asian American feminist resources website made a point not only of willing my prosthetic body into view, but also of identifying themselves as white straight men. Accordingly, I noted that privilege

is not necessarily disrupted by attention drawn to its particularity. I further noted, "The violence of normalization depends upon making natural uneven relations of power and the bodies to which authority accrues; but because fluidity is also a crucial component of gendered and racial hegemony, denaturalizing the social character or the morphological particularity of masculinist hegemony and its attendant racial order by no means guarantees collapse." See Mimi Nguyen, "From Paper to Pixels: Tales of An Asiatic Geek Girl," in *Technicolor: Race and Technology in Everyday Life*, ed. Thuy Linh-Tu and Alondra Nelson with Alicia Headlam Hines (New York: New York University Press, 2001).

42. To quote Kaplan in "The Politics of Location," "In a transnational world where cultural asymmetries and linkages continue to be mystified by economic and political interests at multiple levels, feminists need detailed, historicized maps of the circuits of power" (148).

43. On a broader scale, what has been located as the source of identity—whether the imagined rational self or some substance of gender, sexuality, or race—can be shown to be (also) effects of institutions, practices, and discourses.

Notes on Contributors

John Cheng is assistant professor in the Department of History and Art History and affiliated with the Center for History and New Media at George Mason University. He is the author of the forthcoming *Imagining Science: Science Fiction and the Popular Culture of Science in Interwar America.*

Wendy Hui Kyong Chun is an assistant professor of modern culture and media at Brown University. She has studied both systems design engineering and English literature, which she combines and mutates in her current work on digital media. She is completing a manuscript on the crisis of disciplinary and regulatory power brought about by high-speed telecommunications networks, entitled *Sexuality in the Age of Fiber Optics*, as well as editing a collection entitled *The Archaeology of Multimedia.*

Karen Har-Yen Chow, formerly an assistant professor in English and at the Asian American Studies Institute at the University of Connecticut is now assistant professor at De Anza College in Cupertino, California. She has articles in *Literary Studies East and West, Journal of Narrative Technique,* and has guest-edited two special issues on Asian American Literature and Culture for *LIT: Literature, Interpretation, Theory.* She has served as book reviews coeditor for *MELUS,* and was the Association of Asian American Studies East of California Caucus network co-coordinator from 1999 to 2001.

Vernadette V. Gonzalez is a Ph.D. candidate in ethnic studies at the University of California-Berkeley. She is currently working on her dissertation on the postcolonial and global cultures and political economies of tourism in the Philippines and Hawaii. In her free time, she coedits anthologies on queer ethnic studies theory and Filipino/a transnational youth cultures.

Emily Noelle Ignacio is an assistant professor of sociology at Loyola University in Chicago. She is currently completing her manuscript, *Building Diaspora: Filipino Community Formation on the Internet.* Her new research is an analysis of Filipino cultural productions within Catholic masses held at various homes.

Jerry Kang is a professor of law at UCLA. His teaching and scholarly pursuits include civil procedure, race, and cyberspace. On cyberspace, Kang has published recently in the Stanford and Harvard law reviews on the topics of cyberspace privacy and cyberrace (the technosocial construction of race in cyberspace).

He is also the author of *Communications Law and Policy: Cases and Materials*, a leading casebook in the field.

Aeju Kim is an assistant professor in the Department of English, Dongguk University, in Seoul, Korea. She received her Ph.D. from Dongguk University in 1995. Her book, *A Critical Study of Toni Morrison* (in Korean), was awarded the Author's and Editor's Recognition Award in 2000 by the Toni Morrison Society. In addition to focusing on black female writers such as Toni Morrison, Alice Walker, and Zora Neale Hurston, Kim's current research interests include cyber literature in Korea.

Vinay Lal teaches history at UCLA. He has recently edited *Dissenting Knowledges, Open Futures: The Multiple Selves and Strange Destinations of Ashis Nandy* and is the author of *The Dialectic of Civilization and Nation-State: Essays in Indian History and Culture*, and *The Empire of Knowledge: Culture and Plurality in the New Global Economy*.

Rachel C. Lee, associate professor of women's studies, English, and Asian American studies at UCLA, specializes in Asian American literature and performance culture. She is the author of *The Americas of Asian American Literature: Gendered Fictions of Nation and Transnation*, which addresses current debates on the relationship among Asian American ethnic identity, national belonging, globalization, and gender.

Kim-An Lieberman is a Ph.D. candidate in the English department at University of California-Berkeley, where she is completing a dissertation on Vietnamese American literature. Her essays and poems have appeared in several journals, including *Prairie Schooner, Quarterly West, Threepenny Review, Critical Sense*, and the *Asian Pacific American Journal*. She lives and works in Seattle.

Mimi Nguyen is a Ph.D. candidate in comparative ethnic studies at the University of California-Berkeley, with a designated emphasis on women, gender, and sexuality. Her dissertation work focuses on U.S. Vietnamese cultural production and the politics of diasporic citizenship. She is also working on projects examining the politics of race and sex in reproductive rights discourse, sex-positive feminisms, digital technologies, riot grrrl culture, drag, and other spaces of performance and performativity.

Jeffrey A. Ow is a Ph.D. candidate in the University of California-Berkeley's comparative ethnic studies program, exploring Asian American history and cultural studies. While not engaged in his dissertation work investigating the transformation of Angel Island and Ellis Island from immigration detention centers to social history museums, he spends much of his free time consuming and critiquing Asian American cultural productions on his website at <http://www.enemyalien.com>.

Robyn Magalit Rodriguez is currently a Ph.D. candidate in the Department of Sociology at the University of California-Berkeley. She is currently working on her dissertation, entitled, "The Labor Brokering State: The Philippine State and the Production and Export of Filipina/o Migrant Labor." Rodriguez also works collaboratively with colleagues from a range of disciplines on Filipina/o trans/nationalisms including studies of youth cultures and trans/national political struggles.

Yuan Shu is an assistant professor of English at Texas Tech University. He teaches contemporary American literature as well as Asian American studies. His research interests include technology, transnationalism, and Asian American literature.

Pamela Thoma is assistant professor of women's studies and American studies at Colby College. She teaches courses on Asian Americans; race, ethnicity, and gender; feminist theory and activism; and global feminisms/women's movements. She has published articles in *Genders* and *Frontiers*, and her current project is a book manuscript on the politics of consumption in Asian American women's cultural studies.

Thuy Linh Nguyen Tu is a Ph.D. candidate in the American studies program at New York University, and the coeditor with Alondra Nelson (and Alicia Headlime Hines) of *Technicolor: Race, Technology and Everyday Life*. She is currently completing her dissertation on immigration and the emergence of Asian American popular culture.

Linta Varghese is currently working on her dissertation in cultural anthropology at the University of Texas-Austin. Her current research looks at the effects of the liberalization of the Indian economy on Indian diasporic participation.

Sau-ling Cynthia Wong is a professor in the Asian American studies program, Department of Ethnic Studies, at the University of California-Berkeley. She is the author of *Reading Asian American Literature: From Necessity to Extravagance;* the editor *of Maxine Hong Kingston's* The Woman Warrior: *A Casebook;* and a coeditor of *A Resource Guide to Asian American Literature.* She has published extensively on Asian American autobiography, gender and sexuality, Chinese immigrant literature, and community and diasporic identity.

Index